WEEKEND
GETAWAYS
in Louisiana

The entry road to Afton Villa Gardens in St. Francisville. (Photo by Mary Fonseca)

WEEKEND GETAWAYS
in Louisiana

MARY FONSECA

PELICAN PUBLISHING COMPANY
Gretna 1996

*The word "Pelican" and the depiction of a pelican are
trademarks of Pelican Publishing Company, Inc., and are
registered in the U.S. Patent and Trademark Office.*

Library of Congress Cataloging-in-Publication Data

Fonseca, Mary.
    Weekend getaways in Louisiana / by Mary Fonseca.
       p.   cm.
    Includes bibliographical references and index.
    ISBN 1-56554-096-4 (pbk. : alk. paper)
    1. Louisiana—Guidebooks.   I. Title.
F367.3.F65 1996
917.6304'63—dc20   96-16515
                                                      CIP

*Information in this guidebook is based on authoritative data
available at the time of printing. Prices and hours of operation of
businesses listed are subject to change without notice. Readers are
asked to take this into account when consulting this guide.*

Manufactured in the United States of America
Published by Pelican Publishing Company, Inc.
1101 Monroe Street, Gretna, Louisiana 70053

To my children and grandchildren, and to all who preserve and cherish the mysterious beauty and intriguing diversity of Louisiana.

CONTENTS

ACKNOWLEDGMENTS

Tourism representatives throughout Louisiana gave me invaluable assistance with this book. I am particularly grateful to Betty Stewart, Hyatt Hood, Nathalie Dantin, Betty Reed, Kelly Strenge, Jane Breaux, Debbie Melancon, Rachel Hall, Carolyn Andre, Carola Ann Andrepont, Judy Lowentritt, Sue Edmunds, Betty Jones, Rama Chance, Mary Gibson, Ann Timmons, Gayle Brown, Stacy Brown, Kaye LaFrance, Marie Adams, Sue Normon, Sue Gruber, Donna Perret, Sue Hebert, Nikki Sotile, Judy Davis, Macon Riddle, Alma Cutrer, Martha Palmer, Keitha Donnelly, Anita Young, JoAnn Connell, Pat Guercio, Jo Branch, Randy Slagle, Coe Haygood, Tesa Laviolette, Sarah Klumpp, Martha Royer, Rodessa Simon, Pat Herpin, Allen May, Joan and Dick Williams, and Laura and Mark Norris.

Thanks also to the hospitable innkeepers who sheltered me; and to my daughter, Michelle Fonseca Lucio; my husband, Ron Fonseca; and Maria Ward McIntosh for their indispensable technical assistance and generous support.

INTRODUCTION

While gathering information for this book, I hiked and traveled by car, horseback, bicycle, and buckboard wagon through Louisiana's cities, towns, and villages. I explored her picturesque bayous, lakes, and rivers by canoe, airboat, motorboat, pontoon boat, and steamboat. I visited the grassy hill country just south of the Arkansas border, a sandy chenier island off the Louisiana coastline, and most of the intriguing countryside in between. In the spring, I saw carpets of lavender waterlilies in the Atchafalaya Basin roll out before me as far as I could see. In the fall I watched the sunset on Lake Concordia from the wharf at a stately plantation named Lisburn Hall.

Pathways bordered by brilliant flowers enticed me to walk through peaceful gardens, and gigantic oak trees sheltered me in their shade. Cajun musicians set my toes tapping with their songs, restaurateurs tempted me with spicy Louisiana dishes, and new friends greeted me with broad smiles.

It is a privilege to share my experiences with you. I hope they will make your travels more enjoyable as you explore the mysterious beauty and intriguing diversity you can discover with *Weekend Getaways in Louisiana*.

How to Use This Book

The getaways are designed for a two- to three-day stay. But in some areas, there is so much to do and see you will want to savor a few attractions, restaurants, and shops on your first visit, and save others for a return trip.

An (F) just below the title of a getaway indicates it is a trip I consider suitable for, but not limited to, family travel. Several other getaways will also entertain young people, depending on their ages and interests. Destinations where at least one hostelry offers a golf package are noted with a (G).

Area codes, travel directions, attractions, shops, information centers, accommodations, restaurants, guide services, and major annual events are listed at the end of each chapter. There are many appetizing restaurants and enticing shops in Louisiana that are not listed. I have mentioned those I had occasion to visit, plus a few that were recommended to me by people whose opinions I trust. The listed guide services are those that escort individuals as well as groups. No attraction, hostelry, restaurant, or shop has paid to be included in this book.

Always call ahead when planning to visit an attraction, historic site, restaurant, or shop on a holiday. Holiday closings are not noted unless they are unusual, such as Audubon Zoo's closing on the first Friday in May for its Zoo-To-Do fund-raising party. Hours of operation listed were in effect at time of publication. Attractions that charge admission are specified, but exact prices and fees are not listed because they change so frequently.

There are more than twenty-five swamp tours available in south Louisiana. Each is unique and flavored with the personality of the tour operator, who often entertains with music and/or humor. I have reviewed several that are representative of what you see on such a tour. If you are visiting an area that does not have a swamp tour included in the list of attractions, inquire at the tourist information center.

In several chapters I write about traveling on Louisiana's Scenic Byways. Signs with a logo depicting an old-time car mark this network of two-lane highways and country roads that traverse scenic areas, put you in close touch with regional history and culture, and take you to intriguing wayside attractions. A brochure detailing roads that are now part of the state's still-expanding system of byways may be obtained from the Louisiana Office of Tourism, P.O. Box 94291, Dept. #5179, Baton Rouge, LA 70804-9291, 1-800-633-6970.

If this is your first experience traveling in Louisiana, you may be confused by the use of the word *parish*. A parish is the state's equivalent of a county; the term dates to the Catholic foundations of the area.

Lagniappe may also be a word that is unfamiliar to you. It means a little something extra at no charge, such as complimentary instructions in Cajun dancing offered at many restaurants and dance halls in Acadiana.

Bring an open mind, a friendly smile, and an extra ice chest with you as you travel. The first will make you receptive to new experiences, the second will invite those experiences, and the third is for the Cajun sausages, scrumptious pastries, and other gastronomical treats you will want to take home with you!

You may find it convenient to book rooms at a Bed and Breakfast through a reservation service. If the listed inns are full, reservationists may be aware of others that eluded our search, or opened after this book was published. Bed and Breakfast services that reserve rooms in Louisiana include:

B & B, Inc., 1021 Moss St. (P.O. Box 52257), New Orleans, LA 70152-2257. (504) 488-4640 or 1-800-749-4640.

New Orleans Bed & Breakfast Reservation Service, 671 Rosa Ave., Metairie, LA 70005. (504) 838-0071 or 838-0072.

Southern Comfort, P.O. Box 13294, New Orleans, LA 70185-3294. (504) 861-0082 or 1-800-749-1928.

A fee is charged for reservation services.

You may also request a copy of the Louisiana Bed and Breakfast Association's annual directory at Louisiana welcome centers or by calling the Louisiana Office of Tourism—1-800-633-6970.

If you have comments or updates on information included in *Weekend Getaways in Louisiana,* please contact me in care of Pelican Publishing Company, P.O. Box 3110, Gretna, LA 70054.

May your travels be adventurous, your companions agreeable, and your memories of Louisiana as delightful as mine.

WEEKEND GETAWAYS
in Louisiana

LOUISIANA

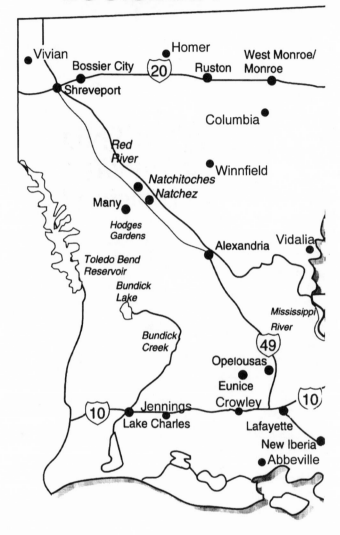

Mississippi
River

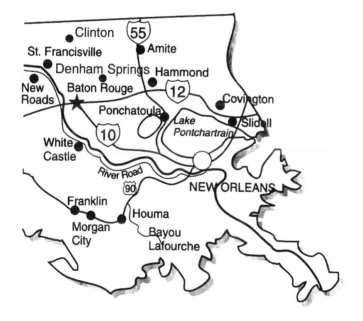

Clinton

(55)

St. Francisville

Amite

Denham Springs

Hammond

New
Roads

Baton Rouge

(12)

Covington

Ponchatoula

Slidell

Lake
Pontchartrain

White
Castle

(10)

River Road

(90)

NEW ORLEANS

Franklin

Houma

Morgan
City

Bayou
Lafourche

1

ANTIQUES, ART, AND APPLAUSE

An hour or two after the last of the merry-makers on Bourbon Street shuffle off to their lodgings, the rising sun shines through a row of shop windows on Royal Street—the genteel, elegant neighbor of New Orleans' rambunctious "party" street. Its beams ignite prisms in crystal chandeliers, cast a shimmering glow on antique tables and armoires, and awaken the brilliant sparkle that sleeps in precious gems.

The exquisite accoutrements embraced by the sun are marketed by knowledgeable French Quarter merchants. Some shopkeepers who turn keys in **Royal Street's** vintage portals and follow the sun beams into their beguiling shops walk in the footsteps of their ancestors. Their great-grandparents started businesses on Royal Street when nineteenth-century New Orleans was a center of fashion and culture. If these ingenious tradesmen could stroll down Royal Street today they would probably feel right at home. The facades of their historic shops, facing Royal between Iberville and St. Ann streets, look much as they did a century ago. But, if they crossed the thresholds and looked inside, they would stare in amazement at an accumulation of fine antiques and cherished collectibles never dreamed of in days gone-by.

If you are looking for a certain eighteenth- or nineteenth-century English or French piece to complete your decor, it is very likely waiting for you in one of Royal Street's distinctive shops. In others, dazzling arrays of heirloom jewelry, Fabergé eggs, rare stamps, and fine photographs present collectors with the happy dilemma of trying to choose what to buy and what to regretfully leave behind. Elaborately decorated hand-guns, valuable coins, and art expressed in many forms are also among the "finds" you may sight while window-shopping on Royal Street. All of these offerings, and the particular shops that sell them, are summed up in a brochure published by the **Royal Street Guild,** an association concerned with maintaining the integrity and ambiance of one of New Orleans' most prestigious streets.

Chartres Street, one block east of Royal, also has evolved into a noteworthy avenue. Its sidewalks give entry to a variety of enchanting **boutiques** devoted to one item or theme. Multicolored tribal emblems are displayed next door to collections of delicate nativity scenes and dolls. A quaint button shop nestles close to a store displaying elegant tester beds, handsome tables, and grandiose chests.

Shoppers sometimes feel overwhelmed by the extraordinary medley presented on Royal and Chartres streets and pause to consider their choices over a cup of coffee in one of several neighborhood cafes. When their shopping is done, they top off a successful day with dinner at **Brennan's Restaurant** or at Chef Paul Prudhommme's **K-Paul's Louisiana Kitchen.** Both are in the midst of the Royal and Chartres streets' shops. And more restaurants with equally tempting menus are just a short walk away.

Although the shops on Royal and Chartres are bulging at the seams, they do not hold all the fine furnishings and artistic creations available in New Orleans. Appealing merchandise awaits buffs and browsers on **Magazine Street,** a six-mile corridor of shops, galleries, and restaurants that extends from Canal Street to the city's Audubon Park.

With a guide compiled by the **Magazine Street Merchant's Association** in hand you can easily find your way to the street's colorful shops. The delightful mélange includes the gallery of famed furniture designer, **Mario Villa,** and two reputable auction houses specializing in estate sales. There are also shopkeepers who deal in discontinued silver, china, and crystal; potters and woodworkers who fashion lovely, hand-crafted items on site; purveyors of fine and not-so-fine antiques; craftsmen who repair or duplicate architectural accents, plus some who restore damaged art works.

Cafes and restaurants tucked between Magazine Street's inviting shops offer fare as varied as the inventory in neighboring galleries and boutiques. **PJ's Coffee & Tea Company's** specialty brews, **Casemento's** seafood, the **Upperline Restaurant's** Creole menu, and **Reginelli's: An Eating Gallery's** grilled entrees are a few enticing examples.

Comfortable shoes and casual clothes make Magazine Street shopping more enjoyable. Leave cameras and other paraphernalia that mark you as a tourist at your hotel. Then, use a **VisiTour Pass** on the Regional Transit Authority's Magazine Street bus or purchase a ticket for **Gray Line's Loop Tour bus.** Both buses allow unlimited on-and-off privileges to riders exploring Magazine Street's intriguing shops.

Art enthusiasts also may enjoy a pleasurable sight-seeing and shopping excursion to New Orleans' art museums and galleries. The city's historic St. Charles Avenue streetcar deposits you at **K&B Plaza,** the starting point of this tour. But, if you prefer to travel by car, ask about complimentary parking at one of the Julia Street galleries included in the tour or bring plenty of change for a parking meter.

Passengers who exit the streetcar in front of the plaza—on St. Charles Avenue by Lee Circle—are greeted by two eye-catching sculptures christened *Streetcar Stop I and II.* These interactive works are part of the Virlane collection, New Orleans' most important assemblage of modern and contemporary art. The remainder of the sculptures and paintings in the collection are exhibited at K&B Plaza, where the Virlane Foundation, a private organization dedicated to cultivating public interest in the arts, displays more than sixty-five works of art.

Isamu Noguchi's towering granite fountain, entitled *The Mississippi,* is the dominant outdoor sculpture on K&B's ground-floor piazza. More fascinating works grace other sections of the plaza, plus seven floors of the K&B building.

After viewing the Virlane collection, cross St. Charles Avenue and walk around part of Lee Circle to Howard Avenue. As you turn right on Howard to Camp Street you will pass the Romanesque Revival Patrick R. Taylor Library, and other buildings that are being readied as quarters for the Roger Houston Ogden Museum of Southern Art, plus studios and retail space for artists and an administrative and conference center for the University of New Orleans, the Arts Council, and the Entergy Arts Business Center. The museum, expected to open sometime between 1998 and the year 2000, will contain approximately six hundred examples of nineteenth-century Louisiana art, plus contemporary paintings and sculptures from the twentieth century donated to the University of New Orleans Foundation by Roger Houston Ogden.

A left turn on Camp takes you to the **Contemporary Arts Center (CAC)** in the middle of the block. This dynamic twenty-year-old center is housed in an historic building donated by the K&B Corporation. Its dated appearance belies a sleek, modern interior where rotating exhibits by local, national, and international artists are displayed in five spacious galleries. In two well-equipped theaters next to the exhibit spaces, audiences applaud original plays, mainstream productions, and recitals by up-and-coming performers.

The development of the CAC spawned a growing colony of contemporary art galleries in a nearby neighborhood known as the Warehouse or Art District. A brochure published by New Orleans' Downtown Development District pinpoints the location of these galleries, plus inviting shops and restaurants in the Art District. Request a copy of the leaflet at the CAC or at one of the Art District galleries.

Most of the galleries border Julia Street between St. Charles Avenue and Commerce Street. To reach them from the Contemporary Arts Center, stroll up Camp Street one-and-a-half blocks to Julia Street. Of particular note in this area is **Galerie Simonne Stern,** the oldest contemporary art gallery in the city. The Stern gallery offers contemporary paintings, master prints, photographs, and sculptures created by talented locals and outstanding international artists.

As you wander in and out of other alluring galleries in the Art District, you may view unusual crafts from all over the world, admire original, hand-carved furniture, watch local artisans shape molten glass into functional pieces or captivating ornaments, and delight in the gaily painted chairs designed by young people associated with the nationally acclaimed **YA/YA (Young Aspirations/Young Artists) Gallery.** Openings (usually scheduled on the first Saturday of each month, fall to spring, 6–9 P.M. and other special events held in the Art District are highlighted in the "Lagniappe" section of the Friday edition of New Orleans' daily newspaper, *The Times-Picayune.*

Art District restaurants range from casual to elegant. You may opt to taste local color, and a New Orleans po' boy sandwich, at **Louisiana Products Deli and Grocery** on Julia Row or lunch while enjoying the folk art displayed in **Doug's Steak House.** Other choices include the first-class soul food served at **The Praline Connection** and the classy cuisine prepared at **Emeril's, L'Economie,** or **Mike's on the Avenue.**

No tour of New Orleans art sectors is complete without a visit to the city's cherished **New Orleans Museum of Art (NOMA).** The neo-classical building housing this highly regarded museum overlooks languid lagoons in spacious City Park. To reach it by public transit from downtown, board the Canal Street bus and transfer to the Carrollton line. The driver can direct you to the stop closest to the museum, which also can be accessed readily by car from the City Park/Metairie Road exit of Interstate 10.

Allow at least a half-day to explore the exquisite artworks on display at NOMA. A recent, $23 million expansion and renovation elevated the museum to a state-of-the-art facility. It shelters a 35,000-piece permanent collection valued at $200 million. Highlights of the collection include fine examples of seventeenth-, eighteenth-, and nineteenth-century French art, Spanish Colonial art, European, and American twentieth-century art, the Lupin Foundation Center for the Decorative Arts, and the Matilda Geddings Gray Foundation Fabergé collection.

Exhibits on NOMA'S second floor help visitors trace the

Aida. (Photo courtesy New Orleans Opera Association)

New Orleans Museum of Art. (Photo by Alan Karchmer, courtesy New Orleans Museum of Art)

development of art in Louisiana over the past two hundred years. One of the newly created exhibitions showcases the museum's extensive photography collection—considered the finest in the Southeast. In others, a breathtaking assemblage of exquisite glass pieces dating from ancient Rome to the present day captures your attention.

Art enthusiasts also can look forward to viewing many world-class traveling shows in NOMA's expansive exhibit space. The first such exhibit, a collection of late works by French Impressionist master Claude Monet, was hosted by the museum in 1995. There is so much to see at the "new" NOMA that you may need a respite from walking through the exhibits. If you do, enjoy a light lunch or snack, and a pleasing view of City Park, in the museum's **Courtyard Cafe.**

Round out your gallery-hopping with an entertaining evening in one of New Orleans' many theaters. On practically any weekend of the year, troubadours embellish the city's cornucopia of art with music, dance, and theatrical productions worthy of your applause. For example, **Le Petit Théâtre du Vieux Carré,** New Orleans' oldest community theater, presents six mainstage productions, plus several performances geared to the younger set, every year. Audiences of all ages enjoy Broadway musicals, plus a variety of star-studded concerts at the **Saenger,** a handsomely decorated Beaux Arts theater on Canal Street. A few blocks away, the magnificent **Orpheum Theater,** a turn-of-the-century hall noted for its exceptional acoustics, provides a fitting backdrop for the master musicians of the **Louisiana Philharmonic Orchestra.** Devotees of the symphony also attend the orchestra's programs of classical and contemporary music at the **Pontchartrain Center,** an easily accessible suburban facility.

Opera buffs in the know purchase tickets to the memorable performances staged by the **New Orleans Opera Association** well in advance. For the past four or five seasons, all eight performances of the four operas staged at the city's **Mahalia Jackson Theatre of the Performing Arts** were sold out.

Productions presented in New Orleans' traditional theaters are complemented with programs to suit every taste and fancy.

A Drover with Sheep and Cattle Beneath
a Pollarded Willow *by Paulus Potter.*
(Photo courtesy Windsor Court Hotel)

Edward VIII when
Prince of Wales *by*
Edward March.
(Photo courtesy
Windsor Court
Hotel)

St. George's Hall *by Joseph Nash.* (Photo
courtesy Windsor Court Hotel)

They range from ballet to Shakespeare to gospel music and are staged in settings as intimate as **True Brew Coffee House** or as expansive as the **University of New Orleans' Lakefront Arena.** Professional touring companies and recording stars are the usual performers at the university's amphitheater, but on the campuses of New Orleans' six universities—**University of New Orleans, Loyola, Xavier, Dillard, Southern,** and **Tulane**—you can also enjoy quality productions involving talented students and visiting artists.

A comprehensive Arts Directory indexing these facilities plus New Orleans' art galleries, auditoriums, dance companies, theatrical and musical troupes, and museums is published annually by the **Arts Council of New Orleans.** The Arts Directory, coupled with the **New Orleans Metropolitan Convention and Visitors Bureau's** calender of events, can be your key to more art-full weekends in New Orleans.

Visitors can also find the services offered on a free, interactive phone network sponsored by WWL-TV and the Crescent City Trade Exchange helpful. Callers who dial FYI-1515 (394-1515) can hear descriptions of the cuisine and make reservations at local restaurants; get information on and purchase tickets to attractions, special events, performances, and exhibits; listen to a local weather forecast; and order a taxi.

When planning your getaways, be sure to allow time for a delightful afternoon at **Windsor Court Hotel.** This elegantly appointed hotel, listed as the best in the United States in the 1994 Zagat survey, is frequently referred to as one of the topnotch hostelries in the world. On the Saturday afternoon of your choice, treat yourself to a sumptuous tea in the relaxing atmosphere of Windsor Court's elegant **Le Salon,** then enjoy a complimentary tour of the hotel's fabulous collection of art and antiques.

Most of the pieces displayed at Windsor Court Hotel are of British origin with an emphasis on works depicting Windsor Castle and the Royal Family's life there. You also will see two stunning marquetry screens (made from many varieties of wood) expressly created for the hotel's Grill Room by Viscount Linley, son of HRH Princess Margaret. A set of twenty-five hand-finished chromolithographs commissioned by Queen Victoria and Prince Albert in 1848; paintings by masters such as Reynolds, Gainsborough, and Van Dyck; and many skillfully crafted antique furnishings round out the fabulous collection.

Area Code: (504)

Getting There:

Interstates 10, 55, and 59 take you to New Orleans in the southeast section of Louisiana. The city is served by Amtrak. Commercial flights land at New Orleans International Airport.

Where and When:

Arts Council of New Orleans, 821 Gravier St., Suite 600, New Orleans, LA 70112-1581. 523-1465. Mon.-Fri., 9 A.M.-5 P.M.

Contemporary Arts Center, 900 Camp St., New Orleans, LA 70130. 523-1216. Gallery hours: Mon.-Sat., 10 A.M.-5 P.M.; Sun., 11 A.M.-5 P.M. Free to CAC members, admission for nonmembers. Box office: Thurs.-Sat., 3-8 P.M.; Sun., noon-3 P.M. Tickets also available through Ticketmaster. 522-5555. Call 528-3800 for recorded ticket information.

Chartres Street Shops. Generally open Mon.-Sat., 9:30 A.M.-5 P.M. A few have slightly different hours and may be open on Sunday. Call before visiting.

Dillard University, 2601 Gentilly Blvd., New Orleans, LA 70119. Art: 286-4692. Music: 286-4760. Theater: 286-4762.

Galerie Simonne Stern, 518 Julia St., New Orleans, LA 70130. 529-1118. Mon.-Fri., 10 A.M.-6 P.M.; Sat., 10 A.M.-5 P.M.

K&B Plaza, 1055 St. Charles Ave., New Orleans, LA 70130. 586-1234. Interior art may be viewed Mon.-Fri., 8 A.M.-4:45 P.M. Exterior art may be viewed daily during daylight hours. Free.

Le Petit Théâtre du Vieux Carré 616 St. Peter St., New Orleans, LA 70116. Box Office: 522-2081. Open Mon.-Fri., 10 A.M.-5 P.M. Business telephone: 522-9958. Schedule sent upon request.

Louisiana Philharmonic Orchestra, 821 Gravier St., Suite 605 (P.O. Box 56579, New Orleans, LA 70156-6579). 523-6530. Mon.-Fri., 10 A.M.-3 P.M. Tickets available by mail or by phone. Schedule sent upon request. Pontchartrain Center tickets may be purchased through Ticketmaster at 522-1314 or the Pontchartrain Center Box Office, 468-6671.

Loyola University, 6363 St. Charles Ave., New Orleans, LA 70118. Louis J. Roussel Performance Hall: 865-3492; Marquette Theatre: 865-3824.

Magazine Street Merchants Association, 3025 Magazine St., New Orleans, LA 70115. Mon.-Sat., 10 A.M.-5 P.M. Telephone information available 9 A.M.-10 P.M. at 897-6915 or 1-800-828-2311.

Mahalia Jackson Theatre of the Performing Arts, Armstrong Park, 1201 St. Peter St., New Orleans, LA 70116. 565-7470. Tickets for events may be purchased at the Louisiana Superdome Box Office, Sugar Bowl Drive, New Orleans, LA 70112. 587-3663. Box Office open Mon.-Fri., 9 A.M.-4:30 P.M.

Mario Villa Gallery, 3908 Magazine St., New Orleans, LA 70115. 895-8731. Tues.-Fri., 11 A.M.-6 P.M.; Sat., 11 A.M.-5 P.M.

New Orleans Museum of Art, City Park (P.O. Box 19123, New Orleans, LA 70179-0123). 488-2631. Tues.-Sun., 10 A.M.-5 P.M. Closed Mondays and all legal holidays. On Thursdays, from 10 A.M.-noon, the museum is open free to Louisiana residents with valid identification. Admission at all other times.

New Orleans Opera Association, 333 St. Charles Ave., Suite 907, New Orleans, LA 70130. 529-2278. Mon.-Fri., 9 A.M.-4:30 P.M. Schedule sent upon request.

Orpheum Theater, 129 University Place, New Orleans, LA 70112. 524-3285.

Pontchartrain Center, 4545 Williams Blvd., Kenner, LA 70065. Box Office: 468-6671.

Royal Street Guild, 828 Royal St. (Box 522), New Orleans, LA 70116. 949-2222. Mon.-Sat., 9 A.M.-5 P.M. Or, if it is more convenient for you to call after business hours, your message will be recorded and your call returned.

Royal Street Shops. Generally open Mon.-Sat., 9:30 A.M.-5 P.M. A few have slightly different hours and may be open on Sunday. Call before visiting.

Saenger Theater, 143 N. Rampart St., New Orleans, LA 70112. 524-2490. Box office open Mon.-Fri., 10 A.M.-5 P.M. Tickets also available through Ticketmaster, 522-5555.

Southern University, 6400 Press Dr., New Orleans, LA 70126. Fine Arts: 286-5267. Music: 286-5247.

True Brew Coffee House, 200 Julia St., New Orleans, LA 70130. 524-8441. Box Office: 522-2907. Open noon-7 P.M.

Tulane University, 6823 St. Charles Ave., New Orleans, LA 70118. Theatre Department Box Office: 865-5106.

University of New Orleans, UNO Lakefront, New Orleans, LA 70148. Drama Department Performances: 286-7469. Lakefront Arena Box Office: 286-7469. Open Mon.-Fri., 10 A.M.-3 P.M. Performance times: 7-8 P.M.

Xavier University, 7325 Palmetto St., New Orleans, LA 70125. Art: 483-7556. Music: 483-7597.

YA/YA (Young Aspirations/Young Artists), Inc., 628 Baronne St., New Orleans, LA 70113. 529-3306. Mon.-Fri., 9 A.M.-6 P.M. Frequently open on Saturday. Call before visiting.

Windsor Court Hotel, 300 Gravier St., New Orleans, LA 70130. Art and antiques tour every Saturday at 4 P.M. Call 596-4798 for reservations. Free.

Transportation:

Gray Line Loop Tour bus. Tickets available at any Gray Line outlet or from Loop Tour bus drivers. Exact change required for tickets purchased on bus. Call 587-0861 for more information.

Regional Transit Authority VisiTour Pass. A one-day or three-day VisiTour Pass allows unlimited transportation on all RTA bus and streetcar lines. The passes may be purchased at the Sheraton, Fairmont, and Marriott hotels, the Riverwalk,

Jackson Brewery, and other locations. A foldout VisiTour Map in *Where* magazine, available free at hotels and tourist information centers, outlines the routes of bus and streetcar lines most often used by visitors. For more information on buses or streetcars, call the Regional Transit Authority at 569-2700.

Information:

The **Arts Directory** may be obtained from the Arts Council of New Orleans, 821 Gravier St., Suite 600, New Orleans, LA 70112-1581. Enclose a stamped, self-addressed, legal-sized envelope.

New Orleans Metropolitan Convention and Visitors Bureau, 1520 Sugar Bowl Dr., New Orleans, LA 70112. 566-5068 or 566-5031. Welcome Centers are at New Orleans International Airport and 529 St. Ann St., facing Jackson Square.

Guide Services:

Let's Go Antiquing, 1424 Fourth St., New Orleans, LA 70130. 899-3027. Even with the help of brochures and maps, the vast wealth of antique and fine art sources in New Orleans can be overwhelming. Let's Go Antiquing is a customized service created to help shoppers with little time find what they are looking for quickly. Shopping consultant, Macon Riddle, or one of her well-trained assistants, will pick you up at your hotel and bring you back at the end of your shopping excursion. Half- or full-day shopping assistance is offered.

Accommodations:

New Orleans has numerous chain and independent hotels and motels and Bed and Breakfasts. For a complete listing of accommodations, request "A Visitors Guide" from the New Orleans Metropolitan Convention and Visitors Bureau.

Note: Serious antique collectors may want to take advantage of a special package offered by the **Omni Royal Orleans Hotel,** 621 St. Louis St., New Orleans, LA 70116. 529-5333. "The King's Ransom" offer includes transportation to and from the airport, caviar and champagne upon arrival, two nights' stay for two people (with one candlelight dinner) in the hotel's Royal Suite, brunch on Saturday or Sunday or a weekday lunch in the hotel restaurant, a personalized tour of Royal Street antique shops by **Let's Go Antiquing,** a complimentary limousine for one evening, and a Mississippi River cruise on the steamboat *Natchez.*

Restaurants:

Brennan's Restaurant, 417 Royal St., New Orleans, LA 70130. 525-9711. Breakfast: Daily, 8 A.M.-2:30 P.M.; Dinner: Daily, 6-10 P.M. Lunch: Mon.-Fri., 11:30 A.M.-2:30 P.M.

Casemento's Restaurant, 4330 Magazine St., New Orleans, LA 70115. 895-9761. Tues.-Sun.: Lunch, 11:45 A.M.-1:30 P.M.; Dinner, 5:30-9 P.M. Closed Mondays and during the summer.

Courtyard Cafe, New Orleans Museum of Art, City Park. 488-2631. Tues.-Sun., 10:30 A.M.-3:30 P.M.

Doug's Steak House, 748 Camp St., New Orleans LA 70130. 527-5433. Lunch: Mon.-Fri., 11 A.M.-2:30 P.M. Dinner: Daily, 5-10 P.M.

Emeril's Restaurant, 800 Tchoupitoulas St., New Orleans, LA 70130. 528-9393. Lunch: Mon.-Fri., 11:30 A.M.-2 P.M. Dinner: Mon.-Sat., 6-10 P.M.

K-Paul's Louisiana Kitchen, 416 Chartres St., New Orleans, LA 70130. Lunch: Mon.-Sat., 11:30 A.M.-2:30 P.M. Dinner: Mon.-Sat., 5:30-10 P.M.

L'Economie Restaurant, 325 Girod St., New Orleans, LA 70130. 524-7405. Lunch: Tues.-Fri., 11:30 A.M.-2 P.M. Dinner: Tues.-Thurs., 6-9:30 P.M.; Fri. and Sat., 6-10:30 P.M. Closed Sundays and Mondays.

Le Salon, Windsor Court Hotel, 300 Gravier St., New Orleans, LA 70130. 596-4513. Afternoon tea served daily 2-5:30 P.M. Reservations required.

Louisiana Products Deli and Grocery, 618 Julia St., New Orleans, LA 70130. 529-1666. Mon.-Fri., 6:15 A.M.-5:30 P.M.; Sat., 8 A.M.-3 P.M.

Mike's on the Avenue, 628 St. Charles Ave., New Orleans, LA 70130. 523-5273. Lunch: Daily, 11:30 A.M.-2 P.M. Dinner: Daily, 6-10 P.M.

PJ's Coffee & Tea Company, 5432 Magazine St., New Orleans, LA 70115. 895-0273. Mon.-Fri., 7 A.M.-11 P.M.; Sat. and Sun., 8 A.M.-11 P.M.

The Praline Connection, 542 Frenchmen St., New Orleans, LA 70130. 943-3934. Mon.-Sat., 11 A.M.-10 P.M.; Sun. 11 A.M.-6 P.M.

Reginelli's: An Eating Gallery, 3923 Magazine St., New Orleans, LA 70115. 895-9229. Lunch: Mon.-Sat., 11:30 A.M.-2:30 P.M. Dinner: Mon.-Thurs., 6-10 P.M.; Fri.-Sun., 6-11 P.M. Closed Mondays.

Upperline Restaurant, 1413 Upperline St. (near 4800 block of Magazine), New Orleans, LA 70115. 891-9822. Wed.-Mon., 5:30 P.M.-'til. Closed Tuesdays.

Major Annual Events:

Art for Art's Sake, Art District, New Orleans—First Saturday in October.

Home and Art Tour, New Orleans Museum of Art—Spring.

Odyssey Ball, New Orleans Museum of Art—Fall.

SweetArts Ball, Contemporary Arts Center—February.

More annual events in New Orleans are listed in "A Is for Aquarium, Z Is for Zoo," and "Cities of the Living, Cities of the Dead."

2

CITIES OF THE LIVING, CITIES OF THE DEAD

Musicians perform in the streets. Artists and street players circle the central square. Tantalizing aromas drift from a "food court" that is unmatched anywhere. Church bells chime, buggy whips crack, and a calliope whistles a merry tune. In the midst of this convivial pageantry, shoppers meander in and out of nearly 1,000 businesses that are part of Louisiana's oldest and largest "festival marketplace"—the French Quarter.

Within the French Quarter's 90 square blocks, bordered by Canal Street, Esplanade Avenue, Rampart Street, and the Mississippi River, visitors with enough stamina, and a good pair of walking shoes, can peruse nearly 150 gift stores and more than 100 antique shops and art galleries. You can also wander through a mixture of music clubs, book shops, clothing stores, and other retail outlets.

The historic Quarter is more than a shopping district, however. It has been a collage of shops and residences since the 1800s. Several thousand people still live in brick-walled homes that front the narrow streets. At the **New Orleans Metropolitan Convention and Visitors Bureau's** Welcome Center on St. Ann Street you can request a map showing the location of vintage French Quarter dwellings open for tours. Visit some of these centuries-old homes and glimpse life as it was in the old city.

The **1850 House** is next to the St. Ann Street welcome center, across from Jackson Square (see "A Is for Aquarium, Z Is for

Zoo"). The three-story home is decorated with furnishings typical of those found in a mid-nineteenth-century New Orleans home.

The **Beauregard-Keyes House,** on the corner of Ursulines and Chartres streets, is four blocks downriver from Jackson Square. The raised cottage was built in 1826 by Joseph Le Carpentier, a prosperous auctioneer, but is most associated with Confederate Gen. Pierre G. T. Beauregard, a native Louisianian who lived in the home for 18 months and Frances Parkinson Keyes, an acclaimed novelist who used New Orleans as a setting for several of her books.

The **Old Ursuline Convent,** the oldest building in the Mississippi Valley, is across the street from the Beauregard-Keyes House. Visitors who tour the 1745 convent walk through one of only two buildings that escaped the flames of a great fire that destroyed the Church of St. Louis and 856 homes in 1788. The Ursuline sisters founded the oldest school for girls in the United States at an earlier convent on the site. They continued their work in the convent that is now open for tours. Here, orphans of French Colonists slaughtered at Fort Rosalie in Natchez, destitute Negro and indian girls, and daughters of the city's wealthy families all received guidance and care from the Ursuline nuns. Beautifully restored **St. Mary's Church,** built in 1845 as the Chapel of the Archbishops, is next to the convent. It is maintained as a sacred, historic edifice affording limited religious services for the convenience of neighbors and visitors.

Gallier House, the 1850s home of architect James Gallier, Jr., is one block down Ursulines, and around the corner on Royal Street. Gallier designed New Orleans' cherished (but no longer existing) French Opera House and many homes in the city's Garden District. His father planned the Pontalba Apartments (see "A Is for Aquarium, Z Is for Zoo"), St. Louis Cathedral, and other treasured landmarks.

After you tour the Gallier home, walk upriver on Royal Street six blocks to the **Historic New Orleans Collection** in the 1792 Merieult House and the ca. 1880 home of Gen. and Mrs. L. Kemper Williams, founders of the Historic New Orleans

Collection. The Merieult home is one of the few structures that escaped a disastrous fire that destroyed New Orleans in 1794. Exhibits in the two homes interpret the city's culture and history.

No tour of the Crescent City's remarkable homes would be complete without a taste of the savory cuisine favored by Creoles (New Orleanians of French and Spanish descent) who settled the old city. The Brennan family has prepared these French-flavored specialties for generations at **Brennan's Restaurant,** one block up from the Historic New Orleans Collection.

The restaurant's pink-faced building was erected in 1795. It was originally a home, but served as quarters for the Banque de la Louisiane from 1805 to 1820. The bank's *BL* monogram still adorns the renowned eatery's iron-railed balcony. In the mid-1800s, the building was the home of Paul Morphy, who became the first American world chess champion before he was twenty-one years old.

After you indulge in Brennan's fine cuisine, walk to the **Hermann-Grima Historic House** on St. Louis Street, 1½ blocks from the corner of Royal and St. Louis streets. This 1831 home has the only working 1830s Creole kitchen in the area and the last private stable in the Vieux Carré (old square).

The Hermann-Grima home is one of the few American-style homes in the French Quarter. Outsiders who came to New Orleans after the Louisiana Purchase in 1803 were not well received by close-knit Creoles who controlled most of the property in the fledgling city. The ingenious newcomers developed their own neighborhoods on the other side of Canal Street. The spacious homes they built are now part of New Orleans' esteemed Garden District.

The diversity of architecture in this prominent residential section is the focus of a Faubourg Promenade Tour conducted by Jean Lafitte National Historical Park and Preserve rangers (see "A Is for Aquarium, Z Is for Zoo"). The New Orleans Metropolitan Convention and Visitors Bureau's brochure, "New Orleans Self-Guided Walking and Driving Tours," also gives directions to distinguished Garden District homes.

While you are in the Garden District, treat yourself to the exceptional cuisine prepared at **Commander's Palace.** Residents of the American sector first supped at Emile Commander's Washington Avenue eatery in 1880. The Victorian structure has housed a restaurant continuously since that time.

In January 1815, Creoles cast aside their scorn of the Americans and joined with them to face a stronger challenge to their way of life. British forces under Sir Edward Packenham were on the verge of attacking the city when Andrew Jackson assembled merchants, planters, free men of color, Indians, pirates, backwoodsmen, and others into a fighting unit. The ragtag army defeated well-trained British forces during the Battle of New Orleans.

Although the battle was fought two weeks after a peace treaty ending the War of 1812 had been signed, it has been called one of the most important in American history. It unified the nation and secured America's control of the Mississippi River and the Louisiana Purchase Territory.

The Battle of New Orleans is recalled through guided tours and films at **Chalmette National Historical Park,** the site of the battle. The park, a unit of the Jean Lafitte National Historical Park and Preserve, is visited by the *Creole Queen* riverboat. You can also reach it by taking Interstate 10 East to the Chalmette exit (Louisiana 47). Travel south to St. Bernard Highway and turn right.

Fewer than ten American lives were lost in the Battle of New Orleans. The heroes who gave their lives are buried in a massive tomb in St. Louis No. 1 Cemetery. It is among the many elaborate, raised monuments in one of New Orleans' oldest "cities of the dead."

After discovering that the city's low water table could disinter their loved ones, early residents learned to bury their dead above the ground. Several famous and infamous New Orleanians rest in burial "houses" beside the heroes of the Battle of New Orleans. They include Etienne Boré, the city's first mayor and the inventor of the process used to granulate sugar, and Paul Morphy, the young chess champion. The grave

St. Roch Cemetery, a typical New Orleans graveyard. (Photo by Mary Fonseca)

Metairie Cemetery. (Photo by Mary Fonseca)

that draws the most attention, however, is that of voodoo queen Marie Laveau. Her tomb is often emblazoned with voodoo markings and offerings from local believers.

Tour guides regale their clients with tales about Marie Laveau and other notables interred in New Orleans' ostentatious tombs. Their interesting commentary would be reason enough to engage them, but they provide safety as well as information. New Orleans' intriguing resting places often hide vandals and thieves. *Please visit the cemeteries only on an escorted group tour.*

If your cemetery excursion includes Metairie Cemetery, the largest, and some say the most elaborate of the city's resting places, you will be just a few blocks from **Longue Vue House and Gardens.** Longue Vue was the home of Edgar Bloom Stern, a prosperous New Orleans businessman, and Edith Rosenwald Stern, a daughter of Julius Rosenwald who directed Sears, Roebuck & Company during its growth to one of the largest merchandising establishments in the world. The classic, twentieth-century estate is a museum of the decorative arts, filled with architectural innovations and artistic treasures collected by the Sterns. End your day with a visit to this prized mansion and a stroll through the lovely, eight-acre garden that surrounds it.

Area Code: (504)

Getting There: (see "Antiques, Art, and Applause")

Where and When:

1850 House, 523 St. Ann St. (Louisiana State Museum, 751 Chartres St., New Orleans, LA 70116.) 568-6968. Tues.-Sun., 10 A.M.-5 P.M. Guided tours. Admission.

Beauregard-Keyes House, 1113 Chartres St., New Orleans, LA 70116. 523-7257. Mon.-Sat., 10 A.M.-3 P.M. Guided tours. Admission.

Chalmette National Historical Park, 8606 St. Bernard Hwy., Chalmette, LA 70043. 589-4430. Daily, 8 A.M.-5 P.M. Extended summer hours. Guided tours. Audiovisual Program. Free.

Gallier House, 1118-32 Royal St., New Orleans, LA 70116. 523-6722. Mon.-Sat., 10 A.M.-4:30 P.M. Open selected Sundays. Guided tours. Admission.

Hermann-Grima Historic House, 820 St. Louis St., New Orleans, LA 70112. 525-5661. Mon.-Sat., 10 A.M.-3:30 P.M. Guided tours. Admission.

Historic New Orleans Collection, 533 Royal St., New Orleans, LA 70130. 523-4662. Tues.-Sat., 10 A.M.-4:45 P.M. Guided tours of Williams residence at 10 A.M., 11 A.M., 2 P.M., and 3 P.M. Admission.

Longue Vue House and Gardens, 7 Bamboo Rd., New Orleans, LA 70124-1065. 488-5488. Tues.-Sat., 10 A.M.-4:30 P.M.; Sun., 1-5 P.M. Guided tours offered. Admission.

Old Ursuline Convent, 1100 Chartres St., New Orleans, LA 70116. 529-3040. Guided tours: Tues.-Fri., 10 A.M., 11 A.M., 1 P.M., 2 P.M., and 3 P.M.; Sat. and Sun., 11:15 A.M., 1 P.M., and 2 P.M. Admission.

St. Mary's Catholic Church, 1100 Chartres St., New Orleans, LA 70116. 529-3040. Guided tours given as part of Old Ursuline Convent tours. Call for schedule of services.

Transportation/Tours:

Cemetery Tours—

Cukie's Travels, Inc., 4610 Redwood St., New Orleans, LA 70127. 244-9679.

Gray Line of New Orleans, 1300 World Trade Center, New Orleans, LA 70130. 587-0861 or 1-800-535-7786. Cemetery visit included in city tour.

Magic Cemetery Tours, 593-9693, conducts daily tours of St. Louis Cemetery No. 1. Tours leave daily from the Wax Museum, 917 Conti St., New Orleans, LA 70112 in the French Quarter at 10:40 A.M. and 1:40 P.M.

Save Our Cemeteries, 2045 Magazine St., Suite D, New Orleans, LA 70130. 588-9357. Call for times and reservations.

Chalmette National Historical Park—Boat Tours
Creole Queen Paddlewheeler, Poydras Street Wharf, New Orleans, LA 70130. 529-4567 or 1-800-445-4109.

Longue Vue House and Gardens—Tours
Call Longue Vue House and Gardens, 488-5488, or the New Orleans Metropolitan Convention and Visitors Bureau, 566-5011.

Information:

FYI—A free, interactive phone network sponsored by WWL-TV and the Crescent City Trade Exchange. Callers who dial FYI-1515 (394-1515) can hear descriptions of the cuisine and make reservations at local restaurants; get information on and purchase tickets to attractions, special events, performances, and exhibits; listen to a local weather forecast; and order a taxi.

New Orleans Metropolitan Convention and Visitors Bureau, 1520 Sugar Bowl Dr., New Orleans, LA 70112. 566-5068 or 566-5031. Welcome centers are at New Orleans International Airport, 467-9276, and 529 St. Ann St., facing Jackson Square, 566-5031.

Guide Services:

Request "A Visitors Guide" from the New Orleans Metropolitan Convention and Visitors Bureau.

Accommodations:

New Orleans has numerous hotels, motels, and Bed and Breakfasts. For a complete listing request the New Orleans Metropolitan Convention and Visitors Bureau's "A Visitors Guide."

Restaurants:

Brennan's Restaurant, 417 Royal St., New Orleans, LA 70130. 525-9711. Breakfast: Daily, 8 A.M.-2:30 P.M. Dinner: Daily, 6-10 P.M. Lunch: Mon.-Fri., 11:30 A.M.-2:30 P.M.

Commander's Palace, 1403 Washington Ave., New Orleans, LA

70130. 899-8221. Lunch: Mon.-Fri., 11:30 A.M.-2 P.M.; Sat., 11 A.M.-2 P.M.; Sun., 10:30 A.M.-2 P.M. Dinner: Daily, 6-10 P.M.

For a complete listing of New Orleans restaurants, request the New Orleans Metropolitan Convention and Visitors Bureau's "A Visitors Guide."

Major Annual Events:

"A Creole Christmas"—French Quarter component of Christmas in New Orleans—December 1-31.

French Market Tomato Festival—First weekend in June.

French Quarter Festival—Mid-April.

Mardi Gras Day—Tuesday before Ash Wednesday.

New Orleans Jazz & Heritage Festival—Last weekend in April–first weekend in May.

Spring Fiesta—One week beginning the first Friday after Easter.

Aquarium of the Americas. (Photo courtesy Audubon Institute)

White alligator on exhibit at Audubon Zoo. (Photo courtesy Audubon Institute)

Louisiana Swamp Exhibit at Audubon Zoo. (Photo courtesy Audubon Institute)

3

A IS FOR AQUARIUM, Z IS FOR ZOO

(F)

Engraved squares of red bricks line the walkway in front of New Orleans' **Aquarium of the Americas.** The bricks, etched with the names of aquarium patrons, are symbolic of the enthusiastic reception the aquatic museum has received since it opened on the banks of the Mississippi River in 1990. The aquarium is the perfect place to start a tour of some fine family attractions offered by the Crescent City. Attendance at this world-class marine facility at the foot of Canal Street has exceeded records set by most other American aquariums.

When you enter the aquarium's exhibit areas, you are surrounded by a magnificent glass archway filled with sky-blue water. Shimmering, rainbow-hued fish circle all around you. When you finally tear yourself away from their mesmerizing spell, you come face to face with several hundred more curiosities of the sea.

The aquarium's lively displays focus on ecosystems in the Caribbean Reef, the Amazon Rainforest, the Gulf of Mexico, and the Mississippi River. Kids love to accept the management's invitation to "Sea Life Up Close" at "touch me" stations and a microlab. The whole family can enjoy lunch and a fabulous view of the Mississippi River from the water wonderland's glass-fronted River Cafe before they see one of the spectacular films shown next door at the aquarium's **IMAX Theater**.

Or you can board the *John James Audubon* riverboat just

outside the front door to take a 45-minute Mississippi River cruise to the **Audubon Zoo,** internationally acclaimed as one of the best zoos in America. The menagerie houses more than 1,800 of the world's rarest animals in a tranquil setting of flower-lined paths that circle whimsical statues and peaceful lagoons. Some of the critters star in educational shows at Wendy's Wildlife Theater and are featured on the Discovery Walk in Wisner Children's Village. You may see both of these presentations on your tour of the zoo.

While you are strolling through the exhibits, pause to taste some of Louisiana's Cajun cuisine at the Cypress Knee Cafe in the Louisiana Swamp Exhibit. Or, if your taste buds are not that adventurous, you can enjoy pizza, hamburgers, and other American snack foods offered by other concessionaires.

When you are ready to leave the animal kingdom, catch the zoo's free shuttle bus at the entrance gate near the Zootique and Zoovenir shops. It will bring you to St. Charles Avenue, where you can board the oldest continuously operating street railway in existence for a pleasant ride past the universities, mansions, and monuments that line one of New Orleans' loveliest thoroughfares.

When the streetcar reaches Canal Street—the city's main downtown boulevard—transfer to any one of the RTA (Regional Transit Authority) buses running along Canal Street and ride back to the riverfront. Cross the Riverfront Streetcar tracks and step up to Spanish Plaza and the **Riverwalk Marketplace.** Here, you can explore more than 140 specialty shops, restaurants, and cafes.

To learn more about life along the Mississippi River, read the informative plaques stationed along Spanish Plaza, the brick walkway behind Riverwalk Marketplace, and the shopping center's second-floor balconies. Then, take a ride across the Mississippi's muddy waters on the **Canal Street Ferry.** The fifteen-minute trip gives you a riverboat pilot's view of the New Orleans skyline.

The ferry ties up at a west bank dock where you can board a complimentary van that will transport you to Blaine Kern's Mardi Gras World. The vehicle usually meets each ferry, but delays can occur during busy seasons. Call the attraction from the ferry terminal if the van is not waiting when you arrive.

Mardi Gras World is part of the largest parade float enterprise in the world. In the huge construction shed, you can chat with artists and craftspeople as they create magical, movable works of art.

If you enjoy boating on the Mississippi River and long for more watery adventures, stop by one of the booths in Spanish Plaza, Riverwalk Marketplace, Jackson Brewery, the French Market, or Woldenberg Park. Representatives will give you information on extended river tours and boat trips to Louisiana's fascinating bayous and swamps.

Woldenberg Park spans the riverfront between the Aquarium of the Americas and Jackson Brewery. Relax on a bench near its grassy sculpture garden and watch the endless parade of ships that constantly sail into the Port of New Orleans and the upriver Port of South Louisiana. Together, these two ports form the second largest cargo facility in the world.

Jackson Brewery is a festival marketplace on the edge of Jackson Square. The two-building complex contains many appealing shops and restaurants. A retail museum, featuring the work of Louisiana artisans, tops the Jackson Brewery's Millhouse at the corner of Toulouse and Decatur streets. The shopping center is named for the brewery that built the Romanesque Revival building in 1891 and concocted its popular beer there until 1974.

Step out of the Brewery's front door and cross the street to **Jackson Square,** the historic center of the French Quarter. In the 1700s, the square served as a parade ground. It was made over into a garden park in 1856, a few years after Baroness Pontalba built the red-bricked Pontalba Apartments that face each other across the square. The **Cabildo** and **Presbytere,** governmental centers of the old city, also front the square. They shelter relics of New Orleans' colorful past in several floors of intriguing exhibits and buttress the graceful spires of **St. Louis Cathedral,** one of the most photographed churches in America.

Watch the diversified procession of artists, street players, and mule-drawn carriages that converges on Jackson Square while you sip a cup of *café au lait* (a hot coffee and milk mixture) at **Café du Monde** in the French Market. Be sure to sample some *beignets* (ben-yays), traditional square doughnuts dredged with a coating of powdered sugar.

Folks have been trading goods at the site of the **French Market** for more than two hundred years. In Dutch Alley, behind Café du Monde, lifelike statues depict buyers and sellers who frequented the stalls many years ago. Today, a beguiling mélange of boutiques, vegetable stands, and flea market booths fills the market and spills out into the street.

At the **Jean Lafitte National Historical Park and Preserve Visitors Center** in Dutch Alley, Louisiana folkways are celebrated with a variety of programs, including musical performances and craft demonstrations. Enjoy one of the complimentary French Quarter walking tours that leave the center daily and inquire about ranger-conducted tours in other areas of the city.

If your youngsters are tired of sight-seeing, walk to the riverfront behind the French Market and hop aboard one of the bright red streetcars that roam the 1.9-mile Riverfront Streetcar route. Get off at Julia Street and walk four blocks to the **Louisiana Children's Museum,** between Tchoupitoulas and Magazine streets.

At the museum, toddlers enjoy a special indoor playscape while older siblings try out hands-on exhibits that allow them to form bubbles taller than themselves, construct building-block castles, and indulge in a bit of washable face painting. They can also step into a studio and pretend they are anchoring an evening newscast, or shop at a miniature supermarket. These are but a few of the many fun things to do in the recently expanded museum.

When everyone has explored all the presentations at the Louisiana Children's Museum, board RTA's Magazine Street bus (heading toward Canal Street) at the corner of Camp and Julia streets. Exit at Poydras Street, a few blocks before Canal Street, and walk one block away from the Mississippi River to St. Charles Avenue. Here you can board the Claiborne-Poydras bus and ride to the **Louisiana Superdome.**

Inside the largest domed stadium in the world, you will be treated to a guided tour of locker rooms used by the New Orleans Saints and visiting NFL teams, see the press box, and visit one of the dome's prized VIP suites. Many family-oriented events such as circuses and ice shows are scheduled at the Louisiana Superdome. To learn about them, and plays and entertainments for the younger set produced on other stages around the city, request a calendar of events from the New Orleans Metropolitan Convention and Visitors Bureau.

Area Code: (504)

Getting There:

Interstates 10, 55, and 59 take you to New Orleans in the southeast section of Louisiana. The city is served by Amtrak. Commercial flights land at New Orleans International Airport.

Where and When:

Aquarium of the Americas, 1 Canal St., New Orleans, LA 70130. 861-2537. Sun.-Thurs., 9:30 A.M.-6 P.M.; Fri. and Sat., 9:30 A.M.-7 P.M. Admission.

Note: In the spring and fall, the aquarium schedules several overnight adventures for children ages 2-12 called "Z-z-z in the Seas." Children bring camping gear for the sleep-over and must be accompanied by an adult. Continental breakfast is served. Call the aquarium's education department for more information. Special charge in addition to aquarium admission price.

Audubon Zoo, 6500 Magazine St. (P.O. Box 4327), New Orleans, LA 70178. 861-2537. Apr.-Sept.: Daily, 9:30 A.M.-5:30 P.M.; Oct.-Mar.: 9:30 A.M.-4:30 P.M. Closed first Friday in May in addition to some major holidays. Admission.

Note: Audubon Zoo offers a "Nocturnal Adventure" for children ages 2-12 on several weekends in the spring and fall. Children receive special education and viewing of animals in selected areas of the zoo. They spend the night sleeping in their camping gear in the zoo's educational building. An adult must accompany children on "Nocturnal Adventures." Continental breakfast is served. Special charge in addition to zoo admission price.

Cabildo, Louisiana State Museum, 751 Chartres St., New Orleans, LA 70116. 568-6968. Tues.-Sun., 10 A.M.-5 P.M. Admission.

Café du Monde, 800 Decatur St., New Orleans, LA 70116. 581-2914. Open 24 hours, daily.

Canal Street Ferry, Marine Dept., Crescent City Connection Division, 2001 Victory Park Dr. (P.O. Box 6297), New Orleans, LA 70174-6297. Daily, 5:45 A.M.-9:30 P.M. Leaves the east bank on the hour and half-hour, the west bank on the quarter-hour.

French Market, 1008 N. Peters St., New Orleans, LA 70116. 522-2621. Shops: Mon.-Sat., 9 A.M.-5 P.M. Farmers Market and Flea Market: Daily, 8 A.M.-7 P.M.

IMAX Theater, 1 Canal St., New Orleans, LA 70130. 581-IMAX. Call for information and schedule. Admission.

Jackson Brewery, 600 Decatur St., Suite 300, New Orleans, LA 70130. 566-7245. Sun.-Thurs., 10 A.M.-9 P.M.; Fri. and Sat., 10 A.M.-10 P.M. Restaurants open later.

Jean Lafitte National Historical Park and Preserve Visitors Center, 916 N. Peters St., New Orleans, LA 70116. 589-2636. Daily, 9 A.M.-5 P.M. Free guided tours.

John James Audubon, New Orleans Steamboat Company, Suite 1300, World Trade Center, New Orleans, LA 70130. 586-8777. Departs from Aquarium at 10 A.M., noon, 2 P.M., and 4 P.M. Departs from Audubon Zoo at 11 A.M., 1 P.M., 3 P.M., and 5 P.M. Admission.

Louisiana Children's Museum, 428 Julia St., New Orleans, LA 70130. 523-1357. Tues.-Sun., 9:30 A.M.-4:30 P.M. Admission.

Louisiana Superdome, Sugar Bowl Drive, New Orleans, LA 70112. 587-3810. Tours daily at 10 A.M., noon, 2 P.M., and 4 P.M., except during some Superdome events. Admission.

Mardi Gras World, 233 Newton St., New Orleans, LA 70114. 361-7821. Daily, 9:30 A.M.-4:30 P.M. Admission.

Presbytere, Louisiana State Museum, 751 Chartres St., New Orleans, LA 70116. 568-6968. Tues.-Sun., 10 A.M.-5 P.M. Admission.

Riverwalk Marketplace, #1 Poydras St., New Orleans, LA 70130. 522-1555. Mon-Thurs., 10 A.M.-9 P.M.; Fri. and Sat., 10 A.M.-10 P.M.; Sun., 11 A.M.-7 P.M. Restaurants may open early and close late.

St. Louis Cathedral, 615 Pere Antoine Alley, New Orleans, LA 70116. 525-9585. Mon.-Sat., 9 A.M.-5 P.M.; Sun., 1-5 P.M. between services. Free guided tours.

Note: Although farther afield, the Barataria Unit of Jean Lafitte National Park and Preserve, Chalmette Battlefield, City Park, museums in Kenner's Rivertown, and the Louisiana Nature and Science Center (not included in this car-free taste of New Orleans family attractions) are all ideal family destinations that you may want to explore on a longer, or additional, visit.

Transportation:

All attractions on this getaway can be reached by walking or using public transportation. A one-day or three-day VisiTour Pass allows unlimited transportation on all RTA bus and streetcar lines. The passes may be purchased at the Sheraton, Fairmont, and Marriott hotels, the Riverwalk, Jackson Brewery, and other locations. A foldout VisiTour Map in *Where* magazine, available free at hotels and tourist information centers, outlines the routes of bus and streetcar lines most often used by visitors. For more information on buses or streetcars, call the Regional Transit Authority at 569-2700.

Information:

FYI—A free, interactive phone network sponsored by WWL-TV and the Crescent City Trade Exchange. Callers who dial FYI-1515 (394-1515) can hear descriptions of the cuisine and make reservations at local restaurants; get information on and purchase tickets to attractions, special events, performances, and exhibits; listen to a local weather forecast; and order a taxi.

New Orleans Metropolitan Convention and Visitors Bureau, 1520 Sugar Bowl Dr., New Orleans, LA 70112. 566-5011. Welcome centers are at New Orleans International Airport, 467-9276, and 529 St. Ann St., facing Jackson Square, 566-5031.

Guide Services:

Request a copy of "A Visitors Guide" from the New Orleans Metropolitan Convention and Visitors Bureau.

Accommodations:

New Orleans has numerous chain and independent hotels and motels and Bed and Breakfasts. For a complete listing of accommodations, consult the New Orleans Metropolitan Convention and Visitors Bureau's "A Visitors Guide."

Restaurants:

New Orleans offers excellent restaurants in every price range. Moderately priced, casual restaurants close to getaway attractions include:

Gumbo Shop, 630 St. Peter St., New Orleans, LA 70116. 525-1486. Daily, 11 A.M.-11 P.M.

Johnny's Po-Boys, 511 St. Louis St., New Orleans, LA 70130. 524-8159. Daily, 11 A.M.-9 P.M.

La Madeleine French Bakery & Cafe, 547 St. Ann St., New Orleans, LA 70116. 568-9950. Daily, 7 A.M.-9 P.M.

Mother's Restaurant, 401 Poydras St., New Orleans, LA 70130. 523-9656. Mon.-Sat., 5 A.M.-10 P.M.; Sun., 7 A.M.-10 p.M.

Note: Youngsters can enjoy the wonderful variety of music available in New Orleans at the following locations:

Mulate's, The World's Most Famous Cajun Restaurant, 201 Julia St., New Orleans, LA 70130. 522-1492. Daily, 11 A.M.-11 P.M. Children's menu. Live Cajun music nightly at 7:30 P.M.

O'Flaherty's Irish Channel Pub, 508 Toulouse St., New Orleans, LA 70130. 529-1317. Presentations of authentic Irish music start at 7:30 P.M. during the fall, winter, and spring; 8:30 P.M. in the summer. No food service in performance area. Nominal cover charge.

Preservation Hall, 726 St. Peter St., New Orleans, LA 70116. Day: 522-2842. Night: 523-8939. New Orleans jazz played from 8 P.M.-midnight (line forms early). Admission.

Sunday gospel, jazz, or blues brunches are offered at several hotels and restaurants. Consult "A Visitors Guide" published by the New Orleans Metropolitan Convention and Visitors Bureau or seek advice from your hotel concierge.

Major Annual Events:

Christmas in New Orleans—December 1-31.

French Quarter Festival—Mid-April.

Mardi Gras Day—Tuesday before Ash Wednesday.

New Orleans Jazz & Heritage Festival—Last weekend in April–first weekend in May.

Spring Fiesta—One week, beginning the first Friday after Easter.

At an average speed of eight miles per hour, the Mississippi Queen's
(c. 1976) decks provide an inviting front row seat to enjoy the setting sun.
(Photo courtesy The Delta Steamboat Company)

River Royalty–The National Historic Landmark Delta Queen *is one of
only three paddle-wheel steamboats to still ply America's rivers on overnight
cruise vacations.* (Photo courtesy The Delta Steamboat Company)

4

ALL DECKED OUT

(F)

The two *Queens* were all decked out for their "Old-fashioned Holiday" house party. The elegant grand dame wore a jewel-toned costume; her younger sibling was glamorously swathed in a pretty, patterned brocade. In honor of the Yuletide season, both of the royal ladies wore festive wreaths and bright red ribbons that fluttered merrily in the breeze. They proudly stood by while accomplished aides welcomed their guests and smiling stewards made sure each was comfortable and content. Some of their houseguests came from distant shores, but others were old friends who lived nearby. With remarkable *savoir faire* and impeccable good taste, the *Queens'* well-trained staff wined them, dined them, and treated them to satire and song.

Overseeing such a splendid party is not a once-in-a-lifetime fling for these experienced hostesses, they do this sort of thing all the time. The regal septuagenarian is the world-renowned *Delta Queen,* the only authentic, fully restored steamboat in the world. Her stylish, twenty-year-old sister, the *Mississippi Queen,* retains the traditional silhouette of her fabulous ancestors but enhances it with contemporary refinements.

Last summer, the *American Queen,* a sophisticated beauty endowed with splendid innovations in steamboat design, joined her famous sisters berthed at the Robin Street Wharf along the Mississippi River in New Orleans.

Cruising the illustrious river Mark Twain called "the majestic, the magnificent Mississippi" on one of the *Queen*s is a marvelous way to celebrate a noteworthy occasion, or escape from everyday cares, especially when the music, food, and entertainment harmonizes with appealing themes such as "Dixie Fest," "In the Good Old Summertime," and "Old-Fashioned Holidays."

For instance, the "Dixie Fest" cruise creates an exhilarating mood with a spirited, jazz send-off. Then, as the steamer's paddle wheel churns along the fabled river, passengers enjoy a potpourri of Southern-flavored activities that may include a guest historian who interprets the legends and music of the region, a tongue-in-cheek "Madams of Bourbon Street" competition, or a "Foods of the Deep South" buffet. The day is brought to a joyful conclusion with an energetic, second-line parade to the music of Pete Fountain, the Preservation Hall Jazz Band, or other great musicians.

These convivial cruises on The Delta Queen Steamboat Company's "floating wedding cakes"—a nickname inspired by the steamboats' elaborate architectural decorations—recapture the romance of America's legendary steamboat era. On delightful, three-night excursions from New Orleans, the *Queen*s steam up the mighty Mississippi to St. Francisville, the charming town described in "A Feliciana Parish Treasure Hunt," and stop at either Houmas House or Oak Alley Plantation along the way. Passengers are offered shore excursions at these intriguing locales for an additional fee, but the spellbinding lore and mesmerizing lure of the Father of Waters is theirs for the taking.

Steamboat riverlorians—crew members who are well versed in the history, navigation, and landmarks of the many rivers the paddle-wheelers ply—distribute charts that identify mile markers and sites along the river and share their treasure trove of river trivia with interested passengers.

The facts and figures presented by the riverlorian kindle an appreciation of the knowledgeable captains who guide the steamboats through the Mississippi's erratic twists and turns. This is enhanced when you tour the pilothouse and learn that these officers must be able to draw from memory every component of the Mississippi River's shores and channels that their boat travels before they are granted a license for that section of the river.

With their well-being in such capable hands, passengers relax and savor the luxury of communing with the river. Some nestle in comfortable rockers on the *Delta Queen*'s decks to gaze at the passing scene and are lulled to sleep by the rhythm of her big, red paddle wheel. Others reserve *Mississippi Queen* or *American Queen* staterooms with private verandas so they can enjoy a singular kinship with the river.

Folks who prefer to socialize while admiring the passing procession of river traffic gather at the Calliope Bar and refreshing spa pool on these two steamers. Passengers on the colossal *American Queen* may also observe the diversity of life on the waterway from an airy forward deck dubbed the "front porch of America."

Some passengers spend idle moments reading *Steamboatin' Times,* a daily newspaper published on board each paddle-wheeler. The journal capsulizes the history and flavor of fascinating places visited on the cruise and lists the day's events. The schedule may include a cooking demonstration by a famous chef, a calliope concert, or perhaps a singalong led by a vivacious banjo-picker. Many passengers embrace every engaging diversion mentioned in the *Times,* but those who prefer the tranquility of a deck chair are not disturbed.

Although their leisure time preferences may differ, everyone agrees that meals prepared by the cruise line's talented chefs are exceptionally delicious. On the *Delta Queen,* the accommodating dining room staff waits on 174 hungry passengers. Their counterparts on the *Mississippi Queen* serve 420, and the *American Queen* staff offers quality service to 436. Mealtime dress is casual except for the Captain's Dinner and the Captain's Champagne Reception, gala events that highlight every cruise.

The activities, dimensions, and decor particular to each steamer contribute to her personality. Thousands of *Delta Queen* passengers cherish the communion with the past they enjoy aboard this National Historic Landmark and return again and again to sit among the antique furnishings in her beautiful parlors and to spend music-filled evenings in her intimate Texas Lounge. And those who claim the *Mississippi Queen* as their favorite are enthralled by an unusual combination of steamboat aura and cruise ship luxury that offers them an elevator and movie theater along with a grand staircase and showboat-style entertainment. Steamboat buffs are sure to find the *American Queen*'s blend of state-of-the art technology, nostalgic grandeur, and modern amenities just as irresistible. The newest steamboat on America's waters has the same modern conveniences as the *Mississippi Queen,* plus a two-story theater reminiscent of an opulent opera house, a lavish dining room accented with filigree woodwork and brilliant chandeliers, and four handsome decks that encircle her grand, yet graceful, hull.

Area Code: (504)

Getting There:

The Delta Queen Steamboat Company's three *Queen*s are berthed at the Robin Street Wharf in New Orleans.

Information:

Contact The Delta Queen Steamboat Company at 1-800-543-1949 or call your travel agent.

5

ACROSS THE LAKE
(F) (G)

New Orleanians have been going "across the lake" for years. Early residents sought the clean air and healthful waters on the north shore of Lake Pontchartrain to escape dreaded plagues of yellow fever. Cool breezes, whispering through towering pines, lured later generations to summer homes along the lakefront and the area's scenic rivers.

Going "across the lake" is still a great idea; the setting is tranquil and the life-style of the area is relaxing. Brochures, available at the **St. Tammany Parish Tourist & Convention Commission** in the Hollycrest Shopping Center on U.S. 190 between Interstate 12 and Covington, will help you get the lay of the land.

Mandeville's lovely, laid-back lakefront is a great place to start your north shore getaway. To get there, turn east off of U.S. 190 onto Monroe Street (Louisiana 1087), about four miles south of the Tourist & Convention Commission office. Then follow one of the "preferred route" signs to the lake.

Ride or stroll past Mandeville's quaint cottages and the historic summer resorts on Lakeshore Drive, then yield to temptation and lounge on the patio of one of several inviting restaurants with a cool drink in your hand. If the wind is right, you can watch sailboats glide across Lake Pontchartrain's rippling water.

Some vacationers spend whole weekends just lazing in the sun on Mandeville's balmy lakefront. But, if it is your first trip across the lake, or you like a little activity between your lackadaisical lapses, be sure to explore the north shore's family attractions, historic sites, and inviting shops.

Make **Wind Haven House** antique shop on Lakeshore Drive and **Small Mall Antiques,** three blocks off the lakefront on Gerard Street, your first stops. While you are at the mall, check on play dates at the **North Star Theatre.** The playhouse, located at the rear of the mall, is the pride of Mandeville.

The town was carved out of Fontainebleau, Bernard Marigny de Mandeville's sprawling sugar plantation. Approximately 2,700 acres of Mandeville's estate were later incorporated into **Fontainebleau State Park.** The green space is one of several enjoyable destinations along U.S. 190 East between Mandeville and Slidell. The eighteen-mile route is part of a well-marked Louisiana Scenic Byway that connects St. Tammany's historic towns. Motorists following the byway stretch their legs on trails in Fontainebleau State Park or on the interpretive nature trail at **Northlake Nature Center** across from the park.

A few miles beyond Fontainebleau and Northlake and one mile left on Lacombe's Fish Hatchery Road (Louisiana 1072), visit the grottolike **Our Lady of Lourdes Shrine** erected by Father François Balay in the early 1800s. Spring water flows into a basin in the little chapel where pilgrims leave mementos.

On Fish Hatchery Road, you will notice a sign advertising **Bayou Lacombe Museum.** Open only on Sunday afternoons from March through October, the museum focuses on the area's earliest inhabitants, the Choctaw Indians, and the folkways of European pioneers who followed.

If you happen upon Lacombe in time for lunch or supper, you will have a tough time deciding on a place to eat. You can choose between the Italian and seafood specialties offered at **Sal & Judy's,** the elegant French cuisine served at award-winning **La Provence,** or the steak and seafood fare at **Sal's Place** (all on U.S. 190).

About ten miles past Lacombe, where U.S. 190 intersects U.S. 11 in Slidell, turn right and go about a mile to Cousin Street, the entrance to the city's Olde Towne neighborhood.

Shopkeepers gladly hand you a Slidell Antique District brochure that pinpoints the area's offerings. You can wander through several of the attractive shops, visit the **Slidell Museum,** and sip a soda at the **Old Town Slidell Soda Shop.** If you didn't stop for lunch in Lacombe, enjoy a light lunch or afternoon tea at Sue Claverie's **Victorian Tea Room** on Carey Street. Here, you can enjoy freshly made soups, salads, sandwiches, or quiches in an lovely setting. Be sure to save room for one of the tearoom's luscious desserts. They are Mama Sue Willis's (Sue's mother) specialty.

Complete your tour of Slidell's vintage neighborhood with a visit to **Salmen-Fritchie House.** Fritz Salmen built this magnificent home in the 1890s when his brick, lumber, and shipbuilding companies were going strong. Homer and Sharon Fritchie welcome visitors who tour their elegantly furnished home and those who enjoy it as bed-and-breakfast guests. To reach Salmen-Fritchie House, return to U.S. 11 and drive two blocks past Cousin Street to Cleveland Avenue.

To continue on, return to U.S. 11, travel south about one mile, and turn left onto Old Spanish Trail. Three miles down the road, at **Slidell Factory Stores,** you can select discount-priced clothes, textiles, housewares, and other attractive merchandise.

If you dream about wearing space gear instead of a stylish ensemble, do some window-shopping at the **National Space Technology Laboratories'** oceanographic and environmental labs. The Visitors Center is approximately fifteen miles down Interstate 10 east of Slidell, on Mississippi 607.

When you are ready to come down to earth, consider landing in the Honey Island Swamp. Sightings and stories about this pristine wilderness's Bigfoot abound, but the monster is not likely to join you. As guides from **Gator Tours, Swamp Monster Tours,** and **Wagner's Honey Island Swamp Tours** steer their boats along the bayous, you are more likely to see flame-colored azaleas, blue herons, dusky green alligators, and other wonders of nature. Maps showing the locations of these tours are on brochures available from the St. Tammany Parish Tourist & Convention Commission.

Christ Episcopal Chapel. (Photo by K. Parsons, courtesy St. Tammany Parish Tourist & Convention Commission)

Chapel at St. Joseph's Abbey. (Photo by Hyatt Hood, courtesy St. Tammany Parish Tourist & Convention Commission)

A Honey Island Swamp tour. (Photo by Hyatt Hood, courtesy St. Tammany Parish Tourist & Convention Commission)

If you don't have time for a tour, drive to the rest area at the intersection of U.S. 90 and U.S. 190 southeast of Slidell and stroll the 300-foot boardwalk Chevron Companies and the Nature Conservancy of Louisiana built in the White Kitchen eagle preserve. Bring your binoculars and enjoy an excellent view of the oldest documented bald eagle nesting spot in Louisiana. Eagles live in the treetop nest between September and May and have returned to it for more than eighty years.

A visit to Madisonville is a pleasant way to end one day of your north shore getaway. Take Interstate 12 west to Exit 1077 to reach this Victorian gem. The quaint village offers appealing boutiques and antique shops, plus historical exhibits in an old courthouse and jail that now serve as the **Madisonville Museum.**

Al fresco dining is offered in several restaurants along the Tchefuncte River. After dinner, enjoy a twilight walk past Madisonville's gingerbreaded cottages and century-old churches.

In nearby Covington, passersby always take delight in picture perfect **Christ Episcopal Chapel.** The tiny chapel looks as if it was set up on the edge of town by a film crew as the setting for a romantic country wedding. Its turreted bell tower reaches toward the heavens; its clapboard walls are encircled by flower beds and a white picket fence.

Christ Episcopal Chapel is Covington's oldest building. To see it, and the town's other historic buildings and attractions, take U.S. 190 Business into Covington or Louisiana 21, the Louisiana Scenic Byway route between Madisonville and Covington.

U.S. 190 Business becomes Boston Street as you cross the Bogue Falaya River into Covington. Christ Episcopal Chapel is near the entrance to Bogue Falaya Park, a picnic area at the end of New Hampshire Street, south of Boston Street. At the **St. Tammany Art Association** building, across the street from the church, you can contemplate works by local artists and get directions to several more Covington galleries. Art enthusiasts especially enjoy the showrooms during the coordinated opening sponsored by the galleries in May and October.

Youngsters take delight in plays staged by the St. Tammany Art Association's **Discovery Theater** and exhibits mounted at the group's **Discovery Center.** Projects and artworks by St. Tammany Parish students are displayed here along with traveling shows on world culture, science, art, history, and mathematics.

Art is not displayed at **H. J. Smith's Son** museum and old-time country store on Columbia Street (one block east of New Hampshire Street across Boston Street), but there are a lot of fascinating articles in these side-by-side landmarks.

H. J. Smith's grandson, or great-grandson, might welcome you to the family's farm supply and hardware store next to the century-old emporium his forefather founded in 1876.

In the newer store, there is a 150-year-old corn crib full of kerosene lamps, cast-iron pots, and enamelware. A few steps away, and a hundred years back in time, in the dimly lit, nineteenth-century store, antique appliances rest amid a hodge-podge of farm tools and household implements.

When you go to H. J. Smith's Son, park in one of Covington's ox lots—parcels of land, such as the one behind the store, that were once used by teamsters who came to town with wag-onloads of produce to sell.

There are several antique shops in the vicinity of H. J. Smith's Son. A St. Tammany Parish Tourist & Convention Commission handout lists them plus many more Covington shops that are fun to explore. Some are located in **The Market,** a collection of smart boutiques behind the town's former railroad station. When you have had your fill of shopping, enjoy the delicious lunches and tea cakes served in **The Victorian Tea Room,** a popular gathering place affiliated with **Jefferson House,** a gift and interiors shop.

If you liked The Market, you will love Covington's enticing **Lee Lane Shops.** They are housed in a row of nineteenth-century Creole cottages near the Boston Street entrance to town. An assortment of goods vies for your attention here. Among them are unique kitchen utensils, quilts, decorative items, books, and clothing. More delectable refreshments are offered at **Coffee Rani** on the lane. There are also **Sterling to a Tea,** on the corner of Lee Lane and East Boston Street, and **Tyler Downtown Drugstore and Soda Fountain,** one block away on North Florida Street.

Side trips from Covington lead to some pleasing places. Abita Springs, a once-popular health resort three miles east of Covington via Louisiana 36, is now an old-fashioned village. Drive around town, or follow the walking tour booklet distributed at Abita Springs Junior High School, to see Victorian homes and churches built during the yellow fever epidemics. In Abita Springs Tourist Park, a pavilion built for the 1884 World's Industrial and Cotton Centennial Exposition rests on the site of one of the springs that gave the town its name. The park affords visitors easy access to the **Tammany Trace,** a rail-to-trail conversion of an abandoned Illinois Central Railroad corridor that extends through scenic woodlands and marshes. When it is completed, the 31-mile recreational trail will link Covington, Abita Springs, Mandeville, Lacombe, and Slidell. Hikers, skaters, and cyclists presently enjoy 8½ miles of paved trail between Abita and Mandeville. And the nine-mile section connecting Mandeville and Lacombe is scheduled to open by December 1996. A separate equestrian trail parallels the ten-foot-wide asphalt path. Bicycles may be rented at **Tour de Trace** in Mandeville, located next to the caboose that serves as headquarters for the Tammany Trace Foundation.

Many people still believe in the curative powers of Abita Spring's water and buy it by the jug. Others find it more appealing after the **Abita Brewing Company** adds malted barley, hops, and yeast to it. The micro-brewery recently moved to larger quarters and opened a brew pub in the center of town on the site of its former factory. Here customers can taste several thirst-quenching beers brewed in Abita, plus many other fine brews.

If you are visiting Abita Springs on a Friday night, rub elbows with locals playing bingo in **Abita Springs Town Hall.** Regulars have been selecting their lucky cards in the town hall every Friday night since 1948. Some of them are also in the audience when the **"Piney Woods Opry,"** a monthly country music show, is broadcast live from Abita Springs Town Hall on radio station KSLU (90.9 FM) and Channel 13, the local community-access television channel in Abita and Covington.

The section of the Louisiana Scenic Byway that follows Louisiana 21 between Covington and Bogalusa passes graceful country homes and pastoral views. But gourmands from miles around know it as the route to the **House of Seafood,** a popular, roadside restaurant midway between Covington and Bogalusa. The eatery's unimpressive exterior gives no hint of the sumptuous seafood buffet served inside.

In another unobtrusive building on the outskirts of Bogalusa, the **Double D Meat Company** entices customers with freshly made pork sausage and bacon, locally ground corn-meal, pork-end pellets used to make "pig skins," and a smorgasbord of other delicatessen items.

History buffs also consider the **Louisiana Museum of Ancient Indian Culture and the Bogue Lusa Pioneer Museum** in Bogalusa's Cassidy Park an alluring destination. To reach the park, turn north onto Louisiana 1075 near Sun before you reach Bogalusa and continue for about five miles to Willis Avenue. (Louisiana 1075 becomes Avenue F in Bogalusa.) Turn left on Willis and drive to the park entrance. (*Note:* If you want to stop at Double D Meat Company, backtrack to Louisiana 21 to visit the museum.)

Junketeers in the mood for a two-hour circular drive through the countryside can take Louisiana 10 from Bogalusa to Franklinton and continue on Louisiana 25 to Covington.

Every spring, brilliant azaleas and white-blossomed dog-woods line Louisiana 25 between Covington and Franklinton. Three miles outside of Covington, a sign signals the entrance to St. Joseph Seminary College on the beautiful grounds of **St. Joseph's Abbey.** Call the abbey and arrange for one of the Benedictine monks to give you a tour of the glorious frescos Dom Gregory Dewit painted on the walls and ceilings of the abbey's church and dining hall in the early 1950s.

Folsom, a crossroads village between Covington and Franklinton, is the center of Louisiana's multimillion-dollar horse industry. Many streets are bordered by wooden-fenced pastures where colts frolic under the watchful eyes of their mothers. Exotic animals moved in next door to the equine capital at Global Wildlife Center, eight miles west of Folsom. See "A Louisiana Safari" for directions to this wildlife education and conservation center where you can watch more than nine hundred animals roam the range.

As it winds through the gently sloping hills between Folsom and Franklinton, Louisiana 25 passes several wholesale nurseries that welcome retail customers. Orchards where you can pick blueberries and peaches are also located in this area. To arrange a visit, call the phone numbers noted in the St. Tammany Parish Tourist & Convention Commission's brochure, "St. Tammany: A Family Place." The leaflet describes many other facilities families can enjoy such as boat and canoe rentals, skating rinks, playgrounds, and parks. Two amusement centers, Sillyville and Live Oak Family Amusement, are recent additions to the list.

Sillyville, in Mandeville, delights and entertains the preschool set with rides, games, and soft play equipment. But Slidell's **Live Oak Family Amusement** is the place to bring those hard to entertain pre-teens and teenagers. A 27-hole miniature golf course, batting cages, a slick go-kart track, and a video game room keep young people happy for hours. Adults and teens enjoy Live Oak's lighted nine-hole (par three) golf course and lighted 300-yard golf driving range. Live Oak Family Amusement is just off Exit 83—the Louisiana 11 and Slidell/Pearl River exit—on Interstate 12.

At the end of a leisurely weekend across the lake, families driving back to New Orleans like to linger awhile at **Trey Yuen Cuisine of China.** This landmark eatery at the foot of the Lake Pontchartrain Causeway was recently voted one of the best Chinese restaurants in the United States by readers of *Conde Nast's Traveler.*

Area Code: (504)

Getting There:

From New Orleans, take Lake Pontchartrain Causeway to the north shore.

From the east or west, take Interstate 12.

From the north, connect with Interstate 12 via Interstate 55 and Interstate 59.

Where and When:

Abita Brewing Company, Inc., P.O. Box 762, Abita Springs, LA 70420. 893-3143. Call for schedule of complimentary tours.

Abita Springs Town Hall, Abita Springs, LA 70420. 892-0711. Bingo—Fri., 8 P.M. Admission.

Bayou Lacombe Museum, P.O. Box 63, Lacombe, LA 70445. Mar.-Oct., Sun., 2-5 P.M.; Nov.-Feb., 1st Sun. only, 2-5 P.M. Donations appreciated.

Christ Episcopal Chapel, 120 N. New Hampshire St., Covington, LA 70433. 892-3177.

Discovery Center, North Park Corporate Center, 109 N. Park Blvd., Covington, LA 70433. 892-8650 or 898-0976. Sat., 10 A.M.-5 P.M.; Sun., 1-5 P.M. Call 892-8650 for information on the Discovery Theater.

Double D Meat Company, 11518 LA 21 South, Bogalusa, LA 70427. 735-6581 or 735-6582. Mon.-Fri., 7 A.M.-4 P.M.

Fontainebleau State Park, P.O. Box 152, Mandeville, LA 70448. 624-4443. Daily, 8 A.M.-7 P.M. Admission.

Gator Swamp Tours, P.O. Box 2082, Slidell, LA 70459. 1-800-875-4287 or 649-1255 (Slidell), 484-6100 (New Orleans). Call for reservations and pick-up times.

H. J. Smith's Son, 308 N. Columbia St., Covington, LA 70433. 892-0460. Mon., Tues., Thurs., and Fri., 8:30 A.M.-5 P.M.; Wed., 8:30 A.M.-noon; Sat., 8:30 A.M.-1 P.M.

The Jefferson House, 619 Jefferson St., Covington, LA 70433. 892-6841. Mon.-Sat., 10 A.M.-5 P.M.

Lee Lane Shops, Lee Lane, Covington, LA. For information, contact Lee Lane Merchants Association, 227 Lee Lane, Covington, LA 70433. 893-3533.

Live Oak Family Amusement, 300 Brownswitch Rd., Slidell, LA 70458. 641-5500. Sun.-Thurs., 8 A.M.-10 P.M.; Fri. and Sat., 8 A.M.-11 P.M.

Louisiana Museum of Ancient Indian Culture and the Bogue Lusa Pioneer Museum, Cassidy Park, Bogalusa, LA. Call the Washington Parish Tourist Commission for information. Open Sat., 8 A.M.-4 P.M., Sun., 1-4 P.M. Donations appreciated.

Madisonville Museum, 201 Cedar St., Madisonville, LA 70447. 845-2100. Sat. and Sun., noon-4 P.M.

The Market, 500 N. Theard St., Covington, LA 70433. 893-5278. Tues.-Sat., 10 A.M.-5 P.M.; Sun., 12-4 P.M.

National Space Technology Laboratories, John C. Stennis Space Center, Bay St. Louis, MS 39529. (601) 688-2370. Daily, 9 A.M.-5 P.M.

Northlake Nature Center, U.S. 190, Mandeville, LA. For more information, contact the St. Tammany Parish Tourist & Convention Commission.

Our Lady of Lourdes Shrine, Fish Hatchery Road, Lacombe, LA. For more information, contact Sacred Heart Church, 28088 Main St., Lacombe, LA 70445. 882-5229. Daily, sunrise-sunset.

"Piney Woods Opry" country music show—Abita Springs Town Hall. One Sat. a month, 7-9 P.M., spring–fall. Arrive 45 minutes early, hall fills up fast. Call 892-0711 for more information. Donations appreciated.

St. Joseph's Abbey, St. Benedict, LA 70457. 892-1800. Tours, 8-10:30 A.M. and 1-5 P.M. Call for reservation. Donations appreciated.

St. Tammany Art Association, 129 N. New Hampshire St., Covington, LA 70433. 892-8650. Tues.-Sat., 10 A.M.-4 P.M.; Sun., 1-4 P.M.

Salmen-Fritchie House, 127 Cleveland Ave., Slidell, LA 70458. 643-1405. Tours, Tues.-Sat., noon-4 P.M. Call for reservation. Admission.

Sillyville, 4700 LA 22, Mandeville, LA 70448. Tues.-Thurs., 10 A.M.-6 P.M.; Fri. and Sat., 10 A.M.-8 P.M.; Sun., 1-7 P.M. Admission.

Slidell Factory Stores, 1000 Caruso St., Slidell, LA 70461. 646-0756. Mon.-Sat., 9 A.M.-9 P.M.; Sun., 12:30-5:30 P.M.

Slidell Museum, P.O. Box 1564, Slidell, LA 70458. 646-4380. Mon., Wed., and Fri., noon-4 P.M. Volunteer-operated, best to call ahead.

Small Mall Antiques/North Star Theatre, 347 Gerard St., Mandeville, LA 70448. 626-9510. Tues.-Sat., 10 A.M.-4:30 P.M.

Swamp Monster Tours, Indian Village Road, Slidell, LA 70461. 1-800-245-1132 or 641-5106 (day), 643-2878 (night). Call for departure time. Admission.

Tammany Trace, Tammany Trace Foundation, 21411 Koop Dr., Mandeville, LA 70448. Daily, 7 A.M.-sunset. For information on access points, trail facilities, and use, call 1-800-43-TRACE.

Tour de Trace, Tammany Trace, Koop Drive, Mandeville, LA 70448 (107 Brookter St., Slidell, LA 70461). For reservations, call 639-4002, 1-800-696-9469, or 643-8748. Sat. and Sun., 8 A.M.-sunset.

Wagner's Honey Island Swamp Tours, Inc., 106 Holly Ridge Dr., Slidell, LA 70461. 641-1769. Two-hour tours morning and afternoon. Call for departure times and reservation. Admission.

Wind Haven House Antiques, 2143 Lakeshore Dr., Mandeville, LA 70448. 626-3374. Daily, 9 A.M.-5 P.M.

Information:

St. Tammany Parish Tourist & Convention Commission, 600 U.S. 190 North, Suite 15, Covington, LA 70433. 892-0520 or 1-800-634-9443. Daily, 8:30 A.M.-4:30 P.M.

Washington Parish Tourist Commission, 608 Willis Ave., Bogalusa, LA 70427. 735-5731. Mon.-Thurs., 9 A.M.-noon, 1-5 P.M.; Fri., 9 A.M.-noon, 1-3 P.M.

Guide Services:

St. Tammany Parish Tour Guide Association, St. Tammany

Parish Tourist & Convention Commission, 600 U.S. 190 North, Suite 15, Covington, LA 70433. 892-0520 or 1-800-634-9443. Daily, 8:30 A.M.-4:30 P.M.

Accommodations:

Chain and independent motels are available in Slidell, Covington, Abita Springs, Lacombe, and Mandeville.

Bed and Breakfasts:

Little River Bluffs, P.O. Box 1466, Folsom, LA 70437. 796-5257.

Magnolia House, 904 Main St., Madisonville, LA 70447. 845-4922.

Millbank Farms, 75654 River Rd., Ramsey, LA 70435. 892-1606.

Pollyanna, 212 Lafitte St., Mandeville, LA 70448. 626-4053.

Riverside Hills Farm, 96 Gardenia Dr., Covington, LA 70433. 892-1794.

Salmen-Fritchie House, 127 Cleveland Ave., Slidell, LA 70458. 643-1405.

Trail's End, 71648 Maple St., Abita Springs, LA 70420. 867-9899.

Windy Pines Bed and Breakfast, 736 Lafayette St., Mandeville, LA 70448. 626-9189.

Woodshole Inn, 78253 Woodshole Lane, Folsom, LA 70437. 796-9077.

Restaurants:

Coffee Rani, 226 N. Lee Lane, Covington, LA 70433. 893-6158. Daily, 8 A.M.-5:30 P.M. Lunch served 11:30 A.M.-2:30 P.M.

House of Seafood, 81790 LA 21, Bush, LA 70431. 886-2231. Thurs.-Fri., 4-10 P.M.; Sat., 3-10 P.M.

La Provence, U.S. 190, Lacombe, LA 70445. 626-9598. Wed.-Sat., 5-11 P.M.; Sun., 1-9 P.M.

Old Town Slidell Soda Shop, 301 Cousin St., Slidell, LA 70458. 649-4806. Daily, 11 A.M.-9 P.M.

Sal & Judy's, U.S. 190, Lacombe, LA 70445. 882-9443. Wed.-Fri., 5-9:30 P.M.; Sat., 5-11 P.M.; Sun., noon-8 P.M.

Sal's Place, Corner of U.S. 190 and LA 434, Lacombe, LA 70445. 882-6680. Mon., Tues., and Thurs., 11 A.M.-3 P.M., 5-9 P.M.; Fri., 11 A.M.-3 P.M., 5-10 P.M.; Sat., 11 A.M.-10 P.M.; Sun., 11 A.M.-9 P.M. Closed Wednesdays.

Sterling to a Tea, 806 E. Boston St., Covington, LA 70433. 893-7968. Tues.-Sat., 10 A.M.-5 P.M.

Trey Yuen Cuisine of China, 600 N. Causeway Blvd., Mandeville, LA 70448. 626-4476. Lunch: Wed.-Fri., 11:30 A.M.-2 P.M. Dinner: Mon.-Thurs., 5-10 P.M.; Fri. and Sat., 5-11 P.M.; Sun., 11:30 A.M.-9:30 P.M.

Tyler Downtown Drugstore and Soda Fountain, 322 N. Florida St., Covington, LA 70433. 892-7220. Mon.-Fri., 8:30 A.M.-6:30 P.M.; Sat., 9 A.M.-7 P.M.

The Victorian Tea Room, 2228 Carey St., Slidell, LA 70458. 643-7881. Lunch: Tues.-Sat., 10 A.M.-3 P.M. Tea, sandwiches, and dessert plates: noon-3 P.M.

The Victorian Tea Room at Jefferson House, 619 S. Jefferson St., Covington, LA 70433. 892-6841. High tea: Mon.-Sat., noon-4 P.M. Light lunch: Wed., Thurs., and Fri., noon-4 P.M.

For a complete listing of St. Tammany Parish restaurants, request the St. Tammany Parish Tourist & Convention Commission's "Dining Guide."

Major Annual Events:

Bayou Lacombe Crab Festival—June.

Celtic Nations Festival, Madisonville—October.
Christmas in the Country, Lee Lane, Covington—December.

Madisonville Wooden Boat Festival—September.

Mandeville Seafood Festival—July.

St. Tammany Parish Fair—Week-long fair in late October or early November.

Slidell Antique District Street Fair—Last weekend in April and October.

Slidell Jazz Festival—May.

World Championship Annual Pirogue/Canoe Races—July.

The addax, an endangered species, has not been seen in the wild since 1986. (Photo courtesy Global Wildlife Center)

Grant's zebra is the only variety of zebra whose stripes extend down to the hooves. (Photo courtesy Global Wildlife Center)

6
A LOUISIANA SAFARI
(F)

If you daydream about seeing exotic animals roaming wild across the plains, but your bank balance makes a trip to the African veldt an unlikely possibility, do not abandon your dream. Zip up your jeans, load your camera, and set out on a safari to **Global Wildlife Center.**

The center, a nonprofit wildlife education and conservation facility located just north of Interstate 12, between Baton Rouge and New Orleans, is home to more than nine hundred animals and birds from all over the world.

Giraffes, camels, bison, zebra, crowned cranes, emus, elands, red lechwes, scimitar horn oryx, and Dama gazelles are among the fascinating wildlife you see, learn about, and feed while crossing Global's spacious grasslands in a tractor-pulled, rubber-wheeled covered wagon.

Many of the creatures that roam the nine hundred acres of sloping fields and placid ponds are endangered species. The Père David's deer and the addax, a screwhorn antelope native to North Africa, are two examples.

The wagon tour is one of several extras included in the "Overnight Special" that Global Wildlife Center offers guests at its **Safari Lodge.** Lodgers may also participate in the daily roundup of the center's reticulated giraffes, who must be housed for the night because they are vulnerable to extreme temperature changes. When the giraffes see the center's camouflaged truck approaching, they follow it back to the barn where the roundup crew rewards them with supper served in their quarters.

Safari Lodge guests sit down to a family-style meal in the inn's pleasant dining room. Get-acquainted conversations often include stories of encounters with animals that nibble corn from plastic cups proffered by wagon riders.

Rooms at the lodge are large and comfortably furnished. All have private baths and picture windows that look out on a field and pond frequented by moose and other animals. A "hot wire" is fixed around the lodge at night to keep Global Wildlife Center's four-legged population on its own turf. Hamlet, a pot bellied pig, and Willie and Danielle, two miniature Sicilian donkeys, are the only animals allowed near the lodge. The trio welcomes a bit of petting from visitors who stroll the walkway in front of the guesthouse.

Hamlet, Willie, and Danielle are the only animals guests are encouraged to approach outside of the covered wagons. Although some of Global Wildlife Center's animals appear to be tame, they *are* wild animals and can be aggressive if they feel threatened.

Most of the time, the animals peacefully roam the range. Deer nibble leaves at the edge of a thicket and gazelles and antelopes leap across open meadows. Stalk-legged waterfowl may be seen feeding in the preserve's well-stocked ponds.

If you want to try your luck in one of Global Wildlife Center's fishing holes, a staff member will take you on an early-morning expedition. With a good-sized bass or catfish in tow, or a good story about the one that got away, you will return to the lodge ready for the hearty breakfast served by a friendly kitchen crew.

Visitors who want to snap some outstanding wildlife pictures make reservations for a Global Wildlife Center Photo Safari. The reasonably priced jaunt (not included in the price of the overnight special) lets you focus your camera or camcorder on the animals you choose while safely perched on a metal-railed platform atop the same camouflaged truck used to herd the giraffes. When you are ready for a break, your driver will oblige with coffee and pastries.

If you are spending two nights at Global Wildlife Center, begin your second day with a horseback tour of the park—another exciting extra you can enjoy for an additional fee. Then explore the surrounding countryside and return to the lodge in time to watch the sunset. Many of the destinations described in "Tangipahoa Town Tour" and "Across the Lake" are less than a thirty-minute drive from Global Wildlife Center.

Breakfast and supper are included in the price of Global's overnight special. Lunch can be purchased at **Global Wildlife Center's Snack Bar** or at several good restaurants in surrounding towns. The center's staff will be happy to advise you.

Area Code: (504)

Getting There:

If approaching from Baton Rouge, travel east on Interstate 12. Take Exit 47 (Robert) and go north 10½ miles on Louisiana 445 to Louisiana 40. Travel east (right) one mile to Global Wildlife Center.

If approaching from New Orleans, cross Lake Pontchartrain Causeway. Travel U.S. 190 west and continue as the roadway changes to Louisiana 25. Follow Louisiana 25 to Folsom. In Folsom, turn onto Louisiana 40 West (left) one block before the traffic light at the intersection of Louisiana 25 and Louisiana 40 East. Travel eight miles to Global Wildlife Center.

Where and When:

Global Wildlife Center, Louisiana 40 West, Folsom, LA 70437. 624-WILD. Daily, 9 A.M.-sunset. Admission. Call ahead for tour schedule. Tours are also available to individuals and groups not staying at Safari Lodge.

Information:

Global Wildlife Center, Louisiana 40 West, Folsom, LA 70437. 624-WILD.

Tangipahoa Parish Tourist Commission, 2612 S. Morrison Rd., Hammond, LA 70403. 542-7520. Daily, 9 A.M.-5 P.M.

Accommodations:

Safari Lodge, Global Wildlife Center, Louisiana 40 West, Folsom, LA 70437. 624-WILD. Overnight special includes breakfast, supper, wagon tour, giraffe roundup, fishing guide, and transportation to pond (you must furnish your own tackle).

Restaurants:

Global Wildlife Center's Snack Bar—hamburgers, sandwiches, hot plates, snacks, and soft drinks.

7

TANGIPAHOA
TOWN TOUR

Variety, that elusive spice of life, often turns up where you least expect to find it—along the highways linking five small Tangipahoa Parish towns, for instance. Ponchatoula, the oldest incorporated city in Tangipahoa Parish, is the one that offers the most enticing assortment of things to do and see.

If you travel two miles east on U.S. 51, off of Interstate 55, you come to a stop right in front of Ponchatoula's mascot, Old Hardhide. Hardhide is the only alligator in the world with his own newspaper column and his own bank account.

Although old by alligator standards, Hardhide is younger than most items on display in the two-block downtown historic district that surrounds him. Ponchatoula, already famed as the "Strawberry Capital of the World," has lately been dubbed, "America's Antique City."

Nearly forty shops on Pine Street (Louisiana 22), Ponchatoula's main thoroughfare, are bursting at the seams with period clothing and furniture, collectible china and bric-a-brac, and outmoded implements of every sort. Wander in and out of the vintage stores and continue your search for bargains at weekly sessions conducted by the **Ponchatoula Auction Company,** the largest antique auction in the South.

Just a few blocks west of Hardhide's digs, at **The Louisiana Furniture Gallery** on Railroad Avenue (U.S. 51), you can see exceptional furniture and artwork in several media fashioned

Antique shops in Ponchatoula.
(Photo by Mary Fonseca)

Collinswood School Museum.
(Photo by Mary Fonseca)

by members of the Louisiana Furniture Industry Association. You are welcome to place orders for custom-made pieces with their talented artisans.

Galleries featuring watercolor paintings by internationally recognized artist Carmel Foret (**Carmel Foret Creations**) and wildlife photographs by equally prominent wildlife photographer Julia Sims (**Gateway Gallery**) are also tucked in among Ponchatoula's antique emporiums. Works from the palettes of other local artists are exhibited in the **Mail Car Art Gallery,** next to Old Hardhide's cage.

In a recycled train depot next to the Mail Car Gallery, **Ponchatoula Country Market's** colorful booths tempt buyers with an astounding array of regional crafts, homemade foods, antiques, and collectibles.

Make your selections, then cross Pine Street to see mementos and artifacts of Ponchatoula's past at the **Collinswood School Museum.** When children of the 1870s learned their ABCs in the Collinswood schoolhouse, it was situated on the Collinswood estate just west of town. It was restored and moved to Pine Street during America's bicentennial celebration.

When you need a breather from browsing Ponchatoula's sights and engaging shops, "sit and rest a spell." Enjoy the Continental cuisine at **C'est Bon,** a fine-dining restaurant on Railroad Avenue, or indulge in some of the authentic Bavarian sausages, breads, and pastries served at **Taste of Bavaria Bakery and Restaurant.** This family-owned bakery/cafe is on Louisiana 22 West, a few miles west of Interstate 55.

After lunch, continue your shopping expedition in several antique-filled outbuildings behind Mount's Villa, a turn-of-the-century estate next door to Taste of Barvaria. They house old-time goods and furnishings sold by **The "Carriage House" Antiques.**

One mile east of the "Carriage House" (turn right at Wagner Street and follow the signs), alligators older and younger than Hardhide laze in murky ponds at **Kleibert's Turtle and Alligator Tours** on Yellow Water Road. Here you can have a close (but not dangerous) encounter with the alligators, plus more than 100,000 turtles. After a fascinating tour of this commercial breeding and harvesting facility, step up to the snack bar and try some gator steak, a gator po' boy or some Alligator Sauce Picante.

On the 1,000-foot boardwalk extending over the Joyce Wildlife Management Area, south of Ponchatoula, you might see yet another alligator sunning on a log or a nutria swimming among the cypress knees. A **Joyce Wildlife Management Area Swamp Walk** brochure, available at the **Tangipahoa Tourist Commission's** Information Center (Interstate 55, exit 28) identifies hundreds of birds, mammals, amphibians, reptiles, and aquatic plants that may be sighted on the Swamp Walk. To enhance your enjoyment of the area, wear flat-heeled walking shoes, tread softly, and take some binoculars with you.

To reach the Swamp Walk, head south from Ponchatoula on U.S. 51, toward Interstate 55. (Do not get on the interstate.) Go over the overpass on U.S. 51, then take exit 22 to Frontage Road. Pass under the elevated section of Interstate 55 to the entrance to the Swamp Walk. Take note of the warning that fast trains ride the rails you must cross to the boardwalk.

Fish and crabs in Lake Maurepas, the productive neighbor of the Joyce Wildlife Management Area, are meant to be tasted rather than observed. **Middendorf's Restaurant** is a good place to do just that. The waterside eatery has been serving Louisiana seafood specialties in Manchac, a tiny fishing village eight miles south of the Swamp Walk, since 1934. The restaurant is so popular that a second Middendorf's was built next to the original to accommodate weekend crowds.

Lake Maurepas' seafood has attracted fishermen to Tangipahoa Parish for many years, but it was the area's extensive forests that interested Peter Hammond, a Swedish immigrant. In the 1820s, Hammond processed large tracts of pine into kegs, barrels, turpentine, and tar. In the town named for this pioneer woodworker, moss-draped trees (some planted when Hammond was developed shortly after the Civil War) shade graceful, century-old homes.

Take U.S. 51 into Hammond. Cross the railroad tracks on West Charles, West Robert, or West Church streets and drive through the neighborhood of stately old residences. On East

Charles Street an ancient oak guards the tombs of Peter Hammond and his family. After touring Hammond's historic area, recross the railroad tracks, turn right on Railroad Avenue, and drive to the campus of **Southeastern Louisiana University.** Here, you can view the current exhibit in Clark Hall Gallery and inquire about performances and special events scheduled at the university.

Then continue your Tangipahoa town tour in Albany's Hungarian Settlement. Street sign sentinels are stationed in the settlement's tidy Presbyterian cemetery, about ten miles west of Hammond on Interstate 12. They are stenciled with the names of Hungarian families who emigrated to the area at the close of the nineteenth century. The Breckenridge lumber mill that offered them plots of cutover timberland in return for their labor is gone, but clapboard Presbyterian and Catholic churches, where residents of the close-knit Hungarian Settlement worshipped, still stand on Louisiana 43, one quarter-mile south of Interstate 12.

The history and culture of Italian immigrants who settled the town of Independence are remembered at the **Independence Italian Culture Museum.** And, foods that were, and still are, part of traditional Italian menus are sold at **Black Cat Grocery,** a renowned local landmark at the intersection of U.S. 51 and Black Cat Road. Goodies available at the store include locally produced ricotta cheese, pickled pig's lips, and Italian sausage plus imported olives and pasta Milanese mix (used in St. Joseph Day dishes). To visit Independence's Italian Culture Museum and Black Cat Grocery, take the Tickfaw exit off of Interstate 55, go east to U.S. 51, and north two miles to Black Cat Road. Continue on Black Cat Road into Independence to visit the museum. On the way there, you can visit two interesting enterprises: Liuzza Produce Farm and Amato's Winery.

Italian settlers were drawn to Independence by the area's thriving strawberry industry. It is said that strawberries from Tangipahoa Parish are the sweetest in the world. You can judge their quality firsthand at **Liuzza Produce Farm,** three-quarters of a mile west from U.S. 51 on Black Cat Road. The Liuzza family farms more than four hundred acres of strawberries and fresh vegetables. They sell flats of strawberries and crates of seasonal produce to drive-by customers. Family members also show visitors their fields and trade gardening tips if they are not caught at a busy time.

Liuzza Produce Farm does not open its fields to visitors who want to pick their own flats of strawberries. But a list of Tangipahoa Parish's "you pick 'em" farms may be obtained from the Tangipahoa Parish Tourist Commission.

Strawberries grown by local farmers such as the Liuzzas are the only ones that go into the three varieties of strawberry wine Henry and Jessie Amato make at **Amato's Winery.** If you call for an appointment, the Amatos will give you a short tour of their plant, just a few miles west of the Liuzza farm. You can also taste their dry, semisweet, and sweet strawberry wines. If you don't have time to visit the Amatos, look for their wines at Black Cat Grocery, Sunflower Stores, or Berry Town Produce in Ponchatoula.

When you leave Independence, continue your Tangipahoa town tour by taking Interstate 55 north. Exit at Louisiana 16 and travel east to Amite. In the last half of the nineteenth century, this country town was a busy way station on the New Orleans, Jackson, and Great Northern Railroad. A small hotel at the "Amite Station" welcomed travelers and became a favorite place to dine and relax. Amite still extends a cordial welcome to travelers and offers respite at **Blythewood Plantation, Dr. C. S. Stewart's Cottage,** and **Elliott House,** three charming Bed and Breakfasts on the town's tree-shaded, flower-rimmed streets. Blythewood is also open for tours.

After a delectable dinner at one of Amite's appetizing restaurants and a restful night in the Bed and Breakfast of your choice, spend the morning exploring **Camp Moore State Commemorative Area,** located about twelve miles north of Amite on U.S. 51. Camp Moore was established in 1861 as a training base for Confederate recruits. A museum on the grounds contains artifacts and documents relating to Louisiana Civil War history.

Kentwood, the last town on your Tangipahoa tour, is a few

miles north of Camp Moore on U.S. 51. Here, you can enjoy an appetizing lunch at **Sheila's,** a delightful restaurant/gift shop that serves soups, salads, and a daily selection of freshly prepared entrees. And, if you have called for an appointment, you can take an entertaining tour of the **C. A. Kent Home.** This American Colonial-style house was built in the 1890s by Charles Kent, son of Amos Kent, who was the founder of Kentwood. Kent's elegant estate, centered on three acres of landscaped grounds, was retained by his descendants until 1984.

Before driving home, stop for supper at **Skinny's,** a U.S. 51 landmark near the Mississippi border that is famous for its tangy barbecue dishes and creamy potato salad. If you are heading south, try the homestyle fare at **LaFleur's Restaurant,** a casual, twenty-four–hour eatery in Kentwood Plaza just off the Interstate 55 exit to Kentwood. The restaurant's decor salutes the scenic dairy farming country around Kentwood.

Area Code: (504)

Getting There:

Interstate 55 follows the western border of Tangipahoa Parish.

Interstate 12 crosses the parish's southern section near Hammond.

Where and When:

Amato Winery, Inc., 12415 W. Black Cat Rd., Independence, LA 70443. 878-6566. Complimentary tours by appointment only. *Note:* Due to local laws, wines may be tasted but not sold on Sundays.

Black Cat Grocery, 130 W. Black Cat Rd., Independence, LA 70443. 878-9651. Daily, 6 A.M.-9 P.M.

Blythewood Plantation, P.O. Box 155, Amite, LA 70422. Call 345-6419 to arrange a tour. Admission.

C. A. Kent Home, 701 Avenue E, Kentwood, LA 70444. 1-800-749-5365 or 229-2283. Daily, 10 A.M.-3 P.M. by appointment.

Camp Moore State Commemorative Area, U.S. 51, Tangipahoa, LA 70465. Tues.-Sat., 10 A.M.-4 P.M. For more information, contact Camp Moore Historical Association, Inc., Tangipahoa, LA 70465. 229-2438. Admission.

Carmel Foret Creations, 101 W. Pine St., Ponchatoula, LA 70454. 386-4221 or 1-800-543-2541. Mon.-Sat., 10 A.M.-5 P.M.; Sun., noon-5 P.M.

The "Carriage House" Antiques, P.O. Box 308, Ponchatoula, LA 70454. 386-2449. Mon.-Sat., 10 A.M.-5 P.M.; Sun., 1-5 P.M.

Collinswood School Museum, Pine Street, Ponchatoula, LA 70454. 386-4291 or 386-2533. Hours vary. Inquire at Ponchatoula Tourist Information Center. Donations welcomed.

Gateway Gallery (Julia Sims), 125 E. Pine St., Ponchatoula, LA 70454. 386-6529. Tues.-Sat., 10 A.M.-5 P.M.; Sun., noon-5 P.M.

Independence Italian Culture Museum, P.O. Box 813, Independence, LA 70443. Call Chris Ackman, 878-6871, for directions and an appointment.

Joyce Wildlife Management Area Swamp Walk, Tangipahoa Parish Tourist Commission, 2612 S. Morrison Blvd., Hammond, LA 70403. 542-7520. Sunrise to sunset.

Kleibert's Turtle & Alligator Tours, Inc., 1264 W. Yellow Water Rd., Hammond, LA 70401. 345-3617. Open daily, Mar. 1-Nov. 1, noon-sunset. Admission.

Liuzza Produce Farm, Inc., 415 W. Black Cat Rd., Independence, LA 70443. 878-4606. Daily, 9 A.M.-4 P.M. Closed Jan., Feb., July, and Aug.

Louisiana Furniture Gallery, 495 S.W. Railroad Ave., Ponchatoula, LA 70454. 386-0471. Mon.-Sat., 10 A.M.-5 P.M.; Sun., noon-5 P.M.

Mail Car Art Gallery, #10 Pine St., Ponchatoula, LA 70454. 345-2857 or 345-2867. Thurs.-Sat., 10 A.M.-4:30 P.M.; Wed. and Sun., 1-4:30 P.M.

Ponchatoula Antique Shops, Ponchatoula Merchants Association, P.O. Box 306, Ponchatoula, LA 70454. 386-2533.

Hours vary with individual merchants. Some are open on Sunday.

Ponchatoula Auction Company, 140 N. Baronne St., Ponchatoula, LA 70454. 386-4970 or 386-2512. Auctions at 6 P.M., every Saturday. Call for information and reserved seating. Previews at 2 P.M., day of auction.

Ponchatoula Country Market, #10 Pine St., Ponchatoula, LA 70454. 386-9580. Mon.-Sat., 10 A.M.-5 P.M.; Sun., noon-5 P.M.

Southeastern Louisiana University, Hammond, LA 70402. For general campus information, call 549-2000. Clark Hall Gallery: Mon.-Fri., 8 A.M.-4 P.M. Music Department: 549-2185. Drama Department: 549-2105.

Note: Zemurray Gardens in Loranger is a worthwhile *seasonal* attraction. A meandering azalea and camellia-lined path encircles twenty-acre Mirror Lake. Native trees, shrubs, and flowers add to the springtime beauty. Call 878-6731 or 878-2284 for *seasonal* dates and times. Admission. Global Wildlife Center (see "A Louisiana Safari"), ten miles from Hammond, can also be toured on this getaway.

Information:

Amite Chamber of Commerce, 101 S.W. Central Ave., Amite, LA 70422. 748-5537. Mon-Fri., 9 A.M.-4 P.M.

Ponchatoula Tourist Information Center, Pine Street (P.O. Box 306), near Country Market, Ponchatoula, LA 70454. 386-2533. Mon.-Fri., 10 A.M.-4 P.M.

Tangipahoa Parish Tourist Commission, 42271 S. Morrison Blvd., Hammond, LA 70403. 542-7520 or 1-800-542-7520. Mon.-Fri., 9 A.M.-5 P.M.; Sat. and Sun., 10 A.M.-4 P.M.

Guide Services:

FPC Tours, Route 1, Box 137, Loranger, LA 70446. 878-9877.

Harmony Tours, P.O. Box 969, Pontchatoula, LA 70454-0969. 386-4979.

Accommodations:

Chain and privately owned motels are available in Hammond.

Bed and Breakfasts:

Bella Rose Mansion, 255 N. 8th St., Ponchatoula, LA 70459. 386-3857.

Blythewood Plantation, P.O. Box 155, Amite, LA 70422. 345-6419.

Dr. C. S. Stewart's Cottage, 116 E. Chestnut St., Amite, LA 70422. 748-3700.

Elliott House, 545 N. Duncan Ave., Amite, LA 70422. 748-8533.

Grand Magnolia, 225 W. Hickory St., Ponchatoula, LA 70454. 386-6414.

Guest House, 248 W. Hickory St., Ponchatoula, LA 70454. 386-6275.

Reservations for Bed and Breakfasts in Amite may also be made through the Amite Chamber of Commerce, 748-5537.

Restaurants:

C'est Bon, 131 S.W. Railroad Ave., Ponchatoula, LA 70454. 386-4077. Lunch: Tues.-Sun., 11 A.M.-2:30 P.M. Dinner: Fri. and Sat., 5-9:30 P.M. Champagne brunch on Sundays.

LaFleur's Restaurant, Kentwood Plaza, 802 Avenue G, Kentwood, LA 70444. 229-7800. Menu ordering available 24 hours. Lunch Buffet: Sun.-Fri., 11 A.M.-2 P.M. Seafood buffet Saturday nights.

Middendorf's Restaurant, Manchac, LA 70454. 386-6666. Mon.-Sat., 10:30 A.M.-9:30 P.M.; Sun., 10:30 A.M.-9 P.M.

Sheila's, 206 Avenue F, Kentwood, LA 70444. 229-7100. Mon.-Fri., 9 A.M.-4:30 P.M.

Skinny's, 78136 U.S. 51, Kentwood, LA 70444. 229-4142. Mon.-Thurs., 11 A.M.-10 P.M.; Fri., 11 A.M.-11 P.M.

Taste of Bavaria Bakery and Restaurant, LA 22 West, Ponchatoula, LA 70454. 386-3634. Wed.-Sun., 7 A.M.-6 P.M.

Major Annual Events:

Amite Oyster Festival—Third weekend in March.

Italian Festival, Independence—Last weekend in April.

Kentwood Dairy Festival—First Saturday in June.

Strawberry Festival, Ponchatoula—Usually second weekend in April (movable if Easter falls on that weekend).

Tangipahoa Parish Free Fair, Amite—October.

The cypress swing on the fishing dock at the Tree House in the Park. (Photo by Mary Fonseca)

The gazebo at the Tree House in the Park. (Photo by Mary Fonseca)

8

A TREE HOUSE
IN THE PARK

Have you ever longed to recapture that "on top of the world" feeling children experience in leaf-curtained tree houses shared with childhood friends? If you are adventurous enough to follow the winding country roads that lead to **Tree House in the Park,** a unique Bed and Breakfast built atop eleven-foot stilts, you can come close to recapturing this nostalgic feeling. But a lofty perch is all Tree House in the Park has in common with the ramshackle clubhouses youngsters erect in their backyards.

If those fabled treetop lovers, Tarzan and Jane, could climb the stairs to Tree House in the Park's guest rooms, they certainly would be impressed by the queen-sized water beds and private hot tubs provided for their modern counterparts. These soothing amenities are two of many offered by hosts Fran and Julius Schneider.

From their well-appointed rooms, guests look out on a swimming pool and a five-acre green space bordered by a peaceful lagoon. On the lagoon's bank, a cypress swing on a fishing dock entices you to rest a spell and try your luck. Alongside the tree house, a gazebo centered in a picturesque pond encourages quiet interludes and intimate conversations amidst the whispering pines.

The serene atmosphere at Tree House in the Park is mirrored in the pastoral countryside surrounding it. Here, close to the Livingston/Ascension parish border, east of Interstate 10 between New Orleans and Baton Rouge, shady back roads curve through the rural landscape adjoining the neighboring communities of Port Vincent and French Settlement. On the outskirts of the villages, tranquil rivers glide through grassy banks fringed with fishing camps.

A wealth of good restaurants near the border makes this scenic, rural area even more inviting. Among them are a popular quartet of eateries and night spots at the intersection of Louisiana 42 and Louisiana 431.

Fifty-year-old **Berthelot's Steak and Seafood Restaurant** is carefully tended by owners Erwin and Donna Villar. Donna's award-winning seafood gumbo whets your appetite for the restaurant's generous helpings of seafood and steaks. Renowned Chef Paul Prudhomme calls Villar's gumbo—winner of the Baton Rouge Culinary Classic's silver medal—"a true Louisiana gumbo."

On the other side of a bridge that spans the Amite River as it zigzags past Berthelot's, the **Amite River Seafood Restaurant and Lounge** serves a tasty mix of seafood entrees. Lagniappe offerings at two neighboring night spots are relished by regular patrons. **June Bug's** cooks up boiled crawfish and Cajun dishes for customers enjoying cool beverages, while practically nonstop band music makes **Fred's on the Amite River** the liveliest watering hole on the river on Sunday nights.

The Biscuit Shack is the gathering place favored by early risers. It is just a stone's throw from Fred's, at the intersection of Louisiana 42 and Louisiana 16. Commuters, fishermen, hunters, and travelers down dozens of the busy bakery's fresh donuts and melt-in-your-mouth biscuits.

Some Biscuit Shack customers live a few miles east of the intersection, in French Settlement. Many residents of this historic town are descendants of eighteenth-century Frenchmen who settled in *La Côte Française* (French Hill), a village built on a ridge parallel to the Amite River. Steamers ferrying furniture and provisions from New Orleans to French Settlement docked nearby, in Colyell Bay, the largest, eastern tributary of the Amite River.

The Creole House Museum in French Settlement. (Photo by Mary Fonseca)

Bayview Tavern offers lively camaraderie to travelers on the site of the old steamer landing at the foot of Colyell Bay Bridge on Louisiana 16. Lucky wayfarers who stop by Bayview Tavern while one of the tavern's arts and crafts sales or Cajun heritage parties (organized for bus tours) is in progress are invited to join in the fun. If nothing special is going on, you can still refresh yourself with a frosty drink at the tavern and arrange a motorboat tour of the languid swamp that extends into the bay. At your request, Bayview Tavern's staff will even prepare lunch for you to enjoy on your leisurely float. If your schedule is tight, you can sample the eerie beauty of Louisiana's wetlands by strolling on the boardwalk in the rear of the tavern.

Streets in French Settlement are lined with several cypress-board, Creole-style homes, distinguished by pitched roofs and two front doors. **Creole House Museum,** an 1898 home typical of the area's architecture, houses mementos of the town's early days. Creole House curator Mercy Lobell brings the museum and the old village to life as she shares anecdotes and memories gleaned from relatives and friends.

One of Creole House's rustic artifacts is a door wreath decorated with bottled spices. When it catches the attention of Creole House visitors, Mercy directs them to the home of **McCoy Berthelot,** just down the road from the museum. Berthelot's house is flagged with a red pepper sign. In a shed behind his cottage, he grinds red pepper and gumbo filé, funnels the spices into amber-colored pharmaceutical bottles (to help retain color and flavor), and sells them at his home and to local stores. Berthelot enjoys showing visitors his garden and grinding house and telling them about the serrano pepper seeds that have been passed down through his family for more than a hundred years. **Tee Pete's,** a few steps away from the Berthelot home, and **Bordelon's,** near another Amite River bridge at the eastern edge of French Settlement, are two more good, homestyle restaurants you can enjoy while visiting French Settlement.

Some highways that connect French Settlement, Port Vincent, and other towns in this area are part of the Louisiana Scenic Byways system. The byways form a network of country roads chosen for their scenery and for their wayside attractions, such as Creole House Museum.

Most Louisiana welcome centers and tourism offices distribute maps showing the network of byways. Those in Livingston and Ascension parishes are easily accessed from Denham Springs in Livingston Parish or from Gonzales, an Ascension Parish city on the eastern border of Interstate 10. These communities offer attractions of their own plus more of Louisiana's fabulous cuisine.

Every year, more than 40,000 Cajun food lovers converge in Gonzales when the town lives up to its title, "Jambalaya Capital of the World," by hosting a two-day Jambalaya Festival. If you can't make it to the June celebration, you will have to be content tasting the spicy jambalayas and other flavorful dishes served in Gonzales' congenial dining rooms. Friendly volunteers at the **Gonzales Welcome Center** on Louisiana 30, .8 miles east of the Louisiana 30 exit on Interstate 10, offer complimentary maps of Gonzales and Ascension Parish and can direct you to the town's landmark restaurants.

Among them is **Vintage Country Kitchen,** famous for its fried chicken, fresh vegetables, and homemade corn bread and biscuits. Customers feast on their heaping platters at cozy tables set amidst artwork and gifts sold in Vintage's combination restaurant and shop. **Dalton's Family Restaurant,** on South Burnside Avenue (Louisiana 44) serves a zesty jambalaya every day, along with a wide array of traditional Louisiana dishes. A few blocks away, at **Marchand's,** boiled seafood is the specialty of the house.

Welcome center personnel distribute an East Ascension Sportsman's League map pinpointing public boat launches and fishing areas to visitors who prefer to catch their own supper. Numerous freshwater lakes and rivers in the area yield bass, sac-a-lait, and catfish.

The Gonzales Welcome Center doubles as an art gallery where works by local artists are exhibited. The **"Tee Joe" Gonzales Museum,** next to the center, displays furnishings and tools used by the community's early settlers. In 1887, "Tee Joe" opened a general store and post office on the site of present day Gonzales. His neighbors and customers included children of Acadian exiles and Spanish colonists as well as homesteaders granted tracts of land in 1880.

More than a century of change has taken place in Gonzales since Tee Joe opened his store. He surely would be amazed at the wide range of shops that have supplanted his emporium. Just west of Interstate 10, on Louisiana 30, the sixty-store **Tanger Factory Outlet Center** offers the latest innovations in fashions, electronics, and housewares. In central Gonzales, stores ranging from an enormous Wal-Mart to intimate boutiques serve the locality. Two of the smaller stores may be especially attractive to visitors. **Roussel's,** on Louisiana 30 east of the Gonzales Welcome Center, delights the eye with tasteful antiques, collectibles and decorator ornaments. And **The Gift Basket of Gonzales,** on East Cornerview Street (Louisiana 3038), packs souvenir goodies in miniature pirogues and prepares specialty baskets to suit every occasion.

The specialty foods prepared at **Reno's Bait, Tackle & Seafood,** except for the highly prized beef jerky, are best carried home in an ice chest. The popular store is well-known for its smoked chickens, fresh and boiled seafood, and *andouille,* Cajun, and Italian sausages. Reno's, located at the intersection of Louisiana 22 and Louisiana 935, also carries alligator tooth necklaces and alligator head bookends. These novelty items are fun, but connisseurs of alligator hide accessories will better appreciate the exquisite belts and wallets the store shows only on request. They are made by the Pritchard family, relatives of David and Veronica Pritchard, who own Reno's. Family members fashion the leather goods at their **Black Bayou Farms.** Call for directions if you would like to tour this alligator farm.

You may also enjoy a visit to **Oak Haven Farms,** a business that offers more than your usual garden-variety nursery. There, you may pick blueberries and blackberries in season, wander through lovely theme gardens (including one that features fragrant antique roses), and try out a large putting green with balls and clubs available in the nursery's gift shop. Golfers who bring their own clubs may even test their skills on a three-hole course next to a picture-perfect picnic area. Bring your own lunch, or call ahead and Oak Haven Farms will have an appetizing meal waiting for you. No matter who prepares the food, you are sure to enjoy it under the moss-draped oak trees that shade Oak Haven's lovely, pond-side setting. A map on Oak Haven Farms' brochure, available at the Gonzales Welcome Center, will show you the way.

In the decade before the Civil War, a health resort William Denham developed around mineral springs flowing on his property attracted city dwellers fleeing the horror of yellow fever. Today, more than 15 **antique shops** on Denham Springs' Range Avenue (Louisiana 16) are drawing an increasing number of visitors to this Livingston Parish city. **The Ant and Grasshopper Cafe,** tucked in among the shops, is convenient for browsers who want to take a coffee break in this tiny spot. To reach the antique shops, take the Denham Springs

(Louisiana 3002) exit from Interstate 12, turn on Range Avenue, and drive north. Cross Louisiana 190 (Louisiana 3002 becomes Louisiana 16 here) and the railroad tracks, and you will be in the antique village.

After a morning of antiquing, you may enjoy a picnic lunch at the springs for which the city is named. A pavilion, barbecue pit, and picnic tables are available at the historic site on River Road. To get there, drive north on Range Avenue, turn left on Centerville Street, and continue on Centerville until it dead ends at River Road. Turn right on River Road to the pavilion, about one block away on your left.

Lunch or dinner at **Crawford's Family Restaurant,** a few blocks north of Interstate 12 near the corner of Rushing Road and Range Avenue, is also a tempting idea. The Crawford family claims their unique preparation method results in the flakiest, most tender catfish you've ever eaten. In fact, they call it "the South's best catfish." If youngsters are in your party when you test their motto, they are sure to be amused by the collection of "sight gags" Ken Crawford keeps on hand to entertain them—such as "an eleven-foot pole for people I wouldn't touch with a ten-foot pole."

Folks who like to fry catfish at home say cornmeal sold at an honor-system gristmill (you leave payment for what you buy) on the south side of Florida Boulevard (U.S. 190), between Denham Springs and Walker, is the best that can be had. They like the freshly ground wheat flour that is sometimes available, too. A Gristmill sign on the highway calls attention to the shed of the large, white Creole-style house where you can help yourself to both products. Don't forget to leave payment for the miller.

Farther east along Florida Boulevard, near Walker, families congregate in **Old South Jamboree's** huge music hall to hear old-time blue grass, gospel, and country music. A sign alongside the highway directs you to the hall, a Livingston Parish landmark since 1968.

Holden, about twelve miles east of Walker, harbors a fairly new family attraction. A sign on Florida Boulevard (U.S. 190) points the way to **Fontenot's Trading Post and Native American**

Replica of an indian village at Fontenot's Trading Post and Native American Center. (Photo by Mary Fonseca)

Center, a unique museum the Fontenot family opened to showcase its collection of Native American and Civil War memorabilia. The fledgling enterprise has grown to include a replica of an Indian village; a small buffalo herd; a fishing pond; and a shop offering authentic Native American jewelry, baskets, and rugs.

Visitors who have time to explore more of Livingston Parish may want to continue east for approximately five miles on U.S. 190 to Albany. Here, in Hungarian Settlement, are the quaint churches and cemeteries described in "Tangipahoa Town Tour." From Albany, you can access Louisiana 43 and tour another section of the Louisiana Scenic Byways system.

Drive south along this pleasant corridor to Louisiana 22 and continue south on this route until it connects with Louisiana 16 near French Settlement. Follow Louisiana 16 north to return to Denham Springs. (While motoring along Louisiana 22, stop for some more good regional cooking at **Tin Lizzie's** on the banks of the Amite River or at **Kevin's Cajun Cafe** in Maurepas.)

You may recognize some of the vintage landmarks and wetland vistas that decorate the walls of Kevin's Cajun Cafe. Kevin's expertise in Acadian cookery is complemented by **Connie Hanna's** delightful sketches of places she knows and loves. With her skillful brush and discerning eye, Hanna immortalizes the enchanting landscapes that surround the Tree House in the Park.

Area Code: (504)

Getting There:

Denham Springs is accessed from the Louisiana 3002 exit off of Interstate 12 east of Baton Rouge.

Gonzales is east of Interstate 10, approximately 25 miles southeast of Baton Rouge. To reach the Port Vincent/French Settlement area from Gonzales, take the Louisiana 30 exit off of Interstate 10. Louisiana 30 becomes Louisiana 431 after it crosses U.S. 61 (Airline Highway) in Gonzales. Follow 431 to the intersection of Louisiana 42.

Where and When:

Black Bayou Farms, 1119 Stringer Bridge Rd., St. Amant, LA 70774. 675-5715 or 737-7251. Tours by appointment. Admission.

Connie's Sketches, 15352 Picou Rd., Maurepas, LA 70449. 695-3828. Call for an appointment.

Creole House Museum, Louisiana 16 (P.O. Box 365), French Settlement, LA 70733. 923-2357. Open the second Sunday of every month except May, 3-5 P.M. Open all day on the second Sunday in September for Creole Festival. Admission.

Denham Springs Antique Shops:

Antiques, Etc., 230 Range Ave., Denham Springs, LA 70726. 664-9130. Tues.-Sat., 10 A.M.-5 P.M.; Sun., 1-5 P.M.

Backwards Glance, 222½ N. Range Ave., Denham Springs,

LA 70726. 667-9779 or 275-5710. Tues.-Sat., 10 A.M.-5 P.M.; Sun., 1-5 P.M.

Benton Brothers Antique Mall, 115 N. Range Ave., Denham Springs, LA 70726. 665-5146. Tues.-Sat., 10 A.M.-5 P.M.; Sun., 1-5 P.M.

The Diamond Mine, 201 N. Range St., Denham Springs, LA 70727. 664-6463. Tues.-Sat., 10 A.M.-5 P.M.; Sun., 1-5 P.M.

The Front Room, 212 N. Range Ave., Denham Springs, LA 70726. 664-5271. Tues.-Sat., 10 A.M.-5 P.M.; Sun., 1-5 P.M.

Georgann's Boutique, 225 N. Range Ave., Denham Springs, LA 70726. 667-4962. Tues.-Sat., 10 A.M.-5 P.M.; Sun., 1-5 P.M.

Hart to Heart Antiques, 219 Range Ave., Denham Springs, LA 70726. 667-4018. Tues.-Sat., 10 A.M.-5 P.M.; Sun., 1-5 P.M.

J & B Crafts, 226 Range Ave., Denham Springs, LA 70726. 665-0800. Tues.-Sat., 10 A.M.-5 P.M.; Sun., 1-5 P.M.

Lesleigh House, 218 Range Ave., Denham Springs, LA 70726. 665-8345. Tues.-Sat., 10 A.M.-5 P.M.; Sun., 1-5 P.M.

Live Oak Antiques and Collectibles, 235 N. Range Ave., Denham Springs, LA 70726. 665-0488. Tues.-Sat., 10 A.M.-5 P.M.; Sun., 1-5 P.M.

The Painted Lady Antiques, 220 N. Range Ave., Denham Springs, LA 70726. 667-1710. Tues.-Sat., 10 A.M.-5 P.M.; Sun., 1-5 P.M.

Romantique, 104 N. Range Ave., Denham Springs, LA 70726. 667-2283. Tues.-Sat., 10 A.M.-5 P.M.; Sun., 1-5 P.M.

Southern Heirs Antiques, 215 N. Range Ave., Denham Springs, LA 70726. 664-9210. Tues.-Sat., 10 A.M.-5 P.M.; Sun., 1-5 P.M.

Theater Antiques, 228 Range Ave., Denham Springs, LA 70726. 665-4666. Tues.-Sat., 10 A.M.-5 P.M.; Sun., 1-5 P.M.

Things from the Past, 239 Range Ave., Denham Springs, LA

70726. 665-2803 or 667-0135. Tues.-Sat., 10 A.M.-5 P.M.; Sun., 1-5 P.M.

The Victorian J, 210 N. Range Ave., Denham Springs, LA 70726. 664-7985. Tues.-Sat., 10 A.M.-5 P.M.; Sun., 1-5 P.M.

Vintage Charm Antiques, 226 N. Range Ave., Denham Springs, LA 70726. 664-4630. Tues.-Sat., 10 A.M.-5 P.M.; Sun., 1-5 P.M.

Fontenot's Trading Post and Native American Center, 31994 N. Doyle Rd., Livingston, LA. Mailing address: 31994 N. Doyle Rd., Holden, LA 70744. Open Tues.-Sun., 9 A.M.-5 P.M. Best to call ahead as special events are often scheduled. Admission fee covers museum tour, pavilion, and fishing pond use. No fee is required to shop in the Trading Post.

The Gift Basket of Gonzales, 1030 E. Cornerview St., Gonzales, LA 70737. 644-7717. Mon.-Fri., 10 A.M.-6 P.M.; Sat., 10 A.M.-4 P.M.

McCoy Berthelot, 16567 LA 16, French Settlement, LA 70733. 698-6176. By appointment or by chance.

Oak Haven Farms, 18377 Blythe Rd., Prairieville, LA 70769. 622-1058 (Gonzales area), 383-8211 (Baton Rouge). Mon.-Sat., 9 A.M.-3 P.M. or by appointment. Nominal fee for picnic ground and putting green. Extra charge for three-hole golf course. Blueberry/blackberry season: May/June. Call ahead. Fee.

Old South Jamboree, P.O. Box 5, Walker, LA 70785. 665-4495 (day), 664-4624 (night). Performances scheduled on most Saturday nights. Call ahead for schedule. Show time: 7:30 P.M. Admission.

Reno's Bait, Tackle & Seafood, Inc., 45434 LA 22, St. Amant, LA 70774. 675-5225. Daily, 4 A.M.-8 P.M.

Roussel's, 414 W. Louisiana 30, Gonzales, LA 70737. 647-7995. Mon.-Fri., 9:30 A.M.-6 P.M.; Sat., 9:30 A.M.-5 P.M.

Tanger Factory Outlet Center, Interstate 10 Exit 177, Gonzales,

LA 70737. 647-0521 or 1-800-727-6885. Mon.-Sat., 10 A.M.-9 P.M.; Sun., noon-6 P.M.

"Tee Joe" Gonzales Museum, Gonzales Welcome Center, 1006 W. Louisiana 30, Gonzales, LA 70737. 647-9560 or 647-9566. Mon.-Fri., 8:30 A.M.-4:30 P.M.

Information:

Ascension Parish Tourist Commission, 6474 LA 22, Sorrento, LA 70778. 675-6550. Daily, 9 A.M.-5 P.M.

Gonzales Welcome Center, 1006 W. Louisiana 30, Gonzales, LA 70737. 647-9566. Mon.-Fri., 8 A.M.-4:30 P.M.

Note: A map of Denham Springs is available at the Denham Springs-Livingston Parish Chamber of Commerce, 991 Government Dr. (P.O. Box 591), Denham Springs, LA 70727-0591. 665-8155. There is also an area map showing the Louisiana highways leading to French Settlement and Port Vincent.

Guide Services:

Inquire at the Denham Springs-Livingston Parish Chamber of Commerce or the Gonzales Welcome Center.

Accommodations:

Chain motels are available in Gonzales and Denham Springs.

Independent motels are available in Gonzales.

Bed and Breakfasts:

Bayou Ridge Bed and Breakfast, 32527 Cullom Rd., Springfield, LA 70462. 294-3838 or 386-3653.

Tree House in the Park, Port Vincent, LA (Mailing address: 16520 Airport Rd., Prairieville, LA 70769). 622-2850 or 1-800-LE CABIN.

Whispering Pines, Louisiana 22, Killian, LA (20211 Dendinger Lane, Springfield, LA 70462). 695-3566.

Restaurants:

The Ant and the Grasshopper Cafe, 233 Range Ave., Denham Springs, LA 70726. 664-9022. Tues.-Sat., 10 A.M.-5 P.M.; Sun., 1-5 P.M.

Amite River Seafood Restaurant and Lounge, 18405 LA 16, Port Vincent, LA 70726. 698-6181. Tues., Wed., Thurs., and Sun., 10 A.M.-9 P.M.; Fri. and Sat., 10 A.M.-10 P.M.

Bayview Tavern and Tours, Louisiana 16 (P.O. Box 58), French Settlement, LA 70733. 698-3147. Mon.-Sat., 6 A.M.-2 A.M.; Sun., 6 A.M.-midnight. Live music Fri. and Sat., 9 P.M.-1 A.M.; Sun., 7-11 P.M.

Berthelot's Steak and Seafood Restaurant, 4708 LA 42, Port Vincent, LA 70726. 622-1215. Daily, except Wednesdays, 11 A.M.-'til.

The Biscuit Shack, 45070 Manny Guitreau Rd., Prairieville, LA 70769. No phone. Daily, 4:30-10 A.M.

Bordelon's Restaurant, 14365 Mecca Rd., French Settlement, LA 70733. 698-3804 or 695-6903. Wed.-Thurs., 5-9 P.M.; Fri. and Sat., 5-10 P.M.; Sun., noon-9 P.M.

Crawford's Family Restaurant, 164 Rushing Rd. West, Denham Springs, LA 70726. 664-1412. Mon.-Thurs., 11 A.M.-9 P.M.; Fri., 11 A.M.-10 P.M.; Sat., 11 A.M.-9:30 P.M.

Dalton's Family Restaurant, 427 S. Burnside Ave., Gonzales, LA 70737. 644-1222 or 644-7110. Daily, 9 A.M.-11 P.M. Daily lunch buffet with jambalaya. Seafood buffet on Friday and Saturday that features more than twenty seafood entrees.

Fred's on the Amite River, 18158 Rushing Rd., Prairieville, LA 70769. 622-4884. Daily, 6 A.M.-2 A.M. Live music Sun., 3 P.M.-'til.

June Bug's, 45020 Manny Guitreau Rd., Prairieville, LA 70769. 622-4990. Daily, 8 A.M.-2 A.M. Complimentary crawfish boils on Wednesday and Friday in season. Thursday, complimentary Cajun entree.

Kevin's Cajun Cafe, 23563 LA 22, Maurepas, LA 70449. 695-3742. Tues.-Thurs., 10:30 A.M.-9 P.M.; Fri. and Sat., 10:30 A.M.-10 P.M.

Marchand's, 624 N. Burnside Ave., Gonzales, LA 70737. 644-3676 or 644-3704. Fresh, boiled, fried seafood and daily special: Mon.-Fri., 8 A.M.-8:30 P.M.; Sat., 10 A.M.-8:30 P.M.

Tee Pete's, 16475 LA 16, French Settlement, LA 70733-2305. 698-9211. Standard Time: Wed. and Thurs., 4-8 P.M.; Fri. and Sat., 4-10 P.M. Daylight Saving Time: Wed. and Thurs., 5-9 P.M.; Fri., 4-10 P.M.; Sat., 11 A.M.-10 P.M.; Sun., 11 A.M.-9 P.M. Closed Mondays and Tuesdays all year.

Vintage Country Kitchen, 615 E. Ascension St., Gonzales, LA 70737. 644-4661. Restaurant: Sun.-Fri., 11 A.M.-2 P.M.; Friday night only, 5-8:30 P.M. Closed Saturdays. Gift shop: Daily, 9 A.M.-5 P.M.

Major Annual Events:

Albany Christmas Parade—Second Monday in December.

Amite River Christmas Boat Parade, Livingston Parish—December.

Creole Festival, French Settlement—Second Sunday in September.

Denham's Springfest, Denham Springs—Fourth Saturday in April.

Garfish Rodeo, Blind River—June.

Denham Springs Christmas Parade—Saturday before area schools' Christmas vacation.

Denham Springs Mardi Gras Parade—Two Saturdays before Fat Tuesday.

District 2 Fireman's Poker Run, Livingston Parish—Second Saturday in June.

Jambalaya Festival, Gonzales—Second full weekend of June.

Livingston Christmas Parade—mid-December.

Livingston Parish Fair, Livingston—Second full week in October.

Louisiana Pine Tree Festival, Walker—Second week of July.

Port Vincent Annual Mardi Gras Boat Parade—Fat Tuesday.

Springfield Firemen's Festival—September.

Tickfaw River Mardi Gras Boat Parade, Livingston Parish—Saturday before Mardi Gras.

Walker Pioneer Days Christmas Parade—First Saturday in December.

Oak Alley Plantation. (Photo courtesy Oak Alley Foundation)

Houmas House Plantation. (Photo courtesy Hélène Crozat)

9

RIVER ROAD RAMBLE

In the first half of the nineteenth century, lavishly decorated plantation mansions, humble slave cabins, and rippling fields of sugarcane formed a picturesque patchwork along the Mississippi River between New Orleans and Baton Rouge. Twenty-eight antebellum homes lined the west bank of the river; 39 rimmed the opposite shore.

A few of these stately manors still stand in the shadows cast by towering petrochemical complexes that supplanted their neighbors. They weathered war, floods, hurricanes, the changing fortunes of their owners, and the Industrial Revolution. As you step across their thresholds, you summon forth the grace and the ghosts of a bygone way of life.

Three of the antebellum homes included in this getaway offer bed and breakfast, plus a sampling of Southern hospitality, Louisiana style. Several are open for tours.

To begin your River Road ramble, turn into the shell-covered drive in front of **Destrehan Plantation,** just a half-block down River Road from its intersection with Interstate 310. Follow a costumed guide as she relates the saga of the plantation, the oldest intact antebellum home in the lower Mississippi Valley.

Destrehan is a West Indies-style home, built in 1787 for the family of Robert Antoine Robin de Logny. Its massive Doric columns and symmetrical garçonnières (apartments reserved

109

for the young men of the family) were added twenty years later when Greek Revival architecture was in vogue. Legend has it that Jean Lafitte, a famous privateer and frequent visitor at Destrehan, hid some of his treasure within the manor's thick walls. If so, his secret hiding place has yet to be discovered.

As you leave Destrehan, turn right onto River Road and follow the Mississippi as it curves past Shell Oil Company's Norco Manufacturing Complex. Here, River Road rises to the top of the levee and then quickly descends to cross in front of Bonnet Carré Spillway's enormous floodgates. The Spillway was built by the U.S. Army Corps of Engineers in 1931 to keep the river from changing course, and to protect downriver areas from devastating floods. The floodgates can divert three million cubic feet of river water per second into Lake Pontchartrain.

San Francisco Plantation is about twenty-two miles upriver from Destrehan Manor. The mansion is a peach- and blue-trimmed Bavarian confection patterned after ornate paddle-wheelers that once churned the Mississippi's muddy waters. San Francisco was built for Edmund Bozonier Marmillion, but he died before his elaborate residence was complete. His son, Valsin Marmillion, named the house *San Frusquin* (one's all) because he emptied his bank account finishing its sumptuous interior.

One mile upriver from San Francisco, and one mile inland on the town of Garyville's Main Street, the **Timbermill Museum** showcases the very different life-style ushered into the river region at the end of the plantation era.

The Lyon Cypress Lumber Company of Illinois built Garyville in 1903 for workers hired to cut large stands of cypress near the town. Garyville had its own schools, churches, stores, medical and social facilities, and its own currency. More than sixty company-built homes and shops still border Garyville's quiet streets.

The museum, housed in the Lyon Company's headquarters, is filled with implements, records, and office equipment used during the mill town's twenty-five—year life. Lumber sheds, a mammoth sawmill on permanent loan from the Smithsonian Institution, and the man-made millpond behind the company complex help visitors envision the days when the lumberyard was peopled with stalwart woodsmen.

When you leave Garyville, ride across the Mississippi River—and back into antebellum Louisiana—on the **Lutcher-Vacherie Ferry.** The ferry landing is five miles upriver from the intersection of Garyville's Main Street and River Road.

Turn right off of the ferry ramp on the west bank of the river, and travel 1½ miles to **Laura Plantation.** Laura's colorful exterior surprises visitors used to white columned Greek Revival plantations. But the reds, greens, and golds that decorate this distinctive Creole plantation were used in the 1805 home's original color scheme. Thirteen structures on Laura's fourteen acres are being restored. They include the main house, two carriage houses, six slave quarters, two Creole cottages, five barns, and a secondary house used as a hospital during the Civil War. Bed and breakfast will be offered when the restoration is complete. Overnight guests and daytrippers will also enjoy a hedge maze—almost an acre in size—and performances based on the Br'er Rabbit stories. Joel Chandler Harris adapted the stories from Senegalese folktales recorded by Alcee Fortier. Fortier heard the cherished stories at Laura when he was growing up.

When you leave Laura, travel four miles upriver to visit the plantation's esteemed neighbor, **Oak Alley Plantation.** The outstretched limbs of twenty-eight 300-year-old live oak trees (so named because they never lose all of their leaves) form the graceful arch that frames this pink-pillared mansion. The trees, believed to be planted by an unknown French settler, outdate the plantation home by more than a hundred years.

In 1839, Jacques Telesphore Roman and his wife, Celina Pilie, moved their family into newly constructed Oak Alley. On an upstairs hallway door, you can still see where Roman and his contractor, George Swainey, signed their names to celebrate the occasion. The family's exodus from the plantation thirty years later was not nearly as pleasant; they were forced to sell Oak Alley at auction because of losses suffered during Reconstruction.

If a morning of plantation-hopping whets your appetite,

gather around a table at **Oak Alley Plantation Restaurant,** on the grounds behind the mansion, and try some of Louisiana's native dishes. The restaurant is surrounded by five country cottages that provide lodging for overnight guests. They were built for plantation workers in 1866. Bed and Breakfast is also offered at **Bay Tree Plantation,** an 1850s French Creole cottage adjacent to Oak Alley.

When you resume your River Road ramble, continue upriver and pause at the small cemetery on the right side of River Road, about six miles from Oak Alley. Here, a historical marker notes the first recorded settlement founded by the Acadians between 1756 and 1757.

Descendants of the Acadians, exiles from Canada who settled in Louisiana, are more widely known as Cajuns. Their *joie de vivre* (love of life), music, and cuisine are famous all over the world.

Many Cajuns, and other early residents of River Road, are buried in the cemetery. Most were of the Catholic faith and attended services at the original St. Jacques de Cabahanoce Church, which stood across River Road. The present church, St. James, built on the site of the old one, contains furnishings from the first chapel.

The Sunshine Bridge is approximately eleven miles from the cemetery. If you want to sample some of the Cajuns' celebrated cuisine, detour onto the service road parallel to the bridge approach and dine at Chef John Folse's **Lafitte's Landing** restaurant. The restaurant, set in the old Viala Plantation, which was moved from the banks of Bayou Lafourche, is listed in the Nation's Restaurant News Hall of Fame and continues to receive culinary accolades from national and international food critics.

After you feast on Chef Folse's specialties, cross the Sunshine Bridge and take the first exit ramp to River Road. Turn right and travel one mile to **Tezcuco Plantation.**

Tezcuco was built as a raised cottage, having only a one-story living area. A grape-leaf-patterned, wrought-iron railing, unusual in plantation architecture, trims the home's wide galleries.

Three of Tezcuco's outbuildings are original to the plantation; others have been moved to its spacious grounds. Among
the charming collection of dependencies are a private chapel;
a tiny, two-seat gazebo topped by the plantation's bell; and a
child's playhouse fronted by a carousel pony. An antique shop,
Civil War Museum, and African American Museum are housed
in other vintage structures.

Tezcuco is an Aztec word meaning "resting place." The spacious estate offers travelers the respite promised in its name in
comfortable bed-and-breakfast cottages. The plantation also
offers overnighters and casual visitors delectable fare in its
Tezcuco Plantation Restaurant.

About two miles upriver from Tezcuco, signs point to a
group of historic structures less than a mile off River Road that
provide nostalgic ambiance for **The Cabin Restaurant.** Several
slave cabins, a cypress water cistern, and the restored first black
Catholic school in Louisiana are part of the architectural
mosaic.

Houmas House Plantation is one mile upriver from The
Cabin signs on River Road. When Caroline and John Preston
built this majestic home in 1840, they joined it to a four-room,
1700s dwelling on the site by constructing a roof over the carriageway between the two homes. Both residences have
notable architectural features, the most admired being the
free-floating, three-story spiral staircase in the Greek Revival
mansion.

Houmas House lost half of its ancient oak alley to the
encroaching Mississippi River in 1930, but eight of the enormous trees still stand. The 250-year-old Burnside oak and 300-
year-old Crozat oak in front of the mansion were named in
honor of previous Houmas House owners.

If you have time for more River Road rambling, drive downriver eleven miles past the Sunshine Bridge for a roadside view
of Manresa House of Retreats (private). Manresa was formerly
Jefferson College, the first institution of higher education in
the region. It is considered by many to be one of the most
beautiful buildings on River Road. The Catholic retreat house
welcomes men of all religious denominations. It is especially

lovely in the spring when large azalea bushes surrounding it are in bloom (usually mid-March through mid-April).

Hymel's, a restaurant favored by locals who relish well-prepared seafood, is on River Road between the Sunshine Bridge and Manresa. Dine in its informal atmosphere before proceeding to the last stop on your River Road tour, the Cajun Village at the intersection of Louisiana 22 and Louisiana 70, just off Interstate 10, exit 182 (Sunshine Bridge Exit).

The village is an entertaining place to linger before heading home. A group of wooden buildings, including some antique structures moved to the roadside, shelter the **Ascension Parish Tourist Information Center,** a blacksmith shop, an alligator pond, and some enticing specialty stores. You can size up the works of some eighty self-taught artisans in **Southern Tangent Gallery;** select Victorian-themed items at **Victorian Tymes;** or purchase handmade dolls, wall hangings, and country-themed items at **Cajun Country Originals.** Nelson Plaisance, a skilled woodworker, fills his **Bayouland Art** shop with hand-carved replicas of old Louisiana boats. It is next door to **"Cajun Flavor" Louisiana's General Store** where you can find a wide range of Louisiana products such as "shoe-pick" caviar, hot sauces, coffees, and cookbooks. Select what you want for a custom gift basket and the store will ship it for you. Before you leave the Cajun Village, indulge in one last cup of *café au lait* (coffee and hot milk) and a couple of hot *beignets* (square donuts) at the **Coffee House.**

Area Code: (504)

Getting There:

Access River Road close to Destrehan Plantation by taking Interstate 310 South from U.S. 61 (Airline Highway) or Interstate 10. Take the first exit past Louisiana 61 off of Interstate 310 and turn left onto Louisiana 48.

Note: The sign with an arrow pointing right indicates the town of Destrehan, not the plantation.

Travelers approaching from Baton Rouge can elect to reverse

the order of the tour and take Louisiana 44 South from Interstate 10 to River Road. There are not many service stations along the River Road, so it is a good idea to start this getaway with a full tank of gas.

Note: River Road is the collective designation given to several state highways that follow the river. On the Mississippi River's east bank, River Road is usually designated as Louisiana 48 and Louisiana 44, but these numbers change on small stretches of roadway. On the river's west bank, River Road is Louisiana 18.

Where and When:

Bayouland Art, Louisiana 22, Sorrento, LA 70778 (Mailing address: Nelson Plaisance, 310 Zynn St., Raceland, LA 70394). 537-3260. Tues.-Sun., 10 A.M.-5 P.M.

Cajun Country Originals, 6474-1 LA 22, Sorrento, LA 70778. 675-6158. Sun.-Tues., 9 A.M.- 5 P.M.; Fri. and Sat., 9 A.M.-7 P.M.

"Cajun Flavor" Louisiana's General Store, 6470 LA 22, Suite B, Sorrento, LA 70778. 675-6681. Daily, 10 A.M.-5 P.M.

Destrehan Plantation, 9999 River Rd. (P.O. Box 5), Destrehan, LA 70047. 764-9315 or 764-9345. Daily, 9:30 A.M.-4 P.M. Admission.

Houmas House Plantation, 40136 LA 942, Burnside/Darrow, LA 70725. 473-7841 or 522-2262 (New Orleans direct line). Daily: Feb.-Oct., 10 A.M.-5 P.M.; Nov.-Jan., 10 A.M.-4 P.M. Guided tours. Admission.

Laura Plantation, 2247 LA 18, Vacherie, LA 70090. 265-7690. Daily, 9 A.M.-5 P.M. Admission.

Lutcher-Vacherie Ferry, Crosses the Mississippi River every hour on the half-hour from the east bank, every hour on the hour from the west bank. Toll.

Oak Alley Plantation, 3645 LA 18 (Route 2, Box 10), Vacherie, LA 70090. 265-2151 or 523-4351 (New Orleans direct line). Daily: Mar.-Oct., 9 A.M.-5:30 P.M.; Nov.-Feb., 9 A.M.-5 P.M. Admission.

San Francisco Plantation, P.O. Drawer AX, Reserve, LA

70084. 535-2341. Daily, 10 A.M.-4 P.M. Admission.

Southern Tangent Gallery, 6482 LA 22, Sorrento, LA 70778. 675-6815. Mon.-Fri., 10 A.M.-5 P.M., or by appointment.

Tezcuco Plantation, 3138 LA 44, Darrow, LA 70725. 562-3929. Daily, 9 A.M.-5 P.M. Admission.

Timbermill Museum, Main Street and Railroad Avenue, Garyville, LA 70051. 535-3202. Mon.-Sat., 9 A.M.-5 P.M.; Sun., 10 A.M.-5 P.M. Admission.

Victorian Tymes, Louisiana 22, Sorrento, LA 70778 (P.O. Box 576, Geismar, LA 70734). 675-7001. Mon.-Thurs., 10 A.M.-6 P.M.; Fri.-Sun., 9 A.M.-7 P.M.

Information:

Ascension Parish Tourist Information Center, 6470 LA 22, Sorrento, LA 70778. 675-6550. Daily, 9 A.M.-5 P.M.

Louisiana Department of Culture, Recreation and Tourism, Office of Tourism, Inquiry Section, P.O. Box 94291, Baton Rouge, LA 70804-9291. 342-5359 or 1-800-633-6970.

Guide Services:

Request information from the Baton Rouge Area Convention & Visitors Bureau, Inc., 730 North Blvd. (P.O. Box 4149), Baton Rouge, LA 70821. 383-1825 or 1-800-LA ROUGE; or the New Orleans Metropolitan Convention and Visitors Bureau, 1520 Sugar Bowl Dr., New Orleans, LA 70112. 566-5068 or 566-5031.

Accommodations:

Bed and Breakfasts:

Bay Tree Plantation Bed and Breakfast, 3785 LA 18, Vacherie, LA 70090. 265-2109 or 1-800-895-2109.

Laura Plantation, 2247 LA 18, Vacherie, LA 70090. 265-7690. (Call for opening date of bed-and-breakfast facilities.)

Oak Alley Plantation, 3645 LA 18 (Route 2, Box 10), Vacherie, LA 70090. 265-2151 or 523-4351 (New Orleans direct line).

Tezcuco Plantation, 3138 LA 44, Darrow, LA 70725. 562-3929.

Restaurants:

The Cabin Restaurant, Louisiana 44 and Louisiana 22 (P.O. Box 85), Burnside, LA 70738. 473-3007. Mon.-Wed., 7 A.M.-3 P.M.; Thurs., 7 A.M.-9 P.M.; Fri. and Sat., 7 A.M.-10 P.M.; Sun., 7 A.M.-6 P.M.

Coffee House, Louisiana 22, Sorrento, LA (P.O. Box 85, Burnside, LA 70738). 675-8068. Daily, 6 A.M.-9 P.M.

Hymel's, River Road (between Manresa and the Sunshine Bridge) (Route 1, Convent, LA 70723). 562-9910 or 562-7031. Lunch: Mon.-Fri., 11 A.M.-2:30 P.M. Dinner: Thurs., 5-9 P.M.; Fri., 5-10 P.M. Sat., 11 A.M.-10 P.M.; Sun., 11 A.M.-8 P.M.

Lafitte's Landing, P.O. Box 1128, Donaldsonville, LA 70346. 473-1232. Sun., 11 A.M.-8 P.M.; Mon., 11 A.M.-3 P.M.; Tues.-Sat., 11 A.M.-3 P.M., 6-10 P.M.

Oak Alley Plantation Restaurant, Oak Alley Plantation, 3645 LA 18, Vacherie, LA 70090. 265-2151 or 523-4351 (New Orleans direct line). Daily, 9 A.M.-3 P.M.

Tezcuco Plantation Restaurant, 3138 LA 44, Darrow, LA 70725. 562-3929. Daily, 8 A.M.-3:30 P.M.

Note: All of the plantations listed above, except Houmas House, have picnic facilities.

Major Annual Events:

Cajun Village Christmas, Sorrento—December 1-31.

Cajun Village Fall Festival, Sorrento—First weekend in October.

Destrehan Plantation Fall Festival—Second weekend in November.

Oak Alley Plantation Christmas Bonfire Party—Second Saturday in December.

Nottoway. (Photo courtesy Baton Rouge Area Convention & Visitors Bureau)

10

LIVING LIKE A KING
IN THE WHITE CASTLE

When John Hampden Randolph started building his palatial antebellum home on the west bank of the Mississippi River he named it **Nottoway.** But, as the mansion neared completion, neighbors, awed by its immense proportions, dubbed it the "white castle."

Today, Nottoway's grandeur continues to enthrall visitors. Hundreds of people tour the plantation everyday, admiring its richly furnished interior and marveling at the elaborate white ballroom designed to showcase Randolph's seven marriageable daughters.

Those who want to linger in Nottoway's antebellum splendor a while longer can tarry overnight in luxurious accommodations. The magnificent master suite is furnished with Randolph's rosewood bed, dresser, and armoire. A mahogany four-poster dominates the third-floor boudoir of his daughter, Cornelia, a novelist who drew from her experiences at Nottoway to write *The White Castle of Louisiana.*

A hostess's welcoming smile and a complimentary bottle of wine delivered to one of the plantation's thirteen comfortable chambers is only the beginning of the red-carpet treatment afforded Nottoway's bed-and-breakfast guests. If you reserve a room in the mansion or the overseer's cottage, you can wander through the manor house at leisure, once the last daily tour of the home is finished.

Occasionally, romantics summon up the luster of the ante-bellum era by circling the elaborate ballroom with a partner. Lovers of antiques take a closer look at Nottoway's fine fur-nishings and ornate plaster friezes. In the summertime, the walled courtyard garden that surrounds Nottoway's inviting pool is a popular gathering place.

A sunset stroll atop the Mississippi River levee is a delightful prelude to dinner in **Randolph Hall,** Nottoway's elegant gourmet restaurant. On weekends, a pianist entertains diners; the rhythmic music entices couples to the floor for after-dinner dancing.

When you arise from a restful night's sleep on one of Nottoway's antique beds, you are bid good morning with an eye-opening tray of hot coffee and muffins. Later, a plantation breakfast is served in ground-floor rooms where the Randolph clan used to hurl balls down the mansion's private tenpin alley.

Many vacationers spend the day at Nottoway lazily watching the Mississippi River drift by, or curled up in a rocker with a good book. Those who like to be on the go explore the high-ways and byways surrounding Nottoway, where there are some unusual sights to see.

For instance, the Chapel of the Madonna, featured in Robert Ripley's "Believe It or Not" and thought to be the small-est church in the world, is just four miles up the River Road from the plantation. A key encased in a wooden box by the Lilliputian chapel's front door admits pilgrims to the Marian shrine Anthony Gullo built in 1902, after his son recovered from a serious illness.

You can find out about more places to visit at the **Plaque-mine Lock Museum and Tourist Center** on Louisiana 1, in the town of Plaquemine—almost nine miles upriver from Nottoway. The dormant lock, built in 1909, once controlled the flow of water from the Mississippi River into Bayou Plaquemine, the access to waterways west of the Mississippi at that time.

Nautical exhibits and a lookout tower that affords a won-derful view of the Mississippi River are features of the museum area. A gate at the rear of the museum grounds leads to

Turnerville, a quaint, 1800s village that flourished during the prime of the Louisiana cypress industry. You can also drive to Turnerville on Louisiana 1. Cross Bayou Plaquemine and follow the Tour Homes signs on your right. They will direct you to the nineteenth-century homes of Miss Louise and Miss Marietta on North Nadler Street.

The two Victorian ladies are no longer residents of Turnerville, but when you tour Miss Louise's chic bungalow and Miss Marietta's homey cottage with Brenda Blanchard, Miss Marietta's granddaughter, you get to know them very well. In her lively presentation, Brenda relates stories that summon up happy memories for folks who visited their grandmothers in similar turn-of-the-century homes. Some visitors enjoy Turnerville so much that they make reservations for bed and breakfast in Miss Louise's home.

When you leave Turnerville cross the bridge again and explore Plaquemine, a charming 300-year-old town. A walking tour brochure offered at the Plaquemine Museum and Tourist Center guides visitors past many of the community's graceful old buildings. During your stroll, stop to browse through some of the town's well-stocked gift shops. **Reflections** and **Sirs**—both housed in vintage homes on Eden Street (Louisiana 1)—offer a selection of Louisiana foods, cookbooks, antiques, and gifts. And carousel horses, baby clothes, dolls, and music boxes are among the fine gifts displayed at **Carousel Dolls and Gift Shop** on Railroad Avenue.

After your walk, sample the tasty fare served at **City Cafe** on Main Street. The original City Cafe, a well-known landmark for decades, was destroyed by a tragic fire a few years ago. But, the Miranda family, long-time owners of the restaurant, rebuilt in the same location. The po' boys, shrimp dinners, and other delectable dishes at **Humphrey's,** Plaquemine's newest restaurant, are also appealing. It is on Eden Street, just a few blocks from the City Cafe.

If you may have time for more sight-seeing, there are plenty of options to choose. One is the informative industrial tour **Dow Chemical U.S.A.'s Louisiana Division** offers every Wednesday at their plant on Louisiana 1, above Plaquemine.

Dow shows visitors an instructive video on the basic chemicals the company produces. Then a guide follows up with a narrated drive-through of the plant and a tour of Dow Plantation House, the restored Union plantation home the company uses for corporate meetings.

During the sugarcane harvest (October-December), there is a lot of activity along Louisiana 1. The cane is cut down in the fields, then foliage is burned off the felled stalks. Trucks deliver this sweet cargo to several mills in the area. One is the Cinclare Sugar Mill in Brusly, a small hamlet between Plaquemine and Port Allen. Cinclare has been operating since 1871. It is on your right as you follow Louisiana 1 through Brusly to Port Allen.

Port Allen is a crossroads town that spans the intersection of Louisiana 1 and Interstate 10 above Brusly. It is also the home of the Port of Baton Rouge, the fifth largest port in the nation. At the Port Allen Lock you can watch tugboats and barges pass between the Mississippi River and the Intracoastal Waterway.

To reach the lock observation area, turn right off of Louisiana 1 at the Port of Baton Rouge sign and follow similar signs to the fenced-in tract adjoining port facilities. Drive through the gate and up the hill to the parking area. Walk onto the wall of the lock, where you can see vessels ease their way through the 96-ton gates. On a clear day, you are also treated to a marvelous view of Louisiana State University's bell tower and football stadium across the Mississippi River.

If the rooms at Nottoway are full, consider staying at the convenient accommodations in Port Allen. They range from budget motels to full service inns. The **West Baton Rouge Parish Tourist Commission** office, at the intersection of Interstate 10 and Louisiana 415, has information on area hostelries, attractions, and restaurants.

A short drive from the tourist center brings you to **Poplar Grove,** an unusual, Oriental-style manor house built for the Bankers' Pavilion at the 1884 World's Industrial and Cotton Exposition in New Orleans. It was moved to its present location in 1886. If you make arrangements ahead of time, you can tour the plantation's well-appointed rooms.

Poplar Grove's rows of plantation cabins and towering old sugar mill can be seen from Louisiana 1, about three miles above Port Allen. During the Christmas season, the sugar mill complex is outlined with twinkling lights during Port Allen's "Plantation Lights—Christmas on Poplar Grove" celebration. The community is one of the last remnants of the "factory towns" that grew up around thousands of Louisiana sugar mills in the late nineteenth and early twentieth centuries.

Learn more about old-time sugar manufacturing by studying the detailed, twenty-two–foot model of a 1904 mill set up in the **West Baton Rouge Museum.** To reach the museum, turn right onto Louisiana Avenue from Louisiana 1 in Port Allen. The museum is on the corner of Louisiana and Jefferson avenues.

Two antique structures adorn the museum's grounds. The 1830s Aillet House, a well-preserved French Creole cottage, reflects the prosperity of its owner. But the humble Allendale Cabin, a two-family slave dwelling, is furnished with primitive household goods.

If you call for an appointment, you can complement your visits to Poplar Grove and the West Baton Rouge Museum with a visit to **Live Oaks,** a lovely, 1838 plantation on the banks of Bayou Grosse Tete. Live Oaks once had 3,000 acres planted in sugarcane and cotton. Today, on the estate, you can visit the 2½-story mansion and stroll grounds where azaleas and camellias grow in shadows cast by gigantic live oak trees. On these expansive grounds, a slave chapel built in 1840, a washhouse, and other outbuildings evoke the aura of plantation life during the nineteenth century. Live Oak is on Louisiana 77, two blocks past the caution light in Rosedale. To reach it, take the Rosedale exit from Interstate 10 west of Port Allen.

Midway Grocery is an intriguing place to stop on the way to or from Live Oaks. This 1903 store retains the old-time ambiance that inspired Chevrolet to use it in a "Heartbeat of America" commercial, but a few twentieth-century fads, such as frozen Daiquiris and videopoker machines, have found their way through Midway's creaking doors. Locals take advantage of the old country store's drop-off laundry service and favor its homemade candy and hog cracklings. At lunchtime, customers gather at wooden tables to enjoy freshly prepared plate lunches or boiled seafood. And in the evening, the vintage grocery becomes a convivial neighborhood pub.

These sites north of Nottoway are entertaining destinations, but a southbound excursion on Louisiana 1 also leads to some engaging wayside attractions. If you leave Nottoway through the plantation's back entrance and turn left onto Louisiana 1, you are a short drive from the town of White Castle. As you pass through White Castle, stop at **Maggio's** on the southwest side of the highway and search for bargains in this landmark antique store. The town's **White Castle Inn,** a Bed and Breakfast housed in the 1897 Bank of White Castle, is another lodging alternative you can consider on trips to this area.

You get a roadside view of a few more sugar mills as you continue south on Louisiana 1. But, if you call for an appointment during harvesttime, you can take an instructive tour of **Evan Hall Sugar Co-op,** the second oldest sugarcane cooperative in Louisiana. A guide takes you through the mill and explains how sugar is ground and graded before it is sent to refineries and processed into consumer products. This fascinating tour requires a lot of walking up and down steps, some of them coated with residue from the manufacturing process. So, be sure you are fit as a fiddle and have sturdy walking shoes on before you turn into the mill yard at the caution light just north of Donaldsonville.

When you leave Evan Hall, drive into Donaldsonville, a town that was the capital of Louisiana during 1830 and 1831, and a cultural and social center for planters before the Civil War. Donaldsonville is said to have "the finest collection of structures from the pre-Civil War era to the 1930s to be found in any of the river parishes north of New Orleans." They include the 1889 Ascension Parish Courthouse; the 1875 Ascension Catholic Church, noted for its beautiful interior; and St. Peter's Methodist Church, which has continuously served the black community since it was founded immediately after the Civil War.

There are two noteworthy stores that you may want to visit during a stroll through the historic district. **Rossie's Ben Franklin** on Railroad Avenue offers more than the average five-and-dime store. Owner Sandra Imbraguglio has a nice display of antiques in the front of her store and frequently invites local artists to exhibit their works and demonstrate their techniques. In the rear of the store, her son, David, runs a frame shop and has several fine prints available for purchase. **The Apple Core,** on Nicholls Street, a few doors off Railroad Avenue, is an appealing boutique that features fashionable clothes for teens and ladies.

Lafitte's Landing, prominently mentioned in "River Road Ramble," is Donaldsonville's most famous restaurant. But, for casual dining, try the fare at two other Donaldsonville landmarks. The **First and Last Chance Cafe** on Railroad Avenue is the third restaurant bearing this unusual name. The original, 1921 eatery served passengers when trains stopped at the Donaldsonville depot across the street. The present 1936 replacement also cooked tasty fare for railroad travelers. The old depot is gone now, but the cafe continues to offer tempting seafood, steak, and rib dishes to its loyal customers. **Ruggiero's** restaurant is even older than the First and Last Chance Cafe. This local favorite serves well-prepared Italian and American entrees in an 1875 building it has occupied since the turn of the century.

Area Code: (504)

Getting There:

From Baton Rouge, take Interstate 10 West across the Mississippi River bridge. Go west to the Plaquemine exit and follow Louisiana 1 18 miles south to Nottoway.

From New Orleans, take Interstate 10 West, exit at Louisiana 22, and cross the Sunshine Bridge. Drive 14 miles north through Donaldsonville on Louisiana 1 to Nottoway.

Where and When:

The Apple Core, 319 Nicholls St. (P.O. Box 1372), Donaldsonville, LA 70346. 473-3311. Mon.-Fri., 9:30 A.M.-5:30 P.M.; Sat., 9:30 A.M.-4 P.M.

Carousel Dolls and Gift Shop, 23408 Railroad Ave., Plaquemine, LA 70764. 687-8822. Mon.-Fri., 10 A.M.-5:30 P.M.; Sat., 10 A.M.-2 P.M. After hours, by appointment.

Dow Chemical U.S.A.'s Louisiana Division, P.O. Box 150, Plaquemine, LA 70765-0150. 389-6623. Complimentary tours offered on Wednesdays, 1-2 P.M. Reservations should be made two weeks in advance. Children must be at least 12 years old.

Evan Hall Sugar Co-op, Inc., Louisiana 1 (P.O. Box 431), Donaldsonville, LA 70346. Call ahead to arrange complimentary tour during grinding season (usually second week in October–first week in December). Daily, 9 A.M.-3 P.M.

Live Oaks, P.O. Box 202, Rosedale, LA 70772. 648-2346. Tours by appointment only. Admission.

Maggio's, 32040 LA 1, White Castle, LA 70788. 545-3940. Wed.-Sun., 10 A.M.-6 P.M.

Midway Grocery, 17355 LA 77, Rosedale, LA 70772. Mon.-Sat., 8 A.M.-7:30 P.M.

Nottoway, P.O. Box 160, White Castle, LA 70788. 545-2730 (White Castle), 346-8263 (Baton Rouge). Tours: Daily, 9 A.M.-5 P.M. Admission.

Plaquemine Lock Museum and Tourist Center, Iberville Chamber of Commerce, P.O. Box 248, Plaquemine, LA 70765. 1-800-233-3560. Mon.-Fri., 8 A.M.-4 P.M.

Poplar Grove Plantation, 3142 N. River Rd., Port Allen, LA 70767. Call 344-3913 for an appointment.

Port Allen Lock, Port Allen, LA 70767. 343-3752. Daily, 9 A.M.-4 P.M.

Reflections, 23610 Eden St., Plaquemine, LA 70764. 687-1212.

Mon.-Fri., 9:30 A.M.-5:30 P.M.; Sat., 9:30 A.M.-3 P.M.

Rossie's Ben Franklin, 510 Railroad Ave., Donaldsonville, LA 70346. 473-6905. Mon.-Sat., 8:30 A.M.-5:30 P.M.; Sun., 9 A.M.-noon.

Sirs, 24040 Eden St., Plaquemine, LA 70764. 687-3602. Mon.-Fri., 10 A.M.-5 P.M.

Turnerville, 23230 Nadler St., Plaquemine, LA 70764. 687-5337. Mon.-Sat., 10 A.M.-4 P.M.; Sun., 1-4 P.M. Free tours given to bed-and-breakfast guests. Admission for others.

West Baton Rouge Museum, 845 N. Jefferson Ave., Port Allen, LA 70767. 336-2422. Tues.-Sat., 10 A.M.-4:30 P.M.

Information:

Plaquemine Lock Museum and Tourist Center, Iberville Chamber of Commerce, P.O. Box 248, Plaquemine, LA 70765. 1-800-233-3560. Mon.-Fri., 8 A.M.-4 P.M.

West Baton Rouge Visitor Information Center, 2855 I-10 Frontage Rd., Port Allen, LA 70767. 344-2920 or 1-800-654-9701. Daily, 9 A.M.-5 P.M.

Guide Services:

Contact the Baton Rouge Area Convention & Visitor Bureau, Inc., 730 North Blvd., Baton Rouge, LA 70821. 383-1825 or 1-800-LA ROUGE; or the West Baton Rouge Visitor Information Center.

Accommodations:

Chain and independent motels in Port Allen.

Bed and Breakfasts:

Nottoway, P.O. Box 160, White Castle, LA 70788. 545-2730 (White Castle), 346-8263 (Baton Rouge).

Turnerville, 23230 Nadler St., Plaquemine, LA 70764. 687-5337.

White Castle Inn, 55035 Cambre St., White Castle, LA 70788. 545-9932.

Restaurants:

City Cafe, 57945 Main St., Plaquemine, LA 70764. 687-7831. Mon.-Thurs., 11 A.M.-8 P.M.; Fri. and Sat., 11 A.M.-9 P.M.

First and Last Chance Cafe, 812 Railroad Ave., Donaldsonville, LA 70346, 473-8236. Mon.-Sat., 9 A.M.-'til; Sun., 10 A.M.-2 P.M.

Humphrey's, 23466 Eden St., Plaquemine, LA 70764. Mon.-Sat., 10 A.M.-10 P.M.

Lafitte's Landing, P.O. Box 1128, Donaldsonville, LA 70346. 473-1232. Sun., 11 A.M.-8 P.M.; Mon., 11 A.M.-3 P.M.; Tues.-Sat., 11 A.M.-3 P.M., 6-10 P.M.

Midway Grocery, 17355 LA 77, Rosedale, LA 70772. Mon.-Sat., 8 A.M.-7:30 P.M.

Randolph Hall, Nottoway Plantation, P.O. Box 160, White Castle, LA 70788. 545-2730. Daily, 11 A.M.-3 P.M., 6-9 P.M.

Ruggiero's, 206 Railroad Ave., Donaldsonville, LA 70346. 473-8476. Tues.-Sat., 11 A.M.-9:15 P.M.

Major Annual Events:

Addis Mardi Gras Parade, Addis—Sunday before Fat Tuesday.

Annual Big Bird Fly In, West Baton Rouge—First weekend in October.

Brusly Christmas Parade—First Sunday in December.

Christmas Festival and Home Tour, Plaquemine—First weekend in December.

Feast on the Levee, Brusly—Last Sunday in September.

International Acadian Festival, Plaquemine—Third weekend in October.

Krewe of Good Friends of the Oaks Parade, Port Allen—Sunday before Fat Tuesday.

Lagniappe by the River, White Castle—First Monday in August.

Plantation Lights, "Christmas on Poplar Grove," Port Allen—December.

Potpourri Festival, Port Allen—Second weekend in October.

Louisiana State Capitol with statue of Huey P. Long. (Photo courtesy Baton Rouge Area Convention & Visitors Bureau)

11

CAPITAL CITY
CAVALCADE

(F) (G)

Many tall tales have been told about Louisiana's legendary governor, Huey Long, but none top the true story of how he ordered fifty feet added to Louisiana's state capitol to steal the distinction of having the tallest state capitol from the state of Nebraska. This is but one of several "Huey" stories you may hear on a half-hour guided tour of **Louisiana's State Capitol.** To reach the capitol, take the Governor's Mansion exit off of Interstate 110 (you will pass the mansion as you approach the capitol).

Tours start at the **State Capitol Tourist Information Center** in the main lobby. As they lead you through the capitol's imposing halls, knowledgeable guides draw your attention to architectural embellishments in Louisiana's thirty-four–story, Art Deco statehouse—built in an unbelievable fourteen months—and point out bullet holes in the corridor where Governor Long was assassinated three years after the Capitol was completed.

After you finish the tour, take the elevator to the first floor to see an enriching exhibit on Louisiana folklife. Then, zoom up to the twenty-seventh–floor Observation Deck. There, you can get a bird's-eye view of Baton Rouge, water traffic on the Mississippi River, and the capitol gardens. Some walkways in the gardens lead to the **Old Arsenal Museum** quartered in a powder magazine built in the early 1800s. Inscriptions made by soldiers stationed at the magazine, plus uniforms, weapons, and historic documents tell the story of conflicts involving Louisiana as she evolved from a pioneer territory to a state.

Walkways in the beautifully manicured square in front of the statehouse lead to Huey Long's statue and grave site. The red-hued, white-columned buildings across the street from the plot are the Pentagon Barracks, built between 1823 and 1824 to quarter U.S. Army personnel. They now serve as the Capitol Complex Information Center and Gift Shop.

After exploring the capitol area, turn left onto River Road, behind the Pentagon Barracks, and head for Baton Rouge's active, attractive, downtown riverfront. At the **Louisiana Arts and Science Center/Riverside Museum,** a children's Discovery Room, a hands-on Science Station, a collection of Egyptian mummies, and regularly scheduled space shows vie for the distinction of being the museum's most popular presentation. In front of the museum, children are quick to climb aboard a 1918 steam engine and pretend they are pulling into the yard of the 1925 Yazoo and Mississippi Valley Railroad depot. The engine is coupled to four antique railcars, including an 1883 private car used in Grover Cleveland's presidential campaign.

The red archways in Riverfront Plaza, next door to the Louisiana Arts and Science Center/Riverside Museum, symbolize Baton Rouge. It is said that Canadian explorer Pierre Le Moyne, Sieur d'Iberville, sailed past the territory in 1699, sighted a red stick used as a boundary marker by neighboring Indian tribes, and named the region Baton Rouge, which is French for red stick. The plaza is a great spot to watch tugboats, barges, and seagoing vessels ply the muddy waters of the Mississippi River.

On two of the boats berthed in the river, the *Belle of Baton Rouge* and *Casino Rouge,* folks try their luck at games of chance and enjoy the festive atmosphere in the paddle-wheelers' lounges and restaurants.

Captain Kidd never steadied the helm of a Mississippi riverboat, but his likeness looks down on the Father of Waters from the stack of the USS *Kidd,* permanently docked next to Riverfront Plaza. The **USS *Kidd,*** the only surviving World War II

Fletcher-class destroyer not modernized by the United States Navy, offers a thirty-four–point, self-guided tour of rooms on three levels, including sick bay, the captain's quarters, and the combat information center.

In the adjacent **Nautical Center,** a P-40 "Flying Tiger" fighter plane hovers over one end of the exhibit area and the pilothouse of the steamboat *Louisiana* beckons would-be Mark Twains at the other. In between, uniforms, ship models, and films chronicle seafaring history. Names of Louisiana's sons and daughters who served their country in battle are etched into the black granite walls of Memorial Plaza next to the Nautical Center.

The Nautical Center's **Flying Tiger Cafe** or the cluster of small cafes at the end of North Boulevard, near the Old State Capitol, are easy-to-locate eateries in the downtown area. They are within walking distance of the Greek Revival "castle" on North Boulevard at River Road that served as Louisiana's State Capitol until 1932. The beautifully restored **Louisiana's Old State Capitol** is now a center for political and governmental history. Inside the landmark building, "Talking Portraits," activated by touching a screen, present the stories of Louisiana's past governors. Other imaginative exhibits explore the issues and events that shaped Louisiana's history and the roll of the media in politics.

The nearby **Louisiana Arts and Science Center/Former Governor's Mansion,** at 502 North Blvd., was home to nine Louisiana governors. Rooms in the white-pillared mansion that Huey Long modeled after the White House are furnished with fine Louisiana antiques and mementos of governors who served the state.

Some folks like to spend a day in Baton Rouge searching for antiques of their own in the city's huge malls and quaint shops that specialize in heirlooms and fine furnishings. The **Baton Rouge Area Convention & Visitors Bureau,** at 730 North Blvd., two blocks east of the Former Governor's Mansion, has information on several places to go antiquing. One is **Landmark Antique Plaza,** on St. Philip Street by Interstate 10 (a few blocks from the USS *Kidd*). Seemingly unending roomfuls of collectibles fill this building, once an 1847 brick factory worked by slaves. **Westmoreland Antique Gallery,** a 33,000-square-foot antique and collectible showplace, is also a popular destination. It is about two miles up Government Street from the downtown intersection of Government and St. Philip streets. Call for directions to **Fireside Antiques & Interiors** where you can end your antiquing spree with a delicious tea offered at tables set against a backdrop of French antiques and fine furnishing.

Furniture made by eighteenth-century Louisiana craftsmen helps recreate the life-style of wealthy Creole families at **Magnolia Mound Plantation,** one of Louisiana's oldest wooden structures. Indigo, cotton, and sugar were harvested at the plantation and sent to markets on the Mississippi River. The 1790s home that was the center of plantation life sits on a natural ridge facing the river. It is on Nicholson Drive, midway between downtown Baton Rouge and Louisiana State University.

Many plantation owners sent their sons to college at Louisiana State Seminary of Learning and Military Academy in Pineville. The school, forerunner of Louisiana State University, opened in January 1860, one year before the Civil War began. A fire forced moves to interim sites, but **Louisiana State University** (LSU) finally settled at its present south Baton Rouge campus in the 1920s. Visitors are welcome in the university's Union building art gallery, bookstore, and dining areas. They may also visit campus museums and the quarters of Mike, LSU's royal Bengal tiger mascot.

Enter LSU from Nicholson Drive, turn left onto South Stadium Road, then left onto Tower Drive to the nominally priced visitors' parking lot behind the Union. Ask for a complimentary campus map at the Union's Visitor Information Center (on your immediate right when entering the front of the Union), which will help you locate the on-campus museums.

Memorial Tower houses the Anglo-American Art Museum's period rooms, Newcomb pottery, a fine collection of New Orleans-made silver, and changing art exhibits. The Museum of Natural Science in Foster Hall has an impressive collection of North American flora and fauna and displays featuring the diverse wildlife encountered in Louisiana. The Museum of Geoscience offers rocks, fossils, minerals, and dioramas depicting Louisiana's Indian history.

Tiger Cage is the map-listing for Mike, who is "at home" to visitors in his quarters on North Stadium Road near the Maravich Assembly Center.

After your visit with Mike, return to the center of the campus, one block east of Tower Drive, and exit the university complex south on Highland Road. On your way to the **LSU Rural Life Museum,** which is off-campus, you will pass through some of Baton Rouge's prettiest neighborhoods. Follow Highland Road about five miles and turn left onto Staring Lane, which becomes Essen Lane as it nears Interstate 10. On your left, just before the interstate, a white fence marks the entrance to the museum.

A pleasant 1.2-mile drive through the grounds of the Burden Research Plantation leads to the Rural Life Museum's 15 antiquated buildings where the culture and life-styles of Louisiana's pre-Industrial Revolution working class is preserved. A bronze statue representing "the arduous and faithful service" of Louisiana's black workers—nicknamed "Uncle Jack"—greets you. He tips his hat, inviting you to examine the Rural Life Museum's homesteads and its mixed harvest of implements, vehicles, tools, and other artifacts gathered in a cavernous barn.

Look at the intriguing exhibits in the barn and inspect the museum's dogtrot and Acadian-style homes, plus a church built by nineteenth-century Louisiana workers. The builders incorporated traditional folk architecture that had been handed down from generation to generation. In the plantation area, there is a nineteenth-century commissary, an overseer's house, slave cabin, gristmill, and blacksmith shop.

Life was hard before the Industrial Revolution, and workers would certainly have welcomed a relaxing stroll through delightful Windrush Gardens in the rear of the Rural Life Museum. Winding pathways in this five-acre, semiformal garden lead to

outdoor "rooms" adorned with flowers and trees representative of a nineteenth-century plantation garden. Whimsical statues, collected mostly in Europe, are charmingly displayed
against the greenery.

Louisiana's fruitful waterways provided fresh seafood for
plantation kitchens and working-class frypans like the ones
exhibited at the Rural Life Museum. Today, you can sample the
state's aquatic largess or buy some fish, crabs, or shrimp to
bring home at restaurant/shops like **Drusilla's Seafood
Restaurant and Market.** To get there, turn left onto Essen Lane
as you exit the Rural Life Museum, go under the interstate
overpass, and turn right onto Jefferson Highway. Drusilla's is
two blocks away on your left in the Drusilla Shopping Center.

With the help of "The Visitor's Guide," published by the
Baton Rouge Convention & Visitors Bureau, you can discover
Baton Rouge's other fine restaurants on your own. Some of the
chefs turning out the delectable dishes set before you are graduates of **The Culinary Arts Institute of Louisiana.** You can taste
appetizing creations prepared by the Baton Rouge institute's
current class of student chefs at **CAILA's Fine Cuisine,** the only
culinary institute-"white linen" restaurant in the Deep South. In
fact, you may want to plan another weekend getaway so you can
be a short-term student chef at this fully accredited cooking
schoool. The institute's "Culinary Adventure Tours" are billed
as two days of fun and learning featuring a variety of cuisines.

A family-style getaway may also be enjoyed in Baton Rouge.
Energize the way locals do, with breakfast at **Frank's,** a popular,
twenty-eight-year-old Airline Highway cafe. The restaurant can
be reached by taking the Airline Highway (U.S. 61) exit from
Interstate 12 and traveling north about two miles.

After breakfast, browse more than 150 stores at **Cortana
Mall,** Louisiana's largest shopping center. It is located on the
east side of Airline Highway at U.S. 190. Then, head for **Fun
Fair Park,** at the intersection of Airline Highway and Florida
Street. Enjoy the park's eight amusement park rides, seven
children's rides, and several carnival games before heading for
Celebration Station, a fun center on Gwen Adele Avenue at the
intersection of Interstate 12 and Airline Highway.

At Celebration Station, families get into the swing of things by playing a round of miniature golf or testing their batting skills. Pre-teens and teens love to race in the fun center's go-karts while their younger siblings frolic on the kiddie rides.

The exquisite dolls and charming tea sets displayed in Baton Rouge's newest family attraction, **The Enchanted Mansion,** cause little girls to squeal with delight. And exhibits featuring animated and ethnic dolls, and a display of First Lady look-alikes, fascinate most visitors. Call for directions to the spacious museum and spend a few hours enjoying its remarkable dolls.

In the summer, plan to spend a few hours at **Blue Bayou Water Park.** From Interstate 10, near Highland Road on the southern edge of town, you can see Blue Bayou's towering slides. The fifteen-acre waterscape has a kiddie play pool, a wave pool, a swimming pool, and a diving tank. Water sprites with a yen for adventure ride the water park's seven-story, high-speed slide, a six-story serpentine chute, or the Flying Pirogue, a rampage sled-slide that satisfies the hungriest thrill-seeker.

If you are enjoying a fall or spring getaway with your family, balance active outings with a lazy day of canoeing and picnicking on Alligator Bayou. Canoes are offered for rent at **Alligator Bayou Bait Shop & Boat Launch.** The bayou is on the southern edge of Baton Rouge and is easily accessed from the Highland/Perkins Road exit. Call or write for complete directions.

Area Code: (504)

Getting There:

Baton Rouge can be accessed by Interstate 10 from the south and west, by Interstate 12 from the east, and by U.S. 61 or state highways from the north. Commercial flights land at Baton Rouge Metropolitan Airport.

Where and When:

Alligator Bayou Bait Shop & Boat Launch, 9980 Manchac Rd., St. Gabriel, LA 70776. 642-8297.

Belle of Baton Rouge, Catfish Town, South Blvd., Baton Rouge, LA 70821. 378-LUCK or 1-800-266-2692. Closed 3-10 A.M.

Blue Bayou Water Park, 18142 Perkins Rd. (off I-10 Highland Rd. exit), Baton Rouge, LA 70810. 753-3333. Daily, June 1-last weekend in August: 10 A.M.-6 P.M. Call for Labor Day and September hours. Admission.

Casino Rouge, 1717 River Road North, Baton Rouge, LA 70802. 581-7777 or 1-800-44-ROUGE. Closed 3-10 A.M.

Celebration Station, 10111 Gwen Adele Ave., Baton Rouge, LA 70816. 924-7888. Mon.-Thurs., 10 A.M.-10 P.M.; Fri. and Sat., 10 A.M.-midnight; Sun., 10 A.M.-10 P.M. Admission.

Cortana Mall, 9401 Cortana Place, Baton Rouge, LA 70815. 923-4731. Mon.-Sat., 10 A.M.-9 P.M.; Sun., noon-6 P.M.

The Culinary Arts Institute of Louisiana, 427 Lafayette St., Baton Rouge, LA 70802. 343-6233 or 1-800-927-0839.

The Enchanted Mansion, 190 Lee Dr., Baton Rouge, LA 70808. 769-0005. Mon. and Wed.-Sat., 10 A.M.-5 P.M.; Sun., 1-4 P.M. Closed Tuesdays.

Fireside Antiques & Interiors, 14007 Perkins Rd., Baton Rouge, LA 70810. Mon.-Sat., 10 A.M.-5:30 P.M. Tea: Tues.-Sat., noon-3:30 P.M. Reservations required.

Fun Fair Park, 8475 Florida Blvd., Baton Rouge, LA 70815. 924-6266. Spring and fall weekend hours: Fri., 6-10 P.M.; Sat., 10 A.M.-10 P.M.; Sun., 1-7 P.M. Summer hours: Tues.-Sat., 10 A.M.-10 P.M.; Sun., 1-10 P.M. Closed November-February. Admission.

Landmark Antique Plaza, 832 St. Philip St., Baton Rouge, LA 70802. 383-4867. Daily, 10 A.M.-6 P.M.

Louisiana Arts & Science Center/Former Governor's Mansion, 502 North Blvd., Baton Rouge, LA 70802. 344-9463. Sat., 10 A.M.-4 P.M.; Sun, 1-4 P.M. Closed weekdays. Admission, except Sat., 10 A.M.-noon.

Louisiana Arts and Science Center/Riverside Museum, 100 S. River Rd. (P.O. Box 3373), Baton Rouge, LA 70821. 344-9463. Tues.-Fri., 10 A.M.-3 P.M.; Sat., 10 A.M.-4 P.M.; Sun., 1-4 P.M.

Admission, except Sat., 10 A.M.-noon. Train: Tues.-Fri., 10 A.M.-noon; Sat., 10 A.M.-4 P.M.; Sun., 1-4 P.M. Space Shows: call for schedule. Free with museum admission.

Louisiana State Capitol, State Capitol Drive, Baton Rouge, LA 70804. Visitor Information Center, 342-7317. Daily, 8 A.M.-4:30 P.M. Call for tour schedule.

Louisiana State University, Baton Rouge, LA 70803-3300. Visitor Information, 388-5030.

Union Building and Information Center, Mon.-Fri, 7 A.M.-11 P.M.; Sat., 8 A.M.-11 P.M.; Sun., 11 A.M.-11 P.M.

Bookstore, Mon.-Wed., 8 A.M.-6 P.M.; Thurs. and Fri., 8 A.M.-5:30 P.M.; Sat., 10 A.M.-4 P.M.

Anglo-American Art Museum, Mon.-Fri., 9 A.M.-4 P.M.; Sat., 10 A.M.-noon, 1-4 P.M.; Sun., 1-4 P.M.

Museum of Geoscience, Mon.-Fri., 8:30 A.M.-4:30 P.M. Traveling exhibits—Sat., 10 A.M.-5 P.M.; Sun., 2-5 P.M.

Museum of Natural Science, Mon.-Fri., 8 A.M.-4 P.M.; Sat., 9:30 A.M.-1 P.M.

LSU Rural Life Museum, Burden Research Plantation, 6200 Burden Lane (Essen Lane at I-10), Baton Rouge, LA 70808. 765-2437. Mon.-Fri., 8:30 A.M.-4:30 P.M.; Sat., Apr.-Nov., 9 A.M.-4:30 P.M. Admission.

Louisiana's Old State Capitol, 100 North Blvd., Baton Rouge, LA 70802. 342-0500. Thurs.-Sat., 10 A.M.-4 P.M.; Sun. noon-4 P.M. Admission.

Magnolia Mound Plantation, 2161 Nicholson Dr., Baton Rouge, LA 70802. 343-4955. Tues.-Sat., 10 A.M.-4 P.M.; Sun., 1-4 P.M. Admission.

Old Arsenal Museum, Louisiana State Capitol Complex, Baton Rouge, LA 70804. 342-0401. Mon.-Sat., 10 A.M.-4 P.M.; Sun., 1-4 P.M. Admission.

USS *Kidd*/Nautical Center, 305 S. River Rd. (P.O. Box 44242), Baton Rouge, LA 70804. 342-1942. Daily, 9 A.M.-5 P.M. Admission.

Westmoreland Antique Gallery, 3374 Government St., Westmoreland Shopping Center, Baton Rouge, LA 70806. 383-7777 or 383-7787. Daily, 10 A.M.-6 P.M.

Transportation:

If you visit Baton Rouge when the Legislature is in session, it is best to park in the downtown riverfront area and walk or take the downtown shuttle to the Louisiana State Capitol. At other times, parking is usually available close to the capitol building.

Information:

Baton Rouge Area Convention & Visitors Bureau, Inc., 730 North Blvd. (P.O. Box 4149), Baton Rouge, LA 70821. 383-1825 or 1-800-LA ROUGE. Mon.-Fri., 8 A.M.-5 P.M.

State Capitol Tourist Information Center, Louisiana State Capitol, State Capitol Drive, Baton Rouge, LA 70804. 342-7317. Daily, 8 A.M.-4:30 P.M.

Guide Services:

Contact the Baton Rouge Area Convention & Visitors Bureau.

Accommodations:

Chain and independent motels are available in the Baton Rouge area.

Bed and Breakfasts:

Mount Hope Plantation, 8151 Highland Rd., Baton Rouge, LA 70808. 766-8600.

Restaurants:

CAILA'S Fine Cuisine, The Culinary Arts Institute of Louisiana, 427 Lafayette St., Baton Rouge, LA 70802. 343-6233 or 1-800-927-0839. Mon.-Fri., 11:30 A.M.-1:30 P.M.

Drusilla's Seafood Restaurant and Market, 3482 Drusilla Lane, Baton Rouge, LA 70809. Restaurant, 923-0896. Daily, 11 A.M.-

10 P.M. Market, 928-2277. Mon.-Thurs., 9 A.M.-6 P.M.; Fri. and Sat., 8:30 A.M.-7 P.M.; Sun., 10 A.M.-6 P.M.

Flying Tiger Cafe, USS *Kidd*/Nautical Center, 305 S. River Rd. (P.O. Box 44242), Baton Rouge, LA 70804. 342-1942. Daily, 11 A.M.-2 P.M.

Frank's, 8353 Airline Hwy., Baton Rouge, LA 70815. 926-5977 or 924-9728. Daily, 5 A.M.-2:30 P.M.

Louisiana State University:

Plantation Room, LSU Union, mezzanine floor. Mon.-Fri., 11:30 A.M.-1:30 P.M.; Sun., 11:30 A.M. buffet.

Swensen's Ice Cream Parlor, LSU Union, 1st floor. Mon.-Sat., 10 A.M.-10 P.M.; Sun., 1-10 P.M.

Union Cafeteria, LSU Union, 1st floor. Mon.-Fri., 8:30 A.M.-2 P.M.

Union Tiger Lair, LSU Union, 1st floor. Mon.-Fri., 7 A.M.-10:45 P.M.; Sat., 8 A.M.-7 P.M.; Sun., 11 A.M.-2 P.M.

Major Annual Events:

Balloon Festival—September.

Baton Rouge Blues Festival—Last weekend in August.

Christmas on the River—December 1-31.

Fest-For-All—Third weekend in May.

Hollydays Christmas Market—October.

A view of Lawyers Row in Clinton, Louisiana. (Photo by Mary Fonseca)

12

TOURING AND TOASTING IN TWO VINTAGE TOWNS
(G)

Turn-of-the-century residents of Jackson shopped at 11 general merchandise stores, 2 millinery shops, a furniture store, and 2 drugstores. They socialized at a couple of "refreshment parlors," often with students attending the town's 3 colleges. Visitors and business travelers had their choice of 2 first-class hotels, and the thriving community of 800 even owned its own railroad. In 1895, a writer for Jackson's daily newspaper, *The Democratic Record,* was so impressed with the town's institutions of learning, and the Greek Revival architecture of its buildings, that he described the flourishing town in the verdant hills north of Baton Rouge as "the Athens of Louisiana."

In 1824, a site about ten miles east of Jackson was chosen to be the parish seat of newly formed East Feliciana Parish. The town established there was named Clinton in honor of Governor DeWitt Clinton, and it developed into a successful legal center that buzzed with important trials. So many attorneys established offices along a street behind the parish courthouse that the assemblage of buildings became known as "Lawyers Row." In the 1830s, when the Clinton and Port Hudson Railroad was established, cotton traders joined the circle of prominent businessmen who contributed to the town's welfare.

Clinton and Jackson blossomed into prosperous towns in the early years of the twentieth century. But the good life faded into memory when boll weevils mercilessly plundered the cotton fields and the Great Depression spread a melancholy fog over the land.

Fortunately, some of East Feliciana's antebellum and Victorian structures survived the hard times. They give character to the towns and pleasure to visitors who appreciate their history. In Jackson, you can wander through a historic district of nearly 125 homes, schools, churches, and businesses. Shady streets that extend from Clinton's distinguished town square—still embellished with its historic courthouse and Lawyers Row—are also graced with vintage structures. Books collected by the East Feliciana Branch of **Audubon Regional Library** have replaced legal tomes in one of the 1840s offices in Lawyers Row, and the library's genealogy and Louisiana sections are popular destinations for visitors attempting to trace their family tree.

Travelers who overnight in Clinton relax in cozy bed-and-breakfast rooms offered at **Martin Hill,** an 1840 townhouse. **LeBlanc's Restaurant,** on Plank Road (Louisiana 67 South), is conveniently located for lunch and dinner.

Guests who stay in Jackson rest in posh accommodations at **Milbank Historic House,** the town's oldest commercial building, or in well-appointed rooms in the newly restored **Old Centenary Inn.** Milbank was built in the 1830s to be Jackson's first bank. In later years it was a barracks for Union soldiers, an assembly hall, an apothecary, a millinery shop, a small hotel and ballroom, and a publishing house. On tours of Milbank's majestic rooms, docents describe the antique furnishings that replaced the paraphernalia of past pursuits.

Old Centenary Inn was built in 1935 with bricks, columns, windows, and doors salvaged from the East Wing of Centenary College. The eight-room hotel was restored into an inviting bed-and-breakfast inn by Leroy and Lynette Harvey, owners of Milbank.

Costumed interpreters lead visitors through exhibits that focus on student life and education in Louisiana in the rejuvenated West Wing of **Centenary College,** the focal point of a recently refurbished State Commemorative Area. Before the

Civil War, nearly 250 students attended classes at Centenary. But, they exchanged textbooks for rifles when the conflict began. *The Democratic Record* of June 8, 1895, recalled that, "Of all the gallants who went with high hopes to defend the Confederacy, very, very few lived to return."

Jackson's accommodations are just steps away from **Bear Corners,** a praiseworthy restaurant that reflects the name of an early settlement that, tradition holds, evolved into the town of Jackson. Light refreshments, including beverages, pastries, and ice cream may be enjoyed at **Jackson Coffee Company** on College Street.

At **Asphodel Village and Inn,** south of Jackson, a pool, hot tub, and **Blum's** well-stocked gift shop complement an attractive cluster of bed-and-breakfast cottages and townhouses. They are grouped around Levy House, the 1840s home of a former cotton merchant that is now an enticing restaurant. Scenic trails behind the hostelry tempt guests to stroll through the woodsy bird sanctuary that connects Asphodel Village and Inn with its namesake, **Asphodel Plantation.** The plantation home is only open for group tours, but visitors are welcome to saunter around the grounds and photograph the exterior of this historic mansion.

Although some golfers reserve well-appointed rooms at **The Lodge at the Bluffs** so they can conveniently combine a day on the links with tours of the area's historic sites, the Arnold Palmer golf course may be enjoyed by visitors staying in any of the Feliciana's fine accommodations. Weekenders are also welcome to enjoy the fine dining offered at **The Bluffs Restaurant.**

The locations of Centenary, Asphodel, and other points of interest in East Feliciana are included in a brochure prepared by the East Feliciana Parish Tourist Commission. It is available at many shops, accommodations, and historic sites, such as Jackson's **Republic of West Florida Museum and Art Gallery.** Here you can browse through engrossing exhibits ranging from Civil War artifacts to a hearse used in the movie, *Interview with a Vampire.* Some displays relate to the short-lived Republic of West Florida, formed in 1803 by Feliciana residents who were angry at being left out of the Louisiana Purchase. The grievance was settled seventy-four days later when the Republic of West Florida was absorbed into the Territory of Orleans, part of the United States.

Before Feliciana Parish was divided into east and west segments, the 1816 **Feliciana Parish Courthouse** across from the museum was a busy place. The building fell into disrepair over the years but was purchased and refurbished by The Jackson Assembly. It is now a branch office for the East Feliciana Parish Clerk of Court.

The Jackson Assembly is dedicated to renovating, embellishing, and promoting the town of Jackson. The civic organization started this ambitious project thirty-two years ago when it revitalized the McKowen and Pipes-McKowen stores on Charter Street (Louisiana 10). Every spring the spruced up buildings are the setting for the Assembly's major fundraiser, The Jackson Assembly Antique Show & Sale. Attendees select from vintage furnishings and collectibles displayed in both stores and enjoy a delicious lunch prepared and served by assembly members.

In the fall, Jackson's Civil War history is remembered with a living history demonstration on a field outside of town. In the morning, spectators visit Union and Confederate camps, then withdraw to a grandstand to watch costumed participants re-enact the Battle of Jackson Crossroads. In the evening, couples dressed in antebellum attire dance to authentic music of the period at an Old South ball in the candlelit Pipes-McKowen store.

The McKowen stores are used only for special events. But other shops in Jackson and Clinton offer year-long opportunities to purchase a souvenir or keepsake of your visit. The **Old Post Office Gift Shop,** next door to Milbank, carries teapots, cookbooks, Louisiana products, and souvenirs. And **Lawson's Crystals by Rae,** housed in the vintage Johnny Jones store on the corner of Church and Erin streets, sells crystal jewelry and crystal accessories for the home, all created by Jackson artisan Rae Lawson. **Missy's Country Collectibles** Charter Street antique shop may somewhat mollify enthusiasts who miss the Jackson

Assembly's Antique Show & Sale. **Lockridge Cottage Gifts,** Jackson's newest boutique, sells books on the area and handsome gift items at its College Avenue location.

McKnight's, in Clinton, is widely recognized as the most stylish store in East Feliciana. It offers chic apparel created by popular designers that is displayed alongside one-of-a-kind pieces. Discerning shoppers admire McKnight's Kamininski hats from Australia, silver jewelry fashioned from antique luggage tags, and duck decoys carved by Robert Thompson, a local sculptor. Charming prints of Clinton's historic St. Andrew Episcopal Church, painted by hometown artist Aline Madere, and captivating drawings of the Clinton courthouse and Lawyers Row, by Lake Charles artist Jerry Goen, may also be purchased at McKnight's. Complimentary coffee, a booklet about historic Clinton, and friendly conversation with Marquita and Ikey McKnight are cheerfully offered as *lagniappe.*

Marquita, an accomplished artist as well as an experienced shopkeeper, designed the lovely East Feliciana screen that hangs in the **Clinton Bank & Trust Company** building on courthouse square. A brochure available at the bank explains the symbolism of the panels.

The **F. S. Williams Country Store** on Louisiana 19 (about a block off of Louisiana 10 between Jackson and Clinton) was doing business in the same location long before the advent of modern banking. The store is the genuine article—an old-fashioned country emporium that has been owned and managed by three generations of the same family. The variety of merchandise inside the spacious store is amazing. Horse collars and well buckets hang from the walls and the shelves overflow with everything from kerosene lamps to linoleum. Groceries, including Louisiana cane syrup and the Williams' homemade pan pork sausages, surround the check-out station in the center of the wooden sales floor. A large side room holds an extensive stock of hunting gear, plus camouflage outfits in every size from infant to extra, extra large.

While you are enjoying East Feliciana's intriguing shops and historic sites, pause to toast the parish's future at two congenial wineries and a lively brewpub.

St. Andrew Episcopal Church in Clinton. (Photo by Mary Fonseca)

Feliciana Cellars Winery in Jackson. (Photo by Mary Fonseca)

Antique wine casks from Spain displayed in Feliciana Cellars Winery. (Photo by Mary Fonseca)

Follow signs along Louisiana 10 east of Clinton to direct you to the Cazedessus family's **Casa De Sue Winery,** the first winery to be licensed in Louisiana. Near the end of a ten-mile excursion to the Hatcher Road facility, columns of maturing grapevines march alongside the road. In mid-summer these vineyards, and others in the region, are heavy with Muscadine grapes. The Cazedessuses have been cultivating grapes for more than ten years. They graciously welcome visitors to their plant, show them a short film on the wine-making process, and treat them to a brief tour that ends in the tasting room. Here, visitors are offered the winery's nine Muscadine and two blueberry wines. Bottles of these vintages, plus an assortment of homemade jellies and wine-related gift items, are also sold here.

Feliciana Cellars Winery is housed in an eye-catching, Spanish-style building on Charter Street in Jackson. The tasting room is embellished with gigantic clay jars and a lavishly decorated oxcart once used by Spanish winemakers. More wine-making antiques are tastefully displayed alongside gift boxes, copper items, wine carriers, and racks. At its tasting bar, this young winery offers two white wines, one red, and nonalcoholic Muscadine grape juice.

Feliciana Cellars Winery also houses **Rikenjaks Microbrewery** and offers tastings of Rikenjaks three thirst-quenching ales—Old Hardhead, E.S.B., and American Ale.

Area Code: (504)

Getting There:

Jackson and Clinton are on Louisiana 10 between U.S. 61 and Interstate 55.

Where and When:

Audubon Regional Library, Lawyers Row, Woodville Street, Clinton, LA 70722. Mon.-Wed., 9 A.M.-5 P.M.

Blum's, Asphodel, 4626 LA 68, Jackson, LA 70748. 654-0055. Mon.-Sat., 10 A.M.-5 P.M.; Sun., 11 A.M.-3 P.M.

Casa De Sue Winery, 14316 Hatcher Rd., Clinton, LA 70722. 1-800-683-5937 or 683-5937. Mon.-Sat., 10 A.M.-6 P.M. Brochure with map mailed upon request.

Centenary State Commemorative Area, College Street, Jackson, LA 70748. (Mailing address: P.O. Box 546, St. Francisville, LA 70775.) 634-7925. Daily, 9 A.M.-5 P.M. Admission.

Clinton Bank & Trust Company, 12225 St. Helena St., Clinton, LA 70722. 683-3371. Mon.-Thurs., 9 A.M.-4 P.M.; Fri., 9 A.M.-5:30 P.M.

F. S. Williams Country Store, 5949 LA 19, Ethel, LA 70730. 683-8251 or 683-8392.

Feliciana Cellars Winery, 1848 Charter St., Jackson, LA 70748. 634-7982. Mon.-Fri., 10 A.M.-5 P.M.; Sat., 9 A.M.-5 P.M.

Feliciana Parish Courthouse, High Street, Jackson, LA 70742. 634-5623. Mon. and Wed., 8:30 A.M.-4:30 P.M.; Fri., 8 A.M.-noon.

Lawson's Crystals by Rae, 1617 Erin St., Jackson, LA 70742. 634-2452. Mon.-Fri., 10 A.M.-5 P.M.

Lockridge Cottage Gifts, 3259 College Ave., Jackson, LA 70748. 634-5832. Tues.-Sat., 9 A.M.-5 P.M.; Sun., 1-5 P.M.

McKnight's Department Store, 12321 St. Helena St. (P.O. Box 36), Clinton, LA 70722. 683-8267. Mon.-Sat., 8 A.M.-5:30 P.M.

Milbank Historic House, 3053 Bank St. (P.O. Box 1000), Jackson, LA 70748. 634-5901. Tours: Mon.-Fri., 9 A.M.-4 P.M.; Sat., 9 A.M.-2 P.M. Admission.

Missy's Country Collectibles, 1741 Charter St., Jackson, LA 70748. 634-7761. Sat. and Sun., 10:30 A.M.-5 P.M. Otherwise by appointment.

Old Post Office Gift Shop, 3053 Bank St., Jackson, LA 70748. 634-2547. Mon.-Fri., 9 A.M.-5 P.M.; Sat., 9 A.M.-2 P.M.

Republic of West Florida Museum and Art Gallery, 3406 College St. (P.O. Box 1000), Jackson, LA 70748. 634-7155. Tues.-Sun., 10 A.M.-5 P.M. Closed Mondays. Admission.

Rikenjaks Microbrewery, Feliciana Cellars Winery, 1848

Charter St., Jackson, LA 70748. 634-5771. Mon.-Fri., 10 A.M.-5 P.M.; Sat., 9 A.M.-5 P.M. Sun., 1-5 P.M.

Information:

Feliciana Cellars Winery, 1848 Charter St., Jackson, LA 70748. 634-7982. Mon.-Fri., 10 A.M.-5 P.M.; Sat., 9 A.M.-5 P.M.; Sun., 1-5 P.M.

Republic of West Florida Museum and Art Gallery, 3406 College St. (P.O. Box 1000), Jackson, LA 70748. 634-7155. Tues.-Sun., 10 A.M.-5 P.M.

Guide Services:

Rachel Hall, St. Francisville Tours, P.O. Box 89, St. Francisville, LA 70775. 635-6283. Assistance with transportation, lodging, individual tour packets, special amenities.

Accommodations:

Bed and Breakfasts:

Asphodel Village and Inn, 4626 LA 68, Jackson, LA 70748. 654-6868.

The Lodge at the Bluffs, Sunrise Way, The Bluffs, Louisiana 965 at Freeland Road, St. Francisville, LA 70775. 634-3410.

Martin Hill, 12537 St. Helena St. (P.O. Box 7933), Clinton, LA 70722. 683-5594.

Milbank Historic House, 3053 Bank St. (P.O. Box 1000), Jackson, LA 70748. 634-5901.

Old Centenary Inn, 1740 Charter St., Jackson, LA 70748. 634-7397.

Hotel, motel, and bed-and-breakfast accommodations are also available less than twenty miles from Jackson in St. Francisville and the surrounding area. See "A Feliciana Parish Treasure Hunt."

Restaurants:

Asphodel Village and Inn, 4626 LA 68, Jackson, LA 70748. 654-6868. Breakfast: Daily, 7:30-9 A.M.; Lunch: Daily, 11:30 A.M.-3

P.M.; Dinner: Tues.-Thurs., 5:30-7:30 P.M.; Fri. and Sat., 5:30-9 P.M.

Bear Corners, 1674 Charter St., Jackson, LA 70748. 634-2844. Lunch: Wed.-Fri., 11:30 A.M.-2 P.M. Dinner: Wed.-Sat., 5:30-9 P.M. Sun. buffet, 11 A.M.-2 P.M.

The Bluffs Restaurant, The Lodge at the Bluffs, Sunrise Way, The Bluffs, Louisiana 965 at Freeland Road, St. Francisville, LA 70775. 634-5088. Lunch: Mon.-Sat., 11:30 A.M.-2 P.M. Dinner: Mon.-Thurs., 5:30-9 P.M.; Fri. and Sat., 5:30-10 P.M.; Sunday buffet, noon-2 P.M. Live music Fridays, 7:30-11:30 P.M.

LeBlanc's, Louisiana 67 (Plank Road), Clinton, LA 70722. 683-3480. Sun.-Thurs., 6:30 A.M.-9 P.M.; Fri. and Sat., 6:30 A.M.-10 P.M.

More restaurants are available in St. Francisville. They are listed in "A Feliciana Parish Treasure Hunt."

Major Annual Events:

Battle of Jackson Crossroads, Jackson—November.

Clinton Christmas Parade—First Saturday in December. Feliciana Spring Sampler, Clinton—April.

Jackson Assembly Antique Show & Sale, Jackson—Last weekend in March.

Norwood Mardi Gras Parade, Norwood—Fat Tuesday.

Octoberfest at Asphodel Inn, Jackson—October.

Pecan Ridge Bluegrass Festival, Jackson—May and September.

Slaughter Christmas Parade, Slaughter—Second Saturday in December.

13

A FELICIANA PARISH TREASURE HUNT
(G)

About twenty miles north of Baton Rouge, U.S. 61 dips and rises through gentle, rolling hills in East and West Feliciana parishes. Hidden in secluded glens bordering the highway, stately plantations, colorful gardens, and fascinating historic sites await discovery by weekend wanderers.

Travelers who have the opportunity to visit the Felicianas— the name means "happy land" in Spanish—more than once savor the bounty offered by this well-favored land at an unhurried pace. They have the opportunity to delve a bit deeper into its cache of accommodations and attractions whenever they can break away from their daily routine.

A leisurely stroll through St. Francisville, a postcard-pretty village that is Louisiana's third-oldest settlement, is a pleasant introduction to a Feliciana tour. The **West Feliciana Historical Society Museum** on Ferdinand Street (the town's main thoroughfare) stocks plenty of information on the community and has some engrossing exhibits. The information center occupies one of approximately 150 historic structures in St. Francisville, a narrow municipality once described as "two miles long and two yards (as in backyards) wide."

A brochure available at the museum outlines a self-guided tour of the community's historic district, laid out in a semi-circle formed by Ferdinand and Royal streets.

Confederate Gen. P. G. T. Beauregard drew the plans for

Our Lady of Mount Carmel Church, which crowns a bluff at one end of Ferdinand Street. Leaflets available in the rear of the 100-year-old church detail the features of this pristine Catholic chapel.

At the foot of Catholic hill, as it is locally known, an iron-fenced cemetery surrounds **Grace Episcopal Church.** The masterful craftsmanship contained in this oft-admired, 1858 house of worship was once marred by shells from Federal gunboats. Today, its restored features are described in handouts available in the rectory.

Snug cottages and imposing townhouses on St. Francisville's Royal and Ferdinand streets have some fascinating stories connected to their history. One often-told tale involves Dora Ross, a daring widow who served meals to Union officers in spite of the wagging tongues that lashed out at her disloyalty to the Confederacy.

Learn more about the town's storied past by spending a night in one of the historic district's bed-and-breakfast homes. Hosts at **Propinquity** and **Barrow House Inn** delight in sharing information about their homes and their historic town. Shirley and Lyle Dittloff, proprietors of Barrow House Inn, even have prepared a special walking-tour tape for their houseguests.

Stores in St. Francisville are brimming with gifts, artworks, crafts, and antiques. **Shadetree,** an airy shop perched on a hill across from Our Lady of Mount Carmel, is a conglomeration of birdhouses and feeders, imported fabrics, folk art, and a selection of quality coffees and teas. Choose a flavorful brew and sip it on the shop's inviting deck while you enjoy the most beautiful view in town. If you are celebrating a special occasion, make prior arrangements with the staff for a luscious gourmet dinner to be served to you in this idyllic setting. Then, settle into one of Shadetree's attractive bed-and-breakfast cottages or climb the stairs in the shop to a cozy loft where you can fall asleep while watching stars twinkle through an overhead skylight.

Just a few blocks from Shadetree, a feast for the eyes awaits you at the Royal Street gallery of Hershel Harrington. In **Harrington Gallery,** this impressionistic artist uses his brushes to capture "the mystical landscapes and tranquil people" of Louisiana, his native state.

Beechwood Gifts, next to the West Feliciana Parish Historical Society Museum on Ferdinand Street, is one of many delightful stores that line Ferdinand Street. The shop offers a fine selection of Audubon prints, along with its framing services and decorator accessories. Across the street, **Shanty Too** stocks appealing gifts, delicate lingerie, and quality linens for all occasions. More unique gifts and keepsakes may be found at **Blum's, Emporium,** and **Belle Lane.** Chestee Harrington's original wood reliefs, limited-edition prints, and sculptures are available at her **Fine Art Gallery.** And, **St. Francis Gallery** showcases more notable works by talented local artists.

Ferdinand Street is also the home of two engaging antique shops—**Somethin' Special** and **C and D Collectibles Then and Now.** Be sure to drop a quarter in the player piano at C and D Collectibles and witness two dancing bears performing in rhythm with the instrument's "five-piece band."

Star Hill Antiques, a hilltop shop on U.S. 61 south of St. Francisville, offers handmade furniture and crafts and fresh cornmeal ground in a local gristmill.

When you are ready for a shopping break, relax in one of St. Francisville's casual restaurants. New Orleans-style po' boys and other enticing lunches are served at **Glory B's Diner** near Shanty Too. At the opposite end of Ferdinand Street you can enjoy delightful beverages and snacks at **Bayou Sara Coffee & Tea Company** in the **St. Francisville Inn** or sample the delicious salads and sandwiches on the menu at the **Magnolia Cafe.**

If you are a nostalgia buff, rent one of the cabins in the recently renovated **3-V Tourist Court** behind the Magnolia Cafe. The comfortably furnished, yet moderately priced cabins, built in the 1920s, are listed on the National Register of Historic Places. They are equipped with stove tops, microwave ovens, and refrigerators.

The Magnolia Cafe neighborhood was once part of St. Francisville's boisterous Red Horse District, so named because teams hauling lumber from the Mississippi River landing were covered with sticky red clay by the time they reached town. **The Red Horse Inn** on Commerce Street is the only remnant of the busy saloons that once enlivened the district. Convivial friends still gather here, especially on Sunday evenings when live music is the draw.

Several cherished antebellum dwellings grace the roadsides surrounding St. Francisville, but none is more prized than **Rosedown,** the exquisite home Martha and Daniel Turnbull built near the town's eastern boundary. Descendants of the Turnbulls lived in Rosedown until 1952, keeping most of the 1835 mansion's decor intact. In the late 1950s, Catherine Fondren Underwood bought the estate and restored it to its former grandeur.

Rosedown's opulent furnishings include a bedroom suite purchased by supporters of Henry Clay. When Clay lost the 1844 presidential election—and the opportunity to move the custom-made furniture into the White House—Daniel Turnbull bought the bedroom set and added a wing to Rosedown to accommodate its massive proportions.

Martha Turnbull was a devoted gardener. Shrubs she cultivated still line Rosedown's shaded walkways. Bricked footpaths connect the garden's secluded arbors, refreshing fountains, and graceful gazebos. After touring hours are over, Rosedown's bed-and-breakfast guests enjoy restful evenings in this beautiful setting.

Catalpa Plantation, a few miles north of Rosedown, is a home that is "lived in, used, and loved," says Mamie Fort Thompson, the present owner. "Miss Mamie" delights in showing visitors the antiques that her grandmother, Sara Turnbull, brought to Catalpa as well as the valuable furnishings accumulated by eight generations of the Thompson family who have lived at Catalpa since the 1800s.

Judge Thomas Butler bought **The Cottage Plantation** near Catalpa in 1810 and added several rooms to the house to accommodate his expanding family. Later, the Butler clan added a bedroom wing that now serves the plantation's bed-and-breakfast clientele.

The parterre *at Afton Villa Gardens in St. Francisville.* (Photo by Mary Fonseca)

At the rambling, two-storied Cottage, guests can relax on the gallery, take a dip in the backyard pool, or play croquet on the lawn. In the evening, tantalizing aromas entice them to **Mattie's House Restaurant,** an attractive eatery on the plantation's grounds.

Breakfast in the Cottage's cozy dining room is followed by a tour of the house, the antiquated outbuildings, and the Butler family cemetery.

While the Civil War brought tragedy and ruin to many Southern plantations, some survived the horrors of war only to meet their demise in later years. Such was the fate of two stunning Feliciana plantations, Afton Villa and Greenwood.

Although Afton Villa no longer graces its parklike setting four miles north of St. Francisville, admirers still enter the burned-out estate's white-pillared gates and follow a serpentine

Butler Greenwood Plantation. (Photo by Mary Fonseca)

road to the plantation ruins. The enchanting drive passes through a natural cathedral beamed with live oaks and bordered with spring-blooming azaleas.

Morell and Genevive Trimble bought the fallen villa in 1972 and transformed it into **Afton Villa Gardens,** a "ruin garden" covered with fragrant blossoms and ferns. Near this unusual garden, walkways lead to a *parterre* (sectioned garden) and descend graded terraces planted with seasonal blooms. An especially pretty show takes place in early spring when trumpet-shaped daffodils coloring the knolls surrounding Afton Villa Gardens' reflecting pond are mirrored in the smooth-surfaced water.

Lightning destroyed **Greenwood Plantation** in a fiery flash, but Walton and Richard Barnes spent fifteen years rebuilding the Greek Revival showplace. Several movie makers have since used the painstakingly restored, twenty-eight–columned plantation as a setting for their films. The producers of *Louisiana* even furnished wallpaper and drapes for the manor's interior, relandscaped the driveway and yard, and constructed an over-seer's house. In 1985, both "North and South" mini-series were filmed at Greenwood, and the cast and crew of *Sister, Sister* used the setting a year later. Greenwood is ten miles west of U.S. 61 via Louisiana 66 and Highland Road.

English-style **Butler Greenwood Plantation** (on U.S. 61, 2.2 miles north of St. Francisville) is very different from the revived colossus that shares its name. The richly decorated home is more reminiscent of the Victorian era than the antebellum period. In the parlor, for instance, gilded French pier mirrors reflect scarlet-upholstered Louis XV rosewood furniture, arranged exactly as it was in 1861. Bed-and-breakfast guests are comfortably accommodated in six appealing cottages that sur-round a pond and pool on Butler Greenwood's extensive grounds.

The facade of **The Myrtles** plantation (on U.S. 61, 1.3 miles north of St. Francisville) also differs from the traditional Greek Revival perspective. Iron grillwork borders the porch of this dormer-windowed manor, more famous for its air of mystery than its architecture. Gadabouts who yearn to encounter the spirit world are enthralled with the ghost stories told by Myrtles tour guides on special evening tours. Intrepid bed-and-break-fast clients sleep in the reputedly haunted mansion, but timid souls opt for lodging in the comfortable wing added to the rear of the house. Casual visitors and overnight guests enjoy The Myrtles' inviting restaurant and the soothing view of a latticed gazebo on the edge of a nearby pond.

When noted naturalist John James Audubon arrived at Oakley Plantation to teach drawing to Eliza Pirrie, the youth-ful daughter of the house, he was so taken with the beauty of the surrounding forest that he noted in his journal, "The rich magnolias covered with fragrant blossoms, the holly, the beech, the tall yellow poplar, the hilly ground and even the red clay, all excited my admiration."

Today, the verdant woodland that so entranced the itinerant teacher is the **Audubon State Commemorative Area.** Admirers of this renowned chronicler of America's birds tour the nearly

200-year-old Oakley and its outbuildings, pausing to reverently scrutinize the tiny, second-floor room assigned to the nomadic painter.

Several original Audubon prints are on display at Oakley (accessed via Louisiana 965, 1.9 miles south of St. Francisville on U.S. 61), and a more extensive collection of the artist's works can be viewed at **Heminbough,** a Bed and Breakfast/conference center with a Grecian atmosphere.

Heminbough is one of several choices available to travelers who prefer to stay in contemporary hostelries while visiting the Felicianas. **St. Francis Hotel-on-the-Lake** offers motel facilities in a waterside setting. **Green Springs Plantation** has a sophisticated mix of antique and modern furnishings in a cottage that is reminiscent of 1800s architecture. And overnight guests at **The Lodge at the Bluffs** enjoy tastefully furnished quarters and a refreshing pool. The resort's golf-related amenities and dining room are available to all visitors.

Weekenders who relax and dine at **Asphodel Village and Inn** appreciate the soothing atmosphere at this inviting Bed and Breakfast. The inn's collection of vintage buildings on Louisiana 68, between U.S. 61 and Louisiana 10, is linked to Asphodel Plantation by a short nature trail. The mansion is only open to group tours but visitors are welcome on the grounds.

Before the Civil War, the only shots heard in the peaceful hills around Asphodel were from guns aimed at wild turkey and deer. In 1863, however, gunfire from fortifications at Port Hudson, a few miles from the plantation, abruptly shattered the serenity of the countryside. The ensuing battle raged for forty-eight days on towering bluffs overlooking the Mississippi River. It was the longest seige in American military history. The **Port Hudson State Commemorative Area's** interpretive center, ten miles south of St. Francisville, vividly recalls the valor of Confederate soldiers who defended this last stronghold of the Confederacy. It also commemorates the courage of the first black soldiers and other regulars in the United States Army who participated in the assault.

Twentieth-century technology seems out of step with the

antebellum luxury and Civil War history immortalized along U.S. 61, so the presence of the River Bend nuclear generating facility, 1.8 miles south of St. Francisville, is a shock to the senses. But visitors who weather the time warp are entranced by the well-planned exhibits in the **River Bend Energy Center.** Included are a simulated 1920s coal-mine elevator, a pedal-power generator, and an exact duplicate of the control room used at the plant.

Spaniards were the first white men to see the rolling hills and lush, green forests they christened "the Felicianas." Twentieth-century "explorers" can get a close up view of the natural beauty that amazed the Spaniards on bicycle tours arranged by the **Feliciana Bicycle Company,** or on trails in the Audubon and Port Hudson State Commemorative Areas and in Mississippi's **Clark Creek Natural Area** (just outside the boundary of West Feliciana Parish). For an unusual, bird's-eye view of the area, take a hot-air balloon ride with licensed pilot **Phil Branstuder.**

To see the Felicianas the way the Spaniards first saw them, ride the **St. Francisville-New Roads Ferry** across the Mississippi River. If time allows, drive into New Roads to see the attractions listed in "A Gift from the Mississippi River."

Area Code: (504)

Getting There:

St. Francisville is just west of U.S. 61, 25 miles north of Baton Rouge and 58 miles south of Natchez.

Where and When:

Afton Villa Gardens, 9247 U.S. 61, St. Francisville, LA 70775. For information: Mr. and Mrs. Morrell F. Trimble, 7020 Green St., New Orleans, LA 70118. 861-7365. Open Mar. 1-June 30 and Oct. 1-Nov. 30. 9 A.M.-4:30 P.M. Admission.

Audubon State Commemorative Area, P.O. Box 546, St. Francisville, LA 70775. 635-3739. Daily: Apr.-Sept., 7 A.M.-10 P.M.; Oct.-Mar., 8 A.M.-7 P.M.

Beechwood Gifts, 11763 Ferdinand St. (P.O. Box 1670), St. Francisville, LA 70775. 635-4223 or 635-6303. Mon.-Sat., 10 A.M.-5 P.M.; Sun., 1-5 P.M.

Belle Lane, 11939 Ferdinand St., St. Francisville, LA 70775. 635-0036. Mon.-Sat., 10 A.M.-5:30 P.M.; Sun., 1-5:30 P.M.

Blum's, 11739 Ferdinand St., St. Francisville, LA 70775. 635-3367. Mon.-Sat., 10 A.M.-5 P.M.; Sun., 1-5 P.M.

Butler Greenwood Plantation, 8345 U.S. 61 (HC 69, Box 438), St. Francisville, LA 70775. 635-6312. Tours: Mon.-Sat., 9 A.M.-5 P.M.; Sun., 1-5 P.M. Admission.

C and D Collectibles Then and Now, 217 Ferdinand St., St. Francisville, LA 70775. 635-3606. Daily, 10 A.M.-6 P.M.

Catalpa Plantation, U.S. 61 (Box 131), St. Francisville, LA 70775. 635-3372. Daily, 9:30 A.M.-5 P.M. Closed December and January, except by appointment. Admission.

Clark Creek Natural Area (both directions and information available at West Feliciana Historical Society Museum), 635-6330.

The Cottage Plantation, 10528 Cottage Lane (HC 68, Box 425), St. Francisville, LA 70775. 635-3674. Daily, 9 A.M.-5 P.M. Admission.

Emporium, 11931 Ferdinand St. (P.O. Box 2247), St. Francisville, LA 70775. 635-0113. Mon.-Sat., 9 A.M.-5 P.M.; Sun., 1-5 P.M.

Feliciana Bicycle Company, 11734 Ferdinand St., St. Francisville, LA 70775. 635-0083. Open daily by reservation. Bicycle rentals or scheduled tours. Free delivery anywhere in West Feliciana Parish.

Fine Art Gallery, 11921 Ferdinand St., St. Francisville, LA 70775. 635-0252 or 1-800-375-0252. Fri. and Sat., 9 A.M.-5 P.M. and by appointment.

Grace Episcopal Church, 11621 Ferdinand St. (P.O. Box 28), St. Francisville, LA 70775. 635-4065. Daily, sunrise-sunset, except during services.

Greenwood Plantation, 6838 Highland Rd. (Route 5W, Box 1480), St. Francisville, LA 70775. 655-4475. Mar.-Nov.: Mon.-Sat., 9 A.M.-5 P.M.; Sun., 1-5 P.M. Nov.-Mar.: Mon.-Sat., 10 A.M.-4 P.M.; Sun., 1-5 P.M. Admission.

Harrington Gallery, 9907 Royal St. (P.O. Box 481), St. Francisville, LA 70775. 635-4214. Mon.-Sat., 10 A.M.-5:30 P.M.

The Myrtles, U.S. 61 North (P.O. Box 1100), St. Francisville, LA 70775. 635-6277. Tours daily, 9 A.M.-5 P.M. Ghost tours: Fri. and Sat., 9:30 P.M. Admission.

Our Lady of Mount Carmel Church, 11485 Ferdinand St. (P.O. Box 67), St. Francisville, LA 70775. 635-3630 (local) or 383-5219 (Baton Rouge). Daily, sunrise-sunset, except during services.

Phil Branstuder, Hot Air Balloon Rides, 11736 Ellen Dr., Baton Rouge, LA 70811. 775-3899.

Port Hudson State Commemorative Area, 756 West Plains-Port Hudson Rd., Zachary, LA 70791. 654-3775. Daily: Apr.-Sept., 7 A.M.-10 P.M.; Oct.-Mar., 8 A.M.-7 P.M.

The Red Horse Inn, 176 S. Commerce St., St. Francisville, LA 70775. 635-4857. Mon.-Sat., 10 A.M.-2 A.M.; Sun., 10 A.M.-midnight. Live music Sundays, 6-10 P.M. Performance schedule varies for other weekend nights.

River Bend Energy Center, U.S. 61 at GSU Road (P.O. Box 220), St. Francisville, LA 70775. 635-5004 (local) or 381-4277 (Baton Rouge). Mon.-Fri., 8 A.M.-4 P.M.

Rosedown, 12501 LA 10, St. Francisville, LA 70775. 635-3332. Daily: Mar.-Oct., 9 A.M.-5 P.M.; Nov.-Feb., 10 A.M.-4 P.M. Admission.

St. Francis Gallery, 11914 Ferdinand St. (P.O. Box 1997), St. Francisville, LA 70775. 635-4199. Mon.-Sat., 9:30 A.M.-5 P.M.; Sun., 1-5 P.M.

St. Francisville-New Roads Ferry, St. Francisville, LA 70775. Daily, 5 A.M.-midnight. Leaves St. Francisville on the hour and half-hour. Fee from St. Francisville to New Roads, free from

New Roads to St. Francisville. For more information, call St. Francisville Chamber of Commerce, 635-6717.

Shadetree, Corner of Royal and Ferdinand streets (P.O. Box 1818), St. Francisville, LA 70775. 635-6116. Mon.-Sat., 10 A.M.-5 P.M.; Sun., noon-5 P.M.

Shanty Too, 11779 Ferdinand St., St. Francisville, LA 70775. 635-4127. Daily, 9:30 A.M.-5:30 P.M.

Somethin' Special, 11911 Ferdinand St., St. Francisville, LA 70775. 635-9804. Daily, 10 A.M.-4 P.M.

Star Hill Antiques and Gifts, 5175 U.S. 61 (HC 69, Box 940), St. Francisville, LA 70775. 635-6215. Daily, 9 A.M.-5:30 P.M.

West Feliciana Historical Society Museum, 11757 Ferdinand St. (P.O. Box 338), St. Francisville, LA 70775. 635-6330. Mon.-Sat., 9 A.M.-4 P.M.; Sun., 1-4 P.M.

Information:

East Feliciana Parish Tourist Commission, 3406 College St. (P.O. Box 667), Jackson, LA 70748. 634-7155. Mon.-Fri., 10 A.M.-4 P.M.

West Feliciana Historical Society, 11757 Ferdinand St. (P.O. Box 338), St. Francisville, LA 70775. 635-6330. Mon.-Sat., 9 A.M.-4 P.M.; Sun., 1-4 P.M.

St. Francisville Town Hall, 11936 Ferdinand St. (P.O. Box 545), St. Francisville, LA 70775. 635-3688. Mon.-Fri., 8:30 A.M.-4:30 P.M.

Guide Services:

Murrell Butler, P.O. Box 1875, St. Francisville, LA 70775. 635-6214. Birding guide services in public natural areas or on the extensive Butler family property.

Rachel Hall, St. Francisville Tours, P.O. Box 89, St. Francisville, LA 70775. 635-6283. Assistance with transportation, lodging, individual tour packets, special amenities.

Accommodations:

3-V Tourist Court, 121 Commerce St., St. Francisville, LA 70775. 635-5209.

Asphodel Village and Inn, Louisiana 68 South (Route 2, Box 89), Jackson, LA 70748. 654-6868 or 1-800-424-6869.

Barrow House Inn, 9774 Royal St. (Drawer 400), St. Francisville, LA 70775. 635-4791. Dinner by advance reservation for overnight guests only.

The Bluffs—The Lodge at the Bluffs, Sunshine Way (P.O. Box 1220), St. Francisville, LA 70775. 634-3410.

Butler Greenwood Plantation, 8345 U.S. 61 (HC 69, Box 438), St. Francisville, LA 70775. 635-6312.

The Cottage Plantation, 10528 Cottage Lane (HC 68, Box 425), St. Francisville, LA 70775. 635-3674.

Green Springs Plantation, 7463 Tunica Trace (LA 66), St. Francisville, LA 70775. 635-4232 or 1-800-457-4978.

Hemingbough, 10591 Beach Rd. (U.S. 61), St. Francisville, LA 70775. 635-6617.

The Myrtles, U.S. 61 North (P.O. Box 1100), St. Francisville, LA 70775. 635-6277.

Propinquity, 523 Royal St. (P.O. Box 516), St. Francisville, LA 70775. 635-6540.

Rosedown, 12501 LA 10, St. Francisville, LA 70775. 635-3332.

St. Francisville Inn, 5720 N. Commerce St. (P.O. Drawer 1369), St. Francisville, LA 70775. 635-6502 or 1-800-488-6502.

St. Francis Hotel-on-the Lake, U.S. 61 and LA 10 (P.O. Box 440), St. Francisville, LA 70775. 635-3821.

Shadetree, P.O. Box 1818, St. Francisville, LA 70775. 635-6116.

For information on additional accommodations in East and West Feliciana parishes contact the appropriate parish tourist commission.

Restaurants:

Asphodel Inn, 4626 LA 68, Jackson, LA 70748. 654-6868. Breakfast: Daily, 7:30-9 A.M.; Lunch: Daily, 11:30 A.M.-3 P.M.; Dinner: Tues.-Thurs., 5:30-7:30 P.M.; Fri. and Sat., 5:30-9 P.M.

Bayou Sara Coffee & Tea Company, St. Francisville Inn, 5720 N. Commerce St., St. Francisville, LA 70775. 635-6502 or 1-800-488-6502. Tues.-Sun., 8:30 A.M.-6:30 P.M.

Beachgrove Restaurant, St. Francis Hotel-on-the-Lake, U.S. 61 and Louisiana 10, St. Francisville, LA 70775. 635-3821. Mon.-Sat., 6 A.M.-2 P.M., 5-10 P.M.; Sun., 6 A.M.-10 P.M.

The Bluffs Restaurant, Louisiana 965 at Freeland Road, St. Francisville, LA 70775. 634-5088. Lunch: Mon.-Sat., 11:30 A.M.-2 P.M. Dinner: Mon.-Thurs., 5:30-9 P.M.; Fri. and Sat., 5:30-10:00 P.M. Sunday Buffet: noon-2 P.M. Live music Fridays, 7:30-11:30 P.M.

Glory B's Diner, 11736 Ferdinand St., St. Francisville, LA 70775. 635-2187. Mon.-Thurs., 10:30 A.M.-4 P.M.; Fri. and Sat., 10:30 A.M.-8:30 P.M.

Magnolia Cafe, 5687 Commerce St., St. Francisville, LA 70775. 635-6528. Mon.-Sat., 10 A.M.-4 P.M.

Mattie's House Restaurant, The Cottage Plantation, 10528 Cottage Lane, St. Francisville, LA 70775. 635-3674. Dinner: 5:30-9 P.M. Closed January.

The Myrtles, U.S. 61 North (P.O. Box 1100), St. Francisville, LA 70775. 635-6277. Daily, 11:30 A.M.-3 P.M. Dinner by advance notice only.

Major Annual Events:

Audubon Pilgrimage, St. Francisville—Third weekend in March.

Christmas in the Country, St. Francisville—First weekend in December.

East Feliciana Pilgrimage, Clinton—Second weekend in April.

Feliciana Peach Festival, Clinton—June.

Garden Symposium, St. Francisville—Second Friday and Saturday in October.

Heritage Festival, St. Francisville—Third weekend in March.

Jackson Assembly Antique Show & Home Tour, Jackson—March.

Mon Coeur. (Photo courtesy Mary Lou Perkins)

14

A GIFT FROM THE MISSISSIPPI RIVER

A few centuries ago, the Mississippi River doubled back on itself about twenty miles upriver from Baton Rouge. Several eighteenth-century spring floods later, the unpredictable Father of Waters had deposited enough sediment to cut off this oxbow bend and create lovely False River. French settlers named the spot where the mighty river built a new bank Pointe Coupée (French for cut point).

The fertile delta soon attracted sugar and tobacco planters, and eventually, the region grew into Pointe Coupée Parish, a multicrop agricultural community that spreads westward from New Roads, the parish seat nestled on the banks of False River.

Pointe Coupée Parish has much to offer travelers who want to get off the beaten path and relax in a serene, scenic setting. Pleasing accommodations are available in New Roads in seven attractive homes that have been converted to appealing bed-and-breakfast inns.

At **Garden Gate Manor,** a 1900s Acadian-style cottage, roomy chambers named for Southern flowers are decorated with handsome English fabrics. Innkeeper Ivonne Cuendet often entertains guests with special weekend happenings such as "Hearts and Flowers Valentine Celebration," "Springfest Chamber Concerts," and "Victorian Lawn Party."

The **River Blossom Inn** is furnished with exquisite antiques. Many of these showpieces are for sale.

169

Early risers at **Sunrise on the River** enjoy gorgeous sunrises at this elegant, riverside Bed and Breakfast. Later in the day, they doze in a hammock in the inn's gazebo or drop a line into the river and wait for the fish to bite.

A beautiful view of False River, and access to a fishing pier, is also enjoyed by guests who stay at **Mon Reve,** an 1820 Creole plantation that faces the lake.

Eight cozy fireplaces and several tall, breeze-catching front windows are enjoyed by travelers who make reservations at **Jubilee!** Virginia and Ovide DeSoto decorated their restored Creole cottage near the Mississippi River with local crafts and a selection of antiques from their False River Road store, also named **Jubilee!** Many of these items are for sale.

Guests in the Samson-Claiborne House, an 1835 Creole residence, and the Hebert House, a 1902 Victorian home next door, stay in their choice of two tastefully decorated fireplace suites or four spacious rooms with private baths. Wicker furniture and potted greenery on the Hebert House's wraparound porch mesh into an intimate setting for reading or conversation. Both homes are part of **Pointe Coupée Bed & Breakfast,** owned by Al and Sidney Coffee. The enterprising couple also operates **Louisiana Backroads,** a tour company specializing in rural sight-seeing, and **The Coffee House,** a fine Creole-menu restaurant on Main Street.

Six of these charming inns are a short walk from False River. "The river," as locals call their beloved twenty-two–mile lake, is one of two trophy-bass lakes in Louisiana. Several riverside fishing camps are available as weekend rentals.

Fishermen with no boat in tow, or folks who just want to enjoy a lazy float on the water, can rent motorized bateaus from **Bonaventure's Boat Landing,** a few miles southwest of town on Louisiana 1. And a public fishing pier in Kiwanis Park appeals to shoreside anglers. Easygoing brown-baggers often picnic in this downtown park, but folks seeking more substantial fare head for **Morel's Restaurant** adjacent to the park.

Stores in downtown New Roads practice a charming mix of old and new style merchandising. **Roy's Jewelry Store, Hebert's**

Jewelers, and a few other emporiums are dressed in 1940s decor, while their neighbor—**Clyde's** gift and accessory shop—is chic and up-to-date.

On the opposite side of Main Street, Hurst and Nicki Samson wriggle their way through the collection of fine antiques that fills **Samson Galleries, Inc.,** to greet visitors with complimentary wine served on a silver tray.

More antiques may be found at **New Roads Antique Mall, Ol' Man River Antiques, Etc.,** and at **Bebes and Tiques**—a Richey Street store, ½ block off of Main Street, that also specializes in museum quality dolls. Several antique stores in the surrounding area are also noted in an antique shop brochure published by the Pointe Coupée Office of Tourism and the Greater Pointe Coupée Chamber of Commerce.

In the commercial area on Hospital Road, **Pepper's Food & Spirits** and **Chinese Inn** offer additional opportunities to sample local cuisine. They are close to **Pap & Pris Baum's** and **Grezaffi's** well-stocked boutiques where you can choose a keepsake or cookbook to bring home.

Main Street is the local designation for Louisiana 1 as it passes through New Roads. One arm of the roadway extends southwest around False River while another points northwest toward the Morganza Floodway. The floodway's gates control the level of the Mississippi River during the high water season. Floodway visitors enjoy delightful accommodations at **Pop's House,** an inviting bed-and-breakfast cottage in Morganza.

Six miles southwest of New Roads, the highway deposits you at **Pointe Coupée Parish Museum and Tourist Center,** housed in an early Creole cottage that once sheltered workers on Parlange Plantation. With the aid of a walking-tour brochure available at the museum and tourist center, stroll through New Roads' residential neighborhoods and learn more about the life-style and architecture of this agreeable community. Along the way you pass historic homes such as The LeJeune House, a stately Greek Revival-style home (private), and the 1856 Stowall House, which has the 12'-by-12' hand-hewn cypress beams used in the first Catholic Church in New Roads.

Two blocks of Pennsylvania Avenue near the east end of

Main Street are lined with neat Victorian cottages. This quaint row of well-kept bungalows is particularly charming during the Christmas season when their architecture is accented with sparkling lights.

Pointe Coupée Museum and Tourist Center's driving tours also direct you to pleasurable destinations. The most famous of these is **Parlange Plantation,** a historic estate just south of the Pointe Coupée Museum. The handsome mansion that adorns one of Louisiana's oldest plantations is also a unique, lived-in home. It reflects the giving nature and enthusiasm for life of its mistress and frequent tour guide, Mrs. Walter C. ("Miss Lucy") Parlange.

The Parlanges are descendants of the original owner, the French Marquis de Ternant. When the Marquis built his two-story, French-colonial home in 1750, he put wide galleries on both floors to provide respite from the south Louisiana sun.

The galleries were used as sleeping quarters for soldiers when the Civil War mistress of the plantation, Madame Virginie de Ternant Parlange, opened her larder to both Union and Confederate officers in order to save her home. On one occasion she even turned over the keys to the wine cellar and storerooms to Union General Nathaniel Banks.

Today, in the same antique-filled rooms where generals once planned battle strategies, children's toys and a pine cone "every season" tree await the youthful whims of the "Parlange Playmates," a group of neighborhood children who frequently play in the home.

Mon Coeur, a mansion near Parlange that offers bed and breakfast, is surrounded by gardens created by noted Louisiana horticulturist Steele Burden. Mon Coeur is a recreation of the Old Bigman Plantation that once stood on the site.

More plantations line the roadways encircling False River, but most can only be viewed from the road. Pause along the scenic False River route at Alma Sugar Plantation's store and study photos of nineteenth-century plantation life on display in the grocery's well-worn cases. A bench on the store's weathered porch entices you to sit a spell while enjoying the link of *boudin* (rice and pork sausage) and cold soft drink you can purchase inside.

Years ago, workers who lived in the quarter houses that line the gravel road in front of the grocery were given script to spend at this former company store. Drive past the row of houses to see the eighteenth-century Alma sugar mill and a red-painted dormitory that houses extra workers during the grinding season (October–December).

When it is time for supper, choose one of several good restaurants that face the highways just outside of New Roads. A scenic drive around False River is a fine prelude to a delectable seafood dinner at **Dailey's** in Ventress. South of Mon Coeur, near the intersection of Louisiana 78, the **Oxbow Restaurant** entices diners with a full menu of well-prepared dishes and an outstanding view of False River.

A line of hungry patrons often snakes out from the door of another popular eatery—**Joe's "Dreyfus Store" Restaurant** on Louisiana 77 in Livonia, about fifteen miles southwest of New Roads via Louisiana 78. The celebrated eatery, quartered in an old general merchandise store, features fresh seafood and Creole/Acadian cuisine.

Louisiana 10 replaced the traditional route that connected False River plantations and the Mississippi River. Take another pleasant drive on this "new road" that gave the parish seat its name and turn left onto Pointe Coupée Road, which borders the Mississippi River. Here, you can view Conquest (private), a Victorian home built in the early 1800s, and Jubilee!, one of New Road's congenial Bed and Breakfasts.

St. Francis Chapel is just down the road from Jubilee! An eighteenth-century wood carving of St. Francis, crafted by Tunica Indian converts, is treasured by the congregation. This small, 1895 church still uses some furnishings salvaged from a chapel built on the same site in the early 1700s. Guests are welcome to join in the gospel music Mass offered here every Sunday morning.

Just beyond the chapel, Suzanne Cannon's rough-hewn log house is surrounded by twenty herb gardens and dozens of rows of pepper plants. After a look at Suzanne's herbs and peppers, your green thumb may start to itch. If it does, this homegrown horticulturist will show you how to start your own herb garden. The flavorful peppers and herbs harvested from Suzanne's plants season her **Suzanna's** label vinegars.

If time permits, when you leave Suzanne's garden, veer right on Pointe Coupée Road from Louisiana 10 and follow the Mississippi River levee to the **New Roads-St. Francisville Ferry** landing. Ride across the river and spend a pleasant afternoon exploring St. Francisville, Louisiana's third-oldest settlement (see "A Feliciana Parish Treasure Hunt").

Area Code: (504)

Getting There:

From the north or south: Follow U.S. 61 to St. Francisville. Cross the Mississippi River on the St. Francisville-New Roads Ferry and travel Louisiana 10 into New Roads.

From the south: Take Louisiana 415 north from Interstate 10 between Baton Rouge and Lafayette. Go northwest on U.S. 190 until it intersects with Louisiana 1. Follow Louisiana 1 into New Roads.

Where and When:

Bebes and Tiques, 124 Richey St., New Roads, LA 70760. 638-8695 or 638-9985. Thurs.-Sun., 11 A.M.-4 P.M.

Bonaventure's Boat Landing, 6716 False River Rd., Oscar, LA 70762. 627-6336. Daily, sunrise-sunset.

Clyde's, 208 E. Main St., New Roads, LA 70760. Mon.-Fri., 9 A.M.-5 P.M.; Sat., 10 A.M.-2 P.M. 638-8881.

Grezaffi's Custom Framing & Gifts, River Birch Plaza, 1111 Hospital Rd., New Roads, LA 70760. 638-7527. Mon.-Sat., 9 A.M.-5 P.M.

Hebert's Jewelers, 102 E. Main St., New Roads, LA 70760. 638-9024. Mon.-Sat., 9 A.M.-5 P.M.

Jubilee! on the River, 9253 False River Rd. (LA 1) (Route 2, Box 59-A), New Roads, LA 70760. 638-3505. Tues.-Sat., 10 A.M.-5 P.M.

New Roads Antique Mall, 200 W. Main St., New Roads, LA 70760. 638-7676. Open every weekend, 10 A.M.-5 P.M.

New Roads-St. Francisville Ferry, LA 10, New Roads, LA 70760. 638-3737. Daily, 5 A.M.-midnight. Leaves New Roads landing on the quarter-hour. Fee for return trip from St. Francisville.

Ol' Man River Antiques, Etc., 9554 False River Rd. (LA 1), New Roads, LA 70760. 638-4488. Wed.-Sun., 10 A.M.-5 P.M.

Pap & Pris Baum's, 2211 Hospital Rd. (P.O. Box 428), New Roads, LA 70760. 638-6781. Mon.-Sat., 8 A.M.-5 P.M.

Parlange Plantation, 8211 False River Rd. (LA 1), New Roads, LA 70760. 638-8410. Daily, 9:30 A.M.-5 P.M. Admission.

Roy's Jewelry Store, 113 W. Main St., New Roads, LA 70760. 638-7674. Mon.-Sat., 9 A.M.-5 P.M.

St. Francis Chapel, Pointe Coupée Road, New Roads, LA 70760. 638-8165. Open by appointment.

Samson Galleries, Inc., 155 E. Main St., New Roads, LA 70760. 638-8644 or 638-8952. Mon.-Sat., 10 A.M.-4 P.M. Sun., by appointment.

Suzanna's, 9282 Pointe Coupée Rd., New Roads, LA 70760. 638-7360. Open by appointment.

Information:

Pointe Coupée Museum and Tourist Center, 8348 False River Rd. (LA 1), New Roads, LA 70760. 638-9858. Thurs.-Sun., 11 A.M.-4 P.M.

For information or brochures, call or stop by the Pointe Coupée Office of Tourism and the Greater Pointe Coupée Chamber of Commerce in the Courthouse Annex, 116 E. Main St. (P.O. Box 555), New Roads, LA 70760. 638-3500. Mon.-Fri., 8 A.M.-4 P.M.

Guide Services:

Louisiana Backroads, 401 Richey St., New Roads, LA 70760. 638-6254 or 1-800-832-7412.

Accommodations:

False River Rentals, 336 E. Main St., New Roads, LA 70760. 638-4468.

Glen Grezaffi, 1111 Hospital Rd., New Roads, LA 70760. 638-7527. Camp rentals.

Ken Major Realty, 113 W. Main St., New Roads, LA 70760. 638-3310 or 627-4547. Camp rentals.

Morel's Motel, 221 W. Main St., New Roads, LA 70760. 638-7177.

Point Breeze Motel, 2111 False River Dr. (LA 1), New Roads, LA 70760. 638-3414.

Raymond's Resort Rentals, 303 E. Main St., New Roads, LA 70760. 638-7550 or 638-3625.

Bed and Breakfasts:

Garden Gate Manor, 204 Poydras St., New Roads, LA 70760. 638-3890 or 1-800-487-3890.

Jubilee!, 11704 Pointe Coupée Rd., New Roads, LA 70760. 638-8333.

Mon Coeur, 7739 False River Rd., Oscar, LA 70762. 638-9892 or 638-4488.

Mon Reve, 9825 False River Rd. (LA 1), New Roads, LA 70760. 638-7848 or 1-800-324-2738.

Pointe Coupée Bed & Breakfast, 401 Richey St., New Roads, LA 70760. 638-6254 or 1-800-832-7412.

Pop's House, 13378 Bayou Fordoche Rd., Morganza, LA 70759. 694-2470 or 694-3435.

River Blossom Inn, 300 N. Carolina St., New Roads, LA 70760. 638-8650 or 1-800-368-8240.

Sunrise on the River, 1825 False River Dr. (LA 1), New Roads, LA 70760. 638-3642 or 1-800-644-3642.

Restaurants:

Chinese Inn, 300½ Hospital Rd., New Roads, LA 70760. 638-7511. Sun.-Thurs., 11 A.M.-9 P.M.; Fri and Sat., 11 A.M.-10 P.M.

The Coffee House, 124 W. Main St., New Roads, LA 70760. 638-7859. Lunch: Mon.-Fri., 11 A.M.-2 P.M. Dinner: Wed. and Thurs., 5-8 P.M.; Fri., 5-10 P.M. Weekends: Sat., noon-10 P.M.; Sun., noon-3 P.M.

Dailey's Seafood, Inc., 8204 Island Rd. (LA 413), Ventress, LA 70783. 638-9222. Mon., Tues., and Thurs., 5-9 P.M.; Fri. and Sat., 5-10 P.M.; Sun., noon-8 P.M.

Joe's "Dreyfus Store" Restaurant, Louisiana 77, Livonia, LA 70755. 637-2625. Lunch: Tues.-Sun., 11 A.M.-2 P.M. Dinner: Tues.-Thurs., 5-9 P.M.; Fri. and Sat., open until 9:30 P.M.

Morel's Restaurant, 210 Morrison Pkwy., New Roads, LA 70760. 638-4057. Sun.-Thurs., 9 A.M.-9:30 P.M.; Fri. and Sat., 9 A.M.-11 P.M.

Oxbow Restaurant, Louisiana 1, Oscar, LA 70762. 627-5285. Lunch: Tues.-Fri., 11:30 A.M.-1:30 P.M. Dinner: Tues.-Sat., 5-9:30 P.M.; Sun., 11:30 A.M.-8:30 P.M.

Pepper's Food & Spirits, 455 Hospital Rd., New Roads, LA 70760. 638-7505. Lunch: Mon.-Sun., 11 A.M.-2 P.M.; Dinner: Mon.-Sat., 5-9 P.M.

Major Annual Events:

Annual Antique Show and Sale, New Roads—Last full weekend in April.

Annual Blessing of the Boats, New Roads—Sunday of Memorial Day weekend.

Brown Bag Concerts, New Roads—April and October.

Children's Christmas Parade, Fordoche—December.

Christmas Tree Lighting Ceremony, New Roads—December.

Farmers Market and Crafts Bazaar, New Roads—Saturday in late June and Saturday in mid-October.

Fall Festival and Bazaar, New Roads—First full weekend in October.

Holiday Memories from Pointe Coupée, New Roads—Weekend before Thanksgiving.

July 4th Boat Parade, Jarrau, New Roads.

Le Krewe du Noel's Christmas Parade, Morganza—December.

Les Bon Vieux Temps Sur Le Chenal, Jarreau—Second-to-last full weekend in September.

Mardi Gras, Batchelor and New Roads—Fat Tuesday.

Mardi Gras, Livonia—Sunday before Fat Tuesday.

Mardi Gras, Maringouin—Saturday before Fat Tuesday.

Pennsylvania Avenue Candlelight Walking Tour, New Roads—December.

"Rockin' on the River," New Roads—Sunday in late June.

St. Stephen's Family Day Fair, Innis—Mid-October.

15

GREAT LAKES!
GREAT BOLLS OF COTTON!
GREAT BALLS OF FIRE!

It's a bit of an adventure to drive on sections of Louisiana 3196. The paved highway tops one of the few Louisiana levees where prolonged driving is allowed. It meanders northeast from Vidalia, an agricultural center on the west bank of the Mississippi River linked physically by bridge, and historically by fate, to Natchez, Mississippi. As you motor along you can look out over Lake Concordia and Old River, an oxbow lake cast off by the Mississippi River.

A 4¼-mile ride on this atypical highway is part of the rather unique route to **Lisburn Hall,** a Greek Revival antebellum home as elegant as any of her Natchez neighbors. To complete the jaunt, the mansion's bed-and-breakfast guests follow a lane that slopes away from the levee, crosses a cotton field, and passes through a border of trees.

As the black-topped lane curves toward Lisburn Hall, first-time visitors often pause to take in the breathtaking view before them. Their eyes sweep across a grove of sturdy trees fringed with mossy beards, and follow a broad, green lawn up to the three-story home's columned porches. A drive through this serene setting leads to a brick patio and another mesmerizing view. Some of Lisburn Hall's forty acres of luxuriant greenery extend from a screened veranda in the rear of the house, encircle a lovely garden, and slope down to the banks of Lake Concordia. A pier extends from the

Lisburn Hall. (Photo by Mary Fonseca)

The gazebo and pier at Lisburn Hall. (Photo by Mary Fonseca)

shore to an enticing, over-the-water gazebo where weekenders can fish, enjoy a variety of water sports, or watch glorious sunsets over the lake's placid waters.

Although Lisburn Hall looks as if it weathered the elements for more than a century on the banks of Lake Concordia, the magnificent home was built in 1852 near Waterproof, Louisiana. It was moved into town—minus its brick-paved floor—at a later date. Then, in 1974, Jim Brown, a well-known Louisiana politician, purchased the 122-year-old plantation home and moved it to its present, parklike setting. He restored the brick floor and porches and re-installed the original slate roof. Carol Becnel, the present owner, renovated the interior and decorated it with a tasteful blend of antiques and reproductions.

Quite often, guests at Lisburn Hall are so charmed by its hospitable amenities and peaceful vistas that they spend the entire weekend roaming the grounds or chatting in comfortable rockers on the front porch. But sometimes, after enjoying Carol's scrumptious breakfast, and a second cup of complimentary coffee at the **Louisiana Welcome Center** on U.S. 84 in Vidalia, guests set off to explore the surrounding countryside. Maps and brochures distributed at the Welcome Center help them find their way around Vidalia.

The town was incorporated in 1870 and expanded on land once farmed by wealthy planters who built exquisite mansions in Natchez. After the Civil War, the little settlement that hugged the banks of the Mississippi River blossomed into a thriving port. Then its prosperity was trounced by a series of disasters, including a destructive fire, voracious boll weevils, and several devastating floods. But Vidalia triumphed over all because, in 1940, the entire town was moved back about a mile from the river and ringed with protective levees.

Some structures from the original town are still in use today. Vidalia's nineteenth-century town hall found new life as the Masonic lodge that stands on the corner of Oak and Texas streets near the Concordia Parish Courthouse. Two law offices, across Oak Street from the courthouse, are also old town buildings. The one at #10 North Oak Street was once Vidalia's post office. To see them, turn north off of Carter Street (the local name for the sections of U.S. 65 and U.S. 84 that converge as they pass through Vidalia) on Oak Street, alongside the court-house, and drive one block to Texas Street.

Several churches and homes from the old town are now part of a quiet neighborhood in back of Vidalia City Hall on the corner of Spruce and Carter streets. A driving tour pinpointing their locations is available at the Louisiana Welcome Center.

The oldest house in Vidalia, built around 1857 as a wedding gift for an early settler, is situated west of Carter Street on Pine Street. It was moved there from its second location on Texas Street, where it served as a rectory for Our Lady of Lourdes Catholic Church. In 1994, Jim and Dot Sanders renovated the historic home into an inviting bed-and-breakfast named **Serendipity.**

The Sanders make their guests feel right at home. Dot also welcomes visitors who want to tour Serendipity, if they call for an appointment. She delights in telling guests about Seren-dipity's ghost, believed to be a Catholic priest who died on the former rectory's front porch. He used to bang doors and make other noises, especially during a storm. But, lately, he makes himself known as an elusive presence in the house.

You can see more of old Vidalia by viewing historic photo-graphs on display in **City Hall.** They offer marked contrast to the scale model of a project, intended to shape Vidalia's future, that is also exhibited there. It shows the hotel, shops, and restaurant, plus facilities such as an open-air amphitheater planned for the broad levee that surrounds the very spot where Vidalia began. The development is being coordinated by Sidney A. Murray, Jr., retired mayor of Vidalia. Murray, a vision-ary leader, was the guiding force behind the Sidney A. Murray, Jr., Hydroelectric Station, a unique enterprise that continues to bring worldwide recognition to Vidalia. It is the largest pre-fabricated power plant in the world. At the present time, visi-tors can only get a look at the hydroelectric station from the levee, but a visitor center is planned for the future. Its displays will tell the amazing story of how the power plant was floated upriver from New Orleans and placed into the U.S. Corps of Engineers' Old River Control Complex. A forty-mile drive, south of Vidalia on Louisiana 15, is the route to the unique facility the Vidalia town council named in honor of the intrepid "dreamer" who conceived it.

After your sight-seeing, choose one of three appetizing alternatives offered in the old-town, civic center neighborhood. Chefs at **The Sandbar, Paul & Randee's,** and **West Bank Eatery** prepare flavorful Louisiana seafood entrees and tender steaks with their own special, creative touch. You may also enjoy the tangy barbecue dinners at **T.G. Ribs,** on the west side of U.S. 84, between Vidalia and Ferriday.

Other pleasant excursions outside Vidalia lead to engaging, wayside sights. For instance, on the way to Ferriday, about eight miles north of Vidalia, a sign on the right (about a mile past the Louisiana Welcome Center) points to a seasonal farmers' market set up on Tuesdays, Thursdays, and Saturdays. Arts and crafts are also offered here. To the far right, behind the marketplace, you can see Tacony Plantation.

This historic plantation home, now in a state of disrepair, was a second residence of planter A. V. Davis, who owned Dunleith, a still magnificent Natchez mansion. He stayed at his Louisiana plantation when visiting his overseer to discuss the progress of his crops. During these sojourns, Davis became aware of the innate intelligence of John R. Lynch, a youngster born into slavery at Tacony. Davis shifted this young slave's duties to Dunlieth and taught him to read. Lynch, whose only other formal education was four months of night school sponsored by the Freedman's Bureau, became the first African-American to hold public office in Mississippi. He was appointed justice of the peace for Natchez at twenty-one, elected to the Mississippi House of Representatives, and chosen to fill the esteemed position of speaker of the Mississippi House by the time he was twenty-four. He was barely twenty-five when he became, at that time, the youngest man ever elected to the U.S. Congress.

Tacony is now the site of Vidalia's annual Jim Bowie Festival. Bowie, a defender of the Alamo, used his deadly Bowie knife in a duel he fought on a Mississippi River sandbar at the foot of the Mississippi River Bridge.

From Tacony, continue into Ferriday past the point where

U.S. 84 curves westward from U.S. 65. A delicious lunch can be enjoyed at **Brocato's Restaurant,** a local landmark on the western side of U.S. 65. The restaurant, which specializes in down-home Southern cooking, is directly across from one of two museums that entertain visitors with out-of-the ordinary displays. The **Ferriday Museum,** on U.S. 65, showcases five native sons and one daughter who became national or international celebrities. With the help of audiovisual aids, you can become better acquainted with journalist Howard K. Smith; television evangelist Jimmy Swaggart; and the acclaimed interior designer Ann Boyar Warner, who married Hollywood czar Jack L. Warner. Recordings by the other honorees, trombonist Pee Wee Whitaker, country music performer and songwriter Mickey Gilley, and rock-and-roll star Jerry Lee Lewis, add to the appeal of this intimate, interactive museum.

You will feel like a close friend of Lewis, and his cousins Mickey Gilley and Jimmy Swaggart, after you tour Ferriday's other museum, **The Lewis Family Living Museum.** Jerry Lee Lewis's sister, Frankie Gene Lewis Terral, converted the "Ferriday Fireball's" boyhood home into a fan's delight. Here, you can see hundreds of Lewis family photographs, plus nostalgic items collected by Frankie Gene. These include Lewis's baby shoes, the piano he played as a boy, and sermons he wrote during his career as a preacher. Fifty of Jimmy Swaggart's suits, plus some of his records, are also displayed here, in the same unpretentious house where he was born. Frankie Gene brings all these mementos to life with stories about Lewis and his well-known kinsmen. The Lewis Family Living Museum is accessed through the family's Quick Stop store on U.S. 84 and Eighth Street.

When you leave the Lewis museum, continue west on U.S. 84 to explore more of the countryside. From mid-September through mid-November the two-lane highway is rimmed by snow-white cotton fields that thrive in the area's rich, Mississippi Delta soil. You may see giant combines harvesting the fluffy bolls and depositing them in modules alongside the road. Most of the collected cotton is brought to **Tanner Cotton Gin,** a state-of-the-art processing plant that comes into view on

Old Place Restaurant in Aimwell, Louisiana. (Photo courtesy Old Place Restaurant)

your left as you pass near Frogmore, a tiny village seven miles west of Ferriday. Visitors who stop at the gin office are given a complimentary auto tour of the gin. From the comfort of a car, you can watch cotton modules being sucked into a huge dryer and follow the process of pressing out the seeds, cleaning off the lint, and baling the end product.

Buddy and Lynette Tanner, the hospitable owners of Tanner Gin, also arrange a tour of one of their catfish farms for visitors with a deep-seated interest in agriculture. Frogmore Plantation (private), an 1830s home the Tanner family renovated, is about a quarter-mile west of the gin on U.S. 84.

On Saturday nights, many locals follow U.S. 84 past Frogmore, turn north on Louisiana 124 for three miles, and head northwest on Louisiana 26. Their destination is **Old Place Restaurant,** an Aimwell, Louisiana, eatery just off Louisiana 26. Old Place's scrumptious, home-cooked food and country atmosphere reward diners who make the approximately 60-minute drive from Vidalia. The restaurant spreads out over the first floor of a long white house, trimmed with an equally long porch. Glynn McGuffee's grandparents built the comfortable-looking home in 1892 on land homesteaded by Benjamin Franklin McGuffee after the Civil War. Glynn greets guests in the seating area while his wife, Ida, and fellow cook, Russell Posey, whip up house specialties such as catfish, prepared blackened or "creek bank fried," and tasty chicken breasts, served hot off the grill. After a satisfying dinner, everyone crosses the yard to the McGuffee barn to listen to old-time country and blue grass tunes skillfully played by the Old Place band. The toe-tapping music starts at 6:30 P.M. and ends around midnight when die-hard fans finally head home.

Another delightful daytrip from Vidalia includes visits to three prosperous enterprises offering locally made products, plus a couple of hours of rural sight-seeing. Follow the northeast bend of U.S. 65 from Ferriday approximately 12 miles to **Midway Plantation Gourmet Foods,** the first stop on this expedition. This wayside manufacturing and sales facility was established to handle the burgeoning, home-based business Nan and Jim Huff started in Midway House, their 1834 plantation home on the banks of the Mississippi River. The delicious Louisiana jams and jellies processed at the roadside store are also shipped to hundreds of mail-order customers. They are made from handpicked fruits tended by the Huffs. Midway Plantation's most popular items, hot pepper jelly and hot pepper pecans, top an expanding product line that includes popcorn rice harvested from the owners' fields, delectable jelly cakes, and a superb assortment of gourmet coffees.

A selection of the more than 2,000 varieties of pecans grown in Louisiana is used in delicious candies, ice-cream sauces, and pecan packages concocted at **Plantation Pecan & Gift Company,** another thriving mail-order and walk-in business next door to the Midway Plantation store. At times, you can watch pecan-flavored products march down Plantation Pecan's assembly line. You can also bring your own backyard pecan harvest and have it cracked in the store's automatic pecan cracker.

Plantation Pecan owners, Harrison and Carol Lee Miller, also offer a wide variety of local agricultural products to drive-by customers. In the summer, expect to find juicy seedless watermelons, cantaloupes, and peaches, plus other fresh fruits and vegetables. The Miller's winter selection includes cabbage,

The Burn. (Photo by Mary Fonseca)

broccoli, and cauliflower. The tempting produce is complemented by Plantation Pecan's home-smoked meats, locally ground cornmeal, and honey gathered from neighborhood hives.

If browsing through all the goodies in these two stores awakens your appetite, step over to **Anna's Restaurant,** on the other side of the Midway Plantation store, and taste her delectable Chinese cooking. Well-prepared seafood plates, salads, po' boys and burgers round out the extensive menu Anna offers.

Hunters and fishermen are most interested in items sold at **Strong Built's** factory outlet store. But anyone who admires good-looking, well-constructed outdoor clothing and equipment will enjoy a stop at this outlet that is just a short hop up the road. Visitors are welcome to turn down Louisiana 568 alongside the store and take a brief tour of the company's manufacturing plant. Here, you can see Strong Built's sturdy deer stands and stitched camouflage cloth items being assembled.

Across Louisiana 568 from the factory, a gravel road cuts through cotton fields leading to The Burn. The name given to this 1850s plantation home comes from Old English words used to describe a watercourse or creek. The house is not open for tours, but visitors are allowed to circle the drive and take pictures.

After viewing The Burn, continue another 10 miles north-east on U.S. 65. Turn right onto Louisiana 128 and drive into St. Joseph, a quaint old steamboat town that has been the seat of Tensas Parish since it was created in 1843. Some of the historic landmarks in the Tensas area decorate a "Chains of the Past" wall hanging in St. Joseph's **Plantation Museum** on Plank Road, the local name for Louisiana 128. The quilt, made to commemorate the sesquicentennial of Tensas Parish in 1993, is one of many intriguing artifacts in the museum. One exhibit contains the powder horn used on one of Teddy Roosevelt's bear hunts in the Tensas swamp. Another features a final issue of *The Vicksburg Daily Citizen,* printed on wallpaper because the Civil War prevented the newspaper from obtaining its usual stock. It announces the surrender of the city to Union troops on the 4th of July, 1863.

Appetizing lunches, plus coffee and snacks, are available at **Emily's House Restaurant** across the street from the museum. This homestyle cafe has been a St. Joseph gathering place since 1947.

Walking-tour brochures, noting some of the 90 buildings of architectural significance in St. Joseph's Historic District, are available at the Plantation Museum and the Louisiana Welcome Center in Vidalia. With one in hand you can easily explore the charming neighborhoods laid out around St. Joseph's New England-style village green. The square is in front of the Tensas Parish Courthouse, a Beaux Art-style building erected in 1905. The greenspace is used by residents for fairs, picnics, and other events throughout the year.

If the thought of a picnic lunch sounds enticing, bring one along on your jaunt and enjoy it at **Lake Bruin State Park.** The park's 53 acres of picnic and camping sites border a 3,000-acre lake about five miles northeast of St. Joseph via Louisiana 604. If you pack a fishing pole, you can cast your line from one of two large piers that jut out into the lake amid a wondrous grove of old cypress trees. Or, you may prefer to angle for one of Lake Bruin's largemouth bass from rental boats available at the park.

To make your ride back to Vidalia more interesting, turn off U.S. 65, about 13 miles south of St. Joseph, and follow Louisiana 568 into Waterproof, a historic community that is the center of Tensas Parish's farm-based economy. Several plantation manors, such as The Burn, are scattered in the countryside around Waterproof. Some are open during the Tensas Garden Club's biannual Christmas tour of homes.

Legend has it that Waterproof was named when the captain of a passing steamboat spied Abner Smalley standing on a small strip of dry land during one of the Mississippi River's frequent floods. "Well, Abner," called the captain, "I see you are waterproof." But Smalley and the original town—a way station for pioneers heading west—proved to be "drip dry" rather than waterproof. The town was moved four times to escape calamity from eroding banks of the Mississippi River. Waterproof's original site is now across the river in the state of Mississippi.

From Waterproof, continue on Louisiana 568 into Ferriday. This scenic route follows the banks of Lake St. John and Lake Concordia. These two lakes, along with Lake Bruin and Cocodrie Lake, make Concordia and Tensas parishes attractive destinations for hunters, fishermen, and vacationers who enjoy water sports. Lakeshore accommodations are available in rustic motels, such as **Cypress Landing** on Lake Bruin. Kitchenette suites, cable television, and furniture that will stand up to children's roughhousing make **Lakeview Lodge,** a new, budget motel on the southeast bank of Lake Concordia, particularly appealing to families looking for waterside vacation accommodations.

Ardent hunters and fishermen enjoy daytrips and weekend packages offered by **Glasscock Lodge,** a hunting and fishing resort on scenic, primitive Glasscock Island. Only archers may stalk big game on Glasscock's more than 15,000 acres of prime Mississippi River bottomland about 15 miles south of Vidalia, but other hunters can take aim at waterfowl, turkeys, squirrels, and other small game. There are more than 40 lakes and ponds on Glasscock's preserve, affording fishermen and duck hunters excellent opportunities for an exceptional catch.

Area Code: (318)

Getting There:

Vidalia is accessed from the east via U.S. 84 and the Mississippi River Bridge connecting Natchez and Vidalia.

From the northeast, U.S. 61 and the Natchez Trace connect with U.S. 84 east of Natchez. The southern leg of U.S. 61 connects with U.S. 84 in Natchez.

West of the Mississippi River, take U.S. 65 from the northeast through Ferriday and U.S. 84 from the west through Ferriday.

From the south, Louisiana 15 connects with Louisiana 131 into Vidalia.

Where and When:

City Hall, 311 Carter St., Vidalia, LA 71373. Mon.-Fri., 8:30 A.M.-4:30 P.M. 336-5206.

Ferriday Museum, Old Concordia Bank Building, Chamber of Commerce Office, U.S. 65, Ferriday, LA 71334. 757-3550. Mon.-Fri., 9 A.M.-4 P.M. Admission.

Lake Bruin State Park, Louisiana 604 (Route 1, Box 183), St. Joseph, LA 71366. 766-3530.

The Lewis Family Living Museum, U.S. 84 and 8th Street, Ferriday, LA 71334. Tues.-Sun., 11 A.M.-9 P.M. 757-4422. Donations appreciated.

Midway Plantation Gourmet Foods, U.S. 65 (HC 62, Box 77), Waterproof, LA 71375. 1-800-336-5267. Mon.-Fri., 9 A.M.-5 P.M.

Plantation Museum, Plank Road, St. Joseph, LA 71366. 766-3222. Tues., Wed., and Fri., 9 A.M.-2 P.M.; Thurs., 9 A.M.-noon; Sat., 10 A.M.-noon. Closed Sundays and Mondays. Admission.

Plantation Pecan & Gift Company, U.S. 65 (HC-62, Box 139), Waterproof, LA 71375. Information: 749-5421 or 749-3770. Orders: 1-800-477-3226. Mon.-Sat., 9 A.M.-5 P.M.

Serendipity Bed and Breakfast, 110 Pine St., Vidalia, LA 71373. 336-9478. Tours by appointment only. Admission.

Strong Built, U.S. 65 (P.O. Box 157), Waterproof, LA 71375. Mon.-Fri., 7 A.M.-5:30 P.M.

Tanner Cotton Gin, U.S. 84, Frogmore, LA 71335. Tours: Mon.-Fri., 9 A.M.-4 P.M. during harvest (mid-Sept.–mid-Nov.).

Information:

Ferriday Museum, Old Concordia Bank Building, Chamber of Commerce Office, U.S. 65, Ferriday, LA 71334. 757-3550. Mon.-Fri., 9 A.M.-4 P.M.

Louisiana Welcome Center, 1401 Carter St. (U.S. 84), Vidalia, LA 71373. 336-7008. Daily, 9 A.M.-5 P.M. Closed major holidays.

Guide Services:

Contact the Louisiana Welcome Station in Vidalia or inquire at the lodging you have reserved.

Accommodations:

Cypress Landing, Route 1, Box 201-F, St. Joseph, LA 71366. 467-5032.

Glasscock Lodge, P.O. Box 1199, Vidalia, LA 71373. 336-8944.

Lakeview Lodge, 1424 Fisherman Dr., Ferriday, LA 71334. 757-CAMP.

Bed and Breakfasts:

Lisburn Hall, P.O. Box 1152, Vidalia, LA 71371. 1-800-972-0127.

Serendipity Bed and Breakfast, 110 Pine St., Vidalia, LA 71373. 336-9478.

Hotel, motel, and bed-and-breakfast accommodations are also available in Natchez.

Restaurants:

Anna's Restaurant, U.S. 65, Waterproof, LA 71375. 749-3187. Mon.-Sat., 10 A.M.-9 P.M.

Brocato's Restaurant, 908 N.E. Wallace Blvd. (U.S. 65),

Ferriday, LA 71334. 757-9985. Mon.-Sat., 5 A.M.-10 P.M.; Sun., 6 A.M.-2 P.M.

Emily's House Restaurant, Plank Road (P.O. Box 12), St. Joseph, LA 71366. 766-4669. Daily, 5:30 A.M.-2 P.M.

Old Place Restaurant, Aimwell, LA 71401. 992-2347. Fri. and Sat., 5-10 P.M. Live country and blue grass music on Saturdays from 6:30 P.M.-midnight.

Paul & Randee's, 103 Carter St., Vidalia, LA 71373. 336-7357. Lunch: Sun.-Fri., 11 A.M.-2 P.M.; Dinner: Daily, 5-10 P.M. Closed for lunch on Saturdays. Second location: Louisiana 568, Lake St. John, Ferriday, LA 71334. 757-2990. Dinner: Tues.-Sun., 5-10 P.M.

The Sandbar, 106 Carter St., Vidalia, LA 71373. 336-5173. Daily, 11 A.M.-10 P.M.

T.G. Ribs, Vidalia-Ferriday Highway (U.S. 84), Ferriday, LA 757-7200. Daily, 11 A.M.-9:30 P.M.

West Bank Eatery, 700 Levee Rd. North (P.O. Box 118), Vidalia, LA 71373. 336-9669. Mon.-Sat., 11 A.M.-10 P.M.

Major Annual Events:

Christian Festival, Vidalia—June.

Christmas Parade and Lights, Ferriday—Parade: First Saturday in December. Lights: Month of December.

Christmas Parade, Vidalia—First Sunday in December.

Jim Bowie Festival, Vidalia—Fall.

16

CITY STREETS, COUNTRY ROADS

Remember the children's story about a city mouse who envied his country cousin's peaceful environment, while the country cousin coveted the amenities his urban relative enjoyed?

Well, it is a sure bet neither of these green-eyed rodents lived in central Louisiana. In Alexandria, the heartland's center, city folk tap a wellspring of pastoral pleasures just minutes away, and rural homesteaders easily access shops and museums in the city.

Spend a weekend in this "crossroads" section of the Pelican State and enjoy the best of both life-styles. Inviting restaurants and appealing attractions are only a short drive from well-appointed rooms in the city or comfortable accommodations in the country. And finding your way is easier with brochures collected at the **Alexandria/Pineville Area Convention & Visitors Bureau** on MacArthur Drive (U.S. 71, U.S. 167) in Alexandria.

"Alex," as the natives call it, was originally a trading post started by Alexander Fulton and William Miller. The partners acquired land from Indians who could not pay their bills and soon had enough acreage to start a town. Because the settlement was at the farthest navigable point of the Red River, it grew into a busy trade center surrounded by prosperous plantations.

Alexandria's good fortune was dealt a severe blow, however, when most of the city, and many neighboring plantations, were burned during the Civil War. **Kent House,** a classic, raised Creole cottage built in 1796, is one of the few survivors. The mansion's courageous owner, Robert Hynson, refused to leave his home, thus preventing Union troops retreating from the battle of Mansfield from setting it afire.

But Hynson could not save his stock or the plantation's outbuildings from the ravaging army. He wrote Confederate Colonel James Wise: ". . . I have lost . . . my corn cribs, grist mill, cotton house . . ., overseer's house, blacksmith shop, hospital and a part of the Negro cabins."

Many of Kent House's bygone structures are now replicated with antebellum dependencies once used on other plantations. Located on Bayou Rapides Road, just west of MacArthur Drive, Kent House and its structures serve as the setting for many living history events throughout the year.

Tyrone Plantation, the stately home of General George Mason Graham, founder of Louisiana State University, is a few miles west of Kent House. William Tecumseh Sherman, the first superintendent of the school—originally located in Pineville, across the Red River from Alexandria—was often a guest of the Grahams. Sherman's attachment to Tyrone is thought to be the reason it was spared when he commanded Union troops during the Civil War. The mansion was enlarged and embellished in the early 1900s and now serves as a bed-and-breakfast inn. It is open for tours by appointment.

Tyrone is one of many buildings improved or constructed during a rebuilding boom in turn-of-the-century Alexandria. Several of these architectural gems are still serving the community. To see them, follow Jackson Street northeast from MacArthur Drive to the downtown section of the city. On the way, notice patches of Alexandria's original brick streets laid in the late 1800s.

In the early years of the twentieth century eleven rail lines extended their tracks to Alexandria, bringing so many new families that the congregation of St. Francis Xavier Catholic Church pitched in to construct a larger house of worship. When the new

The magnificent Hotel Bentley. (Photo courtesy Hotel Bentley)

church was designated **St. Francis Xavier Cathedral** in 1910, ecstatic parishioners graced it with priceless treasures, including Carrara marble statues and handcarved wooden altars. During the following decades, 54 stained-glass windows and other inspirational works of art were installed in this Gothic-style cathedral, located on Fourth Street to the left of Jackson Street. It may be toured by appointment.

Tradition has it that Alexandria owes another of its downtown landmarks, **Hotel Bentley,** to a desk clerk who refused to give self-made lumber magnate, J. A. Bentley, a room at the Rapides Hotel because he was unsuitably dressed. Some locals say Bentley constructed his magnificent neoclassical hotel in 1908 to get the best of the mediocre hostelry that turned him away. Others believe he was just dissatisfied with the service and wanted access to a first-class hotel.

The Bentley is often called the "Waldorf on the Red." Colossal marble columns mark the entrance to the grand lobby where a stained-glass dome reflects colored lights onto the marble floor. A graceful staircase rises to the mezzanine. Elevators with German nickel doors carry guests to their rooms.

At the beginning of World War II, when central Louisiana was the nucleus of a nine-state military training area, the Bentley was crowded with hundreds of servicemen. Among them were Maj. Gen. George Patton, Lt. Col. Omar Bradley, and Col. Dwight Eisenhower. The trio planned military strategies used in the historic conflict while staying at the hotel. Now, artifacts testifying to central Louisiana's role in American military history are on display at the Bentley.

John Wayne, Bob Hope, and Mickey Rooney are just a few of the many notable celebrities who have stayed at the Bentley. If you add your name to the historic hotel's prominent registry, take time to absorb details of the resplendent architecture, brushed to a new lustre during a 1980s renovation.

If you opt for other accommodations, at least treat yourself to dinner in the **Bentley Room,** or lift your glass to the seven jolly tipplers toasting you from the confines of whimsical stained-glass windows in the hotel's **Mirror Room Lounge.**

When you are ready to complete your tour of downtown Alexandria, walk to the **Alexandria Museum of Art** housed in a Rapides Bank building built along the riverfront in 1908. Stimulating regional and national shows often supplement this young museum's growing collection of north Louisiana folk art.

At Alexandria's **River Oaks Square Center,** a few blocks downriver from the art museum, contemporary artists use sculpture, needlework, and other mediums to fashion original creations. View these "works in progress" at the center's busy studios, quartered in the nearly 100-year-old James Wade Bolton House and the adjacent Yaeger building.

The 1890 boyhood home of Arna Bontemps, a well-known author and poet of the Harlem Renaissance, was moved to a site just behind River Oaks Square Center. The modest, wood-frame dwelling contains reminders of Bontemps' career and is being developed into a multipurpose complex, the **Arna Bontemps African-American Museum and Cultural Arts Center.** It will house, among other things, both cultural and culinary arts and the Louisiana Black Hall of Fame.

Since Arna Bontemps was a prominent writer, his descendants know a lot about their ancestry. Other families seeking links to the past may find them at the **Alexandria Genealogical and Historical Library and Museum,** a formidable building on the corner of Washington and Fifth streets. It once housed the first public library built in Alexandria after the Civil War.

To get a better idea of how Alexandria looked decades ago, stop at **Newcomb Camera & Art Supply Center,** on the corner of Murray and Fourth streets. The fifty-year-old business acts as an informal, photographic repository of Alexandria's past. From spring through fall, Newcomb's windows are hung with new additions to a collection of yesteryear portraits and snapshots donated by customers. You can thumb through more pictures inside the store.

After strolling down Newcomb's memory lane, have lunch at **Critics Choice** a few doors away. The restaurant offers delicious Philadelphia steak sandwiches topped with fixings of your choice.

When you are refreshed, cross the Red River at Jackson Street. The bridge connects Jackson Street with Main Street in Pineville. On Main Street you can see centuries-old cemeteries with fenced-in family plots. They surround picturesque Mount Olivet Episcopal Chapel, used as a Civil War hospital by Union forces. Across Main Street from the chapel, a sign directs visitors to Rapides Cemetery, the last resting place of French and Spanish commandants in charge of outposts built on the site in the early 1700s. The burial ground is also a national military cemetery where thousands of men and women who gave their lives in the service of their country are interred.

After exploring Alexandria's past, enjoy some of the recreational and shopping opportunities the city offers. "Do" the **Alexandria Zoo** in Bringhurst Park, take in a performance at the **Crossroads Coliseum,** or scan shops in central Louisiana's largest shopping center, **Alexandria Mall.**

Attractive specialty stores and enticing eateries border Alexandria's Jackson Street Extension, southwest of MacArthur Drive. Among them is **Janohn's** fine restaurant, the choice of many residents who are celebrating special occasions.

You will find unique gifts and Louisiana products at **The Main Dish & More** in the Delchamps Plaza shopping center on Jackson Extension, and at **Pour Vous** on Southampton Drive (the second Jackson Extension intersection past MacArthur Drive).

Snap up colorful Central American imports and hard to find Bill Lewis fishing lures—made in Alexandria—at **Lewis & Reid** on Windsor Place, two blocks south of Southampton Drive. The shop specializes in giftware priced under $15.

When you are ready to explore the countryside, start by checking out the interesting destinations along U.S. 71 South. This highway is possibly the most traveled road leading out of Alexandria. This is not because it is the traditional route to Baton Rouge, but because it passes right in front of **Lea's Lunchroom** in Lecompte. Once folks taste this fifty-year-old restaurant's country cooking, highlighted by fabulous hams and home-baked pies, they find excuses to pass by Lea's again and again.

Follow the crowd to this landmark restaurant, twelve miles south of Alexandria, and enjoy some lip-smacking Southern specialties. If you can decide which kind of pie you want to take home (you will probably end up with at least two), Lea's friendly staff will box it up for you.

Soak up some of Lecompte's small-town atmosphere (and have another opportunity to eat at Lea's) by arranging an overnight stay at **Hardy House.** The recently restored 1880s home is an elegant, but cozy, bed-and-breakfast inn.

Hardy House guests stroll the banks of scenic Bayou Boeuf, pedal complimentary bicycles to Lecompte's old-time hardware and furniture stores, and visit three turn-of-the-century buildings—**Holy Comforter Church, Doctor Whitehead's Office,** and **Old Lecompte High School.** The school closed several years ago, but the 1920s building is being transformed into a history museum, library, and arts-and-crafts center by the town's preservation-conscious citizens.

Cyclists who enjoy longer excursions pedal two miles south on Louisiana 456 to the **"Old Mill Pond"** near the ruins of the Meeker Sugar Refinery. Here you can rent fishing equipment and angle for channel catfish in a heavily stocked pond. Refreshments and edible Louisiana souvenirs are available in the millpond's office.

Hardy House is also a good base from which to canvass some of the 200 wholesale nurseries lining U.S. 165 south from Woodworth to Glenmora, Louisiana 112 from Forest Hill to Lecompte, and U.S. 71 south to Cheneyville. Several Lecompte businesses and the Alexandria/Pineville Area Convention & Visitors Bureau distribute an excellent map pinpointing nurseries who welcome drop-ins.

Untamed by a nurseryman's skill, the Dogwood and Wild Azalea lend their name and beauty to two popular Kisatchie National Forest trails north and south of Alexandria. Hikers enter the 31-mile-long **Wild Azalea Trail** at a U.S. 165 rest area seven miles below the city and at several other points.

The **Dogwood Trail,** accessed from U.S. 165 about thirty miles north of Alexandria, guides motorists along pine-sheltered highways dappled with pastel dogwood blossoms. The best time to follow the circular auto route, and walk its half-mile hiking path, is during March and April.

If you call ahead, you can coordinate a ride on the Dogwood Trail with a garden tour and lunch at **Ridgaway Herb Gardens and Tea Room.** Jean Owen, an herbalist-cook regularly featured on an Alexandria television station, prepares herb-seasoned meals and teas that are a relaxing change from city dining.

From the dining room of **Tunk's Cypress Inn,** you can view one of three forested recreation areas that attract outdoorsmen to central Louisiana. Tunk's overlooks beautiful Lake Kincaid, of **Kincaid Recreation Area,** about seventeen miles west of Alexandria, via Louisiana 28 West. The restful view adds to the enjoyment of diners who relish Tunk's seafoods, well-seasoned gumbos, and Creole-style dishes.

Cotile Recreation Area, in Boyce, fourteen miles north of Alexandria, does not have a restaurant, but the park does offer 2,000 acres of forest shade and freshwater lakes. **Indian Creek Lake Recreation Area,** in the Alexander State Forest off of U.S. 165 south of Alexandria, is the most popular of the three. Campers wait in long lines to get a spot in the ninety-acre campground beside Indian Creek Lake.

Travelers who prefer well-appointed bed-and-breakfast lodging head for Cheneyville—eight miles south of Lecompte—to settle into delightful cottages on the grounds of two antebellum homes. Guests at **Loyd Hall** stay in a recently redecorated, Cajun-style cabin that overlooks the plantation's front lawn or in three new bed-and-breakfast suites in the plantation's former kitchen and commissary. During their stay, guests are treated to a tour of the 1810 manor house. They listen attentively as guides recount a few spine-tingling ghost stories along with a brief history of the three-story mansion.

Bed and breakfast is also offered at **Walnut Grove Plantation House's** Sunniside Cottage, an adaptation of an early 1900s bungalow. The Tudor-style manor house, owned by the McGowan family since 1935, is presently a showcase and salesroom for the clan's fine antiques.

More relics of the past are squeezed into antique shops in Cheneyville and Bunkie, eight miles south of Cheneyville. The friendly vendors proffer a wide range of merchandise including furniture, toys, collectibles, and Americana. After you browse through the antiques, enjoy a homestyle lunch at **Shelly's Market** in Cheneyville or sample the delicious fare offered at **Merchant Planter's Bank Cafe** and **Captain's Galley** in Bunkie.

If time allows, include a complimentary tour of **Producers**

Mutual Cotton Gin in Cheneyville in your excursion. Guests are welcome year-round; but between September and November, when the cotton crop is harvested, you can watch truckloads of fluffy blossoms being sucked up into the mill where the fiber is separated from the seeds.

Many guests at Lloyd Hall and Walnut Grove also visit **Grand Avoyelles Casino** in Marksville. This beautiful new gaming facility on the Tunica-Biloxi reservation is about a half-hour's drive from Cheneyville.

Travelers with a military bent may enjoy another daytrip, or overnight excursion, to the towns of Leesville and DeRidder near Fort Polk, an Army installation about sixty miles west of Alexandria, which played a significant role in preparing American troops for World War II.

A video on view at the **Vernon Parish Tourist & Recreation Commission's** office, at the intersection of U.S. 171 and Louisiana 8 in Leesville, acquaints visitors with the "Louisiana Maneuvers" staged at Camp Polk, as the base was known when it opened in 1940. The tourism office also supplies maps of the area and details on other sites to visit.

If you plan to spend the night, consider bed-and-breakfast accommodations at **Huckleberry Inn,** a charming 1915 home a few miles east of the tourism office. The inn's peaceful setting, attractive rooms, and wraparound porch make it the most appealing lodging in this area.

The **Museum of West Louisiana,** installed in a restored 1916 railroad depot presents an overview of west-central Louisiana history that is a good prelude to your visit to Fort Polk. Its absorbing exhibits include a vintage homestead, archeological artifacts, turn-of-the-century apparel and furnishings, a scale model of the sawmill town Nona Mills, plus mementos of Camp Polk, samples of a natural opalescent quartzite—known as "Louisiana Opal"—found in the Leesville area, and crafts and jellies made by local residents.

A left turn at the Fort Polk sign on U.S. 171 south of Leesville brings you to the base's information center where staff members are on hand Monday through Friday to assist you. A Leesville-Fort Polk map available at the Vernon Parish

The Cypress Lake recreational area in the Kisatchie National Forest in Leesville. (Photo by Mary Fonseca)

Tourist Commission office notes various facilities on the base including the **Fort Polk Military Museum,** where you can browse through several intriguing exhibits pertaining to the "Louisiana Maneuvers," the history of Fort Polk, and exploits of units stationed at the base. A 7th Armored Division flag, signed by members of the unit during World War II, and a stuffed alligator taken from Panamanian president Manuel Noriega's office in 1989 during Operation Just Cause are two of the unusual items exhibited here. In a field next to the museum, military equipment ranging from helicopters to tanks to a Hermes missile is on display.

Two small restaurants in the Fort Polk area offer tasty ethnic dishes that are reasonably priced. German specialties highlight the menu at **Bull's Eye Cafe** on Entrance Road, and delicately flavored entrees and delicious *baklava* are served at **Nick the Greek** on Louisiana 10.

Picnic buffs often head for Little Cypress Park in the Kisatchie National Forest, where they can also enjoy a hiking trail that encircles a small lake. Ask tourist assistants in Leesville and DeRidder about other sylvan spots you can enjoy and the many opportunities for swimming, canoeing, fishing, camping, and hunting that prompt so many military retirees to settle in this area.

DeRidder is just eighteen miles south of the U.S. 171 entrance to Fort Polk. The town's connections to the armed services date to an army air base located there during World War II. During the war, off-duty soldiers from both military installations spent many pleasurable evenings at the **DeRidder USO,** the first facility built for and donated to the United Services Organization, which provided social gatherings and entertainment for the troops. Many of the original furnishings remain in the spacious building, one of the largest of five different sizes of Type A buildings designated for USOs. Visitors are welcome to roam rooms where servicemen and young ladies of the town danced under the watchful eyes of chaperones or enjoyed a chat over coffee and doughnuts. When this historic USO was no longer needed by the armed forces, it became DeRidder's War Memorial Civic Center, dedicated to the 47 Beauregard Parish servicemen who died in World War II and to Generals Bradley, Mark Clark, Eisenhower, Marshall, and Patton who planned strategies and readied troops in Louisiana.

The **Beauregard Parish Tourist Commission,** adjacent to West Park at the intersection of U.S. 171 and High School Drive in DeRidder, distributes maps showing the location of the first USO and other points of interest in the parish. Among these sights is the **Beauregard Parish Museum,** housed, like its counterpart in Leesville, in a depot that once served the town. It contains souvenirs of the days when Beauregard Parish was a lumber and sawmill center.

The museum is on the edge of DeRidder's downtown historic district, a 2½-block area featuring distinctive architecture from the early 1900s. The town's three-story, domed courthouse, built in 1914, is a dignified Beaux Arts structure. Next door to it, connected by an underground tunnel, is the old **Beauregard Parish Jail,** a unique Gothic-style building locally known as "the hanging jail" in reference to a double execution that took place there in 1928. Tours are offered if

Beauregard Parish Jail in DeRidder. (Photo by Mary Fonseca)

The Burk Log Cabin in Merryville. (Photo by Mary Fonseca)

you call for an appointment, or you can muster up your courage and visit the scary spook house set up in the jail every Halloween.

Venetia's Southern Elegance, a congenial restaurant next to the courthouse, offers delectable Southern fare, cooked with a light touch and attractively served. For a tantalizing takeout lunch or take-home goodies, buy some of the German breads, pastries, and sausages sold at **Reichley's Bakery & Delicatessen** located in downtown DeRidder.

If time allows, drive to Merryville, a village seventeen miles west of DeRidder that was originally the home of eighteenth-century Coushatta Indians. The town's **Country at Heart,** an old-time drugstore with several roomfuls of antiques and collectibles, is a fun place to visit. And **Burk Log Cabin and Museum,** which may be toured by appointment, contains antiquated household items and other artifacts from Merryville's early days. No Civil War battles were fought here, but the museum sponsors an annual Civil War re-enactment called "The Battle of Bear Head Creek" to give residents and visitors a better understanding of the daily life of a Civil War soldier.

Area Code: (318)

Getting There:

Interstate 49, U.S. 165, and U.S. 167 are the major routes leading to Alexandria. Commercial airlines fly into the city. Louisiana 28 West connects Alexandria and Leesville.

Where and When:

Alexandria Genealogical and Historical Library and Museum, 503 Washington St., Alexandria, LA 71301. 487-8556. Tues.-Sat., 10 A.M.-4 P.M. Free.

Alexandria Mall, 3437 Masonic Dr., Alexandria, LA 71301. 448-0227. Mon.-Sat., 10 A.M.-9 P.M.; Sun., 12:30-5:30 P.M.

Alexandria Museum of Art, 933 Main St. (P.O. Box 1028),

Alexandria, LA 71309-1028. 443-3458. Tues.-Fri., 10 A.M.-5 P.M.; Sat., 10 A.M.-4 P.M. Admission.

Alexandria Zoo, Bringhurst Park (P.O. Box 71), Alexandria, LA 71309-0071. 473-1385. Summer: Daily, 9 A.M.-6 P.M. Winter: Daily, 9 A.M.-5 P.M. Admission.

Arna Bontemps African-American Museum and Cultural Arts Center, 1327 Third St. (P.O. Box 533), Alexandria, LA 71301. Tues.-Fri., 10 A.M.-4 P.M.; Sat., 10 A.M.-2 P.M. Call 449-5000 to confirm visit. Donations accepted.

Beauregard Parish Jail, East First Street, DeRidder, LA. Tours arranged by Beauregard Parish Tourist Commission.

Beauregard Parish Museum, South Washington Avenue, DeRidder, LA 70634. 463-8148. Tues.-Fri., 1-4 P.M. Admission.

Burk Log Cabin and Museum, Merryville, LA 70653. Call 463-2979 or 825-8083 for more information. Admission.

Cotile Recreation Area. Contact: Mr. Bill Molan, 75 Cotile Lake Rd., Boyce, LA 71409. 793-8995. Open daily, 24 hours.

Country at Heart, 615 Main St., Merryville, LA 70653. 825-6100. Mon.-Fri., 8:30 A.M.-5 P.M.; Sat., 8:30 A.M.-4 P.M.

Crossroads Coliseum, 5600 Coliseum Blvd., Alexandria, LA 71301. 442-9581. Contact the Alexandria/Pineville Area Convention & Visitors Bureau for a schedule of events.

DeRidder USO, War Memorial Civic Center, 200 W. Seventh St., DeRidder, LA 70634. 463-7212. Mon.-Fri., 8 A.M.-4 P.M. and occasional Saturdays.

Doctor Whitehead's Office, Wall Street, Lecompte, LA 71346. Call 776-9497 for tour appointment. Donations appreciated.

Dogwood Trail. Map available at Alexandria/Pineville Area Convention & Visitors Bureau.

Fort Polk, Public Affairs Office, HQ-JRTC & Fort Polk, Bldg. 411, Radio Road, Fort Polk, LA 71459-5060. Visitor information: 531-2911. Information center open Mon.-Fri., 6:30 A.M.-5 P.M.

Fort Polk Military Museum, Fort Polk, LA 71459-5060. 531-7905. Wed.-Fri., 10 A.M.-4 P.M.; Sat. and Sun., 9 A.M.-6 P.M.

Grand Avoyelles Casino, Tunica-Biloxi Reservation, Marksville, LA 71351. 253-1946 or 1-800-946-1946. Open daily, 24 hours.

Holy Comforter Church, Wall Street, Lecompte, LA 71346. Call 776-9497 for tour appointment. Donations appreciated.

Indian Creek Lake Recreation Area, State Forest Complex Manager, Louisiana Office of Forestry, Alexander State Forest, P.O. Box 298, Woodworth, LA 71485. 455-4511. Gate open daily, 8 A.M.-8 P.M.

Kent House, 3601 Bayou Rapides Rd., Alexandria, LA 71301. 487-5998. Mon.-Sat., 9 A.M.-5 P.M. Admission.

Kincaid Recreation Area, State Forest Complex Manager, Louisiana Office of Forestry, Alexander State Forest, P.O. Box 298, Woodworth, LA 71485. 455-4511 or 443-3903. Mon.-Fri., 6 A.M.-9 P.M.; Sat., 7 A.M.-8 P.M.

Lewis & Reid, 1309 Windsor Place, Alexandria, LA 71303. 487-1129. Mon.-Sat., 10 A.M.-5 P.M.

Loyd Hall, 292 Loyd Bridge Rd., Cheneyville, LA 71325. 776-5641. Tues.-Sat., 10 A.M.-4 P.M.; Sun., 1-4 P.M. Admission.

The Main Dish & More, Delchamps Plaza, 1327 Peterman Dr., Alexandria, LA 71301. 448-1830. Mon.-Fri., 10 A.M.-5:30 P.M.; Sat., 10 A.M.-4 P.M.

Museum of West Louisiana, 803 S. Third St., Leesville, LA 71446. 239-0927. Tues.-Sun., 1-5 P.M.

Newcomb Camera & Art Supply Center, 401 Murray St., Alexandria, LA 71301. 448-0544. Mon.-Fri., 8 A.M.-5 P.M.; Sat., 8 A.M.–noon.

Old Lecompte High School, 1610 Charter St., Lecompte, LA 71437. Mon.-Fri., noon-5 P.M.; Sat., 9 A.M.-1 P.M.

"Old Mill Pond," 50 Sugar Mill Rd. (U.S. 71 off I-49), Lecompte, LA 71346. 776-5355. Tues.-Sun., 8 A.M.-6 P.M. Closed during winter months. Admission.

Pour Vous, 1303 Southampton Dr., Alexandria, LA 71303. 445-3200. Mon.-Sat., 10 A.M.-6 P.M.; Sun., 10 A.M.-5 P.M. Closed Sundays during the summmer.

Producers Mutual Cotton Gin, U.S. 71 South (P.O. Box 278), Cheneyville, LA 71325. 279-2145. Tours: Mon.-Wed. and Fri., 8 A.M.-3 P.M. Additional hours during ginning season (Sept.-Nov.): Sat. and Sun., 8 A.M.-3 P.M. Free.

River Oaks Square Center, 1330 Main St., Alexandria, LA 71301. 473-2670. Tues.-Sat., 10 A.M.-4 P.M. Free.

St. Francis Xavier Cathedral, 626 Fourth St., Alexandria, LA 71301. 445-1451. Tours by appointment. Donations appreciated.

Tyrone Plantation, 576 Bayou Rapides Rd., Alexandria, LA 71303. 442-8528. Open by appointment. Admission.

Walnut Grove Plantation House, Route 1, Box 41, Cheneyville, LA 71325. 279-2203. Tues.-Sun., 1-4 P.M. Admission.

Wild Azalea Trail. Map available at Alexandria/Pineville Area Convention & Visitors Bureau.

Information:

Alexandria/Pineville Area Convention & Visitors Bureau, 1470 MacArthur Dr. (P.O. Box 8110), Alexandria, LA 71306. 443-7049 or 1-800-742-7049. Mon.-Sat., 8 A.M.-5 P.M.

Beauregard Parish Tourist Commission, West Park, 624 High School Dr. (P.O. Box 1174), DeRidder, LA 70634. 463-5533 or 464-5534. Mon.-Fri., 9 A.M.-5 P.M.

Vernon Parish Tourist & Recreation Commission, Louisiana 8 (P.O. Box 1228), Leesville, LA 71496-1228. Mon.-Fri., 8 A.M.-noon; 1-4:30 P.M.

Guide Services:

Contact the Alexandria/Pineville Area Convention & Visitors Bureau.

Accommodations:

Chain and independent motels in Alexandria, Leesville, and DeRidder.

Hotel Bentley, 200 DeSoto St., Alexandria, LA 71301. 448-9600 or 1-800-356-6835.

Bed and Breakfasts:

Hardy House, 1414 Weems St., Lecompte, LA 71346. 776-5178.

Huckleberry Inn, 702 Alexandria Hwy., Leesvillle, LA 71446. 238-4000.

Loyd Hall, 292 Loyd Bridge Rd., Cheneyville, LA 71325. 776-5641.

Tyrone Plantation, 576 Bayou Rapides Rd., Alexandria, LA 71303. 442-8528.

Walnut Grove Plantation House, Route 1, Box 41, Cheneyville, LA 71325. 279-2203.

For a complete listing of accommodations in the Alexandria area, contact the Alexandria/Pineville Convention & Visitors Bureau. For a complete list of accommodations in Leesville and DeRidder contact the appropriate tourist information center.

Restaurants:

Bentley Room, Hotel Bentley, 200 DeSoto St., Alexandria, LA 71301. 448-9600. Daily, 6:30 A.M.-10 P.M.

Bull's Eye Cafe, 1171 Entrance Rd., Leesville, LA 71446. 537-2233. Mon.-Sat., 8 A.M.-9 P.M.

Captain's Galley, 412 N.W. Main St., Bunkie, LA 71322. 346-2403. Lunch: Mon.-Fri., 11:30 A.M.-1:30 P.M.; Dinner: Tues.-Sat., 5-8:30 P.M. Seafood buffet on Tuesdays. Closed Sundays except for Mother's Day.

Critics Choice, 415 Murray St., Alexandria, LA 71301. 442-3333. Mon.-Fri., 8 A.M.-10 P.M.; Sat., 8 A.M.-midnight. Second location: 5208 Rue Verdun, Alexandria, LA 71303. 445-1680. Mon.-Sat., 10:30 A.M.-3 P.M.

Janohn's, 5521 Jackson St., Alexandria, LA 71301. 487-6066. Lunch: Mon.-Fri., 10 A.M.-2 P.M. Dinner: Mon.-Sat., 6-10 P.M.

Lea's Lunchroom, U.S. 71 (P.O. Box 309), Lecompte, LA 71346. 776-5178. Mon., 7 A.M.-6 P.M.; Tues.-Sun., 7 A.M.-7 P.M.

Loyd Hall, 292 Loyd Bridge Rd., Cheneyville, LA 71325. 776-5641. Tues.-Sat., 10 A.M.-4 P.M.; Sun., 1-4 P.M. Lunch or dinner by special arrangement.

Merchant Planter's Bank Cafe, 122 S.W. Main St., Bunkie, LA 71346. 346-9458. Tues.-Sun., 9 A.M.-3 P.M. Open evenings, call for hours.

Mirror Room Lounge, Hotel Bentley, 200 DeSoto St., Alexandria, LA 71301. 448-9600. Mon.-Sat., 3 P.M.-2 A.M.

Nick the Greek, 1620 Pitkin Rd. (Louisiana 10), Leesville, LA 71446. 537-0952. Tues.-Sat., 11 A.M.-8 P.M.

Reichley's Bakery & Delicatessen, 219 Washington St., DeRidder, LA 70634. 463-6856. Mon.-Fri., 2:30 A.M.-6 P.M.; Sat., 2:30 A.M.-4 P.M.

Ridgaway Herb Gardens and Tea Room, Louisiana 366 (Route 1, Box 810), Fishville, LA 71467. 765-9294. Call for lunch, dinner, or tea reservations. Mon.-Sat., 9 A.M.-5 P.M.

Shelley's Market, 807 Front St. (U.S. 71) (P.O. Box 333), Cheneyville, LA 71325. 279-2110. Store: Mon.-Sat., 6 A.M.-7 P.M. Breakfast, 7-9 A.M. Lunch, 11 A.M.-1 P.M.

Tunk's Cypress Inn, 9507 LA 28 West, Boyce, LA 71409-9683. 487-4014. Dinner: Mon.-Sat., 5-10 P.M.

Venetia's Southern Elegance, 112 S. Stewart St., DeRidder, LA 70634. 462-3870. Mon.-Fri., 11 A.M.-2 P.M.

Walnut Grove Plantation House, Cheneyville, LA 71325. 279-2203. Lunch or dinner by special arrangement.

For a complete listing of restaurants in the Alexandria area, contact the Alexandria/Pineville Convention & Visitors Bureau. For listings in Leesville and DeRidder, contact the appropriate tourist commission.

Major Annual Events:

Battle of Bearhead Creek Civil War Enactment, Merryville—Last weekend in February.

Beauregard Parish Fair, DeRidder—First Tuesday through Saturday in October.

Beauregard's Country Tour of Christmas Lights—First Saturday in December through January 1.

Boundary Waters Adventure, Leesville—Memorial Day weekend.

Catahoula Lake Festival, Pineville—Last weekend in October.

Cenlabration, Alexandria—Labor Day weekend.

Christmas at the Crossroads, Alexandria—Twelve nights following the first Saturday in December.

Christmas Parade and Festival in West Park, DeRidder—December.

DeRidder Days in the Park—May.

DeRidder Mardi Gras Parade—Fat Tuesday.

Gem and Mineral Show, Leesville—First weekend in November.

Hornbeck Trade Days, Hornbeck—Second weekend in September.

Living Last Supper, DeRidder—Every even year, Thursday before Easter.

Longville Lake Fall Camp-N-Jam, Longville—First weekend in November.

Louisiana Nursery Festival, Forest Hill—Third weekend in March.

Old South Weekend, Alexandria—First weekend in May.

Vernon Arts Festival, Leesville—First weekend in May.

West Louisiana Forestry Festival and Rodeo, Leesville—First weekend in October.

17

WHERE STEEL MAGNOLIAS GROW

Folks in Natchitoches are proud to be living in the oldest town in Louisiana. In soft, Southern inflections, they tell you that their community (pronounced Nak-a-tush by most locals) is also the oldest settlement in the Louisiana Purchase Territory.

Many residents fought to preserve the iron-laced shops, Victorian homes, historic churches, and Creole cottages in Natchitoches's 33-block historic district. Several years ago, determined members of the Association for the Preservation of Historic Natchitoches even blocked a construction crew from tearing up brick-surfaced Front Street in order to update it with a concrete surface. That event has been spun into a local legend, one that typifies the combination of grace and grit that is the theme of *Steel Magnolias,* Robert Harling's stage and screenplay set in his hometown.

Visitors want to see homes and locales used in the film, so many of these landmarks are included in tram and boat tours offered by **City Belle Trolleys and Cane River Cruises.** Both of these delightful excursions depart from the banks of Cane River Lake near Roque House, a restored 1803 dwelling thought to be one of the most outstanding examples of early Creole architecture in the Cane River area.

The boat and tram outings take you past many places that are worth a second look. One is the **Museum of Historic**

The two distinctive buildings of Front Street's Ducournau Square. (Photo by Mary Fonseca)

Wrought-iron spiral staircase on Ducournau Square. (Photo by Mary Fonseca)

Natchitoches dedicated to the town's intriguing history. **Kaffie-Frederick, Inc.,** general store, a Front Street emporium down the street from the museum, is closely entwined with the community's past. It has been serving customers at the same location since 1863. Nostalgia buffs find many items in the store that set them to musing on days gone-by.

At **Just Friends,** a popular eatery a few steps from Kaffie-Frederick, Inc., friends converse over steaming bowls of homemade soup or cool, refreshing salads while they enjoy a soothing view of Cane River Lake.

The restaurant is quartered next door to Ducournau Square, the name given to two restored, wrought-iron-railed buildings on Front Street. **Georgia's Gift Shop** and **Carriage House Market,** a purveyor of fine antiques, are also nestled around the square's arched carriageways.

As you walk through Natchitoches's historic district, notice the street signs. Roadways named for Frenchmen who figured in the town's history are preceded by *rue; street* follows those honoring American historical figures.

The Craft Connection on Rue St. Denis is one of many engaging shops you can include in your stroll. Talented locals sell handmade items in this colorful bazaar's thirty-five booths. And works fashioned by artisans of the past fill several antique malls in the historic district. The malls, and other inviting shops, are listed on a flyer available at the **Natichitoches Parish Tourist Commission** office on Front Street.

You are tempted to sample several fine foods in Natchitoches, but the spicy meat pie that originated in the town is the most tantalizing. The tradition started in the early 1920s when Miss DeDe Breazeale shared her recipe for a pastry-wrapped, seasoned ground-beef filling with her neighbors.

A few generations ago vendors wandered the streets of Natchitoches selling these "hot-a-meat-pies." Now, many restaurants have them on the menu. You can taste one at **Lasyone's Meat Pie Kitchen,** a longtime favorite on Second Street, or at **The Landing** and **Front Street Baking Company,** newcomers to the historic district.

Several new restaurants recently opened in Natchitoches'

historic district. **Merci Beaucoup** offers soups, salads, sandwiches, and tea. Other fine eateries feature Italian and Chinese fare on their menus. Natchitoches Parish Tourist Commission representatives can direct you to these appetizing restaurants and to others outside of the district.

Several celebrities have strolled the quaint streets of Natchitoches. John Wayne and Shirley MacLaine are among the many stars who came to the Cane River area to make films such as *The Horse Soldiers, Steel Magnolias,* and *The Man in the Moon.* These actors, and notables from all walks of life who "contributed significantly to the city and the area through their work, talents and avocations," are remembered in Natchitoches's St. Denis Walk of Honor. Stop to read the tributes as you saunter past the intersection of Second Street and Rue St. Denis.

Some of the notables who come to Natchitoches take part in the city's Christmas Festival of Lights. Every year, more than 150,000 spectators watch the event's jovial parade and the spectacular fireworks display that follows it. When the last glittering starburst fades into Cane River Lake, the grand marshal throws a switch that illuminates more than seventy lighted wirework sculptures that line the banks of the waterway.

The nearly 70-year-old Christmas festival is Natchitoches's most popular celebration, but several other festivals, activities at Northwestern State University, and an annual pilgrimage keep the town humming year-round.

Natchitoches's historic area is especially beautiful in the spring when blossoming azaleas and dogwoods are reflected in Cane River's placid waters. The bewitching river/lake is the heart and soul of the centuries-old community although, by the standards of history, it is a neophyte.

In the early years of its settlement, Natchitoches was a busy trading post on the Red River. French explorer Louis Juchereau de St. Denis founded the village in 1714 and named it for an Indian tribe that befriended him. In the 1830s, when a logjam at the Red River's headwaters was dispersed, the capricious stream chose a different course and ended Natchitoches's reign as a center of commerce.

Cradled by high bluffs carved by its fickle parent, Cane

View of Cane River Lake. (Photo by Mary Fonseca)

Monument commemorating
Louis Juchereau de St. Denis.
(Photo by Mary Fonseca)

Chapel at Fort St. Jean Baptiste.
(Photo by Mary Fonseca)

River—twentieth-century stepchild of the Red—grew into a navigable rivulet. It was dammed to form Cane River Lake.

A replica of **Fort St. Jean Baptiste** stands near the very spot along the riverbank where St. Denis built his outpost. Roam through the primitive buildings, built with pioneer tools, and imagine the fledgling settlement as it was in St. Denis's time. The little village often buzzed with activity as pirogues, steamboats, and other watercraft unloaded goods from New Orleans, took on cargo, and returned downriver.

When you leave the fort, take a drive through the nearby campus of **Northwestern State University.** Pause to look in the windows of the one-room, 1806 schoolhouse near the entrance to the university, and, if you are interested in Louisiana Indian culture, ask directions to the Williamson Museum on the second floor of Keyser Hall. Sports fans may also want to see the Louisiana Sportswriters Hall of Fame in the university's Prather Coliseum.

The beguiling countryside around Natchitoches is known as Cane River Country. A map available at the Natchitoches Parish Tourist Commission office guides visitors to several graceful plantations that border the meandering stream. Four of the homes are open for tours.

Visitors approach **Beau Fort Plantation** under a canopy of live oaks. The Creole cottage, built on the site of a 1760s fort, was constructed by slaves who joined hand-hewn cypress timbers with *bousillage* (a mixture of mud and moss) to form the mansion's walls.

Melrose Plantation, a National Historic Landmark, was originally owned by Marie Thérèse Coincoin, a freed slave. The estate passed through several families before John Hampton and Cammie Garrett Henry bought it in 1898. The couple restored Marie Thérèse's home, the African House built by her family, the 1833 plantation mansion, and several outbuildings and gardens.

The Henrys invited authors and artists from many faraway places to sojourn at Melrose while they worked. But one of the most famous people associated with the plantation is a field hand and cook who lived at Melrose for many decades. The late

Clementine Hunter's primitive paintings, depicting life in the Cane River countryside, are prized by collectors and museums all over America. Her colorful murals adorn the walls of the African House.

Magnolia Plantation, a 2½-story home that has been in the same family since 1753, was one of two holdings west of the Mississippi River singled out as a National Bicentennial Farm. The mansion is still the center of a working plantation where cotton, soybeans, and cattle are raised.

The Cane River Country plantation tour ends in Cloutierville, a French settlement that is almost as old as Natchitoches. Here, in the **Kate Chopin Home/Bayou Folk Museum,** well-informed hostesses explain the local artifacts housed in a Louisiana raised cottage dating to 1813. Articles ranging from "sharp shooter" coffins (tapered at head and foot) to a *prie-Dieu* (prayer stool) that displays the Stations of the Cross on rollers are on display.

The Kate Chopin Home was recently declared a National Historic Landmark. Bayou Folk Museum is named after a collection of short stories by the nineteenth-century novelist. Chopin joined the community in 1880 with her husband and six children. A special exhibit recalls Kate's years as mistress of the residence that houses the museum and the scandal caused by the publication of her unconventional novel, *The Awakening*.

After the plantation tour, return to Natchitoches on Louisiana 1. About six miles north of Cloutierville, a group of craftspeople from the Isle Brevelle community sell handmade quilts, bonnets, and dolls at **LaCour Doll House.** Their trademark doll, Ma-Man, was the official Bicentennial Doll of Louisiana.

When you arrive in Natchitoches, reserve a table at **Mariner's Seafood and Steakhouse,** where you can dine while watching the sun set over Lake Sibley.

The lake is one of many bodies of water around Natchitoches that afford active outdoorsmen numerous opportunities for fishing and watersports. Peaceful trails in nearby **Kisatchie National Forest** beckon those who love to hike in the woodlands. The scenery is spectacular in the spring and fall along the seventeen-mile Longleaf Trail Scenic Byway, an auto trail connecting Louisiana 117 with Louisiana 119 south of Natchitoches and west of Interstate 49.

Area Code: (318)

Getting There:

Natchitoches is accessed via Louisiana 6 off of Interstate 49 between Alexandria and Shreveport or by Louisiana 1 and Louisiana 84.

Where and When:

Beau Fort Plantation, Louisiana 119, Natchez, LA (P.O. Box 2300, Natchitoches, LA 71457). 352-5340 or 352-9580. Daily, 1-4 P.M. Admission.

Carriage House Market, 720 Front St., Natchitoches, LA 71457. 352-4578. Daily, 9 A.M.-5 P.M.

City Belle Trolleys and Cane River Cruises, 612 Williams Ave., Natchitoches, LA 71457. 352-7093. Mar.-Dec.: Daily, weather permitting. Admission.

The Craft Connection, 113 Rue St. Denis, Natchitoches, LA 71457. 357-0064. Mon.-Sat., 10 A.M.-5:30 P.M.

Fort St. Jean Baptiste, Mill Street, Natchitoches, LA 71457. Daily, 9 A.M.-5 P.M. Admission. Call Natchitoches Parish Tourist Commission for information.

Georgia's Gift Shop, 626 Front St., Natchitoches, LA 71457. 352-5833. Mon.-Sat., 10 A.M.-5 P.M.

Kaffie-Frederick, Inc., 758 Front St., Natchitoches, LA 71457. 352-2525. Mon.-Fri., 7 A.M.-5 P.M.; Sat., 7 A.M.-4:30 P.M.

Kate Chopin Home/Bayou Folk Museum, Louisiana 495, Cloutierville, LA 71416. 379-2233. Mon.-Sat., 9 A.M.-5 P.M.; Sun., 1-5 P.M. Admission.

Kisatchie National Forest, Ranger District (P.O. Box 2128), Natchitoches, LA 71457. 352-2568. Headquarters on LA 6 West, a ¼ mile from I-49. Mon.-Fri., 8 A.M.-4:30 P.M. Maps and information available on Kisatchie National Forest Hiking Trails and Longleaf Trail Scenic Byway.

LaCour Doll House, Louisiana 1 South, Natchitoches, LA 71457. 379-2393. By appointment or by chance.

Magnolia Plantation, Louisiana 119, Derry, LA (HC 66, Box 1040, Natchez, LA 71456—mailing address). 379-2221. Daily, 1-4 P.M. or by appointment. Admission.

Melrose Plantation, Junction of Louisiana 493 and Louisiana 119 (General Delivery, Melrose, LA 71452). 379-0055 or 379-2431. Daily, noon-4 P.M. Admission.

Museum of Historic Natchitoches, 840 Washington St., Natchitoches, LA 71457. 357-0070. Daily, 9 A.M.-noon, 1-5 P.M. Open Thurs.-Sun. in January. Admission.

Northwestern State University, College Avenue, Natchitoches, LA 71457. 357-6011.

Williamson Museum, Keyser Hall. Sept.-May: Mon.-Fri., 8 A.M.-3:30 P.M.

Louisiana Sportswriters Hall of Fame, Prather Coliseum. 357-6466. Sept.-May: Mon.-Fri., 8 A.M.-3:30 P.M.

Information:

Natchitoches Parish Tourist Commission, 781 Front St. (P.O. Box 411), Natchitoches, LA 71458-0411. 352-8072 or 1-800-259-1714. Mon.-Sat., 9 A.M.-5 P.M.; Sun., 10 A.M.-3 P.M.

Guide Services:

Tours by Jan, 1438 Washington St., Natchitoches, LA 71457. 352-2324 or 352-2803.

Unique Tours of Historic Natchitoches, Route 2, Box 346C, Natchitoches, LA 71457. 357-8698 or 352-4192.

Accommodations:

Chain and private motels in Natchitoches.

Bed and Breakfasts:

Breazeale House, 926 Washington St., Natchitoches, LA 71457. 352-5630.

Cane River House, 910 Washington St., Natchitoches, LA 71457. 352-9512.

Cloutier Town House, 8 Ducournau Square, Natchitoches, LA 71457. 352-5242.

Dogwood Inn, 225 Williams St., Natchitoches, LA 71457. 352-9812

Fleur de Lis Bed and Breakfast Inn, 336 Second St., Natchitoches, LA 71457. 352-6621.

Green Gables, 201 Pine St., Natchitoches, LA 71457. 352-8672.

Jefferson House Bed and Breakfast, 229 Jefferson St., Natchitoches, LA 71457. 352-5756 or 352-3957.

Lambre-Gwinn Home, 1972 Williams Ave., Natchitoches, LA 71457. 352-4944.

Levy-East House, 358 Jefferson St., Natchitoches, LA 71457. 352-0662

Martin's Roost, 1735½ Washington St., Natchitoches, LA 71457. 352-9215.

Mary's Way, 1818 Washington St., Natchitoches, LA 71457. 352-4550.

River Oaks, 112 S. Williams Ave., Natchitoches, LA 71457. 352-2776.

Starlight Plantation Bed and Breakfast, Louisiana 494 (Route 1, Box 239), Natchitoches, LA 71457. 352-3775.

Tante Huppe Inn B&B, 424 Jefferson St., Natchitoches, LA 71457. 352-8141 (Bobby) or 352-5342 (after 5 P.M.).

William and Mary Ackel House, 146 Jefferson St., Natchitoches, LA 71457. 352-3748.

Restaurants:

Front Street Baking Company, 760 Front St., Natchitoches,

LA 71457. 352-9040. Mon.-Thurs., 7 A.M.-6 P.M.; Fri. and Sat., 7 A.M.-7 P.M.

Just Friends, 746 Front St., Natchitoches, LA 71457. 352-3826. Mon.-Sat., 11 A.M.-3 P.M.

The Landing, 530 Front St., Natchitoches, LA 71457. 352-1579. Tues.-Sun., 11 A.M.-10 P.M. Champagne Brunch on Sundays, 11 A.M.-2 P.M.

Lasyone's Meat Pie Kitchen, 622 Second St., Natchitoches, LA 71457. 352-3353. Mon.-Sat., 7 A.M.-7 P.M.

Mariner's Seafood and Steakhouse, LA 1 Bypass, Natchitoches, LA 71457. 357-1220. Mon.-Sat., 4:30-10 P.M.; Sun., 11 A.M.-9 P.M. Sunday lunch buffet: 11 A.M.-2 P.M.

Merci Beaucoup, 127 Church St., Natchitoches, LA 71457. 352-6634. Mon.-Wed., 10 A.M.-5 P.M.; Thurs.-Sat., 10 A.M.-10 P.M.

Major Annual Events:

Christmas Festival of Lights, Natchitoches—First Saturday in December.

Christmas Lights and Set Pieces, Cane River Lake—First Saturday in December–January 1.

Cloutierville Heritage Festival—First Saturday in September.

Melrose Plantation Arts and Crafts Festival, Melrose—Second full weekend in June.

Natchitoches/Northwestern Folk Festival, Northwestern State University—Third full weekend in July.

Natchitoches Pilgrimage—Second weekend in October.

Statue of Huey Long outside the Winn Parish Courthouse in Winnfield. (Photo by Mary Fonseca)

Earl K. Long Memorial Park in Winnfield. (Photo by Mary Fonseca)

Marker for the Long home in Earl K. Long Memorial Park. (Photo by Mary Fonseca)

18

LONG-ING
(F)

"Why was his family so remarkable? Was it all the result of heredity? Or was it something arising out of the social and political climate of Winn parish—or was it pure accident?"

With these words from his book, *Huey Long*, noted historian T. Harry Williams gives voice to the musings of people still curious about the forces that molded Huey Long into the strong-willed Kingfish and transformed his pugilistic younger brother into the flamboyant Uncle Earl. Those with a strong interest in Louisiana's two most famous governors journey to Winnfield, the Long brothers' boyhood home, to see the environment that shaped the legendary Long dynasty.

A driving tour prepared by the **Winn Chamber of Commerce** directs political aficionados to places once familiar to Huey and Earl. They gaze at a barn and fields that were part of Earl's Pea Patch farm and eyeball a banner in the Heard Insurance Building that marks the window of Huey's first law office. Then, they visit the gravesites of Huey P. Long, Sr., and his cherished wife, Caledonia, in the town cemetery; and stroll through Earl K. Long Memorial Park, erected on the square where the family's spacious log home once stood.

If you find the thought of a similar journey to the Longs' old stomping grounds intriguing, ask the Winn Chamber to send you a copy of the "Huey Pierce Long Centennial Souvenir Edition," published by Winnfield's local newspaper, the *Winn*

Parish Enterprise. It contains reprints of several columns written by Harley Bozeman, Huey's best friend. Bozeman's engaging, often amusing accounts of incidents involving the Long boys, coupled with his descriptions of Winnfield during their youth, are sure to make your Long-ing getaway more enjoyable.

You can get even more in tune with days gone-by if you survey Winnfield from a buckboard wagon pulled by Spider, a handsome Suffolk draft horse. Spider is the pride of wagon driver and local farmer, **Claude O'Bryan.** "Suffolks are one of the oldest draft breeds in the world," says O'Brien, "but their numbers dwindled when they were replaced by modern farm machinery after World War II. Now, there are only about 500 of these gentle, intelligent horses in the world."

As he flicks the reins over Spider's broad back and guides his old-time wagon around town, O'Bryan tells passengers more about Suffolks and spins several tales about the Longs. The sight of the old Winnfield Hotel (rescued from deterioration by local fund raising), for instance, brings to mind the story of how Huey was struck on the head by a falling brick while the hotel was under construction. It rendered him unconscious and ended his short career as a water boy for the construction crew.

A drive by the dignified monument that marks the tomb of Winnfield's other favorite son, Gov. Oscar ("O.K.") Allen, plus colorful stories about other happenings in Winnfield round out O'Bryan's tour. As he passes the old Bank of Winnfield (now the Heard Insurance Company building), he helps you imagine the consternation felt by Bonnie Parker and Clyde Barrow when they attempted their last bank robbery there. The notorious duo came out empty-handed because the Bank of Montgomery had not yet delivered funds to Winnfield that day. You can also imagine the dismay of Bonnie's aunt who lived just a few blocks from the bank and had welcomed her niece as a visitor in her younger, law-abiding days.

O'Bryan usually ends his buckboard tour of Winnfield at the renovated depot that houses the **Louisiana Political Museum & Hall of Fame,** the **Louisiana Forestry Museum,** and the **Winn Parish Museum.** Here, you can leisurely browse through

*The Louisiana Political Museum & Hall of Fame, the Louisiana Forestry
Museum, and the Winn Parish Museum.* (Photo by Mary Fonseca)

exhibits relating to the Longs. The sheet music display of
Governor Huey Long's favorite song, "Every Man a King," con-
trasts nicely with a cookbook featuring Cottolene, a cottonseed
oil-based lard substitute Huey sold on his first job as a hand-to-
mouth, traveling salesman. And, as you look at Uncle Earl's old,
black phone, you can just picture him holding it as he paced
back and forth on the porch of the Pea Patch talking to aides
and constituents. The much-photographed microphone he
used when campaigning from the back of a truck recalls films
showing Earl, standing close to the mike, while he ranted and
raved about his opposition and portrayed himself as the champion of the working class.

The museum's collection of Long mementos is comple-
mented by sketches and memorabilia depicting several
Louisiana politicians and one political cartoonist elected to
the Louisiana Political Hall of Fame. Notables include: Huey
Long's son, U.S. Senator Russell B. Long; William Charles Cole
Claiborne, the first governor of Louisiana; Dudley J. LeBlanc,
state legislator and developer of "Hadacol" tonic; and U.S.
Representatives Hale and Lindy Boggs.

In the section of the museum highlighting the history and

forest-based economy of Winn Parish, a tall trophy adorned with symbols of the timber industry attracts a good deal of attention. It is highly prized by loggers who compete in tests of old-time timber harvesting skills at Winn Parish's springtime Forest Festival.

After seeing the museum and sites connected to the Longs, many visitors enjoy a stroll through downtown Winnfield's appealing stores. Stylish men's and ladies' wear boutiques are tucked among a handful of art, craft, and antique shops. These are pinpointed on a flyer available at the Chamber of Commerce. Some offer unusual, one-of-a-kind items.

Gail Shelton's **Pea Patch Gallery** borrows its name from Earl Long's farm, but is definitely more captivating than the shack with front-and-rear-screened porches that Long pieced together on his property. This spacious art center contains a teaching studio, a small restaurant, well-designed displays of quality antiques, and handsome exhibits of Shelton's artwork. Customers are especially attracted to the artist's renditions of local landmarks and the pen-and-ink drawing Shelton conceived to illustrate "Daddy's Hands," the hit song by country singer, Holly Dunn, Shelton's friend since childhood. Copies of the drawing, along with Dunn's handwritten verse, signed by the songwriter and artist are available at Pea Patch Gallery.

The Flower Box, housed in Winnfield's oldest brick building, offers Battenburg items and fine accessories in addition to its store of fresh and silk flowers. Everyone in town looks forward to the glorious display at The Flower Box during the Christmas season.

Holidays also signal the arrival of themed creations at Ron and Oline McCain's shop, **Governor's Affair.** But other fascinating, handcrafted items are available year-round. Ron makes sturdy racks to hold baseball cap collections, gaily painted bird houses and rocking horses, and made-to-order items. Oline supplies imaginative Victorian and country decorative items plus customers' special requests. A few Louisiana products are also sold here.

At **Karen's Candles,** visitors are charmed by dolls, crocheted doilies, and candles fashioned by local artisans. More candles, plus dolls, bears, and wreaths are sold at **Denise's Creations.**

When you tire of shopping, rest in an ice-cream parlor chair at **O'Kelley's Coffee Bar** and indulge in a cup of reasonably priced, gourmet coffee and a slice of freshly baked cake.

The Pink House Tea Room offers another pleasant setting for refreshments. June Melton prepares festive lunches and intimate, candlelight dinners for patrons who make reservations at her pleasant, airy tearoom. But you can drop in for beverages and desserts—Melton's scrumptious Pink House pie is a perennial favorite—anytime between 10 and 5.

The Pink House is just around the corner from John and Judy Posey's **Southern Colonial Bed and Breakfast.** This inviting, hilltop guesthouse has large, comfortable rooms, plus enticing porches that beckon nappers, readers, and people-watchers. If you are staying at Southern Colonial, you can settle into a cozy corner after a luncheon at The Pink House. If you have other accommodations, request a tour of this handsome home and a stroll through the charming Mary Dee house across the street.

As you enter Southern Colonial's parlor, notice the early model "fire sprinkler" above the door and the anhydrite rocks used in the sturdy fireplace. The stones have the unique ability to re-cement themselves to seal off water and other elements without the addition of other minerals or stabilizing agents. They are from an area near U.S. 84, west of Winnfield, now mined by the WinnRock company. A scenic overlook now being designed will give motorists a bird's-eye view of this unique quarry.

The Poseys point out many other features of the turn-of-the-century home they have lovingly restored. Then, they cross the street to show you the handcrafted cypress stair rails, etched-glass cabinet fronts, and exquisite antiques that embellish the Mary Dee house. The cottage was built by Huey and Earl's brother, Julius Long, and renovated by John Posey's sister.

Homes that Huey and Earl's father and grandfather built in Winn Parish were surrounded by virgin forests. But by 1924, when the Mary Dee home was built, the tall pines had been crudely cut and fed to the smoking sawmills that turned

The Gum Springs Recreation Area in the Kisatchie National Forest. (Photo by Mary Fonseca)

Winnfield into an ugly boomtown. The scarred land was rescued by Franklin D. Roosevelt's Civilian Conservation Corps and the pine seedlings they planted grew into the resplendent Kisatchie National Forest, which surrounds Winnfield today.

U.S. 84 cuts through the forest to connect Winnfield with Natchitoches, the oldest settlement in the Louisiana Purchase Territory. You can spend a pleasant day exploring wayside sites along this thirty-mile stretch of highway, or drive to Natchitoches to see attractions described in "Where Steel Magnolias Grow."

As you turn onto U.S. 84 you are greeted by a replica of an oil well derrick, erected by retired oil worker "Pinkie" Jacobs. His neighbors, **Eric and Michael Kelley,** a remarkably talented pair of woodworkers, display and sell cypress swings and other handcrafted items. Just down the road, the popular **Winn Fish Market** offers tasty lunches. The restaurant is convenient for shoppers browsing through nearby **Country Collectibles,** a quaint, little store specializing in small antiques such as kitchen utensils, glassware, and tools.

Seven miles west of Winnfield on U.S. 84, a caution light signals the entrance to Kisatchie National Forest's Gum

Springs Recreation Area, an inviting picnic and hiking site that is being modernized by the U.S. Forest Service. A hiking and horseback trail is being developed across U.S. 84 from Gum Springs.

A mile or so past Gum Springs, an unmarked road across from Couley Methodist Church leads to Saline Lake, an exceptionally pretty waterway shaded by hundreds of moss-draped cypress trees. The Winn Chamber of Commerce has information on fishing boat rentals if you want to spend some time exploring the lake. Or, you can rent a canoe at **Pat's Country Corner** in Goldonna, about sixteen miles northwest of Winnfield via Louisiana 156, and float down the meandering bayou that flows into the lake.

A two-mile Dogwood Trail gives walkers a chance to immerse themselves in the sylvan beauty of Kisatchie National Forest. The trail extends north from U.S. 84, just before the highway crosses the extension of Saline River that flows southward from the lake.

Ardent outdoor enthusiasts venture further into the forest to visit **Briarwood,** a world-renowned nature preserve that honors and continues the work of Caroline Dormon. Dormon, the first woman employed in forestry in the United States, was largely responsible for the establishment of Kisatchie National Forest. She devoted her life and property to the preservation of native Louisiana trees and plants. Trails in Briarwood lead to her simple cabin and to the tiny retreat where she penned six books and countless articles on Louisiana's native plants. In March, April, and May springtime flowers brighten the preserve. Brilliant Louisiana irises color a bog. Azaleas and other wild flowers wake from a winter's sleep. Hardy summer blooms are next in the preserve's procession of native plants, followed by hardwood trees costumed in red and gold.

To enjoy the changing seasons at Briarwood, follow U.S. 167 north to Dodson. Turn left on Louisiana 126 and travel about 21 miles to the intersection of Louisiana 9. Turn right onto the highway and follow Louisiana 9 for 1.25 miles to the Briarwood sign.

While motoring down the last few miles of Louisiana 126 on

Caroline Dormon's cabin at Briarwood. (Photo by Mary Fonseca)

your way to Briarwood, note the sign pointing the way to
Mirror Lake Lodge. After visiting Briarwood, you may want to
drive here to enjoy a delicious catfish dinner. Winnfield has
some good, casual restaurants, but locals enjoy trekking to this
rustic lodge. Part of its attraction is its informal atmosphere,
reminiscent of a cookout at a relative's home. Indeed, D. C.
Carpenter, the retired educator who owns Mirror Lake Lodge,
treats you like one of his congenial relatives. While you feast on
bountiful servings, D. C. entertains with snappy piano renditions of "Top 40" hits from the past.

Another favorite destination of folks in Winnfield is the
Dodson Fish Market. They drive eighteen miles to this popular
little restaurant to enjoy Lloyd and Nedra Vines' savory fish
dishes and their special alligator pie. The Vines also sell their
own line of condiments, including eight types of hot sauces
and seasonings for wild game.

Area Code: (318)

Getting There:

Winnfield may be accessed by U.S. 167 from the north and
south, and by U.S. 84 from the east and west.

Where and When:

Briarwood, The Foundation for the Preservation of the Caroline Dormon Nature Presrve, Inc., P.O. Box 226, Natchitoches, LA 71457. 576-3379. Open weekends in March, April, May, August, and November. Sat., 9 A.M.-5 P.M.; Sun., noon-5 P.M. or by appointment at any time. Admission.

Country Collectibles, U.S. 84 West, Winnfield, LA 71483. 628-4451. Thurs.-Sat., 10 A.M.-5 P.M.

Denise's Creations, 107 Front St., Winnfield, LA 71483. 628-3438. Call for hours of operation.

The Flower Box, 101 E. Main St., Winnfield, LA 71483. 628-2184. Mon.-Fri., 9 A.M.-5 P.M.; Sat., 9 A.M.-noon.

Governor's Affair, 402 Main St., Winnfield, LA 71483. 628-5353. Mon.-Sat., 10 A.M.-6 P.M.

Karen's Candles, 219 E. Main St., Winnfield, LA 71483. No phone listed. Mon.-Fri., 9 A.M.-5 P.M.; Sat., 9:30 A.M.-1 P.M.

Eric and Michael Kelley, Route 3, Box 150, Winnfield, LA 71483. 628-3442. Cypress swings made by request.

Louisiana Political Museum & Hall of Fame, Louisiana Forestry Museum, Winn Parish Museum, 499 E. Main St., Winnfield, LA 71483. 628-5928. Tues.-Fri., 10 A.M.-4 P.M. Donations appreciated.

Pat's Country Corner, Intersection of Louisiana 156 and Louisiana 479, Goldonna, LA 727-4865. Mon.-Sat., 4:30 A.M.-7 P.M.

Pea Patch Gallery, 108 Abel St., Winnfield, LA 71483. 628-3560. Mon.-Fri., noon-5 P.M.; Sat., 10 A.M.-noon.

Southern Colonial Bed and Breakfast, 801 E. Main St., Winnfield, LA 71483. 628-6087. Admission.

Information:

Winn Chamber of Commerce, Corner of U.S. 167 and Boundary Street (P.O. Box 565), Winnfield, LA 71483. 628-4461. Mon.-Fri., 9 A.M.-4 P.M.

Guide Services:

Claude O'Bryan, 400 W. Oak St., Winnfield, LA 71483. 628-2239.

Accommodations:

Best Western Motel, 700 W. Court St., Winnfield, LA 71483. 628-3993.

Economy Inn, U.S. 84 East, Winnfield, LA 71483. 628-4691.

Southern Colonial Bed and Breakfast, 801 E. Main St., Winnfield, LA 71483. 628-6087.

Restaurants:

Dodson Fish Market, U.S. 167, Dodson, LA 71422. 628-5568. Market: Mon.-Sat., 8 A.M.-7 P.M. Restaurant: Mon.-Thurs., 10 A.M.-7:30 P.M.; Fri. and Sat., 10 A.M.-8 P.M.

Mirror Lake Lodge, Blewer Road (off of Louisiana 126), Winnfield, LA 71483. 576-3688. Mon.-Thurs., 4-9 P.M.; Fri. and Sat., 10 A.M.-10 P.M.; Sun., 10 A.M.-4 P.M.

O'Kelley's Coffee Bar, 113 Main St., Winnfield, LA 71483. 628-6943. Mon.-Sat., 6 A.M.-6 P.M.

Pea Patch Gallery, 108 Abel St., Winnfield, LA 71483. 628-3560. Mon.-Sat., 11 A.M.-2 P.M.

The Pink House, 105 S. Pineville St., Winnfield, LA 71483. 628-1515. Tues.-Sun., 10 A.M.-5 P.M. Closed Mondays, except during Christmas season.

Winn Fish Market, U.S. 84 West, Winnfield, LA 71483. 628-6002. Mon.-Sat., 10 A.M.-8 P.M.

For a complete listing of restaurants in the Winnfield area, contact the Winn Chamber of Commerce.

Major Annual Events:

Christmas Parade and Lighting—First Friday in December.

Drake Salt Works Festival—First Saturday in September.

Governor's Marching Band Festival—October.

Krewe of Kingfish Parade—Saturday before Fat Tuesday.

Louisiana Forest Festival—Fourth weekend in April.

Louisiana Political Hall of Fame Banquet—January.

Piney Hills Black Heritage Weekend—Memorial Day weekend.

Taste Fair—Third Tuesday in October.

Uncle Earl's Catahoula Dog Show and Cattle Roundup—March.

Winn Parish Fair—Last week of September or first week of October.

Wolf Creek Festival—Third weekend in September.

The Schepis Museum. (Photo by Mary Fonseca)

19

DOWN BY THE RIVERSIDE
(F)

When an anonymous composer of the traditional, American sprritual, "Down by the Riverside," wrote, "I'm going to join hands with everyone, down by the riverside," he was anticipating a joyful gathering on a celestial shore. About two years ago, residents of Columbia, a north Louisiana town that hugs the banks of the Ouachita River, adopted the idea expressed in this song. They joined hands, hearts, and minds to complete their vision of a revitalized downtown. Now Columbia's once sleepy Main Street is a lively avenue that encourages new businesses, serves as a pleasant setting for community functions, and enhances the captivating aura that attracts weekenders to this historic town.

Visitors approaching from the north follow U.S. 165 to Columbia, about thirty miles south of Monroe. The highway crosses the scenic Ouachita River, listed as one of America's ten most beautiful rivers by *National Geographic* magazine, then passes through Columbia. A left turn immediately south of the Ouachita River bridge leads to Main Street, one block east of the highway. Another left turn deposits you at **The Schepis Museum,** the most prestigious building in Columbia's rejuvenated downtown.

Before you enter the Schepis Museum, step back and admire the ornate, turn-of-the-century building that is the pride of this close-knit community. The Italian-style structure was built by John Schepis, a Sicilian architect who became a shopkeeper after he emigrated to America. After struggling for many years to build their business, Schepis and his wife moved their prosperous mercantile store to the ground floor of the large structure that now houses the museum and they used the second floor as quarters for their family. Schepis constructed his new building with care, fashioning the exterior with hollow-core cement blocks of his own design. Inside, he created an aura reminiscent of the Renaissance-style palazzos so familiar to him in the old country. Then this talented artisan/architect designed a fitting diadem for his elegant store. He carved clay statues of George Washington and Christopher Columbus, made plaster of Paris molds of his sculptures, and filled them with cement. After the statues hardened, he hoisted them up to the roof of his store where they have withstood the ravages of time to convey the affection Schepis felt for the land he left and his appreciation of the one he chose for his children's future.

When you cross the threshold into the Schepis Museum, you may see a display on wildlife and natural habitats common in north Louisiana, a traveling show from another museum, or an exhibit of local artworks. The museum hosts at least six shows a year, plus musical and dramatic performances. Volunteer docents are on hand to interpret exhibits and assist visitors with information on Columbia and its Caldwell Parish environs.

Stroll down Main Street after you visit the Schepis Museum so you can get acquainted with some of the people and a few of the places that make Columbia such an enchanting town. One of the locals you may happen upon is former governor of Louisiana, John J. McKeithen, who retired from public life after serving two terms as Louisiana's chief executive and resumed his law practice in Columbia. McKeithen treasures his community because it "has retained the dignity inherent in its heritage as a steamboat port and marketplace."

The former governor is an active participant in the affairs of his hometown and readily joins in the many fairs and functions held on Main Street. He and his wife, Dorothy, are usually in the crowd that watches costumed children collect treats from downtown merchants during Columbia's "Witch Way to Main Street?" celebration on Halloween. Among the stores the youngsters visit are **Bebe's Fashions,** a ladies' apparel store; **Main Street Emporium,** a purveyor of local crafts; and **Magnolias, Memories and Antiques,** a fine gift and antique store.

After trick or treating, some families gathered for dinner at the charming **Wisteria Tea Garden,** next door to the Schepis Museum. Folks also socialize over drinks at Main Street's levee-side **Watermark Saloon.** Tasty lunches can be enjoyed at the saloon, the oldest on the Ouachita River, and a restaurant facility on the Watermark's second floor is part of the development plan for Main Street.

On weekends, the Watermark serves as a gathering place for passengers waiting to board the ***Caldwell Belle,*** an old-time paddle-wheeler that regularly cruises the Ouachita River. As the riverboat steams along, you glimpse farms, forests, and intriguing locales such as **Riverton Marina,** home to a community of houseboat owners who relish the mobile life-style they enjoy in their floating homes.

Folks who value stability and fine architecture appreciate the Blanks-Adams house on Wall Street (private), built by a steamboat captain in the 1860s. And visitors can also see the more than 150-year-old Scandinavian Gothic First United Methodist Church and other vintage structures in Columbia's historic district. Inquire at the Schepis Museum if you want to see the handsome interior of the Methodist church, which has skillfully crafted, curved pews and unusual, pale green, stained-glass windows.

Be sure that your tour includes a drive through Columbia Heights Cemetery. This tranquil burial ground, accessed on Stringer Street south of the residential district, is particularly beautiful in the spring when dogwood trees and azaleas are in bloom. But fall color on "cemetery hill" nearly equals the springtime show. This lovely cemetery was built on the highest ground in town because the Ouachita frequently topped its banks before levees were constructed to control its flow.

First United Methodist Church. (Photo by Mary Fonseca)

The Watermark, the oldest saloon on the Ouachita River. (Photo by Mary Fonseca)

Martin Homeplace-Louisiana Art & Folk Center & Museum. (Photo by Mary Fonseca)

The inviting park at the foot of Columbia Heights Cemetery is one of two delightful picnic spots you can enjoy. The other is the Columbia Recreation Area, which overlooks the Ouachita River at the foot of Pearl Street west of U.S. 165.

If you are visiting Columbia on a Thursday in spring or summer, you may want to postpone a picnic or restaurant lunch and enjoy the delicious, reservation only, repast offered at **Martin Homeplace Folk Center & Museum.** Signs on U.S. 165 north of the Ouachita River direct you to the 1870s home built by Ann and George Martin. It housed later generations of their family until 1986 and is now a living history museum containing many articles left by the Martins as well as a folklife center devoted to preserving crafts, customs, and north Louisiana lifestyles. At the center, members of the Louisiana Art & Folk Center & Museum share their expertise in canning, tatting, knitting, quilting, crocheting, chair caning, and other crafts with anyone who wants to learn. You can meet a few of these talented people at the Thursday lunches. And anytime you visit Martin Homeplace, you can view artworks the museum purchases from winners of the annual Louisiana Art & Folk Festival art competition. The October festival—the oldest and largest of its kind in Louisiana—is staged at the Caldwell Parish Fairgrounds on U.S. 165 north of Columbia.

Every spring, several newborn colts nuzzle their mothers in highway-side pastures a mile or so north of the fairgrounds. The picturesque sight is made possible by the meticulous care **Southgate Farms** gives champion stallions and mares. Call and arrange a tour of this outstanding quarter horse farm, home of three-time world champion stallion, Ima Cool Skip. You will learn about breeding and training fine quarter horses and see outstanding stallions such as the handsome champion, Hint of Conclusive.

Berries and grapes gathered at another Caldwell Parish farm are often used in blue-ribbon jellies tasted at the Louisiana Art & Folk Festival. **Pender's Pride** welcomes visitors who want to harvest the farm's muscadine grapes and blackberries. The Pender family's blackberries are usually mouth-watering ripe by the end of May and during the month of June; their muscadines

(Photo by Mary Fonseca)

Southgate Farms stallion, Hint of Conclusive, shows off the breeding and bearing that made him a champion. (Photo by Mary Fonseca)

are ready for picking from mid-August to mid-September. A sign on U.S. 165 near the Ouachita and Caldwell parish border points the way to Pender's Pride, about thirteen miles north of Columbia and 3½ miles west of U.S. 165.

Boscobel Cottage, a charming bed-and-breakfast facility with beautiful grounds bordering the Ouachita River, is one mile past the turn off to Pender's Pride. Boscobel owners Kay and Cliff LaFrance offer cozy quarters in three outbuildings that surround their 1820s cottage. "The Chapel," a former overseer's office, resembles a tiny church; and "The *Garçonniere*," a pleasant second-story apartment, is fronted by an airy balcony. "Wellerman House" is an 1894 dogtrot home that once was part of an old dairy farm.

A very different bed-and-breakfast experience may be enjoyed at **Double G Ranch** eight miles south of Columbia. This equine facility is used as a children's camp from the first weekend in June until mid-August. During the rest of the year, Diane and Buddy Gill offer comfortable, ranch-style accommodations to overnight guests. The Gill's facilities are described in detail in chapter 36, "For Adventurers, and Those Who would Like to Be."

The Double G is the closest Columbia-area accommodation to the **Copenhagen Prairie,** a unique natural area protected and managed by IP Forest Resources Company, a subsidiary of International Paper Company, in partnership with the Louisiana Nature Conservancy. If you plan your getaway three or four weeks in advance you can see this remarkable area in the company of a knowledgeable guide. International Paper's 440 acres of rolling hills and deep ravines are home to the Ogelthorpe oak—a globally imperiled species previously thought to grow only in Ogelthorpe County, Georgia—and to grassland flora once thought extinct. Sixteen plant species not found anywhere else in Louisiana and fossils of animals who once inhabited a prehistoric sea have been found on this unique tract Danish settlers named the Copenhagen Prairie.

If you work up an appetite hiking through this pristine area, sample the fare at one of Caldwell Parish's casual restaurants. **Don Cap** serves smoked-on-the-premises barbecue at his popular, U.S. 165 restaurant just south of Columbia. And about thirteen miles south of Don Cap's, Melvis and Floyce Childress prepare homestyle "Depression era" dishes such as fatback ribs, turnip greens, and cornbread at **Maple Hill Smokehouse,** their hilltop restaurant on U.S. 165. But these three restaurateurs aren't the only ones who stir their pots down by this north Louisiana riverside. In Columbia, diners enjoy the Southern-style menu offered at **Frances',** on Franklin Street just off U.S. 165, and the bountiful salad bar and freshly prepared pizzas at **Pizza Plus** on U.S. 165.

Area Code: (318)

Getting There:

Columbia is accessed from the north and south by U.S. 165 and from the east and west by Louisiana 4.

Where and When:

Bebe's Fashions, 212 Main St. (P.O. Box 824), Columbia, LA 71418. 649-2745. Mon.-Sat., 9:30 A.M.-5 P.M.

Caldwell Belle—Call 649-2138 for cruise schedule and rate information. Admission. Cold soft drinks sold on-board vessel.

Copenhagen Prairie—Call 649-2626 at least three or four weeks in advance to arrange a guided tour. At present, you may only visit Copenhagen Prairie with a guide.

Magnolias, Memories and Antiques, 140 Main St., Columbia, LA 71418. 649-2917. Tues.-Sat., 10 A.M.-4:30 P.M.

Main Street Emporium, 120 Main St., Columbia, LA 71418. 649-9221. Tues.-Sat., 9 A.M.-4:30 P.M.

Martin Homeplace Folk Center & Museum, P.O. Box 196, Columbia, LA 71418. 649-6722. Tues.-Sat., 9 A.M.-4:30 P.M. Lunch on Thursdays in spring and summer by reservation only. Donations appreciated. Separate charge for lunch.

Pender's Pride, 766 Forest Home Rd., Monroe, LA 71202. 323-7001. Daily, 8 A.M.-6:30 P.M. Call to make arrangements. The

Penders will do the picking for you if you prefer. Charge for grapes and blackberries.

Riverton Marina, Route 1, Box 612 BB, Columbia, LA 71418. Contact Ferrand and Mittie Cumpton at 649-9285 for more information.

The Schepis Museum, 107 Main St. (P.O. Box 10), Columbia, LA 71418. 649-2138. Tues.-Fri., 10 A.M.-4:30 P.M.; Sat., 10 A.M.-3 P.M. Donations appreciated.

Southgate Farms, U.S. 165 (P.O. Box 310), Columbia, LA 71418. Call 649-2911 to arrange a complimentary tour.

Information:

The Schepis Museum, 107 Main St. (P.O. Box 10), Columbia, LA 71418. 649-2138. Tues.-Fri., 10 A.M.-4:30 P.M.; Sat., 10 A.M.-3 P.M.

Guide Services:

Not available for this getaway.

Bed and Breakfasts:

Boscobel Cottage, 185 Cordell Lane, Monroe, LA 71202. 325-1550.

Double G Ranch, Route 1, Box 14C, Grayson, LA 71435. 649-9363.

"Homestay" accommodations are offered by several residents of Columbia. Inquire at The Schepis Museum, 649-2138.

Restaurants:

Don Cap's, U.S. 165 South, Columbia, LA 71418. 649-2175. Mon.-Sat., 10 A.M.-9 P.M.

Frances', P.O. Box 1238, Columbia, LA 71418. 649-2306. Daily, 6 A.M.-10 P.M.

Maple Hill Smokehouse, Route 1, Box 59, Kelly, LA 71441. 649-2056. Mon.-Sat., 10 A.M.-7 P.M.

Pizza Plus, 1517 U.S. 165 South, Columbia, LA 71418. 649-7342. Mon.-Fri., 6 A.M.-10 P.M.; Sat. and Sun., 6 A.M.-11 P.M.

The Watermark Saloon, 101 Main St., Columbia, LA 71418. 649-0999. Mon.-Thurs., 11 A.M.-10 P.M.; Fri. and Sat., 11 A.M.-11 P.M. Lunch: Mon.-Thurs., 11 A.M.-3 P.M.; Fri. and Sat., 11 A.M.-8 P.M. Pizza served anytime. Live entertainment on the first Saturday of every month.

Wisteria Tea Garden, 113 Main St., Columbia, LA 71418. 649-6002. Mon.-Thurs., 9 A.M.-3 P.M.; Fri. and Sat., 9 A.M.-8 P.M.

Major Annual Events:

Caldwell Country Christmas, Columbia—First Saturday in December.

Caldwell Rodeo Days, Columbia—Second week in June.

Louisiana Art & Folk Festival, Columbia—Second weekend in October.

"Witch Way to Main Street?," Columbia—Thursday before Halloween.

20

FRATERNAL TWINS
(F) (G)

When applying twin-type labels to the "Twin Cities" of Monroe and West Monroe, fraternal is definitely the suitable choice. The two cities on opposite banks of the Ouachita River in northeast Louisiana have distinctly different profiles and personalities. The **Monroe/West Monroe Convention and Visitors Bureau,** just south of Interstate 20 on State Farm Drive (U.S. 165 Frontage Road), has vital statistics on each of the "twins." Monroe, the larger metropolis, is the business and cultural center of Ouachita Parish; West Monroe projects a more laid-back, suburban atmosphere.

Monroe's Riverside Drive is lined with stately homes, but none is more exquisite than the distinguished residence built by Joseph A. Biedenharn. The first bottler of Coca-Cola, he was also an early promoter of the Monroe-based crop-dusting company that evolved into Delta Air Lines.

Joseph Biedenharn's only daughter, Emy-Lou—an internationally celebrated opera singer—was the last mistress of the Biedenharn home. She decorated the mansion's high-ceilinged rooms with ornate furnishings and rare antiques. Although visitors appreciate the home's artistic decor, the two rooms they favor most are the ones filled with souvenirs of "Mr. Joe's" and Emy-Lou's respective careers.

In back of her home, Emy-Lou developed the Oriental, Italian, and other themed gardens molded into lovely ELsong

Layton Castle. (Photo courtesy Monroe/West Monroe Convention and Visitors Bureau)

ELsong Gardens. (Photo courtesy Monroe/West Monroe Convention and Visitors Bureau)

Cars from Jerry L. Brewster's Dream Cars. (Photo courtesy Monroe/West Monroe Convention and Visitors Bureau)

Gardens (the name deriving from Emy-Lou's initials). As you meander along the gardens' winding paths past graceful fountains and statues, laser beams activate melodies attune to each individual motif. Among them is a "Plants of the Bible" garden, containing flowers and shrubs cited in the Good Book. The garden is suggestive of the Biedenharn Bible Museum next door, the third component of the family properties managed by the **Emy-Lou Biedenharn Foundation.**

In this museum you will probably see more Bibles gathered under one roof than you ever have before. The displays include Bibles brought to America by early English settlers, a copy of the first Bible printed in America, and the first translated into the language of the Algonquin Indians. All are among original and replicated tomes used to demonstrate the significant role of the Bible in American life.

The Biedenharn complex, on the corner of Forsythe Avenue, is easily accessed by turning left onto Louisville Avenue off of U.S. 165, north of Interstate 20, and right onto Riverside Drive when Louisville Avenue dead-ends at the Ouachita River.

Although the Ouachita flows past the Biedenharn estate, the waterway is hidden from view by earthen embankments. On Sunday afternoons from April through October you can enjoy an excellent view of the Ouachita, listed by *National Geographic* as one of America's ten most beautiful rivers, aboard the ***Twin City Queen,*** a triple-decked excursion boat docked a half-block north of the Biedenharn complex.

Outings on the river are a way of life for more than 200 houseboat owners who dock their crafts in nearby marinas. Many of them take part in the gaily-lighted Christmas Flotilla that is a highlight of Monroe's annual Winterfest. During the December festival, special concerts, spectacles, and parades quicken the pace of the holiday season.

Lavish affairs hosted by Eugenia Layton used to enliven Monroe society during the holidays and year-round. During the first half of the twentieth century, the perennial hostess— a flamboyant daughter of Judge Henry Bry—caused such a stir when she embellished her father's South Grand Street cottage with a massive tower, turret, and carriageway that locals nick-named it "Layton Castle."

Layton Castle still sits amid parklike grounds on the banks of the Ouachita River south of Louisville Avenue. Tour its attractive rooms, filled with family heirlooms and portraits. Then take in the **Masur Museum of Art,** which occupies a smaller, Tudor citadel a few blocks away. Special art shows and cultural presentations frequently supplement the institution's permanent collection of works by such twentieth-century artists as Dali and Picasso.

Tourists sight-seeing along the riverfront often pause to mingle with Monroe's downtowners at the **New Orleans Cafe.** The restaurant imports special ingredients for their Cajun and Creole dishes, including New Orleans-baked po' boy bread. Follow Louisville Avenue to Fourth Street and turn right to Washington Street to reach the eatery, housed in the Washington Plaza office building.

At dinnertime, head back to the riverfront to select one of **Warehouse No. 1 Restaurant's** blackened and grilled sea-foods—or some other tempting dishes—while enjoying a levee-top view of the Ouachita River. The popular gathering place is quartered in an old cotton warehouse two blocks south of the intersection of Louisville Avenue and Riverside Drive.

On the second day of your getaway, visit West Monroe's Cottonport Historic District close to the Ouachita River's opposite shore. Cross the Louisville Avenue bridge and turn south onto Trenton Street to access a two-block section of the district known as **Antique Alley.**

Scan the potpourri of colorful wares offered by antique and collectible shops, art galleries, bookstores, and specialty retail-ers along the alley. Then pause for a pick-me-up at one of the quaint cafes sandwiched between the shops. Antique enthusi-asts may enjoy overnighting at **Rose Lee Inn,** a restored, turn-of-the century hotel on the second floor of Chandler's Antique Mall in the center of Antique Alley. Bob and Carolyn Chandler have decorated this five-bedroom Bed and Breakfast with antiques and furnishings reminiscent of the Victorian era.

Just a few blocks south of the Chandlers' hostelry, vintage

Corvettes, Dousenbergs, and Shelbys fill Jerry L. Brewster's time-warped parking lot. You just might find your dream car in the mammoth building that houses **Jerry L. Brewster's Dream Cars** plus a fantasy-fulfilling group of collectible motorcycles.

Although her stock is not as flamboyant as Brewster's, Cherry Whipple is also an imaginative entrepreneur who operates an unusual West Monroe shop. Cherry sells Louisiana-made arts and crafts in her Louisiana Street store, **Just Cherry's.** Useful or decorative items made from recycled materials and homegrown or homemade items such as herbs, loofahs, and scented soaps are the specialties here. To reach Cherry's, take Interstate 20 West to Well Road and travel four blocks north to Louisiana Avenue.

West Monroe's **Kiroli Park Recreation Area** is an oasis that appeals to weary shoppers and sightseers, especially in the fall when the park's hardwoods are dressed in yellow and red. Within the confines of this woodland sanctuary, you may picnic, fish, play tennis, and hike trails that wind beneath towering pines. Check the Twin Cities' Calendar of Events to see if any theater performances, holiday concerts, or other entertainments are scheduled in the park's outdoor amphitheater during your stay.

Several routes lead to Kiroli Park, but heading north on Trenton Street until it turns away from the Ouachita River and becomes Arkansas Road is perhaps the easiest for folks unfamiliar with the city to follow. Arkansas Road intersects with the Kiroli Road entrance to the park in the northwest section of West Monroe.

Entertainment is also offered at the **Monroe Civic Center,** where weekenders may catch one of the many equestrian shows, musicals, and sporting events held at the well-used facility. The auditorium also hosts frequent performances by the Monroe Symphony Orchestra, the Twin City Ballet, or traveling theatrical companies.

About two miles south of the Monroe/West Monroe Convention and Visitors Bureau, another park offers outdoor pleasures. A sign on U.S. 165 directs visitors to the **Louisiana Purchase Gardens & Zoo,** two blocks west of the highway. The

100-acre park's menagerie and its floral beauty can be enjoyed on interconnecting footpaths, from the deck of the *James Monroe* as it meanders the zoo's tranquil waterways, or via a train excursion around the perimeter of the zoo.

During harvesttime (late August-November), cotton fields along U.S. 165 hum with activity. Module builders zip along the rows, pressing cotton into bales and spitting them out into the furrows. Trucks laden with the fluffy crop deliver their loads to the Murray Cotton Gins in Bosco, about 13 miles south of the turn off to the zoo.

If you are interested in cotton farming and other northeast Louisiana agricultural activities, visit a few of the local growers who willingly share their expertise. The Monroe/West Monroe Convention and Visitors Bureau has a list of these "open" farms.

Prolong your visit to Monroe and West Monroe by exploring two engaging destinations northeast of the Twin Cities. **Poverty Point State Commemorative Area,** the most fascinating archaeological site in Louisiana, is about fifty miles from Monroe via Louisiana 139 and Louisiana 134. From 1800 B.C. to about 500 B.C., Poverty Point was the home of prehistoric Indians who constructed several mounds and ridges on the site. The 400-acre area is named for an antebellum plantation that once stood on the spot.

A short video and educational exhibits at the commemorative area's visitor center reveal bits and pieces of information about Poverty Point's ancient residents. From a viewing tower in front of the center, you can see the park's most remarkable landmark, a 70-foot-high, bird-shaped mound that measures 700 by 800 feet at its base. Guided tram tours offer a closer look at the mound and a better understanding of the enormous feat the builders accomplished with primitive tools. A 2.6-mile trail connects other noteworthy points on the grounds.

Louisiana Begins at Lake Providence is the motto of the rural community that hugs the shores of a pretty lake twenty-five miles up Louisiana 134 from Poverty Point. During the Christmas season, lights on 200 enormous trees are reflected in Lake Providence's placid waters. U.S. 65 follows the shore of the lake and passes **Byerley House,** the town's community and welcome center. The vintage dwelling is filled with local crafts and heritage exhibits.

Byerly House representatives can tell you about hunting and other activities in the 6,900-acre **Bayou Macon Wildlife Refuge** or direct you to the **Old Dutch Bakery,** where Mennonite goodies are baked from time-honored recipes. The Byerly House crew also distributes information on a handful of delightful stores scattered around the shores of the lake. Original paintings and photographs are sold at Sherrie Howard's **Straight from the Heart-Art,** while **The Country Loft** specializes in handmade dolls, attractive linens, and table settings. **Hollydays,** a lakeside factory that manufactures children's fashions that are featured in fine stores nationwide, sells its charming creations to drop-in customers.

Louisiana food products are just a short drive away at **Panola Pepper Corporation.** A sign on U.S. 65 points the way to the pepper sauce plant on Holland Delta Road where tours and the zesty items made at the factory are offered. Two of Panola's newest products, Bat's Brew Hot Sauce and Vamp Fire, were inspired by Lake Providence's proximity to Transylvania, the Louisiana outpost of the bloodthirsty Count Dracula.

T-shirts with bat logos, skeleton earrings, and assorted bat-themed goods are sold at the **Transylvania General Store,** ten miles south of Lake Providence on U.S. 65. At the adjacent post office, you can have postcards and letters stamped with the bat-shaped postmark of your choice.

Area Code: (318)

Getting There:

Monroe and West Monroe are at the intersection of Interstate 20 and U.S. 165.

Where and When:

Antique Alley—All shops open Tues.-Sat., 10 A.M.-5 P.M. Some are also open on Mondays. For more information, contact the

Monroe/West Monroe Convention and Visitors Bureau.

Bayou Macon Wildlife Refuge, Louisiana 2 West (Dept. of Wildlife Fisheries, 368 Century Park Dr., Monroe, LA 71203). 343-4044.

The Country Loft, U.S. 65, Lake Providence, LA 71254. 559-1542. Mon.-Fri., 9 A.M.-5 P.M.; Sat., 9 A.M.-noon.

Emy-Lou Biedenharn Foundation, 2006 Riverside Dr., Monroe, LA 71201. 387-5281. Tues.-Fri., 10 A.M.-4 P.M.; Sat. and Sun., 2-5 P.M. Tours begin on the hour: Tues.-Fri., 10 A.M.-3 P.M.; Sat. and Sun., 2-4 P.M. Free.

Hollydays, U.S. 65, Lake Providence, LA 71254. 559-1417. Mon.-Fri., 8 A.M.-noon, 1-5 P.M.

Jerry L. Brewster's Dream Cars, 411 Trenton St., West Monroe, LA 71291. 388-1989. Mon.-Sat., 9 A.M.-5 P.M.

Just Cherry's, 204 Louisiana Ave., West Monroe, LA 71291. 397-2418. Wed.-Sat., 10 A.M.-6 P.M. Open every day in December.

Kiroli Park Recreation Area, Kiroli Road, West Monroe, LA 71291. 396-4016. Daily, 7 A.M.-8 P.M. Admission.

Layton Castle, 1122 S. Grand St., Monroe, LA 71202. 322-4869. Tours by appointment. Admission.

Louisiana Purchase Gardens & Zoo, Ticheli Road (P.O. Box 123), Monroe, LA 71210-0123. 329-2400. Daily, 10 A.M.-5 P.M. Admission.

Masur Museum of Art, 1400 S. Grand St., Monroe, LA 71202. 329-2200. Tues.-Thurs., 9 A.M.-5 P.M.; Fri.-Sun., 2-5 P.M. Free.

Monroe Civic Center, 401 Lea Joyner Expwy., Monroe, LA 71202. Call 329-2225 for a schedule of performances and ticket information.

Panola Pepper Corporation, Route 2, Box 148, Lake Providence, LA 71254. 559-1774. Mon.-Fri., 8 A.M.-4:30 P.M.

Poverty Point State Commemorative Area, HC 60, Box 208-A, Epps, LA 71237. 926-5492. Open daily. Visitors Center and grounds: 9 A.M.-5 P.M. April 1-Sept. 30, grounds and picnic areas open until 7 P.M. Admission for adults. Children and senior citizens admitted free. Guided tram tours begin Easter weekend and end Labor Day weekend. No food service available.

Straight from the Heart-Art, Louisiana 596 (Route 2, Box 75), Lake Providence, LA 71254. 559-0321. Mon.-Fri., 8 A.M.-5 P.M.; Saturday, by appointment or by chance.

Transylvania General Store, U.S. 65 (P.O. Box 88), Transylvania, LA 71286. 559-1338. Mon.-Sat., 5 A.M.-6:30 P.M.

Twin City Queen, 401 Civic Center Blvd. (P.O. Box 300), Monroe, LA 71210. 329-2225. Cruises: April-Oct. on Sun., 2-4 P.M. Call for exact dates of season. Admission.

Note: Many Twin City companies offer plant tours. Among them are Riverwood International Corp.; Plymouth Tube Company; Bancroft Bag, Inc.; and Coca-Cola Bottling Company. Contact the Monroe/West Monroe Convention and Visitors Bureau for more information.

Information:

Byerley House, U.S. 65 (P.O. Box 709), Lake Providence, LA 71254. 559-5125. Mon.-Fri., 9:30 A.M.-4:30 P.M.

Monroe/West Monroe Convention and Visitors Bureau, 1333 State Farm Dr. (P.O. Box 6054), Monroe, LA 71202. 387-5691 or 1-800-843-1872. Mon.-Fri., 8:30 A.M.-5 P.M.

Guide Services:

Ann Cole, 2208 Island Dr., Monroe, LA 71201. 325-4425.

Accommodations:

Chain and independent motels in the Monroe/West Monroe area.

Bed and Breakfasts:

Boscobel Cottage, 185 Cordell Lane, Monroe, LA 71202. 325-1550 or 1-800-749-1928.

Rose Lee Inn, 318 Trenton St., West Monroe, LA 71291. 322-4090 or 322-5998.

For a complete listing of accommodations, contact the Monroe/West Monroe Convention and Visitors Bureau.

Restaurants:

New Orleans Cafe, Washington Plaza, 300 Washington St., Monroe, LA 71201. 323-8996. Lunch: Mon.-Fri., 11 A.M.-4 P.M. Dinner: Mon.-Sat., 4-10 P.M.

Old Dutch Bakery, 208 Lake St., Lake Providence, LA 71254. 559-1574. Tues.-Fri., 6:30 A.M.-5 P.M.; Sat., 6:30 A.M.-4 P.M.

Warehouse No. 1 Restaurant, One Olive St., Monroe, LA 71201. 322-1340. Mon.-Thurs., 5-9 P.M.; Fri. and Sat., 5-9:30 P.M.

For a complete listing of restaurants in the Twin Cities contact the Monroe/West Monroe Convention and Visitors Bureau.

Major Annual Events:

Lights Along the Lake, Lake Providence—Weekend after Thanksgiving–weekend after New Year's Day.

Louisiana Art & Folk Festival, Columbia—Second weekend in October.

Louisiana Soul Food and Heritage Festival, Lake Providence— Second Saturday in June.

Winterfest, Twin Cities—December.

21

A COUNTRY-WESTERN COLLEGE TOWN

(F)

Every Saturday night an expectant crowd gathers in Ruston's Dixie Theater. As the house lights dim, the excitement mounts. Suddenly, the audience erupts into applause as Jimmy Howard steps into the spotlight to start another session of north Louisiana's fastest-growing country music show, the **"Dixie Jamboree."**

After a rousing opener by Myrtle Branch and the Dixie Jamboree Band, rising stars in the Nashville music galaxy test their sparkle before the eager-to-be-pleased throng. The crowd responds by offering floral tributes to performers who have caught their fancy.

The enthusiastic audience is part of the spectacle at these family-oriented shows. Partners of all ages, decked out in denim outfits and leather boots, execute lively steps on the dance floor in front of the stage. To join the agile audience at the eight-year-old "Dixie Jamboree," take Interstate 20 Exit 85 South, follow Trenton Street (U.S. 167 South) to Alabama Street, turn left on Alabama for one block, and right to the theater parking lot on North Vienna Street.

Participating in the "Dixie Jamboree" is one of many pleasurable ways to enjoy yourself in Ruston. Stop by the **Ruston/Lincoln Convention & Visitors Bureau** at 900 N. Trenton Street for information on more sights to see and things to do. Be sure to include the **Lincoln Parish Museum,**

Lincoln Parish Museum, in the Kidd-Davis house. (Photo by Wendy Byers, courtesy Ruston/Lincoln Convention & Visitors Bureau)

on North Vienna Street a few blocks north of the Dixie Theater, in your itinerary. You will enjoy browsing through the museum's delightful exhibits in one of Ruston's oldest homes—the white-columned, eight-gabled Kidd-Davis house. It was built in 1885, one year after Ruston, a post-Civil War railroad boomtown, was established. The museum's spacious rooms are filled with period furniture, antique doll houses, and historical keepsakes of the region.

Ruston's downtown is alive with activity on most weekends. Shoppers meander in and out of busy stores and visit in inviting cafes such as **Anthony's** and **The Coffee Mug.** At **Piney Hills Gallery** they find distinctive merchandise made by regional artisans. The Park Avenue store is a consignment marketing outlet for nearly one hundred juried artists whose mediums include jewelry, wood carving, puppets, pottery, and furniture.

The Antique House, at the foot of Alabama Street, is another unusual venue for shopping. The vintage dwelling is owned by John and Margaret Colvin, who live among the antique beds, sideboards, and other furnishings they sell in their roomy Victorian home. In the Victorian dwelling across the street from The Antique House diners enjoy **The Veranda Restaurant's** delicious steak and lobster dishes.

People-watching from a table in the **Trenton Street Cafe** is also a pleasant way to pass the time. The restaurant caters to the college crowd and features tasty burgers and salads.

Most of the young people you see in Ruston are students at **Louisiana Tech University,** Ruston's mainstay and a wellspring of entertainment and culture. The visitors bureau can alert you to university performances and give directions to some diverting campus attractions. Among them is the Louisiana Tech Gallery, on the fifth floor of the university's Wyly Tower. The gallery showcases creations of regional and national artists. Nearby, the Horticultural Conservatory overflows with cool greenery and delicate flowers and, in December, it is banked with pots of red and pink poinsettias. Christmas plants are also for sale. Zealous green-thumbers may request a tour of Tech's extensive nursery, where all sorts of ornamental plants and vegetables are grown.

Some of the horticultural department's plants and vegetables are sold in the Louisiana Tech Farm Salesroom. Here, you can also find fresh meat, milk, ice cream, and cheese from the university dairy, and fresh roses to take to the "Dixie Jamboree." Shop early because the floral stock is quickly depleted.

The Louisiana Tech Equine Center, locally known as Stallion Station, is to the rear of the Farm Salesroom. Visitors may tour the stables and other facilities and watch the horses exercise.

The Louisiana Tech campus is on U.S. 80 West. Watch for a sign identifying the Farm Salesroom. Wyly Tower and the Horticultural Conservatory are close by.

Ruston has a resident population of about 20,000, but the Louisiana Tech student body helps the community support more than 40 restaurants. Among them are a down-home trio of soul-food kitchens that dish up heaping plates of savory, stick-to-the-ribs food. **Bee's Cafe** and **Annie's Place** are in a neighborhood close to the Louisiana Tech campus; **Sarah's Kitchen** is on Lee Avenue near Interstate 20.

Jimmy Dowling, owner of 22-year-old **Dowling's Smokehouse,** has watched his hometown, and his competition, grow. But, sooner or later, newcomers hear about the incomparable hot sandwiches he makes in his small shop (on the Interstate 20

Service Road). As soon as they taste one, they become regular customers.

Barbecue is big in Western-geared Ruston. After you enjoy a few slices of the **Log Cabin Smoke House's** mouth-watering turkeys and hams in the tidy restaurant, you may want to have one shipped to your home.

At **Bar-B-Que-City,** across Farmerville Highway from Log Cabin Smoke House, the cook expertly turns a cut of beef into tender, saucy slices and loads it on to plates alongside spicy chicken and ribs.

For a change of pace, try the **"Ole" Feed House,** north of the barbecue eateries, where customers enjoy an all-you-can-eat catfish buffet.

A different dining experience is offered by **Jarrell's,** a ladies' fashions and men's accessories store that plans a gourmet brunch and style show for customers on the second Saturday and second and third Tuesday of the month. Take-out orders and recipes are so often requested at these reservation-only affairs that Sharon Jarrell, the proprietress, now stocks a customer-accessible freezer with containers of her gourmet specialties. She also compiled a handy cookbook that is on sale in the store.

Lincoln Parish Park, about three miles north of the Farmerville Highway restaurants, is a good place to go after treating yourself to gourmet goodies or bellying up to the barbecue. In the summer you can work off calories in the park's paddleboats and canoes or take a dip in the lake. When the weather's brisk, walk the 260-acre park's nature trails and enjoy its seasonal palette of scarlet and gold leaves.

Although hardwoods on the forested hillsides around Ruston stage a colorful autumn show, the rolling landscape is called the "Piney Hills Country." Thousands of the lofty evergreens shelter an undergrowth of flowering dogwood that brightens country roads every spring. The tree's pastel flowerets and neighboring fields of similarly hued peach blossoms are woven into a resplendent, pink and white tapestry.

When summer's warmth urges blushing peaches to displace springtime's pale flowers, Rustonians line up at **Mitcham Farms'** peach shed on Louisiana 544 West (West Cooktown Road) to buy some of the juicy, just-picked fruit that is the theme of their annual festival.

Mitcham Farms peaches are graded into three categories: gift box "fancies," harvest that is ripe and ready to eat, and overripe fruit suitable for cooking. To reach the peach shed at the farm, take Exit 84 off of Interstate 20. Go north to a four-way stop sign. Turn left (west) and proceed .7 miles to the Mitcham Farms sign at Louisiana 181. Turn right onto Louisiana 181 and travel 0.7 miles.

Ruston's halcyon country roads take two nationally acclaimed potters home to studios on the outskirts of town. Bruce and Tami O'Dell's West Cooktown Road potting shed, about a quarter-mile from Cooktown Road (Louisiana 544), is stacked with exquisitely decorated clay pieces shaped by Bruce and hand-painted by Tami. The creative duo's handiwork merited first-place honors in the 1992 U.S. Pottery Olympics and also took top honors in the Esthetic Division of the World Pottery Olympics.

The O'Dells use several different firing processes to turn out the one-of-a-kind pieces they sell at the **O'Dell Pottery Studio** in their home and in the **O'Dell Pottery Showroom** in Ruston. Their stock includes rare, high-fired, copper-red pieces as well as stoneware in traditional blues and earthtones.

Kent Follette fashions his own molds for the practical and beautiful stoneware he sells at his Pea Ridge Road workshop and Piney Hills Gallery, but his lead-free, oven-proof, microwaveable cookware is so much in demand that hand-throwing each piece is out of the question. To watch Kent Follette potters at work, call for directions to the **Follette Pottery Studio,** just off Louisiana 3072, west of the Farmerville Highway.

The natural beauty of Lincoln Parish also serves as a setting for performances of the **Louisiana Passion Play.** This moving, outdoor drama, staged on weekends in May through September is presented by a cast and crew who donate their time and talents.

Audiences watching a drama on the life of Christ in the sylvan countryside around Ruston may find it hard to believe that

the wild escapades of two of America's most notorious criminals came to an end just a few miles away. When Bonnie Parker
and Clyde Barrow roamed the highways around Ruston in
1934 they were interested in seeing just one well-known structure—the Ruston State Bank on Trenton Street. The infamous
criminals robbed the bank, kidnapped a local teacher and a
mortician whose car they stole when theirs gave out, and sped
out of town. A few weeks later they were ambushed in Mt.
Lebanon, west of Ruston.

Funeral services for the crime-spree confederates were held
in nearby Arcadia. The town chronicles their criminal
escapades in the **Bonnie and Clyde Museum** and also marks
this bit of local history by naming its monthly art, craft,
antique, and flea market **Bonnie & Clyde Trade Days.** More
than 1,000 dealers take part in this popular fair set up on
Louisiana 9 just south of town.

Some bazaar-browsers extend their shopping binge by visiting Arcadia's **VF Factory Outlet Mall.** Here, brand-name merchandise—sporting Vanity Fair, Lee, and Jantzen labels, to
name a few—is sold at bargain prices.

Area Code: (318)

Getting There:

Ruston is accessed via Interstate 20 from the east and west and
U.S. 167 from the north and south.

Where and When:

The Antique House, 210 E. Alabama St., Ruston, LA 71270.
255-3405. Mon.-Sat., 10 A.M.-5 P.M.; Sun., 2-5 P.M.

Bonnie and Clyde Museum, Arcadia Depot, Railroad Avenue,
Arcadia, LA 71001. By appointment only. Call Arcadia Sheriff's
Dept., 263-8455.

Bonnie & Clyde Trade Days, Inc., P.O. Box 243, Arcadia, LA
71001. 263-2437. Weekend before the third Monday of each
month. Sunrise-sunset. Parking fee. To get there, take Exit 69
off I-20 in Arcadia and proceed south for 3½ miles.

"Dixie Jamboree," Dixie Theater, 206 N. Vienna St., Ruston, LA 71270. 255-0048. Every Saturday night, 7 P.M. CST; 7:30 P.M. DST. Admission.

Follette Pottery Studio, P.O. Box 766, Ruston, LA 71270. 251-1310. Mon.-Sat., 8 A.M.-5 P.M. Call for directions.

Jarrell's, 1317 N. Trenton St., Ruston, LA 71270. 255-3350. Store hours: Mon.-Wed., Fri., and Sat., 9:30 A.M.-5:30 P.M.; Thurs., 9:30 A.M.-7 P.M. Brunch: Second and third Tues. and second Sat. of every month, noon. Reservations required. Admission.

Lincoln Parish Museum, 609 N. Vienna St., Ruston, LA 71273. 255-2031. Mon.-Fri., 8:30 A.M.-5 P.M. Free.

Lincoln Parish Park, Louisiana 33 (P.O. Box 979), Ruston, LA 71270. 255-8023. Summer hours: Mon.-Fri., 8 A.M.-7 P.M.; Sat. and Sun., 10 A.M.-8 P.M. Closes at 5 P.M. daily during the winter. Admission.

Louisiana Passion Play, 3010 S. Vienna St. (U.S. 167 South), Ruston, LA 71270. 255-6277. May: Fri. and Sat., 8:30 P.M. June, July, and August: Thurs., Fri., and Sat., 8:30 P.M. Sept.: Fri. and Sat., 8 P.M.

Louisiana Tech University, Ruston, LA 71272. For visitor information, 257-0211.

Equine Center, 257-4024. Mon.-Fri., 8 A.M.-4 P.M. Weekends by appointment only.

Farm Salesroom, Reese Hall, U.S. 80 West. 257-3550. Mon.-Fri., 8:30 A.M.-5:30 P.M.

Horticultural Conservatory, Lomax Hall, U.S. 80 West. 257-2918. Mon.-Fri., 8 A.M.-4 P.M. Weekends by appointment only. Free. Call 257-2918 for appointment to tour nursery greenhouses.

Louisiana Tech Gallery, Wyly Tower. 257-3077. Mon.-Fri., 8 A.M.-4 P.M. Weekends by appointment only.

Mitcham Farms, Route 2, Box 2644, Ruston, LA 71270. 255-3409.

Peach Harvest: June-July. Call ahead for product availability and hours.

O'Dell Pottery Showroom, 108 N. Vienna St., Ruston, LA 71270. 251-1409. Oct.-Dec.: Tues.-Fri., 10:30 A.M.-5:30 P.M.; Sat., 10:30 A.M.-3 P.M.

O'Dell Pottery Studio, 1805 W. Cooktown Rd., Ruston, LA 71270. 251-3145. Tues.-Sat., 10 A.M.-5 P.M.

Piney Hills Gallery, 206 W. Park Ave., Ruston, LA 71270. 255-7234. Tues.-Sat., 10 A.M.-4 P.M.

VF Factory Outlet Mall, 700 Factory Outlet Dr., Suite 102, Arcadia, LA 71001. 263-8553. Mon.-Thurs., 9 A.M.-7 P.M.; Fri. and Sat., 9 A.M.-9 P.M.; Sun., noon-5 P.M.

Note: Grambling University, home of Eddie Robinson, "the winningest coach in college football," is a few miles west of Ruston. Fans of the popular coach may want to drive to the campus and have a look at Robinson Stadium. This unusual structure is built into the side of a hill and is not visible from ground level. Spectators descend to their seats before the game and climb ramps to the parking lot after the fourth quarter.

Information:

Ruston/Lincoln Convention & Visitors Bureau, 900 Trenton St., Ruston, LA 71273. 255-2031. Mon.-Fri., 8:30 A.M.-5 P.M.

Guide Services:

Not available for this getaway.

Accommodations:

Chain and independent motels in Ruston.

Bed and Breakfast:

Melody Hills Ranch, 804 N. Trenton St., Ruston, LA 71270. 255-7127. Second location in Choudrant, 5 miles from Ruston.

For a complete listing of accommodations, contact the Ruston/Lincoln Convention & Visitors Bureau.

Restaurants:

Annie's Place, 900 Arlington St., Ruston, LA 71270. 251-3288. Mon.-Fri., 11 A.M.-'til. Closed July and August.

Anthony's, 109 N. Trenton St., Ruston, LA 71270. 255-9000. Mon.-Thurs., 11 A.M.-9 P.M.; Fri. and Sat., 11 A.M.-10 P.M.; Sun., 11 A.M.-2 P.M.

Bar-B-Que City, 1911 Farmerville Hwy., Ruston, LA 71270. 255-0535. Mon.-Sun., 10 A.M.-10 P.M.

Bee's Cafe, 805 Larson St., Ruston, LA 71270. 255-5610. Mon.-Fri., 5:30 A.M.-3:30 P.M.

The Coffee Mug, 804 N. Trenton St., Ruston, LA 71270. 255-7127. Daily, 2 P.M.-1 A.M.

Dowling's Smokehouse, East Woodward Avenue (I-20 Service Road East) (P.O. Box 761), Ruston, LA 71273-0761. 255-0028. Mon.-Fri., 9 A.M.-5 P.M. Closed July.

Jarrell's, 1317 N. Trenton St., Ruston, LA 71270. 255-3350. Brunch: Second and third Tues. and second Sat. of every month, noon. Reservations required. Admission.

Log Cabin Smokehouse, 1906 Farmerville Hwy., Ruston, LA 71270. 255-8023. Mon.-Thurs., 11 A.M.-8 P.M.; Fri. and Sat., 11 A.M.-9 P.M.

"Ole" Feed House, Farmerville Hwy., Ruston, LA 71270. 255-6668. Tues.-Sat., 5-9 P.M.

Sarah's Kitchen, 607 Lee Ave., Ruston, LA 71270. 255-1726. Mon.-Sat., 7 A.M.-8 P.M.

Trenton Street Cafe, 201 N. Trenton St., Ruston, LA 71270. 251-2103. Mon.-Wed., 11 A.M.-8:30 P.M.; Thurs.-Sat., 11 A.M.-9 P.M.

The Veranda, 209 E. Alabama St., Ruston, LA 71270. 254-1086. Lunch: Mon.-Sat., 11 A.M.-2 P.M.; Sun., noon-2 P.M.; Dinner: Mon.-Sat., 5-9 P.M.

Major Annual Events:

Christmas in the Pines, Ruston—December.

Dubach Chicken Festival, Dubach—September.

Dubach Chuck Wagon Races, Dubach—First weekend of July.

Louisiana Peach Festival, Ruston—Second week of June.

Mini Car Grand Prix, Ruston—March.

22

LOUISIANA HILL COUNTRY

Folks who live below sea level, in coastal areas of Louisiana, often shake their heads in disbelief when told there is a section of the Bayou State that can be described as "hill country." Their skepticism is probably due to the fact that Louisiana's forested knolls and grassy valleys are somewhat of a hidden treasure, since they are not bisected by a major freeway. But several scenic, two-lane highways do thread through this atypical Louisiana countryside just below the Arkansas border. One, U.S. 79, connects Minden and Homer, two congenial towns that are fun to explore on a hill country getaway.

Since Minden is just thirty miles east of Shreveport, some travelers might assume the community is a trendy suburb of Louisiana's second largest city. But residents of Minden's 160-year-old neighborhoods work together to maintain the small town ambiance they cherish. For instance, ten years ago they enthusiastically embraced the National Office of Historic Preservation's Main Street Program, a plan that has revitalized many small towns. Spurred by community support, the project attracted more than twenty new tenants to thirty restored, turn-of-the-century buildings in downtown Minden. Most of the new businesses are service-oriented, but some of the shops that front Main Street, a brick thoroughfare laid by prisoners in the early 1900s, appeal to visitors.

Temple Hardware is, perhaps, the most intriguing store

along Minden's reawakened Main Street. The building that houses it still has a hand-operated elevator and other nineteenth-century fixtures, including the original tin ceiling installed when Thomas Crichton and his family opened their hardware store in 1882. Crichtons still own the building, but the hardware store bears the name of its new proprietor, Chris Temple.

D Bar D Western Wear and **Her's Bridal** were well-received when they moved to Main Street, and comments by locals about the fashionable apparel featured in these shops soon attracted customers from surrounding towns and cities.

At first glance it seems that three antique, gift, and collectible shops are two too many for Main Street. But **Yesterday's, House of Gifts,** and **The Gift Shop** make a special effort not to duplicate each other's merchandise. Together, these shops plus **Minden Antiques & Gifts** on McDonald Street (at the foot of Main) and **Rose of Sharyan**—a floral enterprise that specializes in dried arrangements and country-style frills— offer a nifty selection of Louisiana foods, decorative items, linens, tableware, and much, much more.

As you leisurely saunter down Main Street exploring these shops and others, pause for refreshment at **Lisa Ellen's Cafe.** Lisa Ellen Vickers says her grandmother "had an apron on me since I was big enough to walk." So Minden owes this matriarch a round of applause for teaching Lisa Ellen skills she uses to prepare the delectable meals she, and her husband, Ken, serve at their cozy restaurant.

The northeast end of Main Street gives way to Minden's residential historic district, comprised of two churches and 69 homes built between the 1850s and 1940s. Most of the buildings reflect Queen Anne and Colonial Revival styles of architecture. The **Minden-South Webster Chamber of Commerce,** on the corner of Sibley Drive (Louisiana 7) and Broadway, has information on the historic district and can advise you of festival dates when some homes are open for tours.

Families who built Minden's oldest homes may have purchased shoes, clothes, and other goods from members of the **Germantown Colony,** a religious commune established in

The doctor's office at the Germantown Colony. (Photo by Mary Fonseca)

1835, six miles north of Minden. Germantown was settled by followers of Bernhard Mueller, a native of Germany who assumed the name and title, Count Leon. The hardy colonists farmed; raised silkworms; operated a cotton gin, a general store, and a blacksmith shop; and made cheese, butter, furniture, and numerous other items to sell.

Minden's Germantown Road leads to this historic site where a tour of three log structures built by the settlers is offered. Furnishings that belonged to "Countess Leon" and other members of the colony help visitors visualize the daily life of these ingenious, hardworking colonists.

Pine-crested slopes on the Germantown Road hint at the natural beauty you may enjoy at two parks near Minden. A four-mile drive on Louisiana 3008, north of Minden, brings you to **Caney Lakes Recreation Area,** a National Forest Service area with tranquil lakes that appeal to fishermen, water skiers, picnickers, and swimmers. Hikers enjoy Caney Lakes' 7.6-mile Sugar Cane Trail, a scenic National Recreation Trail that loops through upland pine groves and bottomland hardwoods in the Kisatchie National Forest.

(Photo by Mary Fonseca)

Caney Lakes provides a sylvan backdrop for the annual Caney-Dorcheat Triathlon. More than 150 athletes gather at the park every August to participate in running, swimming, and biking events included in this competition.

At **Lake Bistineau State Park,** on Louisiana 163, 17 miles south of Minden, outdoor vistas can be enjoyed from screened porches on 14 comfortable cabins, or while you take part in swimming, boating, and other activities offered in this 750-acre natural area. In the evening, join locals who drive to **Franklin's Grocery** on Louisiana 192 near the park to enjoy this old-time grocery/restaurant's delicious seafood and steaks.

Junketeers who favor bed-and-breakfast accommodations may prefer to stay at **Calloway Corners,** an intimate inn with a decidedly romantic decor. The house was used as a setting for four heroines created by a quartet of award-winning romance novelists. Eden, Jo, Mariah, and Tess lived in a fictitious town named Calloway Corners. But due to the efforts of innkeeper Jeanne Woods, the town is no longer a figment of creative imaginations. Since her Bed and Breakfast is outside the city limits of Minden and Sibley, Woods persuaded the Webster Parish police jury to establish a tiny, new town called Calloway

Corners. State highway signs now mark its location, a mere 440
feet on Louisiana 7. Calloway Corners has its own zip code and
a separate listing in the Webster Parish telephone directory.

Moody's, a soul-food restaurant that is a favorite lunch spot
of Minden's business crowd, is just a few minutes away from
Calloway Corners. These folks know good eats when they see
them, so join the crowd and feast on pork chops, turnip
greens, homemade pies, and the rest of Ernestine Moody's
tasty, down-home fare, all accompanied by the restaurant's "lip-
smacking good" hot-water corn bread.

If you are interested in gardens and orchards, be sure to stop
by **Sherwood's Greenhouses** on Louisiana 164 between Sibley
and Doyline sometime during your visit. Here, you can visit with
Sherwood Akin, a lively, unassuming gentleman who started his
small nursery in his retirement years. This unpretentious horticulturist solved a problem that had long confounded nursery-
men when he perfected a technique for growing mayhaw trees
in domestic orchards. Mayhaw fruit makes a delicious jelly, but
it had to be gathered in the wild before Akin developed his
process. He is presently the only nurseryman who sells rooted
cuttings of mayhaw trees. He ships them to 36 states and mails
seeds to 10 foreign countries.

The first mayhaw tree cultivated with Akin's technique is still
growing at his nursery, along with an orchard of nearly 1,000
mayhaw trees. In addition to mayhaws, Akin has a diversified
stock of unusual plants plus "U-Pick-Um" blueberry, blackber-
ry, and muscadine vines.

Memories of Sherwood Akin and other friendly people in
Minden will linger with you as you follow U.S. 79 north to
Homer. The 16-mile route passes near **Tall Timbers Lodge,** a
remarkably inviting Bed and Breakfast nestled in the rolling
landscape a few miles south of Homer. Judy and Meredith Davis
settle guests into Tall Timbers' large bedrooms, tastefully decorated with king-size beds and comfortable rockers, then urge
them to make themselves at home. On cold winter days, guests
like to gather around a massive stone fireplace in the lodge's
"great room." But when the weather warms, they congregate on
a pleasant patio alongside the Davis' private lake. If lucky

anglers catch some fish, Judy prepares them along with other flavorful dishes. While they wait for dinner, weekenders watch the white-tailed deer feed outside the lodge's picture window.

The atmosphere at Tall Timbers is so relaxing that many overnighters spend their days strolling the grounds, reading, and napping for an hour or two. But travelers who enjoy small towns with picturesque courthouse squares find a visit to Homer hard to resist. The town's Greek Revival-style courthouse is one of four antebellum courthouses still in use in Louisiana. Interested visitors are welcome to observe trials in a second-floor courtroom appointed with gleaming, nineteenth-century furnishings, but most folks prefer to take a turn around the courthouse square.

The handsome, 1890s building on the south side of the square once provided lodging for visitors who had business at court and for investors in Louisiana's burgeoning oil industry. Improved transportation robbed the elegant Claiborne Hotel of its high-tone clientele, so the hostelry was transformed into department stores that served the community until 1982. Then the city of Homer bought the historic building and turned it into an impressive museum devoted to the history and culture of north Louisiana.

The first displays in Homer's new **Herbert S. Ford Memorial Museum** were collections of World War I memorabilia and historic bells bequeathed to the town by longtime resident, Herbert S. Ford. Well-planned exhibits now supplement Ford's original collections, including a reassembled, 1860 log cabin that once graced the Claiborne Parish countryside, a hand loom from the Germantown Colony, and fashions from the nineteenth century, plus exquisite wildlife carvings by local wood sculptor, Rev. Cleburn Quaid.

Offices for the **Claiborne Parish Chamber of Commerce** are also located in the Ford Museum. Staff members distribute information on Claiborne Parish and provide visitors with directions and assistance.

Some delightful stores and an inviting restaurant also face the courthouse square. You can find attractive ladies' wear at **Exclusively Yours Boutique;** handicrafts fashioned by local

The historic bell collection at the Herbert S. Ford Memorial Museum. (Photo by Mary Fonseca)

Wildlife wood sculptures by Rev. Cleburn Quaid displayed at the Ford Museum. (Photo by Mary Fonseca)

The general store exhibit at the Ford Museum. (Photo by Mary Fonseca)

artists at **Barnyard Buddies & More!;** and apparel, accessories, gift items, and coffees at **Toni's.** Just a few steps away, you can browse through colorful kitchenware, stylish handbags, and gifts for men and children at **Merle Norman. Gantt's Trading Post** offers collectibles and a few antiques, while gifts of every sort may be found at **Claiborne Drugstore, The Margo Shop,** or **Homer Drugstore.** While shopping on the square, stop in **Lighter Side Restaurant** and try some of Cynthia Hill's scrumptious dishes. Her soups, entrees, and desserts are so good your taste buds fail to remind you that this creative cook's recipes are either fat-free or as low in fat as she can make them.

If one of the many festive events staged at the Claiborne Parish fairgrounds in Haynesville is scheduled during your hill country getaway, take a short, thirteen-mile drive and join in the merriment. At the Northwest Louisiana Dairy Fair and Festival you can watch a colorful parade and enjoy a weekend of music, amusement rides, and country fair events such as pie-baking contests and livestock shows. During Claiborne Parish's annual "Nite at the Fair," you can sample tasty dishes prepared by the best cooks in the area and dance on the fair building's wooden floor.

On the way to Haynesville, you may pass **Linder Motor Lodge and Restaurant,** a good choice for overnighters who like to stay close to town. The restaurant's homestyle food and hot-and-ready coffee pot are popular with Homer businessmen.

During Prohibition, making moonshine was an illegal but profitable occupation in the hills around Homer. In fact, Louisiana 146, which extends southeast from Homer to Vienna, was called "White Lightning Road" in recognition of the rum runners who frequently traveled it. Now, a lovely, seven-mile stretch of the highway takes daytrippers to **Lake Claiborne State Park,** a scenic, 620-acre recreational area that offers excellent fishing and swimming. On a lazy summer day, it is a pleasure to pack a picnic lunch and enjoy it while you gaze at water skiers gliding over the smooth lake.

Watching the moonlight reflect on Lake Claiborne adds to the enjoyment of dining at **Port au Prince Restaurant,** an over-the-water eatery on Louisiana 146 that specializes in charbroiled steaks and all-you-can-eat servings of fried catfish. Locals often gather here before heading to **Claiborne Country,** a country-western dancehall on Louisiana 9 east of Homer. Inside the huge hall, couples, and families with youngsters in tow, dance to the music of the Sounds of Gold band. The energetic musicians lure dancers to the floor with rhythmic waltzes, polkas, two-and three-steps, and line dances.

Area Code: (318)

Getting There:

Minden may be reached by taking Exit 47 from Interstate 20 east of Shreveport and following Louisiana 7 north into town. Access from the northwest is via Louisiana 7, and from the northeast via U.S. 79.

U.S. 79 extends to Homer from the northwest and southwest.

Louisiana 9 gives access from the northeast and Louisiana 2 from the east and west.

Where and When:

Barnyard Buddies & More!, 509 S. Main St., Homer, LA 71040. 927-3414. Mon.-Fri., 10 A.M.-5 P.M.; Sat., 10 A.M.-4 P.M.

Caney Lakes Recreation Area, District Ranger, P.O. Box 479, Homer, LA 71040. 927-2061. Swimming and picnic area closed Oct. 1-April 1. Camping and fishing open all year.

Claiborne Country, Louisiana 9 East, Homer, LA 71040. (501) 863-5462. Fri. and Sat., 8 P.M.-'til. Admission.

Claiborne Drugstore, 511 W. Main St., Homer, LA 71040. 927-3534. Mon.-Fri., 8 A.M.-5:30 P.M.; Sat., 9 A.M.-2 P.M.

D Bar D Western Wear, 619 Main St., Minden, LA 71055. 377-5008. Mon.-Sat., 9 A.M.-5:30 P.M.

Exclusively Yours Boutique, 511 S. Main St., Homer, LA 71040. 927-2929. Mon.-Fri., 9 A.M.-5 P.M.; Sat., 9 A.M.-noon.

Gantt's Trading Post, 513 S. Main St., Homer, LA 71040. 927-3696. Mon., Tues., Thurs., and Fri., 9 A.M.-5 P.M.; Wed., 9 A.M.-noon; Sat., 9 A.M.-4 P.M.

Germantown Colony Museum, Route 5, Box 96, Minden, LA 71055. 377-1875. Wed.-Sat., 9 A.M.-5 P.M.; Sun., 1-6 P.M. Admission.

The Gift Shop, 733 Main St., Minden, LA 71055. 377-6996. Mon.-Sat., 9:30 A.M.-5 P.M.

Herbert S. Ford Memorial Museum, 519 Main St., Homer, LA 71040. 927-9190. Fri., 2-4 P.M.; Sat., 10 A.M.-2 P.M.; Sun., 2-4 P.M.; and by appointment. Admission.

Her's Bridal, 728 Main St., Minden, LA 71055. 377-6669. Mon.-Sat., 9:30 A.M.-5:30 P.M.

House of Gifts, 615 Main St., Minden, LA 71055. 377-3064. Mon.-Sat., 9:30 A.M.-5:30 P.M.; Also Sun., 1-5 P.M., in December.

Homer Drugstore, 522 N. Main St., Homer, LA 70140. 927-3537. Mon.-Fri., 8 A.M.-5 P.M.; Sat., 8 A.M.-noon.

Lake Bistineau State Park, P.O. Box 589, Doyline, LA 71023. 745-3503.

Lake Claiborne State Park, P.O. Box 246, Homer, LA 70140. 927-2976.

The Margo Shop, 515 W. Main St., Homer, LA 70140. 927-2929. Mon.-Fri., 9 A.M.-5 P.M.; Sat., 9 A.M.-noon.

Merle Norman, 501 S. Main St., Homer, LA 71040. 927-6651. Mon.-Fri., 9:30 A.M.-5:30 P.M.; Sat., 10 A.M.-5 P.M.

Minden Antiques & Gifts, 107 McDonald St., Minden, LA 71055. 377-9607. Mon.-Fri., 9:30 A.M.-5 P.M.; Sat., 10 A.M.-4 P.M.

Rose of Sharyan, 712 Main St., Minden, LA 71055. No phone listed. Mon.-Fri., 9:30 A.M.-5:30 P.M.; Saturday, by chance.

Sherwood's Greenhouses, P.O. Box 6, Sibley, LA 71073. 377-3653. Mon.-Sat., 8 A.M.-6 P.M. Price list sent with SASE.

Temple Hardware, 509 Main St., Minden, LA 71055. 377-5065. Mon.-Fri., 8:30 A.M.-5 P.M.; Sat., 9 A.M.-noon.

Toni's, 505 S. Main St., Homer, LA 71040. 927-9155. Mon.-Fri., 10 A.M.-5 P.M.; Sat., 10 A.M.-4 P.M.

Yesterday's, 609 Main St., Minden, LA 71055. 377-7299. Mon., Tues., Thurs., Fri., and Sat., 10 A.M.-5 P.M.

Information:

Claiborne Parish Chamber of Commerce, Herbert S. Ford Memorial Museum, 519 S. Main St., Homer, LA 71040. 927-9190. Mon.-Fri., 9 A.M.-noon and 1-4:30 P.M.; Sun., 2-4 P.M. Call for Saturday hours.

Minden-South Webster Chamber of Commerce, 101 Sibley Rd. (U.S. 79) (P.O. Box 819, Minden, LA 71058-0819.) 377-4240. Mon.-Fri., 8 A.M.-5 P.M.

Guide Services:

Not available for this getaway.

Accommodations:

Privately owned motels in Minden and Homer.

Bed and Breakfasts:

Calloway Corners, Louisiana 7 (P.O. Box 85), Calloway Corners, LA 71073-0085. 317-2058 or 1-800-851-1088.

Tall Timbers Lodge, Route 1, Box 13-T, Homer, LA 71040. 927-5260.

Restaurants:

Franklin's, 2925 Franklin Rd. (LA 192), Minden, LA 71040. 377-3549. Thurs., Fri., and Sat., 5 P.M.- 'til.

Lighter Side Restaurant, 512 N. Main St., Homer, LA 71040. 927-4397. Mon.-Thurs., 8 A.M.-5 P.M.; Fri. and Sat., 8 A.M.-5 P.M. and 6-10 P.M. Boiled crawfish served on Friday and Saturday nights in season.

Linder Motor Lodge Restaurant, Louisiana 2/U.S. 79 North (P.O. Box 328), Homer, LA 71040. 927-2574. Daily, 11 A.M.-2 P.M.; 5-10 P.M. Coffee shop: 5 A.M.-10 P.M.

Lisa Ellen's Cafe, 515 Main St., Minden, LA 71055. 377-2881. Mon.-Fri., 9 A.M.-2 P.M.

Moody's Restaurant, 600 Frazier St., Minden, LA 71055. 377-5873. Daily, 6 A.M.-3 P.M.

Port au Prince, Route 1, Box 175B, Homer, LA 71040. 927-6792. Tues.-Sat., 5-9 P.M.

Major Annual Events:

Caney-Dorcheat Triathlon, Minden—August.

Choral and Lighting Festival, Homer town square—December.

Claiborne Parish Fair, Haynesville—Last week in September.

Claiborne Parish Jubilee and Art Show, Homer—First weekend in May.

Claiborne Parish Oil Patch Festival, Haynesville—Last Saturday in September or first Saturday in October.

Homeplace Acres Bluegrass Festival, Athens—First weekend in June and second weekend in September.

Independence Day Celebration, Homer and Lake Claiborne State Park—4th of July or Saturday following.

Jaycee Fair, Minden—October.

Lumberjack Festival, Springhill—September.

Minden Riding Club Rodeo—August.

Mt. Olive Christian School LRCA Rodeo, Athens—Last weekend in July.

"Nite at the Fair," Haynesville—April.

Oil Patch Pageant, Haynesville—August.

Wildlife Festival, Homer—September.

23

THE ODD COUPLE
(F)

Louisiana 1 starts in sandy Grand Isle, in the toe of boot-shaped Louisiana, and laces diagonally up the length of the state. As the last, forty-mile span of the highway threads northward from Shreveport, it joins Vivian and Oil City, two intriguing communities with styles reminiscent of those Neil Simon assigned to Felix Unger and Oscar Madison in his hit play, *The Odd Couple.*

Vivian is the "Felix" of the two. Her neatness and her appreciation of the finer things of life are reflected in the genteel ambiance that radiates through this turn-of-the-century town. One can easily picture Felix nodding his approval of the tasteful furnishings in **The Rose,** a charming 1890s guesthouse on Tennessee Street. Even overnighters who aren't as well versed in antiques and interior decor as he is are delighted with The Rose's inviting sun porch, its delightful rose garden motif, and its fragrant rose garden.

Bed-and-breakfast guests at The Rose are just a short walk from West Louisiana Avenue, Vivian's main street. On the way there, they saunter through a neighborhood of handsome homes built in the early 1900s. Some of them are dressed in holiday finery during Vivian's annual Christmas Tour of Homes. The tour is part of "Country Christmas," a week-long community celebration that features a Christmas parade and crafts bazaar, plus decorating contests, musical performances, and a Renaissance Christmas feast.

279

Vivian's **Redbud Museum** is housed in the town's former railroad depot at the foot of West Louisiana Avenue. During the Yuletide festival, the museum glows with lights and decorations. Carolers sing traditional songs, and storytellers entrance youngsters with tales of Christmases long ago.

When the sparkle of Christmas dims, Mother Nature redecorates the old depot with lovely, lavender blooms. These usually burst forth in March on a circle of redbud trees planted around the museum. These heralds of spring are the focus of parades, concerts, and other events that are part of Vivian's annual Louisiana Redbud Festival.

During these special events, and throughout the year, the Redbud Museum's volunteer staff greets visitors, explains the significance of displays in the depot, and provides information on local attractions.

Travelers of all ages enjoy **Stagecoach Junction Mall,** on the corner of Louisiana 1 and West Louisiana Avenue. The building's second floor houses a grand mélange of Americana items assembled by mall owners Charles and Cindy Alexander. A guided tour of the charming collection, appropriately displayed in settings such as a country store, a child's room, and even an old jail, is yours for the asking. Inquire downstairs, at **The Unique Shoppe,** a ladies' fashion boutique, or at **Big Boy's Diner** in the rear of the first-floor area.

Tempting though it may be, you may want to forego delving into Big Boy's homestyle fare until evening so you can stroll down West Louisiana Avenue and enjoy a delectable lunch or "Southern Plantation Tea" in **Vivian Antique Mall's** delightful **Garden Tea Room.** Here, you can see how the combined efforts of four talented entrepreneurs—Lafon Monroe, Linda Webb, Ellen Edwards, and Mary Dunn—turned an empty, old downtown building into a charming, well-stocked gift and antique store, accented by an inviting tearoom.

North Caddo Drugstore, a treasured holdover from the 1800s, is next door to Vivian Antique Mall. Sometime during your getaway, perch on one of the red leather stools in front of North Caddo's old-fashioned soda fountain and enjoy hot coffee, tasty sandwiches, and scrumptious ice-cream treats.

RE-Creations Musicke Shoppe & Studio, Vivian Antique Mall's other neighbor, would be remarkable even in a large city. But to discover a music store/studio/workshop specializing in unusual early and folk music instruments flourishing in such a small town is most extraordinary. Some of RE-Creations' shelves are lined with instruments such as *dumbeks* (drums from the Middle East), bowed and plucked *psaltries* (string instruments popular in the Middle Ages), Renaissance flutes, Scottish bagpipes, and American lap and hammered dulcimers. Other shelves hold Irish penny whistles, folk harps, and recorders, plus "mundane" music-makers such as banjos, mandolins, and guitars. Edith Duhon, owner of RE-Creations, makes many of the unconventional instruments featured in her shop and can play every instrument she sells. If RE-Creations doesn't make or stock the musical apparatus you want, Duhon can probably find it for you.

On the fourth Saturday evening of every month, Duhon puts a pot of coffee on, arranges some rocking chairs in a circle, and greets music lovers who look forward to her monthly "gathering." Some come to play their instruments; others to tap their toes to the bluegrass, country, gospel, folk and nostalgic pop music Duhon and her company provide. If you play, carry along your instrument. If not, bring a smile and a handshake and join the fun.

For Friday night entertainment, try the exciting auctions held at **Jones' Auction.** The variety of merchandise going on the block can be seen at Jones' Auction all day Friday. Bid on everything from housewares to jewelry to antiques.

These downtown stores and activities are complemented by two other shops. Crafters come from miles around to purchase inexpensive supplies at **The General Store,** a wholesale mart on Pine Street (Louisiana 1). The ever-changing stock includes dried flowers, picture frames, toys, linens, glassware, seasonal decorations, and baskets.

The map on back of the "Welcome to Vivian" brochure distributed at the Redbud Museum shows the route to **Porcelain Dolls by Deborah,** a home-based classroom, studio, and showroom owned by Deborah Festervand. She gladly explains the doll-making process to interested visitors and shows them some of her finely crafted dolls. If you have an antique or contemporary doll that needs repairs, new clothes, or a general freshening, bring it with you when you visit this knowledgeable and affable artisan.

The drive to Festervand's studio hints at the beauty to be found in the countryside around Vivian. Pretty redbud trees may star in the town's springtime show, but they cannot compete with the hundreds of pink-and-white dogwoods that form graceful chorus lines along surrounding country roads. The lithesome trees must, however, share their outdoor stage with a large corps of pumping jacks, the hard-bodied "soldiers" of the oil industry that rhythmically extract "black gold" from under the grassy blanket that covers the Caddo-Pine Island Oil Field, the largest producing field in north Louisiana.

Pastel-painted dogwood trees also enhance a beautiful garden at the 100-acre estate of Charles and Mable Kirby, in Hosston, seven miles from Vivian, via Louisiana 2. Crimson, violet, white, and pink azaleas pirouette along trails winding down from the Kirby's hilltop home, and their colorful costumes are reflected in a placid lake at the foot of the slope. The Kirbys have lovingly cultivated the hundreds of native and imported plants in their garden and enjoy sharing its beauty with visitors who call for an appointment. Good walking shoes are recommended for easier hillside strolling.

Weekenders who follow Louisiana 2 to the Kirby estate cross a bridge over the serene waters of Black Bayou. The Louisiana Nature Conservancy extols this moss-veiled waterway as "one of the most biologically rich and undisturbed natural places in the entire state." Consider packing a picnic lunch and enjoy it at Robert L. Nance Park, north of the bridge. This 20-acre green space on the banks of Black Bayou Lake offers fine spots for shore fishing, plus playground equipment, tables, grills, and restrooms.

If you would prefer to continue motoring through the countryside to enjoy the springtime color, drive eight miles north on U.S. 71 into Ida when you leave the Kirby estate. Stop to purchase coffee, soft drinks, or snacks at **Carroway's,** an old-time country store a few steps off U.S. 71. Ronnie Carroway oversees the family business his great-grandfather started in Ida in 1926.

From Ida, a seven-mile drive on Louisiana 168 brings you to Rodessa, on Louisiana 1 about seven miles north of Vivian. If youngsters in your party would enjoy the thrill of standing at the intersection of three states at one time, turn north on Highway 1 and drive a few miles to a sign marking the Texas border. Keen eyes are needed to spot the small cement marker at the base of a tree that indicates the common boundary of Louisiana, Arkansas, and Texas. It lies in the roadside clearing, east of the highway and south of the sign, in front of an abandoned store.

After you have experienced the pastoral pleasures in and around Vivian, drive 10 miles south on Louisiana 1 to Oil City, the "Oscar" of this north Louisiana "odd couple."

Oil City was the Ark-La-Tex area's first "wildcat town," born during the Caddo-Pine Island oil boom of the early 1900s. It was a boisterous, tent-town community that took over and spread beyond the boundaries of Ananis, a tiny settlement formed by traders, trappers, and farmers. Considering Oil City's rowdy start, it is not surprising that the town still displays characteristics similar to those of a hardworking roustabout. It is a little rough around the edges, but the town is proud of its heritage and the great contributions it continues to make to Louisiana's oil industry.

Nowhere is Oil City's pride more evident than at the **Caddo-Pine Island Oil and Historical Society Museum.** Signs on Louisiana 1 direct visitors to the museum's new, community-financed facility on Land Avenue, two blocks east of the highway. As you approach the museum, you detect the distinctive smell of oil in the air. It comes from a functioning pumping jack on the museum grounds. The oil-field aura evoked by this display is enhanced by a full-size oil rig and a collection of field equipment from the past and present.

Three historic buildings, all dating to Caddo-Pine Island boomtown days, are also part of the museum. The old Kansas City Southern Railroad depot, across from the main museum

A pumping jack at the Caddo-Pine Island Oil and Historical Society Museum. (Photo by Mary Fonseca)

complex, was often the first building seen by men rushing to Oil City to capitalize on the area's good fortune. Some boom-town period railroading and telegraph equipment is on display here, complemented by a large collection of early Caddo Indian relics and arrowheads. Some of these artifacts are 10,000 years old.

The other two buildings, a turn-of-the-century bank and a vintage post office, were very important to residents of Trees City, a "company town" constructed for workers and their fam-ilies by Benedum & Trees Oil Company. While walking through them, one can imagine the million-dollar deals the partners put together in their offices in the rear of the bank and picture the joy letters from home brought to homesick women who accompanied their husbands to this lonesome town.

But conditions in Trees City, the first company town in the United States, were at least better than those in Oil City. Joe Trees and Mike Benedum provided simple, but comfortable homes for their workers, plus churches, schools, stores, and community gathering places.

The Trees City Post Office.
(Photo by Mary Fonseca)

The Trees City Bank. (Photo by Mary Fonseca)

In the spacious, new building that houses the main exhibits of the Caddo-Pine Island Oil and Historical Museum, you can listen to a dozen or so boomtown residents describe conditions then prevalent in Oil City. Next, you can step through a tent into a full-size diorama of the chaotic canvas city that sheltered most of the area's roustabouts. Through other interactive exhibits, you can learn about the drilling of the first, over-water oil well in the world in nearby Caddo Lake.

These state-of-the-art exhibits, and others depicting the area's history, are supplemented with a host of fascinating presentations that help visitors step from the past to the future of the petroleum industry. These include displays of high-tech drilling equipment, colorful artworks crafted from oil field equipment, and videos that highlight the oil industry's contributions to the progress of the world.

Besides chronicling the history of north Louisiana, and its ongoing relation with the petroleum industry, the Caddo-Pine Island Oil and Historical Society Museum also serves as Oil City's tourist information center. The staff gladly assists visitors with directions, plus information on restaurants and sights in the area.

One of the eateries they always mention is the **Oil City Restaurant,** a tidy cafe a block from the museum. It serves well-prepared, homestyle food for breakfast, lunch, and dinner.

Although huge, unwieldy oil field equipment along Louisiana 1 in Oil City sometimes offends the eye, the terrain surrounding the highway provides some beautiful vistas. If the weather is nice, get a takeout order at the Oil City Restaurant and enjoy it at Earl G. Williamson Park, a 40-acre green space on the banks of scenic Caddo Lake. Looking out over this tranquil waterway, it is difficult to imagine the tumult and commotion one would have seen in 1911 when the first offshore oil well in the world was drilled in this section of the lake. The shore that was once a staging area for that historic accomplishment is now lined with picnic and camping facilities, tennis courts, a lighted softball field, a fenced playground, and swimming and fishing areas. The park entrance is just south of a Louisiana 1 landmark erected by Oil City businessman and booster W. C. ("Dub") Allen. This tower and its giant silver balls proclaim Oil City to be a "city on the ball."

Views of Caddo Lake are also an attraction at **Pelican Lodge** and **Summer Point Landing,** two popular catfish and steak restaurants that offer appetizing fare. A sign on Louisiana 2 directs patrons to Pelican Lodge on Pelican Lodge Road, 3½ miles south of Louisiana 2. Another sign, on Louisiana 169, east of Louisiana 1, shows the way to Summer Point Landing on Crouch Dam Road.

Enjoy even more outstanding views of Caddo Lake by turning west on Louisiana 538 from Louisiana 1. This route, which intersects Louisiana 1 just south of Earl G. Williamson Park, crosses the lake and takes you to the quaint little village of Mooringsport.

The modern bridge that spans Caddo Lake was built to replace an antiquated drawbridge that serviced Mooringsport from 1914. The new bridge affords an outstanding look at its historic predecessor, which had an ingenious, vertical-lift design that allowed tall oil equipment to pass beneath it. It is listed on the National Register of Historic Places.

You can learn more about the drawbridge, and about the history of this 158-year-old steamboat town, at **Mooringsport Mini Museum.** The tiny gallery, established and maintained by the Mooringsport Homemakers Club, is on your right about a block after you leave the bridge and come into town.

One of the museum exhibits tells the story of the *Mittie Stephens,* a paddle-wheeler that caught fire shortly after leaving Mooringsport. Sixty-nine of the more than 100 passengers aboard were lost as she sank into the depths of Caddo Lake. The ruins of the *Mittie Stephens* were recently located by the Mittie Stephens Foundation and docents can furnish more information on the recovery and possible public viewing of articles found on the ship.

Another popular exhibit in the Mooringsport museum highlights the career of native son, and well-known composer, Huddie ("Leadbelly") Ledbetter. Called the King of the Twelve String Guitar, Leadbetter wrote "Goodnight Irene," "Midnight Special," "House of the Rising Sun," and "The Ole Cotton

Fields Back Home." You can listen to these familiar hits at the museum, or, better yet, hear them at Mooringsport's "Leadbelly Era Celebration," an annual tribute to the folk singer held in October.

Across the street from the museum, at **Mooringsport Doll Gallery,** doll enthusiasts can chat with Penny Doyle, a talented professional who expresses her artistry not only by making dolls, but also through original sculptures and clay art.

Complete your visit to Mooringsport with lunch or dinner at Anne Dearing's **Belle of the Bluff** restaurant. This casual restaurant at the foot of the Caddo Lake bridge offers flavorful salads, sandwiches, and seafood dinners.

If you are uncertain about what to do next during your getaway, continue through Mooringsport and follow signs to Uncertain, Texas, so named because residents could not decide on a name for their town. This lakeside community of about 200 citizens is partially populated by weekenders who enjoy cabins by the water. Here you can visit **Caddo Lake State Park,** view works by local artists at **Mossy Brake Art Gallery,** and take a boat tour on Caddo Lake. Three or four small, but good, restaurants overlook the water; and a growing cluster of Bed and Breakfasts offers lodging.

Area Code: (318)

Getting There:

Vivian and Oil City are accessed from the north and south by Louisiana 1. East and west approaches are via Louisiana 2, or Interstate 20 connecting to Louisiana 1.

Where and When:

Caddo Lake State Park, Route 2, Box 15, Karnack, TX. (903) 679-3351.

Caddo-Pine Island Oil and Historical Society Museum, 200 S. Land Ave., Oil City, LA 71061. 995-6845. Mon.-Fri., 9 A.M.-5 P.M.; Sat., by appointment. Admission.

The General Store, 405 S. Pine St., Vivian, LA 71082. 375-5197. Mon.-Fri., 8 A.M.-5 P.M.; Sat., 9 A.M.-4 P.M.

Mooringsport Doll Gallery & Gifts, 127 Croom St. (P.O. Box 96), Mooringsport, LA 71060. 996-5226. Tues.-Fri., 9 A.M.-5 P.M.; Sat., 9 A.M.-3 P.M.

Mooringsport Mini Museum, 124 W. Croom St., Mooringsport, LA 71060. 996-7660 or 996-7490. Sat. and Sun., 2-4 P.M. Weekdays by appointment. Donations appreciated.

North Caddo Drug Store, 144 W. Louisiana Ave., Vivian, LA 71082. 375-2573. Mon.-Fri., 8:30 A.M.-6 P.M.; Sat., 8:30 A.M.-1:30 P.M.

Porcelain Dolls by Deborah, 10139 Festervand Rd., Vivian, LA 71082. 375-4576. Tours Mon.-Sat. by appointment.

RE-Creations Musicke Shoppe & Studio, 140 W. Louisiana Ave., Vivian, LA 71082. 375-4793. Tues.-Sat., 11 A.M.-5 P.M. Closed when owner is participating in Renaissance festivals.

The Unique Shoppe at the **Stagecoach Junction Mall,** 105 W. Louisiana Ave., Vivian, LA 71082. 375-5991 or 375-4580. Mon.-Fri., 10 A.M.-5 P.M.

Vivian Antique Mall, 142 W. Louisiana Ave., Vivian, LA 71082. 375-3300. Tues.-Sat., 10 A.M.-5 P.M. or by appointment.

Information:

Caddo-Pine Island Oil and Historical Society Museum, 200 S. Land Ave. (P.O. Box 897), Oil City, LA 71061. 995-6845. Mon.-Fri., 9 A.M.-5 P.M.; Saturday, by appointment. Admission.

Redbud Museum, West Louisiana Avenue (P.O. Box 1), Vivian, LA 71082. 375-5300. Mon.-Fri., 9 A.M.-4 P.M. Donations appreciated.

Guide Services:

Not available for this getaway.

Accommodations:

Hotels and motels in Shreveport.

Caddo Lake State Park, Route 2, Box 15, Karnack TX 75661. (903) 679-3351.

Country Inn Motel, 1032 S. Pine St., Vivian, LA 71082. 375-4730.

The Rose Bed & Breakfast, 314 Tennessee St., Vivian, LA 71082. 375-5607 or 375-3300.

For information on lodging in Uncertain, Texas, contact Uncertain City Hall, 789-3443; or Texas Tourism information, 1-800-888-8TEX.

Restaurants:

Big Boy's Diner, Stagecoach Junction Mall, 105 W. Louisiana Ave., Vivian, LA 71082. 375-5991 or 375-4580. Mon.-Wed., 10 A.M.-2 P.M.; Thurs.-Sat., 10 A.M.-8 P.M.

Garden Tea Room, Vivian Antique Mall, 142 W. Louisiana Ave., Vivian, LA 71082. 375-3300. Lunch: Tues.-Sat., 11 A.M.-2 P.M.; Southern Plantation Tea: Tues.-Sat., 2-4 P.M. by reservation.

Oil City Restaurant, 118 Land Ave., Oil City, LA 71061. 995-0248. Mon.-Thurs., 7 A.M.-6 P.M.; Fri. and Sat., 7 A.M.-8 P.M.; Sun., 8 A.M.-4 P.M.

Pelican Lodge Catfish Restaurant, 9615 Pelican Lodge Rd., Vivian, LA 71082. 375-3076. Tues.-Thurs., 5-9 P.M.; Fri. and Sat., 5-10 P.M.; Sun., 11:30 A.M.-6 P.M.

Summer Point Landing, Crouch Dam Road, Oil City, LA 996-6045. Tues.-Thurs., 5-9 P.M.; Fri. and Sat., 5-10 P.M.; Sun., noon-9 P.M.

For information on restaurants in Uncertain, Texas, contact Uncertain City Hall, 789-3443; or Texas Tourism information, 1-800-888-8TEX.

Major Annual Events:

Country Christmas, Vivian—Second week in December.

Country Crossroads Festival, Gilliam—Fourth Saturday in March.

Gusher Days Festival, Oil City—Third Saturday in May.

Louisiana Redbud Festival, Vivian—Third Saturday in March.

Monterey Days Festival, Vivian—Third Saturday in October.

Mooring's Port Fall Fest, Mooringsport—Second Saturday in October.

Rodessa Boomtown Day—Last Sunday in September.

The American Rose Center. (Photo courtesy The American Rose
Magazine, American Rose Society)

*The Jane Owen and Quintin T. Hardtner, Jr., Chapel at The Gardens at the
American Rose Center. A popular wedding site, the peaceful chapel is tucked
beneath tall pines and surrounded by the splendor of roses.* (Photo by Ed
Gage, courtesy The American Rose Magazine, American Rose
Society)

24

TIME TO SMELL THE ROSES
(F) (G)

When you feel you need to get away and "take time to smell the roses," there is no better place to do it than Shreveport. **The American Rose Center,** the largest park in the United States dedicated to our national flower, is located just off the Jefferson-Paige Road exit of Interstate 20 west of the city.

At the center, more than 100 acres are planted with 20,000 gorgeous roses. The Hudson Heritage Collection of Old Garden roses, a bed of thornless roses, tony patches of celebrity roses, and the "what's new" garden of beauties who have just made their debut are among 68 resplendent plots spread over the park like a vibrantly colored rug.

A stroll along the American Rose Center's rustic pathways is an excellent way to unwind into a relaxing getaway. Your eyes feast on flower gardens strewn with fountains, statues, and gazebos while you breathe in the delicate floral fragrance that drifts through the air.

The walkways join the headquarters of the American Rose Society with Windsound Carillon Towers, twine around a picturesque wedding chapel, and meander past a replica of a Japanese teahouse. During the Christmas season, these structures, and several holiday displays, are illuminated with the glow of more than one million lights. They serve as scenic backdrops for orchestras, choirs, dancers, and storytellers who entertain audiences at the American Rose Center's annual Christmas in Roseland spectacle.

Flower shows and art exhibits attract year-round crowds to Shreveport's **Barnwell Garden & Art Center,** a downtown complex of exhibit halls complemented by a glass-domed conservatory and an outdoor fragrance garden.

The Barnwell is one of many attractions in a linear park that borders the Red River near Shreveport's central business district. The urban oasis along Clyde Fant Parkway also offers picnic tables, exercise stations, bicycle and walking trails, and a Frisbee golf course. The newest addition to the park, **SciPort Discovery Center,** a hands-on science museum and Omnimax theater, is a favorite destination for youngsters.

The **Shreveport-Bossier City Sports Museum of Champions,** is across Clyde Fant Parkway from the Barnwell Center. At this entertaining museum, you can relive exciting moments in sports by watching videos featuring the approximately 100 north Louisiana athletes the museum honors. National and international champions acclaimed in striking displays include quarterback Terry Bradshaw, motorcyclist Freddie Spencer, golfer Hal Sutton, and an incredible roster of outstanding competitors in sports ranging from kick boxing to duck calling.

Follow your museum visit with a downtown walking tour to get in touch with the city's roots. Brochures available at any **Shreveport-Bossier Convention & Tourist Bureau Visitor Center** map out a route that passes many of the central business district's vintage buildings and churches.

Shreveport and Bossier City were established as settlements after Capt. Henry Miller Shreve and his crew removed a 165-mile logjam from the Red River in 1833. The sister cities' growth into a busy commercial and agricultural center was spurred by cargo vessels that were now able to navigate their way upriver. Shreveport's oldest building is a fitting repository for the **Spring Street Museum's** collection of antiques and mementos that chronicle life in early Shreveport-Bossier.

A block away from this historic building, yesteryear's vehicles and classic cars are the main attractions in a 1920s automobile showroom that is now the home of the **Ark-La-Tex Antique & Classic Vehicle Museum.**

Strand Theatre and the **Municipal Auditorium** joined the downtown skyline in the early 1900s. They are two of several arenas that host performances by the **Shreveport Symphony Orchestra,** the **Theatre of Performing Arts,** the **Ark-La-Tex Roundup,** and visiting artists listed on Shreveport's crowded calendar of events.

When you are on the section of the downtown tour that passes Texas Street, take a break at **Capers Deli.** Enjoy lunch in the popular, casual eatery, or nibble one of the restaurant's irresistible caramel-chocolate brownies.

The fine residences in Shreveport's Fairfield-Highland Historical District are very nice to come home to after a busy day in the CBD. Only a few of the original suburban estates built in the neighborhood survive, but the distinguished showplaces and bed-and-breakfast inns that surround them are just as appealing. Their architecture embraces Victorian, Old South, Colonial, and Mediterranean styles. Outstanding homes in Fairfield-Highland are pinpointed in a driving-tour brochure available at Shreveport-Bossier Convention & Tourist Bureau visitor centers.

The tour of the district includes two sections of Line Avenue, Shreveport's premier shopping street. There is a wealth of unique merchandise available in the avenue's inviting mix of stores. You may, for example, select authentic Williamsburg designs or Walt Disney classics at **The Golden Pineapple** gift shop, quality fashions at **Knox Goodman's Boutique,** hand-tied fly-fishing lures at the **Clearwater Rod & Fly Shop,** and presents for everyone on your list at **The Enchanted Garden.** Other distinctive Line Avenue merchants are listed in a handout available at Shreveport-Bossier Convention & Tourist Bureau visitor centers and Line Avenue shops.

The shopping corridor also offers restaurants to fit a variety of tastes. Gather around a table at **Bon Appetit** to enjoy fresh salads, sandwiches, and entrees while you look over the Louisiana products, kitchen gadgets, and gift items that fill the shelves around you.

Veggies and vitamin-rich drinks prepared at Line Avenue's **Earthereal Restaurant and Bakery** appeal to health-conscious diners. But, one can occasionally throw caution to the wind, cross the street, and indulge in the delicious fare prepared in the **Glenwood Tea Room.** The tearoom's scrumptious English Country House breakfast and hearty farmhouse lunch tea are served Monday through Saturday. Every Saturday friends gather to enjoy "the Queen's Luncheon Tea," a reservation-only event that honors Queen Victoria by featuring goodies associated with her 63-year reign. For tablecloth dining in the evening, try **Monsieur Patou, Your French Restaurant,** a AAA "Four Diamond" restaurant on the corner of Line Avenue and Pierrmont Road, or Line Avenue's **Fertitta's.** Preface your delicious entree at this long-established Italian restaurant with its excellent Anaheim pepper appetizer.

Shreveport's most prominent art museum is a block off of Line Avenue on Creswell Street. A sign along the avenue directs visitors to the azalea-rimmed park that frames the **R. W. Norton Art Gallery** with crimson blooms every spring.

The gallery is widely known for its exceptional collection of works by Frederic Remington and Charles M. Russell. After you view portrayals of life on the American frontier by these Western artists, there are still thousands of other fine artworks to contemplate. These include more than 300 pieces of Wedgewood china, hundreds of tapestries and paintings, and fine collections of early Colonial silver, antique dolls, and rare firearms.

Creations by many artists fill the Norton Gallery, but the **Meadows Art Museum** on the campus of Centenary College was specifically designed to house a 360-piece collection of oil paintings and watercolors by Jean Despujols, a French artist who later became an American citizen. During a 20-month journey from 1936 to 1938, Despujols immortalized the people of what is now Cambodia, Laos, and Vietnam by documenting their disappearing culture with his paintbrushes.

People and places in Louisiana are the focus of the diverse collection housed in the **Louisiana State Exhibit Museum— Shreveport.** Within the unusual, doughnut-shaped building that is the museum's home, there are artifacts ranging from a A.D. 1065 Caddo canoe to a 100-year-old covered wagon.

Children are intrigued by the one-eighth-of-a-mile-long arcade's handcrafted dioramas. Beeswax figures in twenty-two scenes illustrate activities in such industries as petroleum, timber mining, and farming. The museum is presently undergoing a 1.2 million-dollar face-lift that will allow it to add modern, interactive exhibits to the historic items presently displayed.

The state museum, and the **SPAR (Shreveport Parks and Recreation) Planetarium** next door, are two more Shreveport-Bossier City attractions that visitors on a family getaway particularly enjoy. Another is Fairgrounds Field, where baseball fans gather to watch the **Shreveport Captains,** the city's AA Texas League team compete with clubs from Arkansas, Louisiana, Mississippi, Oklahoma, and Texas. And from November through March, the **Shreveport Storm** attract crowds to their exciting basketball games in Hirsch Coliseum.

Crowds also gather at the Louisiana State Fairgrounds, north of Interstate 20, when the ten-day state fair gets under way every October. The popular festival features name entertainers, stunt riders, carnival rides, and concessions, plus traditional livestock, arts and crafts, and 4-H club competitions.

Young people who miss the midway rides at the fair get their thrills on the Thunder Rail Roller Coaster and other exciting rides at **Hamel's Amusement Park.** The park also offers a completely enclosed Kiddie Barn with amusements that delight young children.

Hamel's is on East Seventieth Street at the foot of the Jimmie Davis Bridge in Shreveport—not far from another popular fun spot, **Water Town USA.** The West Seventieth Street water park has splash-down areas suitable for every age.

After enjoying activities at the two amusement parks, spend some quiet time on pastoral nature trails in **Walter B. Jacobs Memorial Nature Park.** Begin your outing with a visit to the spacious interpretive building where youngsters can explore small animal exhibits and a "touch me" table. A flyer available at the tourist information centers gives directions to the park, 14 miles northwest of Shreveport.

You may also want to squeeze in a visit to the **Pioneer Heritage Center** (open only on Sunday afternoons) on the campus of Louisiana State University in Shreveport. A tour of the center's six buildings is so interesting children do not realize they are being educated as well as entertained. Under the tutorship of a trained docent, they learn how North Louisiana pioneers who embraced diverse beliefs and customs built homes, made clothes, grew crops, and coped with sickness and hard times.

If the weather is not suitable for outdoor romps, follow directions on the back of the **Country Crafters' Village** and **Libbey Glass Factory Outlet Store** brochures—available at tourist information centers—and do a little shopping.

At Country Crafters you can find unique creations fashioned by more than eighty of the area's finest artisans. Wooden toys, custom-designed wreaths, appliquéd clothing, and gourmet foods are some of the items attractively displayed in booths that surround the mall's lunch pavilion and extend into several rooms.

A wide assortment of decorative glassware fills the jam-packed aisles at Libbey's outlet store. Tumblers, mugs, plates, and bowls are all offered at bargain prices.

After an enjoyable day, treat yourself to dinner at **Smith's Cross Lake Inn.** Select from the restaurant's full menu and admire the pleasing view of beautiful Cross Lake.

Spend the next day of your getaway sight-seeing in Bossier City. At Barksdale Airforce Base's **Eighth Air Force Museum** you can inspect a piece of the Berlin Wall, a silk escape map used by downed pilots in World War II, and an unusual display of A-2 leather jacket artwork. On the museum's grounds, there is a football field-sized exhibit of airplanes to explore.

Bossier City's **Touchstone Wildlife and Art Museum** offers a nice contrast to the man-made equipment featured at Barksdale. Follow directions on the back of the museum's flyer to see more than a thousand artistically arranged specimens of global wildlife displayed in replicated habitats.

End your excursion in Bossier City at one of Louisiana's finest racetracks, **Louisiana Downs.** Racing fans rave about the facility's luxurious restaurants and the panoramic view they enjoy from the glass-enclosed clubhouse. Off-track betting, year-round racing simulcasts and video poker machines are also offered here.

Louisiana Downs welcomes families to some of their facilities. Parents are encouraged to accompany children to the Kids Korner on the second floor where they can enjoy movies and video games together. Young people six years old and older may join their parents for lunch or dinner in Louisiana Downs' elegant **Pelican Room** or the **Sky Club.**

After the youngsters have had their fun, grown-ups may opt to cap the evening with a visit to Shreveport-Bossier's riverboat casinos. The *Isle of Capri* and *Horseshoe* are docked in Bossier City; **Harrah's** *Shreveport Rose* is berthed on the other side of the Red River.

Area Code: (318)

Getting There:

Shreveport and Bossier City are accessed from the south by Interstate 49, from the east and west by Interstate 20, and from the north by U.S. 71, Louisiana 1, and Louisiana 3. Commercial airlines service the Shreveport airport.

Where and When:

Ark-La-Tex Antique & Classic Vehicle Museum, 601 Spring St., Shreveport, LA 71101. 222-0227. Wed. and Thurs., 10 A.M.-7 P.M.; Sat., 9 A.M.-7 P.M.; Sun., 1-6 P.M. Call for winter hours. Admission.

Ark-La-Tex Roundup, LSU's University Center Theatre, 8600 Youree Dr., Shreveport, LA 71115. 688-5463 or 798-1122. Country and gospel music show: First and third Sat. of each month, 7:30 P.M. Broadcast live on KWKH radio. Admission.

American Rose Center, P.O. Box 30000, Shreveport, LA 71130-0030. 938-5402. Mid-Apr.–Oct.31: Daily, 9 A.M.-6 P.M. Christmas in Roseland: Day after Thanksgiving–Dec. 31, 5-10 P.M. Apr.–May and Sept.–Oct. are prime blooming seasons. Admission.

Barnwell Garden & Art Center, 601 Clyde Fant Pkwy., Shreveport, LA 71101. 673-7703. Mon.-Fri., 9 A.M.-4:30 P.M.; Sat. and Sun., 1-5 P.M. Free.

Bon Appetit, 4832 Line Ave., Shreveport, LA 71106. 868-1438. Store open Mon.-Sat., 9:30 A.M.-5:30 P.M. Lunch: Mon.-Sat., 11 A.M.-2:30 P.M.

Clearwater Rod & Fly Shop, 6505 Line Ave., #16 Pierremont Common, Shreveport, LA 71106. 868-8651. Tues.-Fri., 9:30 A.M.-5:30 P.M.; Sat., 10 A.M.-3 P.M.

Country Crafters' Village, 607 Mt. Zion Rd., Shreveport, LA 71106. 688-3650. Mon.-Sat., 9 A.M.-5 P.M.

Eighth Air Force Museum, Barksdale Air Force Base, Bossier City, LA 71110. 456-3065. June–Sept.: Daily, 10 A.M.-4 P.M.; Oct.–May: Wed.-Sun., 10 A.M.-4 P.M. Free.

The Enchanted Garden, 2429 Line Ave., Shreveport, LA 71104. 227-1213. Mon.-Sat., 10 A.M.-5:30 P.M.

The Golden Pineapple, 6401 Line Ave., #3 Merchants Square, Shreveport, LA 71106. 861-2085. Mon.-Sat., 10 A.M.-5 P.M.

Hamel's Amusement Park, 3232 E. Seventieth St., Shreveport, LA 71105. 869-3566. Spring and fall hours: Sat., 1-10 P.M.; Sun., 1-6 P.M. Summer hours: Wed.-Fri., 6-10 P.M.; Sat., 1-10 P.M.; Sun., 1-7 P.M. Admission.

Harrah's *Shreveport Rose* **Casino,** 401 Market St., Shreveport, LA 71101. 1-800-HARRAHS. Daily, 24 hours.

Horseshoe **Riverboat Casino,** 415 Traffic St., Bossier City, LA 71111. 742-0711. Daily, 24 hours.

Isle of Capri **Casino,** 77 Hamilton Rd., Bossier Ciy, LA 71111. 424-0700. Daily, 24 hours.

Knox Goodman's Boutique, 714 Azalea St., Shreveport, LA 71106. 861-3044. Mon.-Sat., 10 A.M.-5:30 P.M.

Libbey Glass Factory Outlet Store, 4302 Jewella Rd., Shreveport, LA 71109. 631-0367. Mon.-Sat., 10 A.M.-5 P.M., year-round; June-Dec.: Sun., 1-5 P.M.

Louisiana Downs, 8000 E. Texas St. (P.O. Box 5519), Bossier

City, LA 71171-5519. For race dates, times, and reservations call: 747-RACE or 1-800-551-RACE. Live racing: Apr.-Nov.: Wed.-Sun. Video poker and simulcasts offered Wed.-Sun. Call for hours.

Louisiana State Exhibit Museum, 3015 Greenwood Rd., Shreveport, LA 71109. 632-2020. Tues.-Sat., 9 A.M.-4:30 P.M. Admission.

Meadows Art Museum, Centenary College, 2911 Centenary Blvd., Shreveport, LA 71104. 869-5169. Sept.-May: Tues.-Fri., noon-4 P.M.; Sat. and Sun., 1-4 P.M. Call for hours at other times. Admission.

Municipal Auditorium, 705 Grand St., Shreveport, LA 71101. Call 673-5100 for schedule of events.

Pioneer Heritage Center, LSU-Shreveport, 8515 Youree Dr., Shreveport, LA 71115. 797-5332. Sun., 1:30-4:30 P.M. Closed mid-Dec.-Feb. Adult admission, children free.

R. W. Norton Art Gallery, 4700 Creswell Ave., Shreveport, LA 71106. 865-420l. Tues.-Fri., 10 A.M.-5 P.M.; Sat. and Sun., 1-5 P.M. Free.

SciPort Discovery Center, Clyde Fant Parkway, Shreveport, LA 71166. 424-3466. Wed.-Fri., 9 A.M.-5 P.M.; Sat., 10 A.M.-6 P.M.; Sun., 1-5 P.M. Admission.

Shreveport-Bossier City Sports Museum of Champions, 700 Clyde Fant Pkwy. (P.O. Box 1723), Shreveport, LA 71166. 227-0238. Mon.-Fri., 9 A.M.-4:30 P.M. Sat. and Sun., noon-4 P.M. Admission.

Shreveport Captains, Fair Grounds Field, Shreveport, LA 71109. Call 636-5555 or 1-800-467-3230 for game schedule and ticket information.

SPAR (Shreveport Parks and Recreation) Planetarium, 2820 Pershing St., Shreveport, LA 71109. 673-7827. Shows Wed. and Thurs., 1 P.M.; 1st, 2nd, and 3rd Fridays, 1 and 7 P.M.; Sat., 2 P.M. and 4 P.M. Admission.

Shreveport Storm, 401 Market St., #530, Shreveport, LA 71101. 425-SLAM.

Shreveport Symphony Orchestra—Call 222-7496 for schedule and location of performances.

Spring Street Museum, 525 Spring St., Shreveport, LA 71101. 424-0964. April 12-Nov.: Fri.-Sun., 1:30-4:30 P.M. Admission.

Strand Theatre, 619 Louisiana Ave., Shreveport, LA 71101. Call 226-1481 for schedule of performances.

Theatre of Performing Arts, P.O. Box 37404, Shreveport, LA 71122-7404. Call 221-7964 for location and schedule of performances.

Touchstone Wildlife and Art Museum, 3386 U.S. 80 East, Haughton, LA 71037. 949-2323. Tues.-Sat., 9 A.M.-5 P.M.; Sun., 1-5 P.M.

Walter B. Jacobs Memorial Nature Park, Blanchard-Furrh Road, Blanchard, LA 71107. 929-2806. Wed.-Sat., 9 A.M.-5 P.M.; Sun., 1-5 P.M. Free.

Water Town USA, 7670 W. Seventieth St. (P.O. Box 29009), Shreveport, LA 71149-9009. 938-5475. Open weekends in May, daily June-Aug., and Labor Day weekend. Mon.-Wed., 10 A.M.-6 P.M.; Thurs.-Sat., 10 A.M.-8 P.M.; Sun., noon-6 P.M. Admission.

For information on additional things to do and places to visit in Shreveport-Bossier City, request the Shreveport-Bossier Convention & Tourist Bureau's "Visitor's Guide."

Information:

Available at the following Shreveport-Bossier Convention & Tourist Bureau locations:

Business Office, 629 Spring St. (P.O. Box 1761), Shreveport, LA 71166. 222-9391 or 1-800-551-8682. Mon.-Fri., 8 A.M.-5 P.M.

Pierre Bossier Mall Information Center, 2950 E. Texas St., Bossier City, LA 71111. 747-5700. Mon.-Sat., 10 A.M.-9 P.M.; Sun., 1-6 P.M.

100 John Wesley Blvd., Bossier City, LA 71112. 226-8884. Mon.-Sat., 8:30 A.M.-5 P.M.; Sun., 1-5 P.M.

South Park Mall Customer Service Center, 8924 Jewella Rd.,

Shreveport, LA 71118. 686-7627. Mon.-Sat., 10 A.M.-9 P.M.; Sun., noon-6 P.M.

Guide Services:

Jimmy Turner, 4104 Maryland St., Shreveport, LA 71106. 865-9481.

Joyner Tour and Travel, Suite 1, 2829 Youree Dr., Shreveport, LA 71104. 861-4424.

Accommodations:

Chain and independent hotels and motels in Shreveport and Bossier City.

Bed and Breakfasts in Fairfield-Highland Historic District:

2439 Fairfield—"A Bed & Breakfast," 2439 Fairfield Ave., Shreveport, LA 71104. 424-2424.

The Columns on Jordan, 615 Jordan St., Shreveport, LA 71104. 222-5912.

Fairfield Place, 2221 Fairfield Ave., Shreveport, LA 71104. 222-0048.

Other Bed and Breakfasts:

The Lake at Lickskillet, 9760 Sonoma Rd., Greenwood, LA 71033. 938-7859.

The Rose, 314 W. Tennessee St., Vivian, LA 71082. 375-5607 or 375-3300.

For a complete list of accommodations, request the Shreveport-Bossier Convention & Tourist Bureau's "Visitors Guide."

Restaurants:

Bon Appetit, 4832 Line Ave., Shreveport, LA 71106. 868-1438. Lunch: Mon.-Sat., 11 A.M.-2:30 P.M.

Capers Deli, 417 Texas St., Shreveport, LA 71101. 221-1781. Mon.-Fri., 8:30 A.M.-2 P.M.

Earthereal Restaurant and Bakery, 3309 Line Ave., Shreveport,

LA 71106. 865-8947. Mon.-Fri., 9:30 A.M.-4 P.M.; Sat., 10:30 A.M.-2:30 P.M.

Fertitta's, 6301 Line Ave., Shreveport, LA 71106. 865-6301. Dinner: Tues.-Sat., 5 P.M.-'til.

Glenwood Tea Room, 3310 Line Ave., Shreveport, LA 71104. 868-3651. The Victorian Room—Afternoon Luncheon Tea: Tues.-Fri., 11 A.M.-4 P.M., by reservation only; Afternoon Tea à la Carte: Tues.-Sat., 2-4 P.M., reservations not required; The Queen's Luncheon Tea: Sat., 11 A.M. and 3 P.M., by reservation only. The Country Room & Tea Market—Country Breakfast: Mon.-Sat., 9-11:30 A.M.; Country Luncheon: 11 A.M.-3 P.M. No reservations required in The Country Room & Tea Market.

Monsieur Patou, Your French Restaurant, 855 Pierremont Rd., #135, Shreveport, LA 71106. 868-9822. Lunch: Tues.-Fri., 11:30 A.M.-2 P.M. Dinner: Mon.-Sat., 6-11 P.M.

Pelican Room, Louisiana Downs, 8000 E. Texas St., Bossier City, LA 71171-5519. 742-5555. Open during racing season through the seventh race of each day.

Sky Club, Louisiana Downs, 8000 E. Texas St., Bossier City, LA 71171-5519. 742-5555. Open during racing season through the seventh race of each day.

Smith's Cross Lake Inn, 5301 S. Lakeshore Dr., Shreveport, LA 71109. Dinner: Mon.-Sat., 5-10 P.M.

For a complete list of restaurants, request the Shreveport-Bossier Convention & Tourist Bureau's "Visitors Guide."

Major Annual Events:

Christmas in Roseland, American Rose Center—Day after Thanksgiving–New Year's Eve except for Christmas Day.

First Bloom Festival, American Rose Center—April.

Holiday in Dixie, Shreveport and Bossier City—April.

Louisiana State Fair, Shreveport—October.

Mardi Gras in the Ark-La-Tex, Shreveport and Bossier City—
January–Fat Tuesday.

Red River Rally, A Hot Air Balloon Uprising, Shreveport—July.

Red River Revel Arts Festival, Shreveport—October.

Amid the tulips in Hodges Gardens. (Photo courtesy Hodges Gardens)

Scenic view of Hodges Gardens. (Photo courtesy Hodges Gardens)

25

TAKE THE KING'S HIGHWAY TO PARADISE
(F) (G)

El Camino Real (the king's highway) was originally a crude trail pounded into the earth by humpbacked buffalos. As America's frontier moved westward, the dusty track developed into a busy trade route connecting Natchitoches, San Antonio, and Mexico City.

During the first decades of the nineteenth century, travelers avoided the northwest Louisiana section of El Camino Real. The road passed through an ungoverned "no-man's-land" used as a hideout by the most infamous outlaws of the time.

Louisiana 6 is built over this once-dangerous section of the king's highway. It too is a well-used commercial corridor, but today's leisure travelers identify it as the highway that connects two idyllic "paradises," Hodges Gardens and the Toledo Bend Reservoir.

Thousands of professional and amateur sportsmen have fished in Toledo Bend Reservoir, a 186,000-acre, man-made lake that straddles the Louisiana-Texas border. The wooded coves along Toledo Bend's ragged Louisiana shoreline shelter 32 marinas and several scenic parks that offer a variety of clean, reasonably priced accommodations. Most of the lodging is in customized trailers or woodframe motels. Several have kitchen units, restaurants, swimming areas, and other amenities attractive to families. Those that cater to the dawn-to-dusk fisherman are sparsely furnished with a bed, TV, and refrigerator.

New accommodations and recreation areas under development by the Louisiana Sabine River Authority are sure to attract more vacationers to Toledo Bend. The agency is constructing a multimillion dollar recreation complex on the Louisiana shore of the Toledo Bend Reservoir. An 18-hole, par 72 championship golf course with a club house, driving range, and golf academy is nearing completion and is scheduled to open in 1996. A 120-room Radisson hotel, 50 one- or two-bedroom condominiums, and a state-of-the-art conference center will soon follow.

Visitors who enjoy water sports such as swimming, water-skiing, and scuba diving can already enjoy a large, sandy beach area, pavilions, and other facilities at the Sabine River Authority's Twin Island Park. A second swimming area will be adjacent to the resort.

The **Louisiana Sabine River Authority's** Welcome Center, on Louisiana 6 at the foot of the reservoir's Pendleton Bridge, can advise you about the progress of these developments and assist you with finding accommodations that are right for your party. A map furnished by the agency or by the **Sabine Parish Tourist & Recreation Commission** office on U.S. 171 south of Many, will help you locate parks, restaurants, and other points of interest in the Toledo Bend area. Once you are situated, you will find a ready corps of guides, bait shops, boat rentals, and other marine services at your disposal.

There are a few places along Louisiana 6 between Many and the Pendleton Bridge that may catch your fancy. In front of the **Toledo Town** fishing lure factory, there is an outlet store/grill where you can hobnob with local anglers or buy bargain-priced tackle for the fishermen in your family. Just down the road, you can select items from **Armadillo Junction's** collection of folk art, handicrafts, antiques, and pottery, or you can enjoy **Country Skillet's** homestyle foods.

White oak baskets, handcrafted by Johnnie and Anabel Jordan, are exhibited at the Sabine Parish Tourist & Recreation Commission office. Representatives can direct you to the Jordan's **Cabin Crafts** workshop just off U.S. 171 in Florien.

After you have explored these roadside shops, do a little

sight-seeing in the Toledo Bend area. Follow the Louisiana Sabine River Authority's map to Pleasure Point and San Miguel Park or turn south onto Louisiana 191 from Louisiana 6 and motor down to the huge dam at the foot of Toledo Bend Lake. (If you are staying in the Hodges Garden area, drive south to Hornbeck and take Louisiana 473 to Louisiana 191.)

Once there, drive to the designated observation point and enjoy a spectacular view of the reservoir. If you call the Louisiana Sabine River Authority to make an appointment, you may also tour Toledo Bend Dam's hydroelectric plant. It generates electricity for three utility companies serving Louisiana and Texas.

Beautiful Toro Bayou branches off from Toledo Bend just below the dam. If you are enticed by its meandering waters, drive two miles up Louisiana 392 to **Tack-a-Paw Expeditions** Toro Bayou Outpost. Rent a canoe and enjoy a restful float or, if you are an experienced canoeist, ride the bayou's Class I and Class II rapids.

Just before sunset, cross the Pendleton Bridge to the Texas-side of the reservoir. Here, you can feast on **Pendleton Harbor Marina & Restaurant's** generous seafood and Southern-style entrees and enjoy spectacular waterfront scenery.

If you would rather indulge in some of the tasty fare offered on the Louisiana shore, ask welcome center representatives to direct you to **Myrtle's Tamale Hacienda.** Do not be put off by the eatery's nondescript exterior: inside awaits some of the most delicious Mexican food you will ever eat.

After dinner you may be able to join music fans of all ages to enjoy the family-style entertainment staged at **Ken's Country.** Ken's presents occasional shows featuring top Ark-La-Tex country bands and soul-stirring Southern gospel music at a hall two miles east of Toledo Town on the southern border of the highway.

Although it has world-class fishing, abundant wildlife, and numerous facilities for recreation, Toledo Bend may not measure up to your idea of utopia. If your dream world is strewn with magnificent flowers, panoramic vistas, and shady trails, **Hodges Gardens** is your kind of paradise.

When you see this 4,700-acre horticultural park on U.S. 171, about 15 miles south of Louisiana 6, you will be amazed to learn that it was once an abandoned quarry surrounded by an ugly, logged-out forest. The transformation from eyesore to Eden began when pioneer reforester A. J. Hodges and his wife, Nona, bought the property in the early 1900s. They realized that pine seedlings and wild flowers emerging around the quarry's discarded boulders could become the nucleus of a natural scenic garden. With vision and energy, the Hodges laid the foundation for the fabulous park that now surrounds the shores of a 225-acre lake.

There is always something blooming in Hodges Gardens' sixty-acre formal garden. Azaleas, daffodils, and tulips announce the arrival of spring, then step aside so daisies, zinnias, and hibiscus can soak up the summer sun. When the weather cools, the harvest moon casts a glow on chrysanthemums, roses, and other bedfellows blanketed by autumn's leaves. All but the roses join red-dressed hollies for Hodges Gardens' annual Christmas Lights Festival.

The well-attended holiday display is one of many special events held in this glorious garden. An Easter sunrise service draws thousands of visitors to a natural amphitheater on the banks of Hodges Gardens' rippling lake. On July 4, fun-seekers flock to musical performances, craft booths, and water-ski shows topped off with a spectacular fireworks display. Between these seasonal celebrations, amateur horticulturists gather for seminars in the park's educational center.

Casual visitors who seek a more restful communion with nature stroll the formal gardens at leisure, pedal their bicycles along a ten-mile network of paved roads, explore scenic nature trails, or drive two miles of unpaved, winding roads through Hodges Gardens' experimental forest.

Many travelers stay at **Toro Hills Resort** while visiting the gardens. This long-established hostelry is just across U.S. 171 from the gardens' gates. It has a motel complex, nine luxury condominiums, a distinctive restaurant, and a casual lounge. Guests tee off on an 18-hole championship golf course that is rated 73.6 par. They also enjoy a driving range, putting green, two swimming pools, lighted tennis courts, a playground, and a game room.

Toro Hills Resort and Hodges Gardens are about four miles south of Fisher, the only intact sawmill village left in Louisiana. Vintage homes in the hamlet's "silk-stocking row" were built by turn-of-the-century executives who ran the Louisiana Long Leaf Lumber Company. Their two-story office building and old commissary (that now houses the **Fisher Commissary Flea Market and Coffee Shop**) front a square bordered by Fisher's original post office, depot, and church. A charming antique opera house is often the setting for theatrical performances and other entertainments. Some of the box frame houses that extend from the old square still sport whitewashed picket fences and wooden sidewalks. During the Christmas season Fisher's restored buildings sparkle with tiny lights. And, every spring, during "Sawmill Days," the community is enlivened with a weekend of activities that includes music, crafts, horse and wagon rides, and lumberjack skill contests.

Other historical sites in Sabine Parish are remnants of the days when it was the western border of the American frontier. **Los Adaes State Commemorative Area** preserves the site of a Spanish outpost built in 1719. Exhibits, archaeological findings, and an interpretive center tell the story of the fort, which was the capitol of the Province of Texas between 1729 and 1772. Los Adaes was also the residence of the governor and the hardscrabble home of some 100 soldiers who doubled as carpenters, farmers, and herdsmen. The commemorative area is one mile northeast of Robeline on Louisiana 485, just off Louisiana 6.

Once Spain and America settled the boundary dispute that created the Sabine area's no-man's-land, the United States built Fort Jesup and commissioned Col. Zachary Taylor to establish law and order. Eighty-two structures housed officers and men assigned to the fort between 1822 and 1846. The troops secured the area from Indian raids, prevented slave uprisings, and helped to clear the Sabine River.

In 1846, a year after Fort Jesup was used as a staging area for forces entering the Mexican War, its usefulness as a frontier outpost came to an end. Now part of the **Fort Jesup State Commemorative Area,** one small kitchen is the only original structure still standing on the site, six miles east of Many on Louisiana 6. Tours conducted by costumed docents, monthly living history programs, and a reconstructed officers' quarters that houses the Fort Jesup museum help visitors imagine the life of a soldier on the edge of the American frontier.

If you have time to visit some of the attractions in Natchitoches, described in "Where Steel Magnolias Grow," continue east on Louisiana 6 after your visit to Los Adaes and Fort Jesup.

Area Code: (318)

Getting There:

The Toledo Bend and Hodges Gardens areas can be accessed via Louisiana 6 from the east and Texas 21 from the west. Interstate 49 and U.S. 171 are the major north-south routes into the area.

Where and When:

Armadillo Junction, Louisiana 6 West, Many, LA 71449. 256-3477. Daily, 9 A.M.-5 P.M.

Cabin Crafts, (HC 64, Box 630), Florien, LA 71429. 586-3636. Mon.-Fri., 8 A.M.-5 P.M.

Fisher Commissary Flea Market and Coffee Shop, Fisher, LA 71426. Thurs.-Sun., 11 A.M.-5 P.M. No phone available. Call the Sabine Parish Tourist & Recreation Commission for more information.

Fort Jesup State Commemorative Area, Louisiana 6 (Route 2, Box 611), Many, LA 71449. 256-4117. Daily, 9 A.M.-5 P.M. Admission.

Hodges Gardens, U.S. 171 (P.O. Box 900), Many, LA 71449. 586-3523. Daily, 8 A.M.-sunset. Admission.

Ken's Country, Louisiana 6 West, Many, LA 71449. Call 276-5735 for performance schedule. Admission.

Los Adaes State Commemorative Area, Louisiana 485 (P.O.

Box 127), Marthaville, LA 71450. Daily, 9 A.M.-5 P.M. Admission.

Tack-a-Paw Expeditions, Toro Road (P.O. Box 1565), Leesville, LA 71446. 238-0821. Toro Bayou Outpost: 286-9337. Call for information on canoe rentals and shuttle service.

Toledo Town Truck Stop, Corner of Louisiana 6 West and Louisiana 191, Many, LA 71449. 256-5613. Daily, 24 hours.

Information:

Louisiana Sabine River Authority, Louisiana 6 at the foot of the Pendleton Bridge (Route 1, Box 780), Many, LA 71449. 256-4112. Daily, 8 A.M.-4:30 P.M.

Sabine Parish Tourist & Recreation Commission, 920 Fisher Rd. (U.S. 171), Many, LA 71449. 256-5880. Mon.-Fri., 8 A.M.-5 P.M.

Guide Services:

Contact the Louisiana Sabine River Authority for a list of fishing guides and other marine services.

Accommodations:

Toro Hills Resort, U.S. 171 (P.O. Box 460), Florien, LA 71429. 586-4661. For reservations: 1-800-533-5031.

For complete information on accommodations in Sabine Parish, contact the Louisiana Sabine River Authority or Sabine Parish Tourist & Recreation Commission.

Restaurants:

Country Skillet, Louisiana 6 West, Many, LA 71449. 256-0510. Open 24 hours, daily.

Fisher Commissary Flea Market and Coffee Shop, Fisher, LA 71426. No phone available. Thurs.-Sun., 11 A.M.-5 P.M.

Myrtle's Tamale Hacienda, Louisiana 1215, Zwolle, LA 71486. 645-6975. Tues.-Sat., 11 A.M.-9 P.M.

Pendleton Harbor Marina & Restaurant, Texas 21 (P.O. Box 290), Hemphill, TX 75948. (409) 625-4912. Wed.-Sun., 5-9 P.M. or later.

The Sabine Room, Toro Hills Resort, U.S. 171 (P.O. Box 460), Florien, LA 71429. 586-4661. Mon.-Sat., 6 A.M.-10 P.M.; Sun., 6 A.M.-3 P.M. Restaurant will prepare box lunches to enjoy at Hodges Gardens' picnic areas.

Toledo Town Truck Stop, Corner of Louisiana 6 West and Louisiana 191, Many, LA 71449. 256-5613. Daily, 24 hours.

For a complete list of restaurants in Sabine Parish, contact the Sabine Parish Tourist & Recreation Commission.

Major Annual Events:

Easter Sunrise Service—Hodges Gardens.

Fisher Sawmill Days, Fisher—Third weekend in May.

Fourth of July Festival—Hodges Gardens.

Hodges Gardens Christmas Lights Festival—Friday after Thanksgiving–Dec. 31.

McDonald's Tournament, Toledo Bend—First weekend in June.

Oilman's Bass Classic, Toledo Bend—Weekend after Labor Day.

Sabine Free State Festival, Florien—Second weekend in November.

Tamale Festival, Zwolle—Second weekend in October.

Texas Oilman's Bass Invitational, Toledo Bend—Last full weekend in March.

26

THE WILD WEST
(G)

Bands of outlaws have not sought refuge in the coastal marshlands below Lake Charles since nineteenth-century pirate Jean Lafitte sailed into the area's secluded bays with his cohorts. But, in the vast, untamed region south of Louisiana's westernmost major city, cattle still graze in wetland pastures and are herded to market by cowboys sitting tall in the saddle.

These ranch hands do not travel dusty trails cut through buffalo grass. Instead, they use a 105-mile network of black-topped roads collectively known as the **Creole Nature Trail.** The trail begins at Exit 20 off Interstate 10 near Sulphur, Louisiana (just across the Calcasieu River bridge from Lake Charles), and follows Louisiana 27 south to the Gulf of Mexico. It parallels the gulf for more than fifty miles and turns north to rejoin the interstate east of Lake Charles.

Critters wilder than the little doggies rounded up every May and June also search for sustenance in the boggy wilderness surrounding the trail. Many of them live within the protective borders of the **Sabine National Wildlife Refuge**—the largest and most accessible of four federally supervised sanctuaries safeguarding the nutrient-rich ecosystem surrounding the Creole Nature Trail. Motorists driving the trail for the first time are startled by a warning at the border of the refuge: Beware!!! Gator Crossing. The words of caution, posted just below the wilderness-edge town of Hackberry, remind passing motorists,

In the wild on the Creole Nature Trail. (Photo courtesy Lake Charles/Southwest Louisiana Convention & Visitors Bureau and Bill Turnbull)

and sportsmen who cast their nets in roadside bayous rich with crabs and shrimp, that they are outsiders here and must respect the waterfowl and wildlife who inhabit the coastal prairie encompassed by the Creole Nature Trail. At the Sabine National Wildlife Refuge Visitors Center, an audioanimatronic Cajun spokesman urges visitors to familiarize themselves with the estuary while dioramas depicting resident and migratory wildlife ease the learning process.

Nearly four miles south of the Visitors Center, herons and egrets glide above the Sabine National Wildlife Refuge's 1½-mile Marsh Trail. Along the wooden walkway, long-legged shorebirds feed in the grass, mother gators guard fenced-off nests, and amphibians and reptiles slither through pools or sun themselves on the shore. Buzzing insects, especially bothersome deerflies, may be a nuisance to wildlife observers who set out without applying repellant.

If you climb the Marsh Trail's sturdy observation tower in the summertime, you may see fields of yellow American lotus blooming for miles around. During spring and fall, sightings of some of the thousands of migratory birds that rest along the Louisiana coast before continuing their journey on the Mississippi Flyway are a common occurrence. Bring along some binoculars for a closeup view.

Casual wildlife observers often end their exploration of the Creole Nature Trail at the Sabine National Wildlife Refuge Visitors Center, but hunters, fishermen, birders, and adventurous motorists trek by car and boat into the far reaches of the remote wilderness surrounding the trail.

If you decide to follow the Creole Nature Trail along the secluded, starkly beautiful coast, stock up on beverages and picnic provisions, be sure your car is in good condition, and fill the gas tank before setting out. Indoor bathroom facilities at the Sabine Wildlife Refuge Visitors Center are the last open to the public until the town of Holly Beach near the end of the Creole Nature Trail.

You will probably see more shorebirds as the Creole Nature Trail continues south through scenic marshlands, following Louisiana 27 until it intersects with Louisiana 82 along the shores of the Gulf of Mexico. Turn west and follow Louisiana 82 to Constance Beach, one of the few residential communities scattered along southwest Louisiana's isolated coast.

Follow signs to **Mickey's Shell Shop** and meet Mickey Guilbeaux and her husband, Rod, a Cajun raconteur. This amiable couple doles out shelling advice, tourist information, and friendly conversation to passersby. Mickey has shelled beaches all over the world and declares there is none finer than the one outside her front door. Huge containers of shells stacked outside her shop lend credence to this claim. Mickey collects nature's delicate castoffs between October and March—the best months for shelling on Constance Beach—and turns them into jewelry and decorative objects to sell in her store.

Consider renting a rustic apartment at Constance Beach if you want to hunt shells for your own collection, nest close to the nearby Holleyman-Sheely and Henshaw Bird Sanctuary, or just enjoy the peaceful sound of waves lapping outside your window.

Birders may want to engage a local escort to help them find new species to add to their identification list. Guides, charter boats, and rugged accommodations are also available to hunters and fishermen lured to these isolated marshes and bayous by Louisiana's reputation as a "sportsman's paradise."

Constance Beach is part of a 35-mile-long strip of sand fronting the Creole Nature Trail's coastal roadways. Driving is allowed on many sections of the beach, but to avoid an expensive tow out of soft sand, seek local advice before trying this. One popular driving area is east of Constance Beach at Holly Beach, an enterprising seaside community bisected by the Creole Nature Trail.

Grand Isle, a barrier island community described in "The Longest Street in the World," and Holly Beach were both nicknamed, "the Cajun Riviera," by locals and visitors. But, Holly Beach residents enhanced their claim to the title by incorporating into the **Cajun Riviera Association.** The group promotes the beach, its facilities, and the Cajun Riviera Festival held every August.

Holly Beach's fishing camps and tourist cabins are assembled into a sandy village. They offer shelter to swimmers who frolic in the surf, even though Gulf waters along this coast are quite often gray with sediment. On holiday weekends the community is the setting for beach parties that can be loud and boisterous.

Holly Beach fishermen sell fresh shrimp and seafood to drive-by customers, and the community's **G & G's Concessions** offers walk-up, snack-bar fare. Portable restrooms are available on the beach near the snack bar. **Lagneaux's Cafe,** the only full-service restaurant in Holly Beach, offers an appetizing, mostly Cajun menu and clean, indoor restrooms.

Creole Nature Trail souvenirs are available in Holly Beach at **T & T Grocery** along with handicrafts, groceries, and camp and fishing supplies. Three-dimensional shell compositions and sculptures, created by local artist Ron J. Robicheaux, are on sale at **Heck's Beachside Creations.**

When the Creole Nature Trail reaches the outskirts of Holly Beach, it continues east along the Gulf of Mexico until it turns northward (on Louisiana 82) to connect with the car ferry that crosses the Calcasieu River Channel. Keen-eyed passengers sometimes see dolphins curving above the river as they follow schools of shrimp to inland waters.

Louisiana 27 joins Louisiana 82 on the eastern shore of the Calcasieu River as the Creole Nature Trail extends to Cameron, a fishing and petroleum industry town that offers restaurants and overnight accommodations.

Side trips to the **Rockefeller** and **Lacassine** national wildlife refuges may be taken from Cameron. Both refuges are open from March 1 through October 15, but since few roads penetrate these pristine wildernesses, it is best to explore them by boat. The **Cameron Prairie National Wildlife Refuge,** north of Cameron, is under development, but visitors are welcome at the headquarters building. The **Cameron Chamber of Commerce** office on Louisiana 82 is a good source of information on these three refuges and on guides and boat charters available in the area.

Outside of Cameron, on the last leg of the route, the Creole Nature Trail passes the **Boudin Factory** in Hacketts Corner. Some connoisseurs of this Cajun sausage believe the cafe's links set a standard for others to follow. Try some before you end your trek along the Creole Nature Trail.

To complete this wilderness tour, drivers must connect with Louisiana 385 West and Louisiana 385 North when Louisiana 27 ends between Cameron and Lake Charles. Then follow Louisiana 171 back to the Interstate-210 loop.

You can get maps of the Creole Nature Trail from the **Lake Charles/Southwest Louisiana Convention & Visitors Bureau** on Lakeshore Drive near the shores of the city's namesake lake. Representatives also supply information on the city's urban attractions.

The "City on the Lake" started as a sawmill town in the early 1800s. By the time the century was drawing to a close, Lake Charles was a thriving mill center shaped by lumber barons who wanted fine homes built for their families. Since there were no architects in the city, the patriarchs relied on skilled carpenters to design and construct their residences. The craftsmen tried to

House from the Charpentier District in Lake Charles. (Photo courtesy Lake Charles/Southwest Louisiana Convention & Visitors Bureau)

outdo each other and embellished a twenty-block neighborhood of Victorian homes with elaborate fretwork, panelled doors, and other fancy woodwork. The area is now known as the Charpentier (carpenter) District and the carpenter-laced architecture on display is called the "Lake Charles style."

The convention and visitors bureau's Charpentier District walking-tour brochure gives directions to these unique homes, accessed by following Pujo Street from Lakeshore Drive. The district is at its best on Palm Sunday (the Sunday before Easter), when six homes are open and springtime azaleas color the yards. On other days, you can arrange to see the interiors of one or two by contacting the Lake Charles/Southwest Louisiana Convention & Visitors Bureau.

More can be learned about Lake Charles' early years at the **Imperial Calcasieu Museum,** so called because Beauregard, Allen, Jefferson Davis, Cameron, and Calcasieu parishes were once known collectively as "Imperial Calcasieu."

The museum is on the site of a cabin built by Charles Sallier, the first white man to settle the area, and the one honored in the city's name. Well-planned exhibits including three rooms of home furnishings, an apothecary, and a barbershop, plus some fine Audubon prints fill the museum's exhibit areas. Docents enhance the artistic and utilitarian artifacts with educational narratives. To reach the museum, follow Lake Street off of Lakeshore Drive and turn east onto Sallier Street to Ethel Street. After viewing the displays, contemplate the next stop on your itinerary under the sprawling branches of the 300-year-old Sallier oak in the museum's backyard.

If shopping is on the agenda, browse an attractive group of boutiques collectively known as the **Cottage Shops.** They carry gourmet foods, cookware, accessories, Louisiana festival posters, collectors' items, and Victoriana. To reach the Cottage Shops, continue east on Sallier Street until it becomes Twelfth Street. Turn right on Hodges Street—the second red light— and travel two blocks to the shopping area.

Two shops on Common Street, a few blocks away, are also fun to explore. **Francine's,** a specialty boutique and consignment shop, specializes in sizes 14-26. **Rethread's & Accessories** offers new and quality consignment clothing plus watches, jewelry, and accessories.

Collectors, and visitors searching for that "just right" accent for their home, may want to include Lake Charles' three art galleries in their shopping itinerary. Regional and national artists exhibit at the **Fine Art Gallery** on Ryan Street, and **Galerie Melançon,** an elegant Sallier Place showcase, specializes in contemporary art. Members of **Associated Louisiana Artists Gallery by the Lake** welcome visitors to their art classes in an old Melody Music store converted to a downtown studio. The space doubles as a showroom where fine art is offered for sale.

Mary Ann's Cafe, a downtown Lake Charles diner that serves some of the best hamburgers you will ever taste, is a good choice for lunch after your visit to the Associated Louisiana Artists Gallery by the Lake. The restaurant's well-worn interior has been frequented by locals for more than forty years.

If you prefer to sample southwest Louisiana seafood, try **Mr. D's on the Bayou** (near the Cottage Shops) or the **Jean Lafitte Inne,** on College Street just off the Interstate-210 loop. Mexican food aficionados will enjoy the well-prepared "South-of-the-Border" cuisine at **Casa Manana Mexican Restaurant** on Ryan Street.

If you want to enjoy the outdoors, head north of Lake Charles to **Sam Houston Jones State Park.** After picnicking in the approximately 1,000-acre park, you can stroll its scenic nature trails, rent a boat and relax on the West Fork of the Calcasieu River, or view wildlife in a fenced-in deer park.

When you are ready for more sight-seeing, drive to Sulphur, a few miles west of Lake Charles via the interstate, to see the local arts and crafts, including a large display of cornhusk dolls, exhibited at the **Brimstone Museum.** Children will really enjoy this display, but the small gallery's main focus is the mineral for which the town of Sulphur is named. The process of mining sulphur by liquefying it and pumping it out of the ground was developed here around the turn of the century. To reach the museum, turn right on Louisiana 27, left onto Parish Street, and right onto Picard Road at the far corner of Herman Frasch Park.

Adults seeking livelier entertainment enjoy games of chance offered on *Players* **Riverboat Casino** and *Star* **Casino** berthed in Lake Charles, or they cheer their horse across the finish line at **Delta Downs** in Vinton, west of Sulphur.

Area Code: (318)

Getting There:

Lake Charles is accessed by Interstate 10 from the east and west and U.S. 165 from the northeast.

Where and When:

Associated Louisiana Artists Gallery on the Lake, 106 Lawrence St., Lake Charles, LA 70601. 436-1008. Mon.-Sat., 10 A.M.-3 P.M.

Brimstone Museum, 800 Picard Rd., Sulphur, LA 70663. 527-7142. Mon.-Fri., 9:30 A.M.-5 P.M. Additional hours for special shows and exhibits. Free.

Cameron Prairie National Wildlife Refuge, Louisiana 27, ¾ mile north of Gibbstown Bridge (Route 1, Box 643), Bell City, LA 70630. 598-2216. Mon.-Fri., 8 A.M.-4 P.M.

Cottage Shops, Hodges Street, Lake Charles, LA 70601. Request information and directions from the Lake Charles/Southwest Louisiana Convention & Visitors Bureau.

Creole Nature Trail. Request information and map from the Lake Charles/Southwest Louisiana Convention & Visitors Bureau.

Delta Downs, North of I-10 on Louisiana 3063 (P.O. Box 175), Vinton, LA 70668-0175. For reservations: 1-800-737-3358. Lake Charles: 433-3206. Vinton: 589-7441. Thoroughbred season: Sept.-Mar. Quarter horse season: Apr.-Aug. Call for exact dates and hours. Admission.

Fine Art Gallery, 1424 Ryan St., Lake Charles, LA 70601. 439-1430. Mon.-Fri., 10 A.M.-5:30 P.M.; Sat., 10 A.M.-2 P.M. Free.

Francine's, 2700 Common St., Lake Charles, LA 70601. 491-0987.

Galerie Melançon, 241 Sallier Place, Lake Charles, LA 70601. 433-0766. Mon.-Fri., 9:30 A.M.-5:30 P.M.; Sat., 10 A.M.-3 P.M.

Heck's Beachside Creations, Holly Beach (HC 69, Box 12A), Cameron, LA 70631. 569-2589. Call for information.

Imperial Calcasieu Museum, 204 W. Sallier St., Lake Charles, LA 70601. 439-3797. Tues.-Fri., 10 A.M.-5 P.M.; Sat. and Sun., 1-5 P.M. Donations appreciated.

Lacassine National Wildlife Refuge, (HCR 63, Box 186), Lake Arthur, LA 70549. 774-5923. Office: Mon.-Fri., 7 A.M.-3:30 P.M. Refuge: Daily, sunrise-sunset.

Mickey's Shell Shop, Constance Beach (HC 69, Box 121), Cameron, LA 70631. 569-2159. Daily, 8 A.M.-6 P.M. Family owned, open when available.

Players **Riverboat Casino** and *Star* **Casino,** 507 N. Lakeshore Dr., Lake Charles, LA 70601. 1-800-275-6378. Open daily, 24 hours. One boat is docked while the other cruises.

Rethread's & Accessories, 2640 Common St., Lake Charles, LA 70631. 439-1881. Mon.-Fri., 10 A.M.-5 P.M.; Sat., noon-4 P.M.

Rockefeller National Wildlife Refuge, Route 1, Box 20 B, Grand Chenier, LA 70643. 538-2165. Office: Mon.-Fri., 7 A.M.-4:30 P.M. Refuge: Daily, sunrise-sunset.

Sabine National Wildlife Refuge, U.S. Fish and Wildlife Service, Louisiana 27 South (3000 Main St.), Hackberry, LA 70645. 762-3816. Visitors center: Mon.-Fri., 7 A.M.-4 P.M.; Sat. and Sun., noon-4 P.M. Marsh trail and Refuge: Daily, one hour before sunrise-one hour after sunset.

Sam Houston Jones State Park, Route 4, Box 294, Lake Charles, LA 70611. 855-2665. Apr. 1-Sept. 30: 7 A.M.-10 P.M.; Oct. 1-Mar. 31: 8 A.M.-7 P.M. Admission.

T & T Grocery, Holly Beach (HC 69, Box 63), Cameron, LA 70631. 569-2474. Daily, 6 A.M.-9 P.M. (until 10 P.M. during the summer).

Information:

Cajun Riviera Association, Holly Beach (HC 69, Box 63), Cameron, LA 70631. 569-2474.

Cameron Chamber of Commerce, P.O. Box 590, Cameron, LA 70631. 775-5222. Mon.-Fri., 8 A.M.-3:30 P.M.

Lake Charles/Southwest Louisiana Convention & Visitors Bureau, 1211 N. Lakeshore Dr., Lake Charles, LA 70601. 436-9588 or 1-800-456-SWLA. Mon.-Fri., 8 A.M.-5 P.M.; Sat. and Sun., 8 A.M.-3 P.M.

Guide Services:

Birders may want to request the Lake Charles/Southwest Louisiana Convention & Visitors Bureau's excellent "Birding Guide," which details locations and species found on the Creole Nature Trail and in other natural areas around Lake Charles. Guide referrals are also available.

Information on hunting and fishing regulations and guides for these activities are also available from the Lake Charles/Southwest Louisiana Convention & Visitors Bureau and the Cameron Chamber of Commerce.

Accommodations:

Chain and independent motels are available in Lake Charles and Sulphur and independent motels are in Cameron. There are rustic cabins and fishing camps at Cottage Beach, Holly Beach, and other beaches along the Creole Nature Trail.

Restaurants:

Boudin Factory, Louisiana 27, Hacketts Corner, Sweetlake, LA 70630. 598-3448. Mon.-Fri., 8 A.M.-5 P.M.; Sat., 9 A.M.-1 P.M.

Casa Manana Mexican Restaurant, 2510 Ryan St., Lake Charles, LA 70601. 433-4112. Sun.-Thurs., 11 A.M.-9:30 P.M.; Fri. and Sat., 11 A.M.-10 P.M.

G & G's Concessions, Holly Beach (HC 69, Box 99), Cameron, LA 70631. 569-2143 or 569-2162. Mon. and Tues., 10 A.M.-4 P.M.; Thurs.-Sun., 10 A.M.-10 P.M.

Jean Lafitte Inne, 501 W. College St., Lake Charles, LA 70601. 474-2730. Mon.-Thurs., 11 A.M.-10 P.M.; Fri., 11 A.M.-11 P.M.; Sat., 5-11 P.M.

Lagneaux's Cafe, HC 69, Box 24, Holly Beach, Cameron, LA 70631. Mon.-Fri., Lunch: 11 A.M.-2 P.M.; Dinner: 5-8 P.M. Sat. and Sun., 11 A.M.-9 P.M.

Mary Ann's Cafe, 110 W. Broad St., Lake Charles, LA 70601. Mon.-Fri., 10 A.M.-2 P.M.; Sat., 9 A.M.-2 P.M.

Mr. D's on the Bayou, 3205 Common St., Lake Charles, LA 70601. 433-9652. Mon.-Sat., 10 A.M.-10 P.M.

For a complete listing of restaurants in the Lake Charles area request a "Dining Guide" from the Lake Charles/Southwest Louisiana Convention & Visitors Bureau.

Major Annual Events:

Cajun French Music and Food Festival, Lake Charles—July.

Cajun Riviera Festival, Holly Beach—August.

Calca Chew Food Festival, Lake Charles—September.

Cal Cam Fair, Sulphur—October.

Calcasieu Preservation Society Palm Sunday Home Tour—Lake Charles.

Contraband Days, Lake Charles—First two weeks of May.

Louisiana High School Rodeo Championship, Lake Charles—June.

Louisiana National Airshow, Lake Charles—November.

Mardi Gras, Lake Charles—Tuesday before Ash Wednesday.

Southwest Louisiana Christmas Lighting Festival, Lake Charles—December.

Southwest Louisiana Fur and Wildlife Festival, Cameron—January.

Southwest Louisiana State Fair and Exposition, Lake Charles—September.

27

THERE'S MORE HERE THAN MEETS THE EYE
(F) (G)

The terrain in southwest Louisiana is so flat you can gaze across it for miles on a clear day. On some sections of Interstate 10 between Lafayette and Lake Charles, motorists see little more than prairie land and rice fields. But, there is more here than meets the eye. Just beyond the view of highway travelers lay towns that offer some delightful diversions. To learn more about these communities, turn off Interstate 10 at Exit 64 and visit Jeff Davis Parish's **Louisiana Oil and Gas Park.**

The screen of tall pines that shields this delightful area from the rush and noise of the highway also shelters the Jeff Davis Parish Tourist Information Center, picnic and playground equipment, a jogging trail, Lake Cocodrie (*cocodrie* is Cajun French for "alligator"), and a wooden derrick similar to the one used to drill Louisiana's first oil well. The outdated oil field equipment and a historic marker remind visitors that this noteworthy event took place about five miles from the park.

Lake Cocodrie is very popular with local anglers, especially since none of its namesake critters live in the placid waters. Several are housed in Louisiana Oil and Gas Park's *Chateau des Cocodries* (house for alligators), however. Since the thousands of alligators that live in south Louisiana's wetlands usually manage to stay out of sight—especially in the winter—the park staff keeps several young alligators in the chateau so visitors can get acquainted with them and learn about their habits and habitats.

After your rendezvous with these fascinating creatures, chat with the **Jeff Davis Parish Tourist Information Center's** friendly volunteers about the area's many attractions. Many of the places they will advise you to explore are in Jennings, a Jeff Davis Parish town that was recently listed as one of the nation's top ten rural tourism destinations by the U.S. Tourism and Travel Administration. Cross Interstate 10 and follow Louisiana 26 into Jennings to see why this Louisiana prairie community merited such a distinction.

Immediately after you cross the highway, you may notice small aircraft taking off or landing in a field to your right. Pilots of small planes often take advantage of a unique arrangement that allows them to land at the Jennings Airport and taxi up to the Holiday Inn. In October, owners of more than 50 Stearman biplanes—the open cockpit aircraft used to train pilots in World War II—gather in Jennings for the annual Stearman Fly-in. The sport plane enthusiasts who meticulously restore these historic airplanes invite the public to view them at the airfield, and they celebrate their yearly gathering by flying in formation over the area.

The Jeff Davis Arts Council and the Jennings Festival Association host Jennings Alive, a music, food, and crafts festival, on the same weekend as the fly-in. The town's spruced-up Main Street is a fine setting for the festival, which starts early and ends at midnight. Main Street's bricked sidewalks give entry to well-kept businesses such as drug stores and jewelers and to several attractive boutiques that complement the **W. H. Tupper General Merchandise Museum,** a unique country store museum with a fascinating history.

W. H. Tupper sold an astounding variety of goods at the general store he opened in 1910. For thirty-nine years, rural families traveled to Tupper's store twelve miles north of Jennings to buy everyday needs such as hammers, hats, dishes, and medicines, plus toys, candies, and other treats. When the store closed in 1949, there were about 10,000 items on the well-worn, wooden shelves. Bolts of cloth, bars of soap, spools of thread, and an array of other household goods were left in the store until they were moved to a warehouse in 1971. Then, in

1989, W. H. Tupper's grandson, Joe, offered the well-preserved stock to the city of Jennings.

It is fun to stroll through the re-created Tupper store and read price tags that make you long for the "good old days" and critique clothes and accessories considered quite fashionable in the 1930s and 1940s. After you leisurely survey Mr. Tupper's stock, you can step through a door in the rear of the store and enjoy the **Louisiana Telephone Pioneer Museum.** Visitors can view a video presentation on the development of communication through the ages before they study the well-planned exhibits in this walk-through museum. A *lagniappe* video on the land of the Acadians is also available. The audio-enhanced exhibits, built by Louisiana chapters of the Telephone Pioneers of America, show changes that have taken place during 100 years of telephone service.

On your way out of the telephone museum you will stroll past The Back Porch, the setting for a display of colorful, handmade quilts. If you are lucky, you may see expert quilters at work here.

Quilting is one of many crafts practiced by artisans who supply the **Old Magnolia Gift Shoppe.** The appealing store adjacent to the museum specializes in Louisiana-made products. It is jam-packed with handmade jewelry, Coushatta Indian pineneedle baskets, hand-painted china and clothing, plus a great selection of food products, regional books, and cookbooks.

Complimentary coffee is graciously offered at Old Magnolia Gift Shoppe. Enjoy a cup before spending a pleasant hour or two wandering through Main Street's other stores. Enticing boutiques near the museum are stocked with novel gifts, gourmet foods, artworks, and tasteful accessories.

Dedicated shoppers may want to include the **Jennings Antique Mall** and **The Jennings Auction House and Flea Market** in their plans. In the 1,000-square-foot, Main Street mall, dealers sell glassware, furniture, and other antiquated articles in thirty booths. Many customers who shop at the Cutting Avenue (Louisiana 102) flea market's fifty-five booths return to savor the excitement of the establishment's Monday-night auctions.

Antique toy in the W. H. Tupper General Merchandise Museum. (Photo by Burt Tietje, courtesy Jeff Davis Parish Tourist Commission)

Quilting demonstration at the W. H. Tupper General Merchandise Museum. (Photo by Burt Tietje, courtesy Jeff Davis Parish Tourist Commission)

When it is time to take a break from shopping, take a short drive to **Boudin King Restaurant** on West Division Street. Here, you can join the lunch time crowd that lines up to order hearty portions of Chef Ellis Cormier's celebrated *boudin,* or one of his other spicy, Cajun dishes. Head south on Main Street and continue as it curves into West Division Street to reach this popular restaurant. It is about four blocks past Louisiana 26.

If you prefer to sup Cajun-style, two "atmospheric" fast-food restaurants in Jennings may appeal to you at midday. At **Rocket Drive Inn,** a throwback to the '50s on the corner of State Street and U.S. 90, ice-cream treats with names like "Purple Cow" and "Brown Derby" round out a menu that features Frito pies and hamburgers. And at **"Mickey D's,"** across from the Holiday Inn, jukebox selections of '50s oldies entertain diners enjoying McDonald's familiar fare. Nostalgic artworks of the decade surround the center of attention in this '50s-themed restaurant—a red, 1959 Chevy Corvette convertible.

Prints similar to the ones that decorate Mickey D's are often the only art country folks can regularly enjoy in their home-towns. But Jennings philanthropist Ruth B. Zigler made it possible for folks living in, or passing through, Jeff Davis Parish to admire original paintings by world-famous artists such as James Whistler, Clementine Hunter, and C. C. Lockwood any time they want. In 1963, Zigler set up a trust fund to finance the art museum that bears her name and donated her family home to house the paintings and sculptures the museum would acquire. Two wings were added to the Clara Street home to provide additional exhibit space.

More than 200 works of art are shown on a rotating basis at the **Zigler Museum,** but the institution's treasures—a Rembrandt etching, a VanDyke self-portrait, and a Constable oil—are always on display. The Zigler's holdings also include the largest collection of works by noted black artist William Tolliver, fine wood and bronze sculptures, an antique gun collection, and a collection of "Best in Show" of the Wildfowl Carvers Guild. The museum is east of Louisiana 26, between West Division Street and U.S. 90.

The starting point of a driving tour outlined in a Jeff Davis

The Zigler Museum. (Photo by Burt Tietje, courtesy Jeff Davis Parish Tourist Commission)

The Little Brick Jail in Elton. (Photo by Mary Fonseca)

Le Petit Chateau deLuxe *in Mermantau, Louisiana.* (Photo by Mary Fonseca)

Tourist Commission brochure is just a few blocks from the Zigler Museum. The route passes stately, historic homes in Jennings, Lake Arthur, and Welsh. **Creole Rose Manor,** a charming Bed and Breakfast within walking distance of shops on Jennings' Main Street, is the only home open for tours. A Marian Prayer Garden at Our Lady Help of Christians Catholic Church in Jennings is also included in the excursion. People of all faiths are invited to stroll through this serene meditation garden.

The homes and gardens featured in the Jeff Davis Parish driving tour are indeed lovely, but there is a house about six miles southeast of Jennings that outshines them in every way. When you get your first glimpse of *Le Petit Chateau deLuxe* (The Small Luxury Castle), you may wonder if a tornado, like the one that transported Dorothy's house to Oz, picked up a turreted castle in France's Loire Valley and deposited it in Louisiana's broad prairie. Such is not the case. A father's dream and a son's dedication created the thirty-room chateau that majestically stands on the banks of the Mermantau River.

Louis Desormeaux, a native of Mermantau, fell in love with France's beautiful chateaux, and after many trips to France, he designed a magnificent home that incorporates features of four of his favorite chateaux. In 1955, his son, Philip, began landscaping the 19-acre grounds that would provide a proper setting for this jewel, and he has directed construction of the chateau since 1962. Philip did most of the interior work on the castle, using his woodworking skills to embellish three self-supporting staircases and floors and ceilings in several rooms. The younger Desormeaux and his family recently moved into his father's dream house, which is at long last nearing completion. If you follow the map in the chateau's brochure, you can meet Philip Desormeaux and enjoy the splendid tour he gives of *Le Petit Chateau deLuxe.*

The Mermantau river that flows past Desormeaux's home feeds into Lake Arthur, the largest body of inland water in south Louisiana. On the shores of this vast lake, in the town that bears its name, a well-maintained, seven-acre park provides leisure facilities that the whole family can enjoy. **Lake**

Arthur Park picnickers enjoy pavilions shaded by large oak trees. There is a sandy beach for swimming, plus covered cabanas, rental tubes and paddleboats, volleyball, tennis and basketball courts, playground equipment, restrooms, and concessions.

The Jean Lafitte Scenic Byway connects Lake Arthur with the **Lacassine National Wildlife Refuge.** During spring and fall migration, birds of many species rest in fields along Louisiana 14 and Louisiana 101, highways that are part of the byway. Because these roads have no shoulders, it is best not to stop for a closer look at the wildlife. You can do that at Lacassine Wildlife Refuge headquarters where a boardwalk extends into the marsh. You can also view the refuge's informative exhibits and fish from a public pier.

If you are intrigued by the wetland scenery at the refuge, you may enjoy spending a night at **La Retraite Lorrain,** a nearby bed-and-breakfast cottage on the grounds of a private home. Peaceful best describes the atmosphere at this hide-a-way near Bayou Lacassine, even though it is only a 10-minute drive from Interstate 10.

Scenery at the Lacassine Refuge area gives some hint of how southwest Louisiana must have looked to the Coushatta Indians when they migrated here in the late 1800s. Descendants of these native Americans live on a reservation near Elton, a community 16 miles north of Jennings via Louisiana 26. At **Bayou Indian Enterprises,** on U.S. 190 in Elton, an educational video about the Coushattas contains clips of the traditional dances they perform at the annual Bayou Indian Festival held in Louisiana Oil and Gas Park. You can also purchase longleaf pine baskets here, fashioned in designs the Coushattas have handed down for generations. Friendship beads and other Coushatta-made items, as well as handicrafts designed by artisans from other tribes, may also be found at Bayou Indian Enterprises.

A leaflet distributed by the Jeff Davis Parish Tourist Commission explains the history of The Little Brick Jail situated between the Elton Town Hall and Bayou Indian Enterprises. It was built in 1927 during a 30-day period at a cost of $621; the only jail of similar construction is in Texas. Prisoners in the two cells enclosed by The Little Brick Jail's 14-by-14-foot brick walls must have had a miserable confinement.

Before you leave Bayou Indian Enterprises, ask for directions to **Estherwood Rice, Inc.,** a few blocks away. You can take a 40-minute tour of this unique company that found its niche in the milling and packaging of specialty rices. Owner David Bertrand guides you through the milling process and shows you samples of fragrant rices such as popcorn, jasmine, and toro. He also demonstrates how Estherwood imprints the colorfully emblazoned bags the company uses to pack rice for its 700 or so clients. Hundreds of Estherwood customers send fragrant rices to their friends in Christmas-card-designed bags, and Bertrand will plan a special sack for you if you order at least 10 two-pound packs of rice.

Jaunts through the Jeff Davis Parish countryside certainly can wake up your appetite, but fortunately food cravings are easily satisfied in the parish's appetizing restaurants. Great tasting crawfish étouffée tops the menu of king-size Cajun entrees and steaks at **Donn E's** in Jennings. At **Cajun Tales** in Welsh, a fried alligator appetizer and two catfish entrees created by the chef are the most requested dishes. And everyone can find something to please them on **Nott's Corner's** five-page menu. Daily lunch specials are also featured at this Lake Arthur eatery, known for the big red crawfish that hangs outside the entrance.

Some restaurants in the region, such as **D.I.'s** in Basile and **Harris'** in Hayes, combine the attractions of tangy Cajun food and lively Cajun music, but at **The Red Rose Dance Hall** in Lake Arthur, dancing and socializing are the mix.

The Strand Theater in Jennings is another popular night spot. This 350-seat movie palace was renovated in 1993 and is now the home of the A Block Off Broadway Players. The community theater's performances are well-attended, as are the musical presentations, children's plays, and touring shows that fill the theater's calendar.

In January 1995, when the Coushatta tribe opened its **Grand Casino Coushatta,** night life in Jeff Davis Parish took on a glamorous, sophisticated air. The dazzling, 115,000-square-foot gaming hall is Louisiana's largest land-based casino.

Area Code: (318)

Getting There:

Jennings, Elton, Lake Arthur, and Welsh can be accessed from Interstate 10.

Where and When:

Bayou Indian Enterprises, U.S. 190 (P.O. Box 668), Elton, LA 70532. 584-2653. Mon.-Sat., 9 A.M.-5 P.M.

Estherwood Rice, Inc., 10105 Seward Lane, Elton, LA 70532. Call 584-5199 or 584-2391 for appointment Mon.-Fri.

Grand Casino Coushatta, Louisiana 165, Kinder, LA 70648. 738-7263 or 1-800-58-GRAND. Daily, 24 hours.

Jennings Antique Mall, 1019 N. Main St., Jennings, LA 70546. 824-3360. Mon.-Sat., 10 A.M.-5 P.M. and first and third Sundays of each month.

The Jennings Auction House & Flea Market, 202 S. Cutting Ave., Jennings, LA 70546. 824-0683. Mon., Wed.-Sat., 10 A.M.-5 P.M. Closed Tuesdays and Sundays. Auction every Monday at 6:30 P.M.

Lacassine National Wildlife Refuge, HCR 63, Box 186, Lake Arthur, LA 70549. 774-5923. Office open Mar. 1-Oct. 15, 7 A.M.-3:30 P.M. Wildlife observation year-round, daily, dawn-sunset.

Lake Arthur Park, Town of Lake Arthur, P.O. Drawer AK, Lake Arthur, LA 70549. 774-2211. Daily, 7 A.M.-9 P.M. Concessions April-September. Admission for special events.

LePetit Chateau deLuxe, P.O. Box 399, Mermentau, LA 70556. 783-3641. Tours: Tues.-Sat., 10 A.M.-3 P.M. every hour on the hour. Appointments appreciated. Admission 12 years and older.

Louisiana Telephone Pioneer Museum, 311 N. Main St.,

Jennings, LA 70546. 821-5532. Mon.-Sat., 10 A.M.-6 P.M.

Old Magnolia Gift Shoppe, 311 N. Main St., Jennings, LA 70546. 821-5532. Mon.-Sat., 10 A.M.-6 P.M.

The Red Rose Dance Hall, Louisiana 14, Lake Arthur, LA 70549. Call 774-2480 for days, hours, and live band schedule.

Strand Theater, 432 Main St. (P.O. Box 1249), Jennings, LA 70546. Call 821-5500 or 1-800-264-5521 for schedule.

W. H. Tupper General Merchandise Museum, 311 N. Main St., Jennings, LA 70546. 821-5532. Mon.-Sat., 10 A.M.-6 P.M. Admission.

Zigler Museum, 411 Clara St., Jennings, LA 70546. 824-0114. Tues.-Sat., 9 A.M.-5 P.M.; Sun., 1-5 P.M. Admission.

Information:

Jeff Davis Parish Tourist Information Center, Louisiana Oil and Gas Park (P.O. Box 1207), Jennings, LA 70546. 821-5521 or 1-800-264-5521. Mon.-Fri., 8 A.M.-5 P.M.

Guide Services:

Hunting and fishing guides:

Doug's Hunting & Fishing, 310 Calcasieu St., Lake Arthur, LA 70549. 774-2636.

Skipper's Guide Services, 426 E. Plaquemine St., Jennings, LA 70546. 824-4422.

Accommodations:

Bed and Breakfasts:

Creole Rose Manor, 214 Plaquemine St., Jennings, LA 70546. 824-3145. Admission for tours.

La Retraite Lorrain, P.O. Box 27, Hayes, LA 70646-0027. 622-3412.

For a complete listing of motel accommodations, contact the Jeff Davis Parish Tourist Information Center.

Restaurants:

Boudin King, 906 W. Division St., Jennings, LA 70546. 824-6593. Mon.-Sat., 8 A.M.-9 P.M.

Cajun Tales, I-10 Exit 54, Welsh, LA 70591. 734-4772.

D.I.'s Cajun Restaurant, Louisiana 97, Basile, LA 70515. 432-5141. Tues.-Sat., 5 P.M.-'til. Live Cajun Music: Tues., Fri., and Sat. Jam Session: Wednesdays.

Donn E's, Louisiana 26 North (Route 2, Box 704A1), Jennings, LA 70546. 824-3402. Mon.-Thurs., 6 A.M.-8:30 P.M.; Fri. and Sat., 6 A.M.-10 P.M.; Sun., 7 A.M.-7 P.M.

Harris' Cajun Restaurant, Louisiana 14 (P.O. Box 382), Hayes, LA 70646. 622-3582. Tues.-Sat., 11 A.M.-10 P.M.; Sun., 5-10 P.M. Live Cajun music: Wed. and Fri.; Country-Western music: Saturdays.

Mickey D's, 1740 Elton Rd., Jennings, LA 70546. 824-9454. Memorial Day–Labor Day: Daily, 6 A.M.-midnight; Balance of year: Sun.-Thurs., 6 A.M.-11 P.M.; Fri. and Sat., 6 A.M.-midnight.

Nott's Corner, 639 Arthur Ave., Lake Arthur, LA 70549. 774-2332. Daily, 7 A.M.-9 P.M.

Rocket Drive Inn, 1118 State St., Jennings, LA 70546. 824-2120. Daily, 9 A.M.-10 P.M.

Major Annual Events:

Bayou Indian Festival (Cowboy and Indian Festival), Louisiana Oil and Gas Park—June, on Father's Day weekend.

Cajun Food & Fun Festival, Welsh—April.

Fenton Red Beans & Rice Festival, Fenton—September.

Harvest Days, Welsh—Every Saturday in October.

Home Grown Music Festival, Lake Arthur—October.

Jeff Davis Parish Fair, Jennings Fairgrounds—October.

Jennings Alive, Main Street, Jennings—October.

Jennings Christmas Festival, Jennings—December.

Lake Arthur Christmas Hall of Trees, Lake Arthur—December.

Lake Arthur Christmas Parade and Boat Parade, Lake Arthur—December.

Lake Arthur 4th of July Festival—Lake Arthur.

Spring Extravaganza and Beach Party, Lake Arthur Park, Lake Arthur—May.

Stars and Stripes Festival, Jennings—4th of July.

Stearman Fly-in, Jennings Airport—October.

Welsh Fall Arts & Crafts Fest—First Saturday in October.

Welsh 4th of July Festival—Welsh Town Square.

Zigler Museum Christmas Festival, Jennings—December, special activities all month.

(Photo by Mary Fonseca)

One of the many frog murals in Rayne. (Photo by Mary Fonseca)

Waldfohrtshappelle, *a pilgrimage chapel built in 1890 in Roberts Cove.* (Photo by Mary Fonseca)

28

FROGS AND RICE?
OUI, CHERE, THAT'S NICE

On Monday—the traditional washday—nineteenth-century housewives had a mountain of clothes to wash and little time to prepare supper. New Orleans homemakers solved the problem by simmering a pot of red beans on the stove while they scrubbed away on their washboards. When the laundry was done, so were the beans. These hardworking ladies would be surprised to learn that the delicious solution to their washday problem survived the advent of modern washers and dryers to become a popular staple on many Deep South menus.

Red beans are replaced by frogs in the unconventional combination offered on this getaway. The duo is not spiced with the savory condiments used in the traditional dish, but the rich culture and fascinating heritage of three Acadia Parish towns—Rayne, Church Point, and Crowley—make it every bit as pleasing.

Long before Kermit the Frog became a Muppet, some of his deep-throated ancestors were croaking love songs in marshes and ponds around the newborn community of Rayne. The bass-toned ditties were so well received by the fairer sex that, by the 1880s, thousands of little *oua-oua-rons* (pronounced wah-wah-rons), as Acadian settlers called them, were jumping about the countryside. Three brothers, Jacques, Emond, and Gautran Weil, realized that the ample stock of green-backed amphibians could be exchanged for "green backs" they could spend. So, they started harvesting the bullfrogs and shipping them to biological supply houses.

The contributions the *oua-oua-rons* made to science diminished over the years because their habitat was gradually supplanted by more profitable rice fields. But citizens of Rayne came up with a unique way to immortalize the bug-eyed frogs who supplied one of the town's first industries. They adopted the *oua-oua-ron* as their mascot and started painting the town green. Within a few years they transformed Rayne into the "Frog Capital of the World."

Whimsical bullfrogs are featured in more than twenty murals in Rayne. The one on the front of Rayne City Court on North Parkerson Street, for instance, features a courtroom where a web-footed judge, lawyer, and jury are conducting a trial. On the side of Mr. Gatti's Pizza on North Adams Avenue, a frog prince prepares gumbo for his lady love. Who knows what the *oua-oua-rons* will do in ingenious renditions the town will add to reach its goal of fifty murals.

Most of the imaginative paintings are by Robert Dafford, a Louisiana muralist who has embellished many buildings in Europe and America. Others were done by talented residents of Rayne. Together the clever murals provide a distinctive setting for the town's popular frog festival and frog-themed Mardi Gras celebration.

The first frog you meet on a visit to Rayne is the gracious mascot that greets visitors who turn south from Interstate 10 at the Rayne exit. He points the way to this "frog-friendly" town and cordially invites you to "leap on in."

Accept his invitation and drive down the landscaped boulevard that leads to the center of town. On the entryway—appropriately named The Boulevard—colorful banners wave a cheery welcome. A hard-to-miss sign stationed near the **Rayne Chamber of Commerce** cautions you to slow down for a frog crossing. At the Chamber office you can ask for information and buy souvenirs and T-shirts decorated in a frog motif.

At **City Hall,** a few blocks south of the Chamber, you may be welcomed by the mayor himself—if he is not in a meeting. His Honor may even join you for a cup of complimentary coffee or present you with a gold lapel pin in the shape of—you guessed it—a frog.

When you leave City Hall, continue south on The Boulevard, keeping a sharp eye for "frog sightings" along the way. A map distributed by the Rayne Chamber of Commerce makes the fanciful murals easier to find.

The Boulevard becomes Clegg Street for a few blocks before turning southeast to join North Adams Avenue. Tarry near this bend in the road at **Lazy Dazy** and **Antik Dazy,** two charming shops in the 400 block of North Adams. Sara Boudreaux oversees the inventory of frog-figured merchandise, gourmet foods, elegant gifts, and fine collectibles in Lazy Dazy, while her mother, Marie Habetz, keeps tab on the intriguing goods and furnishings in the shop she opened next door to her daughter's.

Rayne's inviting cluster of antique emporiums also attracts shoppers. It takes a leisurely hour or two to cover all the furniture and bric-a-brac at **Comeaux's Antiques & Collectibles** and **Jubilee Rouge Antiques.** Then, dedicated shoppers can browse awhile at **Gwen's Crafts, Balloons & Gifts, Koury's Jewelry & Gifts,** and **People's Drugs & Gifts** to find the perfect present for someone back home.

Worthmore's 5, 10 & 25 Cent Store also offers customers gift items and much more. The five and dime's informal motto is, "If you can't find it here, forget it." You understand why as you make your way down the nearly sixty-year-old store's numerous aisles, which stretch through long counters topped by an amazing conglomeration of articles. Among them are can-can petticoats, cast-iron skillets, French drip coffee pots, hard-to-find hardware items, and frog souvenirs.

Good restaurants are nearby when you are ready for lunch or dinner. **The Warehouse Restaurant and Loading Dock Bar** is just two blocks from Worthmore's, next door to **Maison Daboval,** the well-appointed bed-and-breakfast inn Martha and Gene Royer opened in a nineteenth-century building they restored. Martha is an excellent cook, skilled in preparing traditional Acadian dishes. If you call ahead, she will teach you how to concoct one or two of the delicious recipes indigenous to Acadiana.

One of them, **Michael & Sun's** on East Texas Avenue, is probably the only Cajun/Korean Restaurant in existence. Michael Pinchoff and his wife serve flavorful foods representative of their respective heritages. Occasionally, when local farmers provide them, the restaurant features Rayne frog legs on the menu.

Oriental specialties and tropical drinks are the fare at Rayne's highly regarded **Galaxy Chinese Restaurant** located on North Adams Avenue, across from the Lazy Dazy boutique.

A few doors away, at **Sweet Pea's,** chef/owner Kevin Prejean serves a distinctive cuisine he describes as "progressive Cajun and grilled Louisiana seafood." Casual diners like the well-prepared plate lunches at **Gabe's Cajun Foods,** on The Boulevard, and **Boulevard Mobil's** twenty-four-hour grill and deli.

Entertainments are frequently scheduled at a pavilion and amphitheater on the site of Rayne's former train station near Maison Daboval and The Warehouse. Chamber of Commerce representatives can give you information on the craft markets, musicals, and special events held here.

More Cajun-style diversions may be found in Church Point and Lewisburg, about twelve miles northeast of Rayne, via Louisiana 35. Church Point is home to more Cajun musicians than any other community in Acadiana. Every Wednesday, some of them perform at the town's *Le Parc de Vieux Depot* (the park at the old depot) on Railroad Avenue. The lively jam sessions, held an hour or two before sundown, provide just a small sample of the music and camaraderie enjoyed at the town's **Saddle Tramp Riding Club.**

This vintage structure is most festive the Sunday before Mardi Gras when Church Point's *Courir de Mardi Gras* (Mardi Gras run) gets underway. Jovial riders, wearing homemade costumes and masks, gather there before riding to homes in the countryside. At each of the pre-arranged stops they collect ingredients for a pot of gumbo while engaging in high-spirited repartee. After a glittering parade down Main Street, they join friends and relatives at the clubhouse to feast on gumbo and other delicious goodies. Music and dancing end the fun-filled day.

Sprightly tunes fill the Saddle Tramp's Ebey Street (Louisiana 178) hall once again when **The Cajun Ladies** host their bimonthly *bals de maison* (house parties). At-home parties were one of the few entertainments available to early Acadian settlers because they lived in such an isolated area. In Church Point, for example, buggies were used for all sorts of travel well into the 1940s. Then a road to the town was finally built.

At their *bals,* The Cajun Ladies—a group of French-speaking matrons dedicated to preserving their Acadian heritage—dress in the traditional garb worn by their ancestors. They serve a delectable homestyle meal to their guests and join in dancing the Cajun two-step and Cajun waltz. They even serenade onlookers with Acadian folk songs upon request. Locals who can't make it to the popular *bals de maison* listen to radio station KSLO's live broadcasts of the sessions.

Folks who can't stop their toes from tapping when a Cajun band starts to play are known to gather at two old-time dance halls in Lewisburg, a few miles northeast of Church Point. Every weekend couples waltz and two-step around the wooden dance floor at **Guidry's Friendly Lounge.** There are Saturday and Sunday dances at **Borque's,** too, plus a Friday night jam session for up-and-coming musicians. To try your two-step at Guidry's and Borque's, take Louisiana 178 to Louisiana 357 north from Church Point. Turn left from Louisiana 357 onto Louisiana 759. When the highway dead-ends at a little mission church, turn right. Turn right again at the next street. Guidry's is on your right, about a block away. To reach Borque's, turn right at the Borque's sign on the paved road one block before the church and drive one block into the club's parking lot.

Some of the Cajun musicians who play accordions, fiddles, guitars, and triangles make their own instruments. German accordion factories that used to ship instruments to America were burned during World War II, so Acadian accordionists had to begin putting together instruments from items they could obtain at home. Musicians who played guitars and fiddles followed suit, and these self-taught skills were passed down and honed over the years. Now, talented craftsmen are able to fashion custom-made instruments for clients. One Church

Point accordionist, **Andrew J. Jagneaux,** shares the ins and outs of accordion making with visitors who call for an appointment.

While a succession of local musicians were perfecting their skills, farmers were learning better ways to grow rice, an integral part of Acadian cuisine. By the start of the twentieth century, transplanted wheat farmers from the Midwest, and German immigrants seeking a new life in America, were plowing fields alongside Acadian settlers.

Many German families settled in Roberts Cove, a rural community about four miles from Rayne. Some customs and celebrations they brought from the old country are still observed here. Religious gatherings and processions take place at the enchanting *Waldfohrtshappelle* (chapel in the woods) on the grounds of **St. Leo the Great Catholic Church.**

The *Waldfohrtshappelle* was originally a pilgrimage church, built in 1890 by members of the Benedictine order. A priest would go to the chapel once a month to lead the faithful in prayer. Now the cherished shrine stands on the site of the original St. Leo the Great Church and farm families gather there on the three days preceeding the feast of the Ascension to pray for good crops. On Corpus Christi and Palm Sunday, solemn marchers join processions that wind around the tiny chapel. The *Waldfohrtshappelle* may be reached by following White Oak Road from the foot of The Boulevard close to Interstate 10. A sign here points to Roberts Cove. Stay on White Oak Road until it intersects with Roberts Cove Road, then turn left onto Roberts Cove Road and continue to the church.

Most of the farmers who join their neighbors at the *Waldfohrtshappelle* to pray for a good harvest are rice planters. New varieties of rice, and techniques to cultivate them, developed at the **Louisiana State University Rice Experiment Station** are of great importance to them. At the university's research center on Caffey Road, you can watch an educational video about important elements of rice farming and follow it up with an escorted auto tour of LSU's rice fields. Depending on the time of year, you may see planting, growing, or harvesting methods while you are briefed about research projects in progress at the station. Take Louisiana 90 north from Rayne, turn right onto Caffey Road, and continue on Caffey Road about ¾ mile past Interstate 10 to the Louisiana State University Rice Experiment Station.

Much of the rice bordering roads around Rayne, Church Point, and Crowley feeds Acadia Parish's 11 rice mills, which produce more than 160,000 tons of rice every year. Visitors can get a firsthand look at the milling process at **ADM Milling Company's Doré Rice Mill** in Crowley's Rice Mill Row. To arrange a tour, drop by or call the **Crowley Chamber of Commerce** office, which shares space with the **Acadia Parish Tourist Commission** in the restored Frisco Depot near the Southern Pacific Railroad tracks in Crowley. The 1907 building at the foot of Parkerson Avenue (Louisiana 13) is accessed from the Crowley exit off of Interstate 10.

Tourist Commission representatives can also give you a handout to guide you on a walking/driving tour of East Crowley, the town's oldest residential area. A handful of the graceful, Victorian homes in this National Register Historic District retain their original architecture and decorations, but many others were damaged by hurricanes or updated by owners. Eminent novelist Frances Parkinson Keyes lived in the large house at 625 East Fourth St. more than ten years. Crowley was the setting for *Blue Camellia* and *Victorine*, two of the many novels she wrote there.

Blanchet-Romero House, the Acadian-style home that shelters the **Blue Rose Museum,** had been a family dwelling for fifty years by the time East Crowley's Victorian gems were built. The two-story, mortised-and-pegged cottage was constructed in Youngsville, Louisiana, of handmade bricks, Louisiana cypress, and *bousillage* (mud and moss plaster). Mr. and Mrs. Salmon L. Wright bought the home in 1964 and moved it to their property southwest of Crowley. They named it Blue Rose to honor Mr. Wright's father, Sol Wright, who developed Blue Rose rice and many other varieties. The Wrights furnished their new home with an assortment of valuable, unique, and historic items. Among the intriguing articles you see on an escorted tour are covered wagon chairs, Venetian glass chandeliers, turn-of-the-century wedding dresses, and Catherine of Aquitane's secret hollow liquor holder.

The Blue Rose Museum in Crowley. (Photo by Mary Fonseca)

To reach Blue Rose Museum, follow Louisiana 13 over the Southern Pacific Railroad tracks and drive south of Crowley for approximately 2½ miles. Turn right onto Airport Road and continue past the first stop sign to a shell road marked by a Wright Company sign. Turn left onto the shell road to the museum.

After you tour Crowley's historic homes, stop at some of the town's engaging shops. Artists in the area sell original arts and crafts at **The Gallery,** a North Parkerson Avenue shop sponsored by the Crowley Art Association. **Gail's Gifts** on North Second Avenue carries appealing items for all ages, including a collection of Cajun gifts, Mardi Gras dolls, cookbooks, music, and The Rice Pin—official emblem of Crowley, the historic Rice Capital of America. At **The Gift Box,** on North Parkerson Avenue, you'll find scrumptious Louisiana products plus gourmet coffees, seasonal items, and a fine assortment of gifts.

Hardware stores are not usually associated with romance, but **Dixie True Value Hardware** is an exception. In keeping with a tradition still cherished in some rural communities, brides choose china, small appliances, and housewares from

Dixie's plentiful stock. Their choices are displayed on about 25 "bridal tables" attractively arranged in the front of the store, each bearing cards with the names of the bride and groom. Customers come to Dixie to buy gifts for the betrothed or discuss their selection by phone. A favorite choice is the hard-to-find Metro Rice Steamer sold at Dixie. Unlike steamers made for a variety of uses, this model has a solid pan with holes in the sides to properly steam rice.

Crowley celebrates its long history as a leader in the rice industry with an International Rice Festival. Special events at the two-day fair include rice grading, cooking, and eating contests. Booths at the downtown fairgrounds entice festival-goers with a variety of rice-based dishes and irresistible snacks—all to be enjoyed while listening to a marvelous assembly of talented entertainers.

When the International Rice Festival is not in progress, you can join downtowners at **Ruddock's Bakery** or **Johnny's Cafe** for breakfast and coffee breaks. At noon, they socialize over homestyle plate lunches and sandwiches at **Mae's Cafe.**

When the workweek is through, friends gather at **Belizaire's Cajun Restaurant.** Some come for a Saturday night dinner of spicy Acadian foods, but the Cajun bands featured on weekends—and a large dance floor—are the real attractions here.

Parkerson Avenue is dotted with all sorts of appetizing restaurants, but **Cafe Acadie,** on the Interstate 10 Service Road in front of the Crowley Inn, is the only place you can taste savory dishes prepared by Roy Lyons, one of the area's most accomplished chefs. Spice up your visit to Acadia Parish with one of Lyons' innovative specialties, such as broiled catfish Willie topped with crawfish sauce, or rib eyes topped with special crawfish *étouffée*. The chef's delectable recipes recently merited a gold medal in the Baton Rouge Culinary Classic.

Area Code: (318)

Getting There:

Rayne and Crowley are just south of Interstate 10 between Lafayette and Lake Charles.

Where and When:

ADM Milling Co., Doré Rice Mill Div., Rice Mill Row (P.O. Box 461), Crowley, LA 70526. Call Crowley Chamber of Commerce, 788-0177, to arrange a tour. Free.

Antik Dazy, 405 N. Adams St., Rayne, LA 70578. 334-5699. Wed.-Sat., 10 A.M.-5 P.M.

Blue Rose Museum, 6428 Airport Rd., Crowley, LA 70527. Call 783-3096 for an appointment. Admission.

Borque's Club, Cedar Street, Lewisburg, LA 70525. 948-9904. Daily, 4 P.M.-'til. Dancing: Sat., 9 P.M.-1 A.M.; Sun., 4-10 P.M. Cajun musician jam session on Friday nights.

The Cajun Ladies, 837 E. Ebey St., Church Point, LA 70525. Call The Cajun Ladies at 684-2739 or KSLO, 942-2633, to ensure show will be broadcast on Saturday during your visit. *Bals de maison* are sometimes held at the pavilion in the city park when the weather is good. Fee for meal only. Food service begins about 6:30 P.M. and continues during show. Showtime: 7-10 P.M. Free.

Comeaux's Antiques & Collectibles, 106 E. Louisiana Ave., Rayne, LA 70578. 334-2508. Open first and third weekend of every month, 9 A.M.-5 P.M.

Dixie True Value Hardware, 505 Parkerson Ave., Crowley, LA 70527. 783-3736. Mon.-Sat., 7 A.M.-5 P.M.

Gail's Gifts, 127 N. Avenue E (U.S 90), Crowley, LA 70527. 788-1117. Mon.-Fri., 7:30 A.M.-5 P.M.; Sat., 8 A.M.-noon.

The Gallery, 220 N. Parkerson Ave., Crowley, LA 70526. 783-3747. Mon.-Fri., 10 A.M.-4 P.M.; Sat., 10 A.M.-1 P.M.

The Gift Box, 1028 N. Parkerson Ave, Crowley, LA 70527. 788-3249. Mon.-Fri., 8:30 A.M.-5:30 P.M.; Sat., 9:30 A.M.-5 P.M.

Guidry's Friendly Lounge, Route 1, Box 252, Lewisburg, LA 70525. 942-9988. Daily, 10 A.M.-'til. Dancing: Sat., 9 P.M.-1 A.M.; Sun., 5-9 P.M.

Gwen's Crafts, Balloons & Gifts, 200 N. Polk St., Rayne, LA 70578. 334-2008. Mon.-Fri., 9 A.M.-5 P.M.; Sat., 9 A.M.-noon.

Jagneaux, Andrew J., Cajun Roots Accordions, 161 Edmonia Dr. (Route 3, Box 10 B), Church Point, LA 70525. 684-2672. Call for appointment.

Jubilee Rouge Antiques, 107 E. Louisiana Ave., Rayne, LA 70578. 334-9543. Wed.-Sat., 11 A.M.-5 P.M.

Koury's Jewelry & Gifts, 113 N. Adams Ave. (P.O. Box 85), Rayne, LA 70578. 334-5126. Mon.-Fri., 9 A.M.-5 P.M.; Sat., 9 A.M.-noon.; December: Saturdays, 9 A.M.-5 P.M.

Lazy Dazy, 411 N. Adams Ave., Rayne, LA 70578. 334-3009. Tues.-Sat., 10 A.M.-5 P.M.

Louisiana State University Rice Experiment Station, Caffey Road, Crowley, LA 70527. 788-7531. Mon.-Fri., 8 A.M.-5 P.M.

People's Drugs & Gifts, Inc., 201 Louisiana Ave., Rayne, LA 70578. 334-3745. Mon.-Fri., 8 A.M.-6 P.M.; Sat., 8 A.M.-noon.

Saddle Tramp Riding Club, Ebey Street (Louisiana 178), Church Point, LA 70525. Contact Church Point Area Chamber of Commerce, 684-3030.

St. Leo the Great Catholic Church and *Waldfohrtshappelle*, Louisiana 98, Rayne, LA. 334-5056.

Worthmore's 5, 10 & 25 Cent Store, 100 W. Louisiana Ave., Rayne, LA 70578. 334-3763. Mon.-Sat., 8 A.M.-5 P.M.

Information:

Acadia Parish Tourist Commission, 114 E. First St. (P.O. Box 2125), Crowley, LA 70527-2125. 788-0177. Mon.-Fri., 9 A.M.-noon and 1-4:30 P.M.

Church Point Area Chamber of Commerce, 102 Church Blvd. (P.O. Box 218), Church Point, LA 70525-0218. 684-3030. Mon.-Fri., 8 A.M.-5 P.M.

Crowley Chamber of Commerce, 114 E. First St. (P.O. Box 2125), Crowley, LA 70527-2125. 788-0177. Mon.-Fri., 9 A.M.-noon and 1-4:30 P.M.

Rayne Chamber of Commerce, 1023 The Boulevard, Rayne, LA 70578. 334-2332. Mon.-Fri., 9 A.M.-noon; 1-4 P.M.

Rayne City Hall, 801 The Boulevard, Rayne, LA 70578. 334-3121. Mon.-Fri., 9 A.M.-4 P.M.

Guide Services:

Martha Royer, Certified Tour Guide, 305 E. Louisiana St., Rayne, LA 70578. 344-3489.

Accommodations:

Chain and independent hotels and motels in Rayne and Crowley.

Bed and Breakfast:

Maison Daboval Bed & Breakfast, 305 E. Louisiana St., Rayne, LA 70578. 334-3489.

Restaurants:

Belizaire's Cajun Restaurant, 2307 Parkerson Ave., Crowley, LA 70527. 788-2501. Mon.-Thurs., 11 A.M.-10 P.M.; Fri., 11 A.M.-midnight; Sat., 5 P.M.-midnight; Sun., 11 A.M.-8 P.M. Cajun band: Sat., 8-11 P.M.; Sun., 4-8 P.M.

Boulevard Mobil, 1421 The Boulevard, Rayne, LA 70578. Daily, 24 hours. 334-9588 or 334-9221.

Cafe Acadie, Interstate 10 Service Road in front of Crowley Inn (P.O. Box 302, Crowley, LA 70527). 783-3256. Sun.-Thurs., 5:30 A.M.-9:30 P.M.; Fri. and Sat., 5:30 A.M.-11 P.M.

Gabe's Cajun Foods, 1410 The Boulevard, Rayne, LA 70578. 334-4820. Daily, 10 A.M.-9 P.M.

Galaxy Chinese Restaurant, 406 N. Adams Ave., Rayne, LA 70578. 334-2472 or 334-2473. Lunch: Daily, 11 A.M.-2 P.M. Dinner: Mon.-Sat., 6-9 P.M.

Johnny's Cafe, 414 N. Parkerson Ave., Crowley, LA 70527. 783-4572. Mon.-Sat., 8 A.M.-2 P.M.

Mae's Cafe, 230 W. 2nd St., Crowley, LA 70527. 783-5464. Mon.-Fri., 10 A.M.-2 P.M.

Michael & Sun's Restaurant, 201 E. Texas Ave., Rayne, LA

70578. 334-5539. Mon.-Thurs., 7 A.M.-3:30 P.M.; Fri. and Sat., 7 A.M.-10 P.M.

Ruddock's Bakery, 556 E. Court Circle, Crowley, LA 70527. 783-2962. Tues.-Sun., 5 A.M.-7 P.M.

Sweet Pea's, 607 The Boulevard, Rayne, LA 70578. 334-8494. Sun.-Wed., 6 A.M.-2 P.M.; Thurs.-Sat., 6 A.M.-2 P.M. and 5 P.M.-'til.

The Warehouse Restaurant and Loading Dock Bar, 205 E. Louisiana Ave., Rayne, LA 70578. 334-7741. Tues.-Sat., 11 A.M.-2 P.M. and 5-10 P.M.; Sun., Champagne brunch: 11 A.M.-2 P.M.

Major Annual Events:

Arts in the Park, Crowley—Weekend before Easter.

Buggy Festival, Church Point—First Weekend in June.

Cajun Days, Church Point—Fall.

Courir de Mardi Gras, Church Point—Sunday before Fat Tuesday.

Horseshoe Tournament, Roberts Cove—Spring.

International Rice Festival, Crowley—Third Friday and Saturday of October.

LaFleur De Rue Craft Show, Church Point—November.

Rayne Frog Festival—September.

Rice Capital Christmas, Crowley—December.

Chretien Point Plantation. (Photo courtesy Chretien Point Plantation)

The bell at the Academy of the Sacred Heart. (Photo by Mary Fonseca)

29

NOT JUST THE SAME OLD SONG AND DANCE

Louisiana's world-famous cuisine began when African, Creole, and Cajun cooks combined vittles they had on hand and seasoned the mixture with flavorful herbs gathered from the marshlands. To make dishes such as gumbo or jambalaya, they started with wild game or seafood, added a little of this, a cup of that, and a dash of some tangy spices. And travelers find that the secret to concocting entertaining, off-the-beaten-path getaways in the Pelican State is to imitate these time-honored recipes.

You can, for instance, explore some of the fascinating towns just north of Lafayette, meet some of Louisiana's friendly people, blend in a handful of lively, toe-tapping musicians, add a dollop of Cajun *joie de vivre* (love of life), and stir everything into a fail-proof formula for fun.

Even a sourpuss like Dickens' Ebeneezer Scrooge would have a good time with the warmhearted residents of Opelousas. The town sponsors more than 14 **Main Street Revived** street dances every year. Most of these get-togethers are held on Fridays in the spring and summer, the rest on special occasions during the year. Whatever the time, friends, neighbors, and visitors meet in front of a downtown bandstand to sway to the musical flavor of the day. Sometimes it is Cajun or zydeco (a unique form of black-Creole music indigenous to southwest Louisiana). Now and then, it is the blues or rock 'n' roll.

When the street music winds down, friends often congregate in local restaurants to renew their energy with hearty Cajun food. At **Toby's Country Corner,** an informal restaurant/service station on Louisiana 182, customers relish the tasty fried catfish and freshly boiled seafood. And at **Soileau's Dinner Club,** everyone sits down to bowls of steaming gumbo, platters piled high with seafood, or a tempting combination of Cajun specialties.

Vacationers can find out about more entertaining places to visit at the **Opelousas Tourist Information Center** (just off of Interstate 49 at U.S. 190). The center is surrounded by vintage buildings that make up Le Vieux Village (The Old Village) of Opelousas. A doctor's office, school house, and several other structures are being developed into a living-history museum.

When the aroma of freshly baked donuts drifts through the village, only the most disciplined dieters can resist a coffee break at **Meche's Donuts.** The shop shares a covered pavilion in front of Le Vieux Village with a seasonally full **Farmers Market.**

The book *Opelousas Tours: A Journey Through Louisiana's Third Oldest City,* sold at the center, or a complimentary "Points of Interest" brochure guide visitors to sights around Opelousas. **Sandoz's Hardware,** a family-operated store that celebrated its centennial in 1978, is one of many intriguing places you can visit. It is filled with gadgets and thingamajigs used long ago, as well as an encyclopedic conglomeration of modern implements.

Many tourists have wares from Sandoz's store in hand when they sit down to lunch in Opelousas' oldest restaurant, the **Palace Cafe.** The Doucas family has been serving homestyle cooking here, at the corner of Landry and Market streets, since 1927. **Back in Time,** one of Opelousas' newest restaurants, is just a few doors away. This new kid on the block serves salads and sandwiches named for legendary movie stars and historic happenings. After lunching at Palace Cafe or Back in Time, shop for Louisiana products and gifts at **La Louisiane and Jim Bowie Courtyard,** just a few steps away from the restaurants.

Then, continue a walking tour of Opelousas by viewing Estorge House (private), the 1827, neo-classical home known locally as "the Elegant Old Lady of Market Street."

Thirsty sightseers may want to walk two blocks north of Estorge House to **Country Heirlooms** to sample the charming tearoom's signature coffee blend, La Cafe de Cocoa. Tea, soft drinks, and an array of pastries and gift items are also for sale. If you have time for more shopping, find your way to several antique shops listed in a brochure available from the Opelousas Tourist Information Center.

While you are touring the town, be sure to stop in at the **Opelousas Museum and Interpretive Center** at 329 Main St. Some of the museum's exhibits are devoted to episodes in Opelousas's rich past, including the period when it was the Civil War capital of Louisiana. Others are dedicated to various ethnic and religious groups who settled the area. An enchanting doll display captures the attention of youngsters and a large selection of video tapes—viewed in the museum's audio-visual room—showcases attractions in other areas of Louisiana.

A "cook's" tour of Opelousas is another agreeable way to spend the day. Start by sampling Cajun sausages and cracklins (fried pork skins) at **Kelly's Country Meat Block & Diner** on South Union Street (U.S. 167). Select some take-home items from the store's handsome display of Louisiana specialty foods before departing for **Savoie's Real Cajun Food Products.** Eula Savoie continues her family's tradition of making and selling the real thing at the Savoie factory and store six miles southwest of Opelousas. Pork tasso, *andouille* sausage, dressing mix, light and dark roux, and several other products bear the yellow Savoie family label. Drop by the store anytime, but call ahead to visit the plant.

After a day of touring, enjoy the music at **Slim's Y-Ki-Ki,** a long-established dance hall. Visitors from near and far often join dancers at Slim's who step lively to the spirited rhythms played in this renowned zydeco club. Then relax in comfortable accommodations in Opelousas or in historic Bed and Breakfasts in nearby towns. At **La Maison de Campagne,** a king-size Victorian home moved in four sections to the out-skirts of Lafayette in 1974, Joann and Fred McLemore settle guests into spacious rooms and urge them to "help them-selves" at the bountiful table Joann sets. Travelers who cannot overnight at La Maison de Campagne may tour the home if they call for directions and an appointment.

At **Chretien Point Plantation,** a secluded twenty-acre estate in Sunset, breakfast is graciously served on an 1800s rectory table. Tour guides tell visitors that during the first half of that war-torn century, Barataria's nomadic pirate, Jean Lafitte, was a frequent guest of the Chretiens. Today, tester-covered beds, a refreshing pool, and a sunny tennis court await twentieth-cen-tury overnighters.

If you stay at Chretien Point, you may want to visit Margaret Brinkhaus at **La Caboose,** her backyard railcar store. This Sunset entrepreneur distributes her homemade jams, jellies, preserves, and vinegars to gourmet food stores. But, it is more fun to stop by her home on the way to or from Chretien Point Plantation and select items with her assistance. If Margaret is not busy in the kitchen or working on one of her paintings (also for sale in La Caboose), she will show you the herbs and berries she grows for her products.

The charming village of Grand Coteau is just a few miles from Sunset on the eastern side of Interstate 49. The town is a photographer's delight, so consider spending a few delightful hours snapping pictures of the quaint cottages that line the streets and the oak alleys that shade the grounds of peaceful retreat houses operated by Catholic orders. You may visit pic-turesque **St. Charles Borrommeo Church** and the cemetery behind it; and, if you call for an appointment, you can tour beautiful, historic **Academy of the Sacred Heart** and hear the story of the miracle that took place there. For refreshments and information on the town, stop by **Kitchen Shop Tearoom,** an appealing gift shop and tearoom that offers delicious meals, plus snacks such as coffee and pastries.

More enchanting homes may be seen in Washington, six miles north of Opelousas. About eighty percent of the resi-dences in this former steamboat town are on the National

Register of Historic Places and several offer bed and breakfast. Information on these noteworthy structures is available at the **Historic Washington Museum and Tourist Information Center,** which displays relics of the steamboat era.

Antique interior furnishings are on display in **Camellia Cove Bed & Breakfast, De La Morandiere,** the **Hinckley House,** and the **Nicholson House of History;** but **Magnolia Ridge Antebellum Home and Gardens,** Washington's most prominent home, is not open for tours. The gracious owners of this lovely antebellum mansion do, however, permit visitors to stroll three miles of scenic trails that wind through their beautiful, 60-acre garden on the banks of Bayou Courtableau.

In addition to the fun of historic house-hopping, Washington offers a weekend's worth of browsing in Main Street antique shops and at **O'Connor's Antique School Mall.** Close to fifty antique and collectible dealers display their wares at the mall every weekend. Shoppers take a break to enjoy the plate lunches, salads, and sandwiches served in the gym by **Charlene's Deli & Market** on Saturdays and Sundays.

Charlene's is in the midst of the hodgepodge of shops along Washington's Main Street. You'll find more antiques in several shops plus quality gifts and crafts at the **Acadian Connection,** and cowhide chairs, handmade rockers, rugs, and drums at **Soileau's Cowhide Chairs.**

Nearly every shop along Main Street—even the hardware and auto-parts store—carries sturdy baskets woven by the Edward Harris family. The attractive containers made by the native Washingtonians are much in demand because of their quality workmanship.

After an enjoyable day in Washington, dine at **Steamboat Warehouse** restaurant on the banks of Bayou Courtableau. The chef's well-prepared French and Cajun dishes seem to taste even better in the restaurant's steamboat-era atmosphere.

With generous plantation breakfasts and irresistible Cajun dishes tempting them at every turn, vacationers on a "light diet" sometimes feel they must "brown-bag" it through south Louisiana. Not so. Most restaurants in the area prepare special

A statue of Eunice Pharr Duson. The town of Eunice,
founded by her husband, is named for her. (Photo by
Mary Fonseca)

dishes on request and Enola Prudhomme, proprietress of **Enola Prudhomme's Cajun Cafe,** is particularly accommodating to travelers on "heart-healthy" diets. The innovative chef, sister to famous chef Paul Prudhomme, includes flavorful, slimmed-down versions of several Cajun entrees on the menu of her Frontage Road restaurant. They are listed alongside a full selection of traditionally cooked dishes.

It has been said that if Cajuns aren't eating they are likely to be dancing or playing music. Some of Acadiana's homegrown musical talent is on display every Saturday in the nearby towns of Eunice and Mamou. Here is a plan that will let you enjoy an entertaining day of fiddlin', strummin', and sight-seeing in these hospitable Acadian communities.

After a generous breakfast at **Ruby's Cafe** in downtown Eunice or at one of the area's cozy Bed and Breakfasts, join the party at **Savoy Music Center** on U.S. 190. Mark Savoy spends his weekdays handcrafting Cajun accordions while he chats with visitors from all over the world. But, on Saturday mornings, work is put aside so Mark and other local musicians can "jam" behind his storefront counter. They play for a walk-in audience that sways to the waltzes and taps toes to the two-steps flowing from their instruments.

About midmorning, enjoy a complimentary cup of coffee at **Potier's Drug Store** (on U.S. 190 nearer the center of town), while you shop for souvenirs. Then, head for **Fred's Lounge** in Mamou (ten miles north of Eunice via Louisiana 13).

Live Cajun music has been broadcast from Fred's every Saturday morning since 1946. Early risers start drifting into the pink-walled lounge about 9 A.M., just before the French-speaking commentator from KVPI in Ville Platte announces the first selection by Don Thibodeaux and the Musical Cajuns.

As the morning lengthens the crowd thickens, so onlookers happily squeeze together to make room for more couples who want to dance. The radio show signs off at 11 A.M., but the live music and camaraderie continue until about 1 P.M.

After the last set is played, cross the street to **Cajun Rainbow Specialties** to stock up on Cajun country keepsakes. Then, gather around tables in **Jeff's Seafood and Steak Restaurant** (around the corner on Main Street) to ponder how to spend the rest of the day.

Outdoor types may opt for a couple of hours at **Chicot State Park** and the adjacent **Louisiana State Arboretum.** They are both in the town of Ville Platte, about 15 miles from Mamou. Opportunities for fishing, swimming, picnicking, and hiking are plentiful on Chicot's 6,000-acre expanse, and a quiet stroll along the arboretum's tree-shaded paths brings nature lovers close to almost every type of vegetation native to Louisiana. Many visitors choose a ranger-guided walk so they can learn more about the arboretum's greenery and the animals that feed in this atypical forest.

Some weekenders prefer to spend the afternoon in Eunice. They line up with locals to buy hot *boudin* balls at **Johnson's Grocery** (during winter months, the line extends a half-block outside the store), browse stores in the downtown mall, or shop for fresh sausage or *ponce* (stuffed pig stomach) at **LeJeune's** or **Cormier's** sausage kitchens. With take-home items safely stashed away, there is time to contemplate exhibits in the **Eunice Museum** and the **Jean Lafitte National Historical Park and Preserve Prairie Acadian Cultural Center.**

The town museum occupies an old depot on South C. C. Duson Drive where an 1890s real-estate speculator, C. C. Duson, once auctioned off lots in the new town he planned and named for his wife, Eunice. The depot's displays, which relate to the history, culture, and industry of this unique area, are enhanced by continuously shown video tapes explaining Cajun culture. The **Eunice Chamber of Commerce Tourist Information Center** is adjacent to the museum.

The Prairie Acadian Cultural Center on South Third Street and Park Avenue depicts folkways cultivated by early grassland settlers. Craft and music workshops, as well as a variety of special programs and exhibits, are held at the center. These include frequent performances by Cajun bands and by La Branche Vivant, a choral group dedicated to preserving ancient Cajun canticles.

On the corner of Martin Luther King Drive and Magnolia Street, a small section of Louisiana's once vast prairie is being restored to its natural state. Louisiana State University's **Cajun Prairie Preservation Project** will ensure the survival of grassland plants and provide an opportunity for everyone to see the prairie the way it used to be.

No matter how visitors elect to spend the afternoon, it is a sure bet they will be lined up in front of the national park's **Liberty Center for the Performing Arts** around 4 P.M. to buy tickets for the "Rendez Vous des Cajuns" live radio show.

Broadcast from a restored 1920s movie palace, the show draws enthusiastic crowds every Saturday evening. An enjoyable two-hour program features Cajun and zydeco bands, local humorists, and special guests who converse in French with host Barry Ancelet. Just below the stage, audience members dance to the exhilarating music.

Tickets to the Liberty Theater show are so much in demand that patrons who purchase them when the box office opens at 4 P.M. are advised to be in their seats no later than 5 P.M. While waiting for the six-o'clock show to start, spectators get acquainted with each other and watch preparations onstage. When the theater is filled to capacity, overflow crowds take advantage of a video hookup in the Prairie Acadian Cultural Center theater.

After the show, some theater-goers share their impressions of the performance during conversations at **Nick's on Second Street,** as they choose from the restaurant's wide-ranging menu and relax among newfound friends.

Area Code: (318)

Getting There:

Opelousas, Sunset, and Washington can be accessed from Interstate 49 just north of Lafayette. Eunice is 25 miles west of Opelousas via U.S. 190. Mamou is 10 miles north of Eunice via Louisiana 13.

Where and When:

Academy of the Sacred Heart, P.O. Box 310, Grand Coteau, LA 70541. 662-5275. Donations appreciated.

Acadian Connection, 202 S. Main St. (P.O. Box 11), Washington, LA 70589. 826-3967. Fri.-Sun., 1-3:30 P.M., by appointment, or by chance.

Cajun Prairie Preservation Project, Corner of Martin Luther King Drive and Magnolia Street, Eunice, LA 70535. For information, call 457-2016 or 457-4497.

Cajun Rainbow Specialties, 415-A Sixth St., Mamou, LA 70554. 468-4433. Mon.-Fri., 8:30 A.M.-5 P.M.; Sat., 9 A.M.-3 P.M.

Camellia Cove Bed & Breakfast, 205 W. Hill St., Washington, LA 70589. 826-7362. Tours by appointment or by chance. Admission.

Chicot State Park, Route 3, Box 494, Ville Platte, LA 70586. 363-2403. Apr. 1-Sept. 30: 7 A.M.-10 P.M.; Oct. 1-Mar. 31: 8 A.M.-7 P.M. Admission.

Chretien Point Plantation, Route 1, Box 163, Sunset, LA 70584. 662-5876. Daily, 10 A.M.-5 P.M. Last tour starts at 4 P.M. Admission.

Cormier's Sausage Kitchen, U.S. 190 East (Route 3, Box 573), Eunice, LA 70535. 457-4102. Mon.-Sat., 8 A.M.-6 P.M.

De La Morandiere, Corner of Sittig and St. John streets (P.O. Box 327), Washington, LA 70589. 826-3510. Tours by appointment or by chance. Admission.

Eunice Museum, 220 South C. C. Duson Dr., Eunice, LA 70535. 457-6540. Tues.-Sat., 8 A.M.-noon, 1-5 P.M.; Sun., noon-5 P.M. Free.

Farmers Market, Pavilion, I-49 and U.S. 190, Opelousas, LA 70570. For information, call 948-6263.

Fred's Lounge, 420 Sixth St., Mamou, LA 70554. 468-5411. Saturday only, 8 A.M.-1 P.M. Radio show: 9:15-11 A.M. No cover.

Hinckley House, 405 E. Dejean St. (P.O. Box 291), Washington, LA 70589. 826-3906. Tours by appointment or by chance.

Jean Lafitte National Historical Park and Preserve Prairie Acadian Cultural Center, Corner of South Third Street and Park Avenue, Eunice, LA 70535. 457-8499. Daily, 9 A.M.-6 P.M.

Johnson's Grocery, 700 E. Maple Ave., Eunice, LA 70535. 457-9314. Mon.-Fri., 5:30 A.M.-6 P.M.; Sat., 5:30 A.M.-5 P.M.

Kitchen Shop Tearoom, Corner of Cherry and King streets (P.O. Box F, Grand Coteau, LA 70541). 662-3500. Shop: Mon.-Sat., 10 A.M.-5 P.M. Tearoom: Tues.-Sat., 10 A.M.-5 P.M.

La Caboose, 254 Budd St. (Drawer E), Sunset, LA 70584. 662-5401. By appointment or by chance; daily, 9 A.M.-6 P.M.

La Louisiane and Jim Bowie Courtyard, 153 W. Landry St. Opelousas, LA 70570. 942-2575. Mon.-Fri., 11 A.M.-5 P.M.; Sat. by chance.

La Maison de Campagne, 825 Kidder Rd., Carencro, LA 70520. 896-6529. Tours by appointment only. Admission.

LeJeune's Sausage Kitchen, Old Crowley Road, Eunice, LA 70535. 457-8491. Mon.-Fri., 7 A.M.-5:30 P.M.; Sat., 7 A.M.-5 P.M.

Liberty Center for the Performing Arts, Corner of South Second Street and Park Avenue, Eunice, LA 70535. 457-6575. Saturdays: "Rendez Vous des Cajuns" radio show, 6-8 P.M. Admission. Tickets go on sale at 4 P.M. No advance sale.

Louisiana State Arboretum, Route 3, Box 494, Ville Platte, LA 70586. Daily, sunrise-sunset. Tours: Sat. and Sun., 10 A.M., 2 P.M., or by appointment. Free.

Magnolia Ridge Antebellum Home and Gardens, Louisiana 103 (Prescott Street), Washington, LA 70589. 826-3027. Home—private; Gardens open daily, sunrise to sunset.

Main Street Revived, c/o 441 E. Grolee St., Opelousas, LA 70570. 948-2589, 948-4731, or 942-5712. Schedules available for nominal fee. Dances held on Main Street between Bellevue and Court streets. Free.

Note: For information on more opportunities to hear live music in the Opelousas area, contact the Opelousas Tourist Information Center.

Nicholson House of History, 303 Main St., Washington, LA 70589. 826-3670. Tours by appointment or by chance. Admission.

O'Connor's Antique School Mall, 210 Church St. (P.O. Box 695), Washington, LA 70589. 826-3580. Fri.-Sun., 9 A.M.-5 P.M.

Opelousas Museum and Interpretive Center, 329 N. Main St., Opelousas, LA 70570. 948-2589. Tues-Sat., 9 A.M.-5 P.M.

Potier's Drug Store, 1021 E. Laurel Ave. (U.S. 190), Eunice, LA 457-5698. Mon.-Fri., 8 A.M.-6 P.M.; Sat., 8 A.M.-5 P.M.

St. Charles Borrommeo Church, St. Charles Street, Grand Coteau, LA 70541. 662-5279. Mon.-Sat., 8 A.M.-5 P.M. Services: Sat. (winter), 4 P.M.; (summer) 5 P.M. Sun., 9:15 and 11 A.M.

Sandoz Hardware (J. B. Sandoz, Inc.), 318 N. Main St. (P.O. Box 670), Opelousas, LA 70570. 942-3564. Mon.-Sat., 7:15 A.M.-5 P.M.

Savoie's Real Cajun Food Products, 581 LA 742, Opelousas, LA 70570. 942-7241. Store: Mon.-Fri., 7 A.M.-5 P.M.; Sat., 8 A.M.-noon. Tours: Call Tues. and Thurs., 8:30-9 A.M. for appointment on those days.

Savoy Music Center, U.S. 190 East, Eunice, LA 70535. 457-9563. Store: Tues.-Fri., 9 A.M.-5 P.M. (closed for lunch, 12-1:30 P.M.) Jam Session: Sat., 9 A.M.-noon. Watch for large sign on highway. Free.

Slim's Y-Ki-Ki, Washington Road (U.S. 167 North), (P.O. Box 64), Opelousas, LA 70570. 942-9980. Fri. and Sat., 4 P.M.-2 A.M. Cover charge.

Soileau's Cowhide Chairs, Louisiana 363, Washington, LA 70589. Call 826-5818 or 826-3295 for information.

Information:

Eunice Chamber of Commerce Tourist Information Center, 200 South C. C. Duson Dr. (P.O. Box 508), Eunice, LA 70535. 457-2565 or 1-800-222-2342. Mon.-Fri., 9 A.M.-5 P.M.

Historic Washington Museum and Tourist Center, 402 N. Main St. (P.O. Box 597), Washington, LA 70589. 826-7353. Mon.-Fri., 10 A.M.-3 P.M.; Sat. and Sun., 9 A.M.-4 P.M.

Main Street Opelousas, 329 N. Main St. (P.O. Box 712), Opelousas, LA 70571. 948-2590 or 948-6784.

Opelousas Tourist Information Center, U.S. 190 (west of I-49), Opelousas, LA 70570. 948-6263 or 1-800-424-5442. Daily, 8 A.M.-4 P.M.

St. Landry Parish Tourist Commission, P.O. Box 1415, Opelousas, LA 70571. 1-800-424-5442. Phone only, no office open to the public.

Guide Services:

Carola L. Andrepont, Historic St. Landry Tours, 441 E. Grolee St., Opelousas, LA 70570. 948-6784 or 948-4731.

Accommodations:

Carencro:

Bed and Breakfasts:

Belle of the Oaks Bed and Breakfast, 122 Le Medicin Rd., Carencro, LA 70520. 896-4965.

La Maison de Campagne, 825 Kidder Rd., Carencro, LA 70520. 896-6529.

Eunice:

A list of private motels is available from the Eunice Chamber of Commerce Tourist Information Center.

Bed and Breakfasts:

Cottages on Swan Lake, U.S. 190 East, Eunice, LA 70535. 457-1470.

La Petite Maison, Christian Woodworks, 601 Fort St., Eunice, LA 70535. 457-7136. After hours: 457-1254 or 457-3851.

Potiers Prairie Cajun Inn, 110 W. Park Ave., Eunice, LA 70535. 457-0440.

The Seale Guesthouse, Louisiana 13 (P.O. Box 568), Eunice, LA 70535. 457-3753.

Additional bed-and-breakfast accommodations available in private homes. Reservations through Southern Comfort, 1-800-749-1928.

Opelousas:

Bed and Breakfast:

Coteau Ridge, 120 Bois de Chene, Opelousas, LA 70570. 942-8180.

A list of chain and private motels is available from the Opelousas Tourist Information Center.

Sunset:

Bed and Breakfast:

Chretien Point Plantation, Route 1, Box 163, Sunset, LA 70584. 662-5876. Business address: 2500 Johnston St., Lafayette, LA 70503. 233-7050.

Washington:

Bed and Breakfasts:

Camellia Cove Bed & Breakfast, 205 W. Hill St., Washington, LA 70589. 826-7362.

The Country House Bed & Breakfast, 609 E. Carrier St., Washington, LA 70589. 826-3052.

De La Morandiere, Corner of Sittig and St. John streets (P.O. Box 327), Washington, LA 70589. 826-3510.

La Chaumiere Guest Cottage, 217 S. Washington St., Washington, LA 70589. 826-3967.

LaPlace de Ville, 217 W. Dejean St., Washington, LA 70589. 826-3367.

Maison Garrique Bed & Breakfast, 110 Garrique St., Washington, LA 70589. 826-3967.

Restaurants:

Back in Time, 145 W. Landry St., Opelousas, LA 70570. 942-2413. Mon.-Thurs., 10 A.M.-5 P.M.; Fri., 10 A.M.-4 P.M.; Sat., 11 A.M.-3 P.M. *Note:* Lunch is served 11 A.M.-2:30 P.M., beverages and desserts at all times.

Charlene's Deli & Market, 311 N. Main St., Washington, LA

70589. 826-3926. Daily, 6:30 A.M.-6:30 P.M. Lunch served daily at Deli and on Sat. and Sun., 10:30 A.M.-2 P.M. at O'Connor's Antique School Mall.

Country Heirlooms, 619 Market St., Opelousas, LA 70570. 948-1206. Mon.-Fri., 10 A.M.-5 P.M.

Enola Prudhommme's Cajun Cafe, 4676 N.E. Evangeline Thruway (I-49, Exit 7), Carencro, LA 70520. 896-7694. Tues.-Sat., 11 A.M.-10 P.M.; Sun., 11 A.M.-2:30 P.M.

Jeff's Seafood and Steak Restaurant, 513 Main St., Mamou, LA 70554. 468-2330. Mon.-Fri., 5:30 A.M.-9 P.M.; Fri. and Sat., 5:30 A.M.-10 P.M.

Kelly's Country Meat Block & Diner, 1618 S. Union St., Opelousas, LA 70570. Store: 948-4170. Diner: 942-7466. Tues.-Sun., 10 A.M.-9 P.M.

Kitchen Shop Tearoom, Corner of Cherry and King streets (P.O. Box F, Grand Coteau, LA 70541). 662-3500. Shop: Mon.-Sat., 10 A.M.-5 P.M.; Tearoom: Tues.-Sat., 10 A.M.-5 P.M.

Meche's Donuts, 949 E. Landry St., Opelousas, LA 70570. 942-2128. Daily, 4 A.M.-1 P.M.

Nick's on Second Street, 123 Second St., Eunice, LA 70535. 457-4921. Lunch: Tues.-Fri., 11 A.M.-2 P.M.; Sun., 11 A.M.-2 P.M. Dinner: Tues.-Sun., 6 P.M.-'til.

Palace Cafe, 167 W. Landry St., Opelousas, LA 70570. 942-2142. Mon.-Sat., 6 A.M.-9 P.M.; Sun., 7 A.M.-9 P.M.

Ruby's Cafe, 221 W. Walnut St., Eunice, LA 70535. 457-2583. Mon.-Fri., 5:30 A.M.-6 P.M.; Sat., 5:30 A.M.-2 P.M.

Soileau's Dinner Club, 1620 N. Main St., Opelousas, LA 70570. 942-2985. Sun.-Thurs., 11 A.M.-10 P.M.; Fri. and Sat., 11 A.M.-11 P.M.

Steamboat Warehouse, Main Street, Washington, LA 70589. 826-7227. Tues.-Sat., 5:30-10:30 P.M.; Sun., 11 A.M.-2 P.M.

Toby's Country Corner, Louisiana 182 South, Opelousas, LA 70570. 942-9044. Daily, 11 A.M.-9 P.M.

Major Annual Events:

Cajun Music Festival, Mamou—June.

Christmas in Old Opelousas—Second week of December.

Church Point Buggy Festival—Late May or early June.

Courir de Mardi Gras, Eunice—Tuesday before Ash Wednesday (Mardi Gras).

Cultural A-Fair in Historic Opelousas—Third weekend in September.

Festival de Courtableau, Washington—Second weekend in May.

Here's the Beef Cook-off, Opelousas—Last Sunday in March.

International Cajun Joke Telling Contest, Opelousas—Third weekend in April.

Louisiana Yambilee Festival, Opelousas/St. Landry Parish area—Week of the last full weekend of October.

St. Landry Parish Heritage Festival, Opelousas—Last weekend of April every other year.

Southwest Louisiana Zydeco Music Festival, Plaisance—Saturday before Labor Day.

World's Championship Crawfish Etouffée Cook-off, Eunice—Last Sunday in March unless Easter falls on that date.

30

LAISSEZ LES BONS TEMPS ROULER

(F) (G)

The jovial Cajun yell, "*Laissez les bon temps rouler*!" (Let the good times roll!), is heard in Lafayette more frequently than "Jolie Blanc," a time-honored ballad of lost love adopted as the Cajun "national anthem."

Good times roll often in this Acadian hub—the unofficial "capital" of French Louisiana. Lafayette merchants bring "Downtown Alive!" in the spring and fall with festive "after-five" block parties. The T.G.I.F. crowd boogies to whatever sound is featured—Cajun, zydeco (a unique form of black-Creole music indigenous to southwest Louisiana), rock 'n' roll, or country.

Lafayette's Natural History Museum adds to the springtime fun with a series of Bach lunches—outdoor interludes of jazz, classical, or baroque music played while the audience picnics on their brown-bag lunches or tastes chef specialties served on the museum grounds.

From the beginning of April until Labor Day, racing fans enjoy the thrill of Thoroughbred racing as they cheer their picks to the finish line at the **New Evangeline Downs.**

No matter what the season, patrons waltz and two-step to the music of high-spirited Cajun bands at **Mulate's,** in neighboring Breaux Bridge, and at **Prejean's** or **Randol's,** in Lafayette. Some arrive early to enjoy the spicy Cajun fare served at these genial restaurants.

Weekends offer more opportunities to whirl around the

371

floor. At several dance halls, locals take time to show visitors a step or two so they can join in the fun.

Request maps that will help you locate these convivial places, and others, at Gateway Lafayette, the city's easily spotted information and welcome center in the median of Evangeline Thruway south of Interstate 10 Exit 103-A. The center's wetland setting has made it somewhat of a tourist attraction itself.

Dancing with friends and neighbors has been part of the Cajun life-style since *fais-do-dos* (house parties begun after the children went to bed) were first held in settlements such as Vermilionville, the village that evolved into the city of Lafayette. At **Jean Lafitte National Historical Park and Preserve's Acadian Cultural Center** you can learn more about the Cajun way of life through well-designed, interpretive exhibits plus an excellent, forty-minute film about the deportation of the Acadians from Nova Scotia. The cultural center is on Fisher Road, near the Lafayette airport. You can reach it by following Evangeline Thruway south from Interstate 10 and turning left on Surrey Street.

Two diverse, but intriguing attractions are within a couple of blocks of the Jean Lafitte Acadian Cultural Center. **Combat Aircraft Museum,** located at the airport, is a hands-on museum that offers the public a unique opportunity to witness and participate in the restoration of authentic World War II aircraft. In the winter, you can visit and work with museum members while they repair vintage airplanes. Among them is a World War II, PV II submarine hunter dubbed *Fat Cat Too.* It is the only fully restored, flying PV II in the world. Weekdays, during the summer, the combat museum's planes, plus a developing exhibit of aviation memorabilia, are on display. On summer weekends, the aircraft are flown in airshows around the country.

On Surrey Street, just past the Jean Lafitte Acadian Cultural Center, Lafayette brings **Vermilionville** to life again in a group of authentic and replicated buildings clustered on the banks of Bayou Vermilion. As you wander through the complex, you can pause to listen to the toe-tapping music played at daily *fais-do-dos* and see cooks and artisans re-create folkways ingrained in their heritage.

The Cajun way of life is also celebrated at **Acadian Village,** a charming museum of Acadian architecture, history, and culture set in 10 acres of gardens and woodland. As you stroll the banks of the village's simulated bayou and cross the thresholds of seven antique and four reconstructed dwellings, you get a sense of the closeness and interdependency that was necessary in such isolated villages. There were not many diversions, so weddings like the ones held nearly every weekend in the museum's tiny New Hope Chapel were important social events.

Some of Acadian Village's pioneer structures may have once housed blushing newlyweds. Now, they are showcases of Cajun history. The museum's most unique artifacts are perhaps those displayed in the boyhood home of state Sen. Dudley J. LeBlanc. They trace the lifework of the legislator, and the evolution of Hadacol, his 12-percent-alcohol vitamin tonic—popular in the 1950s—guaranteed to cure all ills.

A 400-year-old dugout and several lethal blowguns are among the many fascinating exhibits in Acadian Village's Mississippi Valley Missionary Museum. They were used by Indians who lived in Louisiana hundreds of years before *"Le Grand Dérangement,"* as Acadians call their exile from Nova Scotia. Some of these Native Americans taught the new settlers survival skills and schooled them in the use of local herbs so important to their cuisine.

The history of the generations that built on the beginning made by stalwart Acadian exiles is chronicled in the **Lafayette Museum.** The museum was once the home of Jean Mouton, a prosperous planter who designed Vermilionville around a chapel and courthouse site he donated to the fledgling settlement. Since his plantation was 10 miles away, Mouton built a "Sunday house" near the chapel for his family to use when attending services or social functions. One chamber of the two-room house, built in 1800, and three rooms added by Mouton's son, Alexandre—the first democratic governor of Louisiana—comprise the first floor of the museum. Vintage articles, such as a quilt stitched by Abraham Lincoln's mother and turn-of-the-century wedding gowns, plus costumes of the city's recent Mardi Gras monarchs are on display here. The

Lafayette Museum. (Photo courtesy Lafayette Convention and Visitors Commission)

Cypress Lake, a microcosm of a cypress swamp, at the University of Southwestern Louisiana. (Photo courtesy Lafayette Convention and Visitors Commission)

carnival king's raiments are emblazoned with *G* for Gabriel, his consort's bear an *E* for Evangeline. Both symbols honor the exiled Acadian couple immortalized in Henry Wadsworth Longfellow's poem, *Evangeline.*

A few blocks away, the magnificent belfry of the **Cathedral of St. John the Evangelist** rises where Mouton's original chapel once stood. The city father lays in eternal rest in a grave in the first line of tombs behind the Cathedral.

The enduring Cathedral Oak next to St. John's was two centuries old when Jean Mouton laid out Vermilionville. This 400-year-old testament to nature's workmanship, whose bowing limbs completely cover the 1916 church's yard, is "vice-president" of the Live Oak Society, an organization started in 1934 to recognize some of the oldest and most renowned oak trees in America.

If you are an antiques enthusiast, you may want to follow up your visits to museums chronicling Lafayette's past with a 1½-hour tour of **Shagwood Manor,** a unique, contemporary home filled with museum-quality furniture and artifacts. J. C. Chargois takes great pleasure in showing visitors the "potpourri of fascinating antiques, objects d'art and memorabilia" he has collected in his home. Some of this well-known interior designer and local historian's fine pieces also decorate Shagwood's inviting guesthouse. The view from the cottage's comfortable sun porch overlooks the Vermilion River. If there are six or more in your party, consider treating yourself to one of J. C.'s gourmet lunches or dinners during a visit to Shagwood Manor.

Nature lovers are surprised and pleased to learn about the many outdoor venues they can visit in Lafayette. One that is particularly unique is the towering group of cypress trees that rests on knobby knees in the University of Southwestern Louisiana's **Cypress Lake.** If there were a society to honor cypress trees, these giants would surely qualify. If you would like to see this unusual, on-campus mini-swamp, turn off Johnston Street (U.S. 167 South) onto McKinley Avenue, which borders the university. Park in the visitors' parking lot on your right and walk through the student union building to the lake.

If youngsters in your party are ready for a break, or you would enjoy a picnic lunch, continue down McKinley for a few blocks to Girard Park, where you will find picnic tables and playground equipment, and the **Lafayette Natural History Museum,** another "kid place" the whole family can enjoy. In a well-supplied Discovery Room, young people use microscopes and magnetism toys to make their own scientific breakthroughs; or they don a cushioned turtle shell, dress-up clothes, or other props to become whatever they want to imagine. And in the main exhibition hall, children explore changing, hands-on exhibits. They are usually delighted with the funny mirrors and neon lights that provide distraction while they wait for the museum's star-studded planetarium show to begin.

Before you leave the Natural History Museum, ask someone to direct you to the **Lafayette Natural History Museum's Acadiana Park Nature Station and Trail,** a few minutes away. Walk down a winding, 0.4-mile-long trail through the park and climb stairs to the Nature Station's treetop-high tower. Here, you can see natural history displays and artifacts found on the site. Acadiana Park was an Indian campground for more than 5,000 years before Pierre Dugat developed it into a prosperous eighteenth-century plantation. Three more miles of forest trails extend from the Nature Station. You can follow them with the Nature Station's self-guiding booklet or join one of the free guided hikes offered on weekends.

The Zoo of Acadiana, two miles south of Broussard, Louisiana, on Lakeview Drive (Louisiana 182), and Lafayette's downtown **Children's Museum** are two more places you may want to visit on a family getaway. The 25-acre menagerie is just a short drive from Lafayette. It accommodates more than 300 animals who live in natural habitats carved out of a forested countryside.

Families can also enjoy the Lafayette area's most outstanding outdoor experience, a boat tour through the scenic Atchafalaya Basin south of Lafayette. Contact **Atchafalaya Experience** in Lafayette or **Angelle's** and **McGee's** boats in Henderson, about thirty miles southeast of Lafayette, to make arrangements.

When the weather isn't attune to nature excursions, the Children's Museum's interactive exhibits provide an enjoyable outlet for youthful energy. While you are downtown, you can also follow the urban trail of murals described in a "Get Downtown Lafayette" brochure, available at the welcome center. Representatives at downtown's **Acadiana Arts Council** and **Artists Alliance** showrooms can direct you to several galleries near the murals. They are part of a seedling art colony being nourished by the city.

If you view the murals around noon, lunch at **Dwyer's,** favored by locals for its homestyle cooking since 1927. Ardent art buffs may prefer to end their gallery hop with a look at the blue dog paintings made famous by artist George Rodrigue. **Rodrigue's Gallery** is in an iron-railed Jefferson Street home nine blocks away. It is just a short walk from the **Cedar Grocery,** where you can sample freshly prepared Greek specialties. After lunch, treat yourself to a cone at **Borden's** old-fashioned ice-cream parlor next door.

Groceries that sell plate lunches and specialty items are very popular in Acadiana. At **Comeaux's** Lafayette locations, the deli selection includes *boudin,* tasso, and quail eggs. The meat case at **Poche's** in Breaux Bridge is brimming with *boudin,* stuffed pork chops, and other delicacies. **Bayou Boudin & Cracklin,** also in Breaux Bridge, features crawfish balls, baked sweet potatoes, and hogshead cheese in addition to its namesake specialties.

For special morning treats, go to **Poupart Bakery, Inc.,** where you can sip a cup of coffee and select a continental breakfast from the delectable danish pastries, croissants, beignets, and breads that the French-trained bakers have prepared. Or drive to Breaux Bridge's **Cafe des Amis** to taste *cush-cush,* a traditional Acadian breakfast cereal, made with cornmeal and served with a topping of milk, cheese, or corn syrup. Follow this up with a tasty *oreille de cochon,* a wafer-thin bit of biscuit dough so named because its ends turn up like a pig's ear when it's fried. They are delicious plain or rolled around *boudin* and coated with powdered sugar or corn syrup. The cafe's scrumptious breakfast is complimentary for guests at **Maison des Amis** Bed and Breakfast located next door to the cafe in the second old-est building in Breaux Bridge.

In the evening, experience fine dining in romantic sur-roundings, at fifty-year-old **Blair House Restaurant & Cafe** or **Cafe Vermilionville,** a Pinhook Road restaurant quartered in Lafayette's first inn. For a change of pace try **LaFonda,** a city landmark not far from Acadian Village that serves delicious southwest Texas/Mexican specialties.

Area Code: (318)

Getting There:

Lafayette is in south-central Louisiana at the junction of Interstate 10, Interstate 49, and U.S. 90. Commercial airlines land at Lafayette airport. There is an Amtrak station. For infor-mation call 1-800-872-7245.

Where and When:

Acadian Village, 200 Greenleaf Dr., Lafayette, LA 70506. 981-2489 or 1-800-962-9133. Daily, 10 A.M.-5 P.M. Admission.

Atchafalaya Experience, 338 N. Sterling St., Lafayette, LA 70501. 233-7816. Admission.

Acadiana Arts Council, Lafayette Art Gallery, 700 Lee Ave., Lafayette, LA 70501. 269-0363. Mon.-Fri., 10 A.M.-4:30 P.M. Free.

Angelle's Atchafalaya Basin Tours, P.O. Box 111, Cecilia, LA 70521. 228-8567. Tours depart daily, 10 A.M., 1 P.M., 3 P.M., and 5 P.M. Reservations advised. Admission.

Artists Alliance, 121 W. Vermilion St., Lafayette, LA 70501. 233-7518. Tues.-Fri., noon-5 P.M.; Sat., 1-5 P.M. or by appointment.

Cathedral of St. John the Evangelist, 914 St. John St. (P.O. Drawer V), Lafayette, LA 70502. 232-1322. Daily, sunrise-sun-set. Descriptive brochures available in back of church.

Children's Museum, 201 E. Congress St., Lafayette, LA 70501. 232-8500. Tues.-Sat., 10 A.M.-5 P.M. Admission.

Combat Aircraft Museum, Lafayette Airport, Surrey Road, Lafayette, LA 70508. 237-7158. Mon.-Fri., noon-5 P.M. Call for seasonal weekend hours. Donations appreciated.

Cypress Lake, University of Southwestern Louisiana, P.O. Box 42611, Lafayette, LA 70504. 231-6954 or 231-6400. Daily, sunrise-sunset.

Jean Lafitte National Historical Park and Preserve's Acadian Cultural Center, 501 Fisher Rd., Lafayette, LA 70508. 232-0789. Daily, 8 A.M.-5 P.M. Free.

Lafayette Museum, 1122 Lafayette St., Lafayette, LA 70501. 234-2208. Tues.-Sat., 9 A.M.-5 P.M.; Sun., 3-5 P.M. Admission.

Lafayette Natural History Museum & Planetarium, 637 Girard Park Dr., Lafayette, LA 70503-2896. 268-5544 or 268-5549. Mon., Wed.-Fri., 9 A.M.-5 P.M.; Tues., 9 A.M.-9 P.M.; Sat. and Sun., 1-5 P.M. Admission charge for some special exhibits.

Lafayette Natural History Museum's Acadiana Park Nature Station and Trail, East Alexander Street (637 Girard Park Dr.), Lafayette, LA 70503-2896. 261-8448. Mon.-Fri., 9 A.M.-5 P.M.; Sat. and Sun., 11 A.M.-3 P.M. Free. Guided tours on Sat. and Sun., 1 P.M. Admission.

McGee's Atchafalaya Basin Tours, McGee's Landing, Henderson, LA (1104 Huval St., Breaux Bridge, LA 70517). 228-8519 or 228-2384. Tours at 10 A.M., 1 P.M., 3 P.M., and 5 P.M. (daylight savings time only). Reservations advised. Admission. Restaurant adjoins landing.

New Evangeline Downs, I-49 North (P.O. Box 90270), Lafayette, LA 70509. Racing season, May-Sept. Call 896-RACE or 1-800-256-1234 in Louisiana for more information. Admission.

Rodrigue's Gallery, 1206 Jefferson St., Lafayette, LA 70501. 232-2180. Mon.-Fri., 10 A.M.-4 P.M.; weekends by appointment.

Shagwood Manor, 1414 E. Bayou Parkway, Lafayette, LA 70508. Open by appointment only. Call 984-1647 or 233-4570. Admission.

Vermilionville, 1600 Surrey St. (P.O. Box 2266), Lafayette, LA 70502-2266. 233-4077 or 1-800-99-BAYOU. Daily, 10 A.M.-5 P.M. Admission.

The Zoo of Acadiana, 116 Lakeview Dr. (Louisiana 182), Broussard, LA 70518. 837-4325. Daily, 9 A.M.-5 P.M. Admission.

For information on area dance halls request a "Cajun Music" brochure from the Lafayette Convention and Visitors Commission.

Note: From mid-March through mid-April, a twenty-mile Azalea Trail, laid out by the Lafayette Jaycees, blooms in Lafayette. A brochure outlining the trail is available from the Lafayette Convention and Visitors Commission.

Information:

Lafayette Convention and Visitors Commission, P.O. Box 52066, Lafayette, LA 70505. 232-3808 or 1-800-346-1958, United States; 1-800-543-5340, Canada. Mon.-Fri., 8:30 A.M.-5 P.M.; Sat. and Sun., 9 A.M.-5 P.M.

Guide Services:

Contact the Lafayette Convention and Visitors Commission.

Accommodations:

Chain and independent hotels and motels in Lafayette.

Bed and Breakfasts:

A Bois des Chenes Inn, 338 N. Sterling St., Lafayette, LA 70501. 233-7816.

Acadian Bed and Breakfast, 127 Vincent Rd., Lafayette, LA 70508. 856-5260.

Bayou Cabins, 100 Mills Ave., Breaux Bridge, LA 70517. 332-6158 or 1-800-884-7329.

Belle of the Oaks Bed and Breakfast, 122 Le Medecin Rd., Carencro, LA 70520. 896-4965.

Chretien Point Plantation, Route 1, Box 162, Sunset, LA 70584. 662-5876 or 1-800-233-7050.

Country Oaks Guesthouse, 1138-A Lawless Tauzin Rd., Breaux Bridge, LA 70517. 332-3093.

La Maison de Campagne, 825 Kidder Rd., Carencro, LA 70520. 896-6529.

A La Maison de T' Frere, 1905 Verot School Rd., Lafayette, LA 70508. 984-9347.

Maison Andre Billeaud, 203 E. Main St., Broussard, LA 70518. 837-3455 or 1-800-960-REST.

Maison des Amis, 140 E. Bridge St., Breaux Bridge, LA 70517. 332-5273.

Mouton Manor Inn, 310 Sidney Martin Rd., Lafayette, LA 70507. 237-6996.

Shagwood Manor Guest House, 1414 E. Bayou Parkway, Lafayette, LA 70508. 984-1647 or 233-4570.

Tante Da's, 2631 S.E. Evangeline Thruway, Lafayette, LA 70508-2168. 264-1191 or 1-800-853-REST.

For a complete listing of accommodations, request "Cajun Country Vacation Guide" from the Lafayette Convention and Visitors Commission.

Restaurants:

Bayou Boudin & Cracklin, 100 Mills Ave., Breaux Bridge, LA 70517. 332-6158. Daily, 7 A.M.-6 P.M.

Blair House Restaurant & Cafe, 1316 Surrey St., Lafayette, LA 70501. 234-0357. Cafe: Mon.-Fri., 11 A.M.-3 P.M. Restaurant: Mon.-Fri., 11 A.M.-10 P.M.; Sat., 5-10:30 P.M.

Borden's Ice Cream Store, 1103 Jefferson St., Lafayette, LA 70501. 235-9291. Sun. and Mon., 11 A.M.-10 P.M.; Tues. and Wed., 2-10 P.M.; Thurs.-Sat., 11 A.M.-10 P.M.

Cafe des Amis, 140 E. Bridge St., Breaux Bridge, LA 70517. 332-5273. Tues.-Sun., 8 A.M.-10 P.M.

Cafe Vermilionville, 1304 W. Pinhook Rd., Lafayette, LA 70503. 237-0100. Mon.-Fri., 11 A.M.-2 P.M., 5:30-10 P.M.; Sat., 5:30-10 P.M.; Sun.,11 A.M.-2 P.M.

Cedar Grocery, 1115 Jefferson St., Lafayette, LA 70501. 233-5460. Mon.-Fri., 9 A.M.-6 P.M.; Sat., 9 A.M.-4 P.M.

Comeaux's Cajun Corner, 1215 Moss St., Lafayette, LA 70501. 233-1612. Mon.-Fri., 8 A.M.-6 P.M.; Sat., 8 A.M.-5 P.M.

Comeaux's Grocery & Market, 2807 Kaliste Rd., Lafayette, LA 70508. 988-0516. Mon.-Fri., 7 A.M.-8 P.M.; Sat., 8 A.M.-8 P.M.

Comeaux's Grocery & Market, 1000 Lamar St., Lafayette, LA 70501. 234-6109. Mon.-Fri., 7 A.M.-6 P.M.; Sat., 8 A.M.-5 P.M.

Dwyer's Cafe, 323 Jefferson St., Lafayette, LA 70501. Mon.-Fri., 4 A.M.-4 P.M.; Sat., 4 A.M.-2 P.M.

LaFonda Restaurant, 3809 Johnston St., Lafayette, LA 70503. 984-5630. Tues.-Thurs., 11 A.M.-10 P.M.; Fri. and Sat., Lunch: 11 A.M.-2 P.M., Dinner: 5-10 P.M.

McGee's Atchafalaya Cafe, Henderson, LA (1104 Huval St., Breaux Bridge, LA 70517). 228-7555 or 1-800-445-6681. Mar.-Nov.: Mon., 11 A.M.-5 P.M.; Tues.-Sun., 11 A.M.-8 P.M. Call for off-season hours.

Mulate's—The World's Most Famous Cajun Restaurant, 325 Mills Ave., Breaux Bridge, LA 70517. 1-800-634-9880, Louisiana; 1-800-422-2586 (1-800-42-CAJUN), U.S. Mon.-Sat., 7 A.M.-10:30 P.M.; Sun., 11 A.M.-11 P.M. Live Cajun music seven nights a week and daily at lunch. Cajun breakfast.

Poche's Market & Restaurant, 3015-A Main Hwy., Breaux Bridge, LA 70517. 332-2108. Daily, 6 A.M.-9 P.M.

Poupart Bakery, Inc., 1902 W. Pinhook Rd., Lafayette, LA 70508. 232-7921. Tues.-Sat., 7 A.M.-6:30 P.M.; Sun., 7 A.M.-4 P.M.

Prejean's Restaurant, 3480 U.S. 167 North, Lafayette, LA 70501. 896-3247. Mon.-Thurs., 11 A.M.-10 P.M.; Fri. and Sat., 11 A.M.-11 P.M. Live Cajun music every evening.

Randol's Restaurant & Cajun Dancehall, 2320 Kaliste Saloom Rd., Lafayette, LA 70508. 981-7080 or 1-800-YO-CAJUN. Mon.-Thurs., 5-10 P.M.; Fri.-Sun., 5-10:30 P.M. Live Cajun music and dancing every night. Home of "Laissez Les Bons Temps Rouler" Cajun music show filmed at Randol's and shown on television channel 15, Saturdays from 4-5 P.M. Call Randol's for shooting schedule.

For a complete listing of Lafayette area restaurants, request

"Cajun Country Vacation Guide" from Lafayette Convention and Visitors Commission.

Major Annual Events:

Cajun Christmas, Lafayette—December 1-31.

Crawfish Festival, Breaux Bridge—First full weekend in May.

Festival Acadiens, Lafayette—Third week in September.

Festival International de Louisiane, Lafayette—Third week in April.

Mardi Gras Day, Lafayette—Tuesday before Ash Wednesday.

Statue of Evangeline. (Courtesy Petit Paris Museum)

31

A LIBERAL SPRINKLING OF SALT AND PEPPER
(G)

Perhaps the Creator was hinting at the zesty dishes Acadian cooks would one day concoct when He whipped up a gumbo of seafood-rich marshes and bayous along the south Louisiana coast, sprinkled it liberally with salt, and added a dash of pepper.

Near the Bayou Teche town of New Iberia two islands whose histories are closely tied to the area's large, prehistoric deposits of salt yield a feast for the eyes. One of the two is also the home of one of the most popular brands of pepper sauce in the world. The **Iberia Parish Tourist Commission** on Louisiana 14, north of U.S. 90, has information on these unique attractions and others you may also enjoy.

The spectacular beauty of **Live Oak Gardens** adorns a hilltop seven miles southwest of the information center. Thousands of flowers cascade down the lofty knoll in front of a Gothic home built by nineteenth-century actor Joseph Jefferson.

You spy familiar blooms and exotic greenery as you climb Live Oak Gardens' blossom-rimmed paths to the famed thespian's winter retreat. You also see the Lafitte Oaks, which shade one of the few places some of the legendary pirate's treasure was actually found. After viewing rare antiques and paintings in the actor's architecturally innovative home, saunter down the walkway to Live Oak Gardens Cafe-by-the-Lake and dine in a picturesque setting overlooking Lake Peigneur.

As you gaze at the peaceful scene before you, you will find it hard to believe that it was once marred by tragedy. On November 20, 1980, barges, a home, and a section of Live Oak Gardens were swallowed up by a whirlpool that drained the lake. You can relive the incredible tale of Live Oak Gardens' misadventure—resulting from an accidental puncture of the salt dome under the lake—by watching a video at the visitors center. The story is also told aboard the boat that offers cruises of Lake Peigneur. Enjoy the boat ride, then end your tour of Live Oak Gardens with a visit to the Gallery of the Gardens, a showcase for national and local artworks, on the edge of the parking area.

Another huge salt dome is located on Avery Island on Louisiana 329. But the island, off Louisiana 14 north of the Iberia Parish Tourist Commission's Information Center, is most famous for the sharp, sinus-clearing aroma of fermenting pepper mash that drifts through its Tabasco Pepper Sauce Factory. Artifacts, and a film shown at the **McIlhenny Company,** recall the history and explain the processing of Tabasco brand pepper sauce.

Edmund McIlhenny fathered the commercial processing of Louisiana pepper sauces when he mixed and aged Capsicum pepper mash, salt, and vinegar, ladled it into 150 perfume bottles (the only containers left after Union troops devastated his island home), and sent them to markets in New York. His family now ships the zingy sauce all over the world.

Pepper plant operations occupy a large section of Avery Island's alluring terrain, but a 200-acre tract of the fertile land has been developed into "The Jungle Gardens of Avery Island."

This entrancing, pastoral sanctuary is planted with camellias and azaleas, plus other exotic plants E. A. ("Ned") McIlhenny, son of the Tabasco sauce founder, gathered from every corner of the world. As you wander through them, you see alligators, nutria, and other animals. The most notable are the snowy egrets Ned saved from extinction.

After a day of "garden-ing," head into New Iberia and become better acquainted with the town's saucy Cajun culture. Follow Louisiana 14 (Center Street) to St. Peter Street. Turn right, and right again, to the **Konriko Rice Mill and Company Store** on Ann Street. Here, you can watch an excellent slide presentation on the history and culture of Acadiana and tour America's oldest rice mill.

After you enjoy the complimentary tasting of Konriko's products that completes the tour, turn right onto St. Peter Street, left at Lewis St (Spur 87), and left again onto Main Street. Drive west on Main Street to a historic neighborhood of graceful residences, shaded by massive oak trees. Since traffic flows quickly along Main Street, you can enjoy New Iberia's Historic District more if you walk for a few blocks. As you pass the ornate Steamboat House (circa 1886–90) at 623 Main St., notice the elephantine oak tree intruding on the entryway and, as you cross Prairie Avenue, the Gebert Oak, planted in 1831 by Mrs. Jonas Marsh over the grave of her son. Its wide-reaching boughs nearly obscure the Gates home at the rear of the picket-fenced yard.

Illness and death were all too familiar to New Iberia's early settlers. Residents lost hundreds of family members to yellow fever, in spite of the loving care rendered by nurses such as Félicité, a black native of Haiti. A historical marker in front of New Iberia's Civic Center—housed in the former St. Peter's College—notes that everyone in town followed her to her resting place when she passed away in 1852.

A few feet away, alongside the Iberia Parish Library, a Lourdes Grotto is dedicated to New Iberians who died in foreign wars. When you cross Main Street by the grotto, you will be near two historic houses that welcome bed-and-breakfast guests. **Maison Marcelline** is a tastefully decorated Eastlake cottage with an inviting patio garden. **The Estorge-Norton House** next door to it is a comfortable turn-of-the-century bungalow.

When you have completed this short, historic district walking tour, continue west on Main Street to **Shadows-on-the-Teche,** a splendid antebellum manor at the intersection of Main and Center streets. Park in front of the Shadows, or in the alley on the far side of the mansion.

Slave artisans built the red-bricked, white-columned mansion in 1834 for David and Mary Clara Weeks. Since then, four generations of the family have lived in the home, leaving behind many of the fine furnishings on display and 40 trunks of clothing, family papers, and plantation inventories in the attic. Shadows-on-the-Teche is one of only 17 houses in the United States designated a National Trust for Historic Preservation Masterplace. All are homes that "preserve a significant part of our national heritage."

You can enjoy fine dining and a pleasant view of The Shadows at **Le Rosier,** a well-appointed restaurant and Bed and Breakfast across the street from the mansion.

When you leave The Shadows, drive onto Weeks Street, which intersects Main Street across from the mansion's parking lot. A half-block away, in front of the New Iberia Savings and Loan Association's building, you can view the city's most unusual landmark—a seven-foot-plus statue of Hadrian, the Roman emperor noted for the 73-mile-long wall he built in England. This towering remnant of an 1,800-year-old culture was a world traveler until 1961, when the financial institution purchased it and enclosed it in glass.

Continue your tour of New Iberia west of the Shadows where you can explore the town's downtown section. Complimentary parking and a stellar view of Bayou Teche are offered at Bouligny Plaza. Information and directions are available at the **Chamber of Commerce** across Main Street from the plaza.

Choose Louisiana-made handicrafts at **Combined Effort,** an artisans' cooperative at the foot of the Duperier Street bridge, two blocks east of Bouligny Plaza. Then, scan items that found their way out of neighborhood attics into a string of flea markets on Iberia Street, around the corner from the Chamber of Commerce.

Then return to Main Street to browse through the enticing assortment of cookbooks, and books on Acadiana and Louisiana, displayed at **Books Along the Teche.** It is to the left, between the Chamber of Commerce and **Lagniappe, Too,** a charming cafe where locals gather to enjoy the restaurant's flavorful Louisiana-French cuisine.

To the right of the Chamber office, **Bayou Art Gallery** displays works by approximately 70 local artists. Two blocks away, you will pass ivy-coated Episcopal Church of the Epiphany, used as a field hospital and prison during the Civil War. Tours can be arranged at the rectory.

In St. Martinville, about nine miles north of New Iberia, three bells—named Marie Angeli, Auguste, and Stephanie—call the faithful to worship at another historic chapel, **St. Martin de Tours Catholic Church.**

The chapel, the mother church of the Acadians, is the centerpiece of St. Martinville's well-preserved town square. It is framed by **Petit Paris Museum,** which houses a collection of Mardi Gras costumes and local crafts, and the church rectory, built in a grand style in 1856 in hopes that it would be used as the bishop's home.

Behind the chapel, a statue of Emmeline Labiche commemorates the tragic separation of Acadian families that inspired Henry Wadsworth Longfellow's poem *Evangeline.* Professional storytellers retell the saga of Evangeline and Gabriel, two star-crossed Acadian sweethearts, under the spreading branches of the Evangeline Oak on the banks of Bayou Teche. The revered tree shelters the traditionally accepted site of the first landing of the Acadians in Louisiana.

The raconteurs may also direct you to **Longfellow-Evangeline Commemorative Area** on the northern edge of St. Martinville. Here, you can visit the legendary home of Gabriel and learn more about happenings that caused the Acadians to be exiled from Canada.

The **Old Castillo Hotel** that stands in the shade of the Evangeline Oak was once a way station for steamboat passengers. Now, the restored hostelry offers tasty meals and bed-and-breakfast accommodations. Travelers can also enjoy continental breakfast at **Danna's Bakery** or a hearty plate of food at **Durand's Quality Meats & Cafe.**

As you stroll along Bayou Teche and meander in and out of the shops surrounding St. Martinville's square, you can hear conversations carried on in a *patois* (dialect) that incorporates ancient words used by French aristocrats who fled to St. Martinville—their *"Petit Paris"*—at the start of the French Revolution. You can also find friendly, bilingual residents and salespeople in shops such as **Acadian Arts and Crafts** and **Les be' Belle,** a gift and clothing boutique quartered in an opera house once prized by the French nobility.

While you are in St. Martinville, cross Bayou Teche at Bridge Street—between Petit Paris Museum and Acadian Arts and Crafts—and explore the sites of two Louisiana legends connected by humble symbols of faith.

Bridge Street leads to Louisiana 96, where a historical marker about two miles away details the story of Charles Durand's Oak and Pine Alley. Turn onto the gravel road by the marker, and drive for more than a mile under a canopy of trees that used to extend two miles farther to Durand's Bayou Teche plantation. Imagine the tree-lined alley as legend says it appeared on the day Durand's daughters were married at a double ceremony—laced with spider webs sprinkled with gold dust.

As you continue on Louisiana 96 to Catahoula, notice the simple, creche-shaped Stations of the Cross strung along the highway. When St. Rita's congregation was blessed with a new church in the early 1950s, church members placed the cypress wood stations from their former church in Catahoula along the road so they could "keep their mind on God" during trips to St. Martinville. The stations are refurbished every few years by Catahoulians who solemnly follow the ten-mile route *en masse* on Good Friday.

The Catahoula Indians, for whom the town is named, worshipped a different god, one that had to be appeased with sacrificial offerings of young maidens. Lake Catahoula, which borders the tiny fishing village, is said to be the burial site of these unlucky virgins.

After your jaunt to Catahoula, return to New Iberia by way of St. Martinville. Stop for refreshments at **Barbara's Restaurant** in **Beno's Motel,** a nineteen-room country inn midway between New Iberia and St. Martinville, or **Possum's,** a mostly seafood eatery near the same location.

If you can spend more time in Acadiana, consider two short, but enjoyable, side trips that start in downtown New Iberia. To follow the first route, cross the Duperier Street bridge, turn right onto Louisiana 87, and drive to its terminus in Jeanerette. On the way, you will pass New Iberia's scenic, rural-residential areas. Just past Alice (private) and Bayside (private) plantations, recross the bayou and drive east for about a mile on Louisiana 182 into Jeanerette. Here, you can visit the sugar-sweetened **Jeanerette Museum,** roam through **Emery's Antiques and Collectibles,** and treat yourself to a loaf of New Orleans-style French bread, baked in original brick ovens used by **LeJeune's Bakery** since 1884. Drive back to New Iberia on Louisiana 182.

If you are in the mood for some excitement, take a "hold onto your hat" airboat ride on Lake Fausse Pointe. The lake, scenic most any time of year, is especially beautiful in early summer when yellow-blossomed American Lotus float atop the shallow water. To reach Lake Fausse Pointe, follow the map on the back of **Airboat Tours, Inc.'s** brochure (available at New Iberia's visitors center) to Loreauville's Marshfield Boat Landing.

Area Code: (318)

Getting There:

U.S. 90 and Louisiana 182 (scenic route) lead to New Iberia. Both St. Martinville and New Iberia can also be reached via Louisiana 31 (Exit 109 South) off of Interstate 10.

Where and When:

Acadian Arts and Crafts, Bridge and Main streets, St. Martinville, LA 70582. 394-4304, 394-5407, or 394-9230. Tues.-Sat., 10 A.M.-4 P.M.

Airboat Tours, Inc., Marshfield Boat Landing (P.O. Box 716), Loreauville, LA 70552. 229-4457. Tues.-Sun. Call for times and reservations. Admission.

Bayou Art Gallery, 143 W. Main St., New Iberia, LA 70560. 369-3014. Mon.-Fri., 10 A.M.-4 P.M.; Sat., 10 A.M.-2 P.M.

Books Along the Teche, 110 E. Main St., New Iberia, LA 70560. 367-7621. Mon.-Sat., 9:30 A.M.-5:30 P.M.

Combined Effort, 121 Burke St., New Iberia, LA 70560. 369-7569. Mon.-Sat., 9 A.M.-5 P.M.

Emery's Antiques and Collectibles, 1522 Main St., Jeanerette, LA 70544. 276-3940. Daily, 9 A.M.-5 P.M.

Jeanerette Museum, 500 E. Main St. (LA 182), Jeanerette, LA 70544. 276-4408. Mon.-Fri., 10 A.M.-noon, 1-4 P.M. Admission.

Konriko Rice Mill and Company Store, 301 Ann St., New Iberia, LA 70560. 1-800-551-3245 or 367-6163. Mon.-Sat., 9 A.M.-5 P.M. Admission.

LeJeune's Bakery, 1510 W. Main St., Jeanerette, LA 70544. 276-5690. Mon.-Fri., 4 A.M.-6 P.M.

Les be' Belle, 214 S. Main St., St. Martinville, LA 70582. 394-1252. Mon.-Fri., 10 A.M.-6 P.M.; Sat., 10 A.M.-4 P.M.

Live Oak Gardens, 5505 Rip Van Winkle Rd., New Iberia, LA 70560. 365-3332. Daily, 9 A.M.-5 P.M. Admission.

Longfellow-Evangeline State Commemorative Area, P.O. Box 497, St. Martinville, LA 70582. 394-3754. Daily, 9 A.M.-5 P.M. Admission.

McIlhenny Company, Avery Island, LA 70513. 369-6243. Tabasco Factory: Mon.-Fri., 9 A.M.-3:45 P.M. Sat., 9-11:45 A.M. Free. Jungle Gardens: Daily, 8 A.M.-5:30 P.M. Admission.

Petit Paris Museum, 103 S. Main St., St. Martinville, LA 70582. 394-7334. Daily, 9:30 A.M.-4:30 P.M. Admission.

St. Martin de Tours Catholic Church, 133 S. Main St., St. Martinville, LA 70582. 394-6021. Daily, sunrise-sunset.

Shadows-on-the-Teche, 317 E. Main St., New Iberia, LA 70560. 369-6446. Daily, 9 A.M.-4:30 P.M. Admission.

Information:

Chamber of Commerce, 111 W. Main St., New Iberia, LA 70560. 364-1836. Mon.-Fri., 8:30 A.M.-5 P.M.

Iberia Parish Tourist Commission, 2704 LA 14, New Iberia, LA 70560. 365-1540. Daily, 9 A.M.-5 P.M.

Guide Services:

In New Iberia:

Barbara Hoyt, 1204 Iberia St., New Iberia, LA 70560. 365-5686.

Cajun Fun Tours, 701 Parkview Dr., New Iberia, LA 70560. 369-6777.

Contact the Lafayette Convention and Visitors Commission, P.O. Box 52066, Lafayette, LA 70505. 232-3808 or 1-800-346-1958 (United States); 1-800-543-5340 (Canada). Mon.-Fri., 8:30 A.M.-5 P.M.; Sat. and Sun., 9 A.M.-5 P.M.

Accommodations:

Chain and independent motels in New Iberia.

Beno's Motel, Louisiana 31, St. Martinville, LA 70582. 394-5523.

Bed and Breakfasts: *area code 318*

Alice Plantation, 9217 Old Jeanerette Rd., Jeanerette, LA 70560. 276-3187.

Chez Herbert, 5304 Stoneline Dr., New Iberia, LA 70560. 367-6447.

The Inn at Le Rosier, 314 E. Main St., New Iberia, LA 70560. 367-5306.

La Maison Bed and Breakfast, Lydia, LA (Route 4, Box 207, New Iberia, LA 70560). 364-2970.

La Maison du Teche Bed and Breakfast, 417 E. Main St., New Iberia, LA 70560. 367-9456.

Maison Bleu Bed and Breakfast, 417 N. Main St., St. Martinville, LA 70582. 394-1215. *3 rooms: ① - king bed + shower $95 ③ queen + shower $75 ② 2 full + trundle + free standing bath $85*

Maison Marcelline, 442 E. Main St., New Iberia, LA 70560. 364-5922.

Old Castillo Hotel, 220 Evangeline Blvd. (P.O. Box 172), St. Martinville, LA 70582. 394-4010 or 1-800-621-3017.

Pourtos House, 4018 Old Jeanerette Rd., New Iberia, LA 70560. 367-7045 or 1-800-336-7317.

disconnected disconnected

For a complete list of area accommodations, request "Iberia Parish Accommodations Guide" from the Iberia Parish Tourist Commission.

Restaurants:

Barbara's Restaurant, Beno's Motel, Louisiana 31, St. Martinville, LA 70582. 394-5523. Lunch buffet: Mon.-Fri., 11 A.M.-2 P.M. Dinner: Sun.-Thurs., 5:30-10 P.M.; Fri. and Sat., 5 P.M.-midnight.

Danna's Bakery, 207 E. Bridge St., St. Martinville, LA 70582. 394-3889. Tues.-Sat., 5:30 A.M.-5:30 P.M.

Durand's Quality Meats & Cafe, 117 W. Port St., St. Martinville, LA 70582. Grocery: 394-5981. Cafe: 394-9880. Sun.-Thurs., 5:30 A.M.-4 P.M.; Fri., 5:30 A.M.-9 P.M.

Lagniappe Too, 204 E. Main St., New Iberia, LA 70560. 365-9419. Lunch: Mon.-Fri., 10 A.M.-2 P.M. Dinner: Fri. and Sat., 6-9 P.M. (summer, 7-10 P.M.)

Le Rosier, 314 E. Main St., New Iberia, LA 70560. 367-5306. Lunch: Mon.-Fri., 11:30 A.M.-2 P.M.; Dinner: Tues.-Sat., 6:30-9 P.M. Reservations required for dinner.

Old Castillo Restaurant, 220 Evangeline Blvd. (P.O. Box 172), St. Martinville, LA 70582. 394-4010 or 1-800-621-3017. Sun.-Thurs., 8 A.M.-9 P.M.; Fri. and Sat., 8 A.M.-10 P.M.

Possum's, 1007 Little Oak Dr. (LA 31), St. Martinville, LA 70582. 394-3233. Lunch: daily, 11 A.M.-2 P.M. Dinner: Sun.-Fri., 5-10 P.M.; Sat., 5-11 P.M.

For a complete listing of area restaurants, request "Iberia Parish Restaurant Guide" from the Iberia Parish Tourist Commission.

Major Annual Events:

Christmas on the Teche, New Iberia—Weekend after Thanksgiving.

Delcambre Shrimp Festival, Delcambre—Third weekend in August.

St. Lucy Festival of Lights, St. Martinville—First Friday in December.

Sugar Cane Festival, New Iberia—Last weekend in September.

Statue of Pere Megret, the founder of Abbeville. (Photo by Mary Fonseca)

St. Mary Magdalen Catholic Church. (Photo by Mary Fonseca)

32

GOOD NEIGHBORS

Traffic zips along U.S. 90 between Morgan City and Lafayette at a steady clip. Trucks carrying cargo on the well-traveled corridor roll alongside motorists and tour buses headed for celebrated attractions in Louisiana's Cajun Country.

Louisiana 14, a two-lane highway that angles westward from Louisiana 90 near New Iberia, is not nearly as busy. But weekenders who turn onto this "road less traveled" discover warm hospitality and delightful Acadian ambiance in the neighboring communities of Erath, Abbeville, and Kaplan.

Comfortable accommodations are available in three countryside Bed and Breakfasts and two tidy inns in Abbeville and Kaplan. On your excursions, invite tête-à-têtes with the amiable folks you meet by offering a handshake or a smile.

Start getting acquainted by visiting the **Greater Abbeville-Vermilion Chamber of Commerce Tourist Information Center** on Veterans Memorial Drive (Louisiana 14 Bypass). In the 1840s, Abbeville was just a vision in the mind of Pere Antoine Megret, a well-heeled Catholic priest. At first, the good Father was just going to build a chapel on property he owned to serve the faithful in the southern part of Vermilion Parish. But, in 1846, Pere Megret became convinced that the land around the chapel would be the best location for the parish seat. To help his dream become reality, he designed a town with two public squares, named it Abbeville after his hometown in Provence,

France, and donated the land on which it was to be built to Vermilion Parish.

A cherished statue of Pere Megret in one of Abbeville's original squares commemorates his generosity. It is only a few steps away from **St. Mary Magdalen Catholic Church,** known as the most beautiful in Acadiana. Walk inside and see the enchanting cherubs that decorate the church's baroque-style organ.

Several shopkeepers in the neighborhood around St. Mary Magdalen offer made-in-Louisiana merchandise. Hazel Roy stocks her **Cajun Cupboard** (across the street from the church) with local crafts and south Louisiana-style confections. Admire the view of St. Mary Magdalen, and indulge in a cup of gourmet coffee, a delicious pastry, or a tempting dessert, while seated at one of Cajun Cupboard's inviting tables.

Grandparents who wander into Roy's **Little Miss & Master** shop next door to Cajun Cupboard do so at their own risk. Once they see the store's exquisite christening and communion outfits, many "Mamams" and "Papas" feel they must buy one to take home. These special occasion clothes—plus other children's apparel—are handmade by nimble-fingered Roy and her talented assistant, Cheryl LeBlanc.

Roma Russo's **Roma LTD,** in the 400 block of Pere Megret Street, has fashionable handbags and accessories, plus sterling silver jewelry made in Louisiana. Crawfish, alligators, and other symbols of Acadiana decorate the finely crafted bracelets, earrings, and necklaces Roma sells.

Cajun themes also embellish T-shirts and aprons at **Abbeville Record Shoppe.** In addition to CDs, you still can purchase 45, 12, and LP records here. The State Street music store also carries a sizeable inventory of old and new recordings by Louisiana musicians. Harmonicas, fiddles, and accordions are available for customers who prefer to make their own music.

Arlene Faulk's charming shop, **The Apple Tree,** is just around the corner from the record shop. Arlene can help you select cards and gifts, or a collectible souvenir, at her Concord Street store.

Some of Abbeville's best restaurants are interspersed with the stores. **Dupuy's Oyster Shop** preserves the name the owner's grandfather, Joseph Dupuy, gave to the South Main Street business in 1887. Joseph sold his freshly harvested oysters by the sack, gallon, or dozen. You can still buy them that way at Dupuy's, or you can select one of the restaurant's delicious oyster specialties. They include a grilled oyster salad, oyster stew, and an oyster and shrimp loaf.

Sacks and gallons of fresh oysters are also available at **Black's Oyster Bar,** but oysters on the half-shell is the specialty here. Black's also features an oyster cocktail, plus many of the same delectable choices offered at Dupuy's. Both eateries serve a variety of seafood fare, but they are renowned for their oyster dishes.

If you are celebrating a special occasion, or want to feel like you are, reserve a table at **Ovide's Riverfront Restaurant** on the banks of the Vermilion River. On weekends a pianist plays soft music while diners enjoy the restaurant's fine cuisine and a pleasing view of Abbeville's downtown district.

For a more casual atmosphere, try **El Camino Restaurant** on Concord Street or **Park Restaurant** across the Vermilion River on Park Avenue. El Camino offers a festive decor and well-cooked Mexican specialties. Park is a good choice for hearty breakfasts and homestyle Cajun dinners.

If you plan your getaway in advance, you can enjoy an entertaining performance after dinner. **The Abbey Players** present well-known comedies and dramas in their recently expanded, professional playhouse located in Abbeville's restaurant/shopping area. Theater buffs from all over Acadiana make up the capacity crowds that applaud the 20-year-old company's four annual productions.

After the final curtain, meet some of the cast members at **Crescent Grill & Tavern,** across the street from the playhouse. The after-theater crowd relishes the restaurant's steak, seafood, and pasta dishes. The convivial setting is enhanced by box office posters of Abbey Players productions.

For a memorable Sunday in Abbeville, join the crowd caught up in the excitement of racing at **Cajun Downs.** Locals gather here to watch youthful jockeys test the mettle of fleet-footed

The Cajun Downs sign. (Photo by Mary Fonseca)

Mary Suire on the porch of Suire's Grocery in Kaplan. (Photo by Mary Fonseca)

quarter horses. They urge their mounts down unique, fenced-lane courses used for these short, thrilling races.

The only changes made at Cajun Downs over the last fifty years are those that were necessary to improve the racecourse. You won't find a plush clubhouse or computerized betting windows. However, friendly wagers are made amongst the spectators. Everyone brings a lawn chair and a picnic lunch, or they buy the barbecued foods sold at the track. It's great fun to watch the races and listen to owners and bettors argue the merits of their horses in Cajun French. Take Louisiana 338 North from the Louisiana 14 Bypass to this vintage bush track.

The Hebert family has owned Cajun Downs for more than a century. When Clement Hebert, the present owner, is not attending to business at Cajun Downs, you can usually find him behind the counter at **Hebert's Slaughterhouse Market.** Some locals say Hebert's *boudin* sausage—sold at the market directly across from the track—is the best in the area.

Larry's Super Foods in Kaplan lacks the old-time atmosphere of Hebert's market but gourmands still extol the supermarket's Cajun specialties. You will find marinated pork, locally known as *grillades;* boneless chickens stuffed with cornbread, rice dressing, or crawfish and rice; plus an array of spicy sausages, turkey *tasso* (smoked turkey slices), *chaudin* (stuffed pig stomach), and rabbits farm-raised in Louisiana.

Fill your ice chest with some of Larry's tasty Cajun foods during a delightful jaunt to the Kaplan area. Early risers can start the day with a flavorful breakfast at **Homestead Steak & Seafood Restaurant,** on North Cushing Street in Kaplan. Between seven and nine, this cafe with its easygoing atmosphere is usually buzzing with sociable locals who converse about affairs of the day in Cajun French. Let them know you are a visitor and they will give you a hearty welcome in English.

You will also be graciously welcomed at two charming shops that offer handmade Louisiana keepsakes and a selection of delightful gifts. At **Victorian Reflections,** on North Cushing Street, Kim Guidrey and Ramona Navarre sell Victorian accessories plus lovely, hand-fashioned items made by Louisiana artisans. They have antique buttons from St. Francisville, ivory buttons from Washington, herbal bath salts and paintings from Lafayette, and hand-painted desks from Lake Arthur. Beautiful decoupaged hat boxes and suitcases are made by the talented shopkeepers.

Janie Forman fills some shelves in her First Street (Louisiana 14) **Granny's Hut** with hand-painted wood crafts. But this talented grandmother also makes high quality Christmas decorations, homemade herbal bath salts, scented soaps, and vinegars. Her daughter, Julie Abshire, helps her turn out the shop's dainty handmade clothing for infants and children.

At **Kaplan City Hall,** on North Cushing Street just a few blocks north of Homestead Steak & Seafood Restaurant, you can request information or maps to help you explore the surrounding countryside. Visitors interested in agriculture also may arrange a visit to a local emu farm at the civic center office.

Valued for their hides, oil, meat, and feathers, emus are the newest critters raised on American farms. As you cruise along Vermilion Parish roads you may catch glimpses of these long-necked cousins of the ostrich, or of farmers tending cattle, crawfish, alligators, and catfish. But, as the huge Riviana and Liberty Mills in Abbeville and Kaplan affirm, rice is the major agricultural interest here.

In the spring, crop duster planes swoop down over flooded fields to release rice seeds. The water is drained off from mid-summer into fall so huge combines can gather the crop. Then the fields are flooded again to usher in the crawfish season. The succulent crustaceans end their hibernation, climb out of their muddy burrows beneath the flooded fields, and feed on hulls and rice left by the harvesters.

Watch for signs of these agricultural activities as you head east out of Kaplan on Louisiana 14. Turn south on Louisiana 35 for approximately twelve miles, then travel eight miles east on Louisiana 82 to Esther. From this point, take Louisiana 333 through Intracoastal City to **Leland Bowman Lock.** The lock is a U.S. Army Corps of Engineers project that prevents salt water from intruding through the Gulf Intracoastal Waterway into the Mermentau Basin rice-growing area. An informative flyer about the lock and the weather-monitoring procedures that take place there is available inside the U.S. Army Corps of Engineers office adjacent to the lock. Restrooms in the building are open to the public.

On your way to the lock, pick up some soft drinks at one of the small stores that line the highway in Intracoastal City. Enjoy your cool beverages while you watch boats and barges pass through the lock from your perch atop a raised gazebo the Corps constructed for visitors. Bring some binoculars, because, depending on the season, you also may spot alligators, deer, and an extraordinary variety of birds.

When it's time for lunch, retrace your route up Louisiana 35 to **Suire's** restaurant and grocery at the intersection of Louisiana 35 and 335. When this local landmark opened for business about seventy years ago, groceries lined shelves in the whole building. Several years later, when Mary Suire started cooking lunches and suppers for her family at the store, customers tantalized by the tangy aroma of her cooking started asking if they could buy a plate of "whatever it is that smells so good." So, Suire's gradually evolved into a restaurant that sells a few groceries.

The old store is imbued with an aura of yesteryear. Old-fashioned utensils decorate the walls. Among them is a washboard—"my husband's first gift to me," says Suire. At long tables covered with crawfish print tablecloths, farmers and visitors enjoy a relaxed camaraderie, and the scrumptious plate lunch Mary cooked that day. At a counter in back of the store, customers order po' boys and burgers or opt for some of Mary's homemade fruit tarts, syrup cakes, and sausage breads. On Saturday and Sunday nights the popular cook prepares steaks and seafoods for a crowd that knows the truth of the motto she prints on her menus, "If you want country cooking, come to the country."

After a leisurely lunch at Suire's, visit Cajuns from the past and present at one of the best small museums in Louisiana. Erath's **Acadian Heritage and Culture Museum** is quartered in the "Old Bank of Erath," one of the oldest buildings in the area. Inside the bank's sturdy walls, The Acadian Heritage & Culture Foundation displays records, artifacts, and memorabilia of the Acadians. There are three roomfuls of informative exhibits; one is devoted to the settlement and development of Erath, while the other two trace the history of the Acadians before and after their banishment from Canada. A collection of videos, books, and documents is available to those interested in researching Acadian history.

If your last name is Broussard, the Erath museum will hold a particular attraction for you. The Beausoleil Broussard family and their descendants settled the town of Erath. Documents pertaining to the village are on exhibit along with a list of other Acadian family names—such as Gaudet—whose members may belong to this family tree. The museum is on the corner of South Broadway and Louisiana 14.

If you are a fan of D. L. Menard, the singer, songwriter, and guitar player known as "the Cajun Hank Williams," drop by Menard's rocking chair factory and say hello while you are in Erath. Menard recently was proclaimed a National Heritage Fellow by the National Endowment for the Arts. But this Hall of Fame musician who has traveled the world with his band, the Louisiana Aces, has no airs about him. He loves people and is always happy to welcome visitors. To reach Menard's factory, drive down Broadway, turn right at Bourque Street, and left on Kibbie Street. Continue on Kibbie until you see a metal building on your left with Menard's rocking chair sign in front of it.

The Louisiana Aces are usually on the road, but other local bands play lively music every weekend at **Pirate's** (pronounced *P-rats*) on Louisiana 14 in Erath. Families and friends gather here to enjoy the restaurant's boiled and fried seafood. Then, they two-step the night away.

If you prefer to return to Kaplan, you can enjoy traditional Cajun cuisine at **Hebert's Steak House,** a family-style restaurant on Louisiana 14 between Kaplan and Abbeville. Although it may seem an odd practice to some, many Acadian families serve potato salad as an accompaniment to the steaming bowls of gumbo they enjoy at home. Hebert's offers this customary side dish with servings of their well-seasoned gumbo. If you decide to dine in this unpretentious restaurant's friendly atmosphere, the owners, Janelle and Gerald LaMaire, will make you feel right at home, just the way you should feel when a good neighbor invites you to dinner.

Area Code: (318)

Getting There:

Erath, Abbeville, and Kaplan may be accessed by turning west onto Louisiana 14 from Louisiana 90. You may also take Louisiana 35 from Interstate 10 (Rayne exit), which intersects with Louisiana 14 a few miles east of Kaplan; or take U.S. 167 from Lafayette into Abbeville.

Where and When:

Abbeville Record Shoppe, 124 State St., Abbeville, LA 70510. 893-3187. Mon.-Sat., 9 A.M.-5 P.M.

The Abbey Players, 200 S. State St. (P.O. Box 1211), Abbeville, LA 70511-1211. To make reservations, call 893-6082.

Acadian Heritage and Culture Museum, 203 S. Broadway, Erath, LA 70533. 233-5832 or 937-5468. Mon.-Fri., 1-4 P.M. or by appointment. Free. Donations appreciated.

The Apple Tree, 119 Concord St., Abbeville, LA 70570. 893-5009. Mon.-Sat., 9 A.M.-5 P.M.

Cajun Cupboard, 313 Pere Megret St., Abbeville, LA 70510. 893-3971. Tues.-Sat., 7 A.M.-9 P.M.

Cajun Downs, Louisiana 338, Abbeville, LA 70510. 893-5688. Race days Sept.-March: Every Sunday, 11 A.M.-2 P.M. (approximate ending time); Apr.-Sept.: Starting the first week in April races are held every other Sunday, 11 A.M.-2 P.M. (approximate ending time).

Note: Animal lovers may be distressed to see a cock-fighting room at Cajun Downs. It is one of several that still exist in Acadiana. Although the practice is lamented by many Louisianians, some Acadians consider it part of their culture.

Cock-fighting is legal in all parishes in Louisiana except Orleans and Jefferson parishes.

Granny's Hut, 110 E. First St. (LA 14), Kaplan, LA 70548. 643-1257. Tues.-Fri., 10 A.M.-5 P.M. Open Saturdays during the Christmas season.

Hebert's Slaughterhouse Market, Louisiana 338, Abbeville, LA 70510. 893-5688. Mon.-Fri., 8 A.M.-5 P.M.; Sat., 8 A.M.-noon.

Larry's Super Foods, 1313 W. First St. (LA 14 West), Kaplan, LA 70548. 643-6492. Winter: Daily, 7 A.M.-8 P.M.; Summer: Daily, 7 A.M.-9 P.M.

Leland Bowman Lock, Route 3, Box 1172, Abbeville, LA 70510. 893-6790. Mon.-Fri., 8 A.M.-3 P.M. Road to lock is closed on weekends.

Little Miss & Master, 313 Pere Megret St., Abbeville, LA 70510. 893-3971. Tues.-Sat., 9 A.M.-5:30 P.M.

Roma LTD, 404½ Pere Megret St., Abbeville, LA 70510. 898-1199. Mon.-Fri., 9 A.M.-5 P.M.; Sat., 9 A.M.-2 P.M.

St. Mary Magdalen Catholic Church, 302 Pere Megret St., Abbeville, LA 70510. 893-0244.

Victorian Reflections, Inc., 313 N. Cushing Blvd. (P.O. Box 9, Kaplan, LA 70548). 643-8223. Tues.-Fri., 10 A.M.-5 P.M. Open Saturdays during Christmas season.

Information:

Abbeville City Hall, 101 N. State St., Abbeville, LA 70510. 893-8550. Mon.-Fri., 8 A.M.-4 P.M.

Greater Abbeville-Vermilion Chamber of Commerce Tourist Information Center, 1905 Veterans Memorial (LA 14 Bypass), Abbeville, LA 70510. 898-4264. Tues.-Fri., 8 A.M.-4 P.M.; Sat., 8-11 A.M.

Kaplan City Hall, 701 N. Cushing Ave., Kaplan, LA 70548. Mon.-Fri., 7 A.M.-4 P.M.

Guide Services:

Contact Abbeville or Kaplan tourist information centers or

Tour Masters, Inc., 402 N. Irving Ave., Kaplan, LA 70548. 643-8481.

Accommodations:

A la Bonne Veillee Guest House, LeBlanc House, Route 2, Box 2270, Abbeville, LA 70510. 937-5495.

Kisinoaks Bed and Breakfast, Route 2, Box 86 (P.O. Box 67), Abbeville, LA. 1-800-749-1928, 893-8888, or 893-7777.

Sunbelt Lodge, 1903 Veterans Memorial (LA 14 Bypass), Abbeville, LA 70510. 898-1453.

Sunnyside Motel, 700 W. First St. (LA 14 West), Kaplan, LA 70548-4798. 643-7181.

For a complete listing of accommodations in Abbeville, contact the Greater Abbeville-Vermilion Chamber of Commerce Tourist Information Center.

Restaurants:

Black's Oyster Bar, 319 Pere Megret St., Abbeville, LA 70510. 893-4266. Tues.-Thurs., 10 A.M.-9:30 P.M.; Fri. and Sat., 10 A.M.-10 P.M.

Crescent Grill & Tavern, 119 S. State St., Abbeville, LA 70510. 893-8826. Mon.-Thurs., 7 A.M.-11 P.M.; Fri., 7 A.M.-midnight; Sat., 4 P.M.-midnight; Sun., 9 A.M.-5 P.M. Closed during August.

Dupuy's Oyster Shop, 108 S. Main St., Abbeville, LA 70510. 893-2336. Mon.-Sat., 11 A.M.-9 P.M.

El Camino Restaurant, 124 Concord St., Abbeville, LA 70510. 898-2710. Mon.-Thurs., 11 A.M.-9 P.M.; Fri., 11 A.M.-10 P.M.; Sat., 4-10 P.M.

Hebert's Steak House, Louisiana 14, Kaplan, LA 70548. 643-2933. Tues.-Sat., 5 P.M.-'til.

Homestead Steak & Seafood Restaurant, 303 N. Cushing St., Kaplan, LA 70548. 643-6660. Mon.-Fri., 6 A.M.-9 P.M.; Sat., 6-10 A.M. and 4-10 P.M.; Sun., 6-9 A.M.

Ovide's River Front Restaurant, 503 W. Port St., Abbeville, LA 70510. 898-0270. Sun.-Fri., 11 A.M.-2 P.M.; Mon.-Sat., 5:30-9:30 P.M.

Park Restaurant, 204 Park Ave., Abbeville, LA 70510. 893-9957. Mon.-Sat., 5 A.M.-8:30 P.M.

Pirate's Restaurant, 709 E. Lastie St. (LA 14), Erath, LA 70533. 937-5037. Wed., Thurs., Sat., and Sun., 5-10 P.M.; Fri., 10:30 A.M.-10 P.M. Live music on Fridays, Saturdays, and Sundays.

Suire's, Louisiana 35 and 335, Kaplan, LA 70548. 643-8911. Mon.-Thurs., 6 A.M.-7:30 P.M.; Fri. and Sat., 6 A.M.-10 P.M.

Major Annual Events:

Bastille Days, Kaplan—July.

Cajun Island Fete, Kaplan—September.

Chic-A-La-Pie Mardi Gras Parade, Kaplan—Mardi Gras Day.

Erath July 4th Celebration, Erath.

Festival of the Islands, Cow Island—April.

Le Jour De Cajun, Kaplan—April.

Les Lumieres du Village, Abbeville—December.

Louisiana Cajun Country Music Festival, Kaplan—May.

Louisiana Cattle Festival, Abbeville—October.

October Fete, Kaplan—October.

Omelette Festival, Abbeville—November.

33

LOUISIANA 182,
WE LOVE YOU!

The southernmost section of Louisiana 182 wraps itself around several moss-draped, plantation-dotted towns and ties some tempting wayside "goodies" into a desirable package. On a leisurely cruise of a short (fewer than 50 miles) span of the highway between Morgan City and Franklin, weekenders can sample these countryside tidbits and relish the distinctly different flavors of two appealing south Louisiana towns.

The authentic Acadian cabin on Myrtle Street off U.S. 90 that houses **Morgan City's Tourist Information Center** is an appropriate place to start this getaway. The rough-hewn structure gives testimony to the community's persevering Cajun heritage, a storied legacy that is shared with visitors at **The Original Swamp Gardens,** a 3½-acre natural swamp across from the tourist center.

Lifelike depictions of Acadian settlers and the hardy Indians who preceded them are stationed along the gardens' paths. A guide "introduces" visitors to these reincarnated swamp dwellers, several native animals, and Morgan City's most famous transient, Tarzan. The "ape-man" used the junglelike swamps around the city as a location for his first movie.

After you bid "*adieu*" to Swamp Garden residents, continue your tour of Morgan City at **Brownell Memorial Park.** In this secluded pocket of greenery, songbirds are accompanied by one of the world's largest and finest cast-bell carillons. A short

Cypress grove in Brownell Memorial Park. (Photo by Mary Fonseca)

St. Mary's Episcopal Church. (Photo by Mary Fonseca)

Oaklawn Manor. (Photo by Mary Fonseca)

trail that passes behind the campanile is curtained by the feathery leaves of towering cypress trees that dip down to beautiful Lake Palourde.

To reach Brownell Park, head West on U.S. 90 and turn right onto Louisiana 70. Circle Lake Palourde, pass Lake End campground, and watch for the park entrance on your right.

When the last note of the park's carillon concert (played every half-hour) fades into the air, drive to **Scully's Restaurant**—a few miles farther on Louisiana 70—where you can chug along the wildlife-rich waters of Bayou Long aboard the *Tom Stephens* and other crafts, or just enjoy good Cajun cooking and a restful bayou view.

Morgan City's other attractions are on the Atchafalaya River side of town, so when you leave Scully's, retrace your route along Louisiana 70. Turn right onto U.S. 90 and left onto Second Street to **Turn-of-the-Century House.** Here, you can immerse yourself in the accoutrements of an upper-middle class, ragtime-era family and be dazzled by the stunning Mardi Gras costumes displayed in a second-floor museum.

Many revelers attired in sequined costumes during the carnival season don shrimpers' boots or roustabouts' hard hats while they work aboard vessels docked in the Morgan City harbor. A few blocks behind Turn-of-the-Century House, you can stroll sections of the harbor's 22-foot-high, 22-mile-long bulwark. From this lofty vantage point, you can see the town's flotilla of butterfly-netted shrimp boats, weathered oil field crafts, and weekend pleasure boats berthed side by side.

Seafood harvested from the Atchafalaya Basin is the main ingredient in many traditional Cajun dishes. They are served up at local eateries such as **Manny's** and the **Dixie Grill,** two popular diners on U.S. 90; and **Bee Bee's,** a downhome restaurant at the foot of the old bridge just west of Morgan City. Louisiana 182 begins here.

If you are in the mood to "pass a good time," drive four miles west of Berwick to Bayou Vista. Complimentary Cajun dance lessons are frequently offered to customers enjoying the good food and camaraderie at the town's **Richard's Restaurant and Lounge** on Thursday nights. And you can two-step to live

Cajun music at Richard's on occasional Sunday afternoons.

After an enjoyable day, and a revitalizing rest in Morgan City, start an adventurous ramble along Louisiana 182. On the eastern edge of Patterson, pause at the St. Mary Parish Tourist Center to gather brochures on the area. You may want to board **Cajun Jack's** tour boat at a bayou landing next to the tourist center and glide through a section of the Atchafalaya Basin that Jack describes as a "twisting maze of bayous, lakes, and channels." From the deck of the excursion boat you glimpse alligators and waterfowl, see dwellings in secluded areas of the basin, and inspect a 114-year-old houseboat still used as a trapper's camp.

Once you are dock-side again, enjoy a picnic lunch under the oaks surrounding the tourist center. Or, if you so desire, backtrack about a mile to Universe Street, alongside the Plantation Inn in Bayou Vista, to enjoy **Harbor Seafood's** generous luncheon buffet.

After lunch, resume your drive along Louisiana 182 past Patterson's tidy Victorian cottages and restored historic homes. Pause on the outskirts of town to visit the **Wedell-Williams Memorial Aviation Museum** at the Harry P. Williams Memorial Airport. In the 1930s, the airport was the home of Wedell-Williams Air Service, Louisiana's first commercial airline.

Learn more about the airline and the tragedy-shortened lives of aviation pioneers James R. ("Jimmy") Wedell and Harry P. Williams via the museum's informative video presentation. Then, roam through the museum, a flight-fancier's wonderland filled with airplanes and aviation memorabilia that mirror the history of flying. Models of Wedell-Williams' innovative, low-winged monoplanes, logs of the duo's record-breaking flights, and their competition trophies are prominent features of the museum's eye-catching displays.

The square-columned, antebellum cottage across the road from Harry P. Williams Memorial Airport once belonged to Williams and his wife, silent-screen heroine Marguerite Clark. The couple started restoration of Calumet (private) several months before Williams, a native of Patterson, crashed to his death in 1936.

About 1½ miles past Calumet, Louisiana 182 briefly joins U.S. 90, then veers off toward postcard-pretty Centerville. Several structures in this charming hamlet were built during the 1800s, when the town was a shipping center for local sugar planters. Notable among them are the quaint, clapboarded Presbyterian Church; the stately Shakespeare-Allen and Vetter homes just past the chapel (both private); the Old Kennedy Hotel, now a branch of the Commercial Bank and Trust Company of Franklin; and the Joshua Cary House (private), at the intersection of Louisiana 182 and Louisiana 317.

While you're in Centerville, spend a delightful hour or two at **Oakwood on the Teche,** also known as the "House of Needlework." This New England stone-ender style home, whose exterior is partially faced with the tan and brown stone that surrounds a huge fireplace in the kitchen, is filled with hooked rugs, needlepoint, quilts, and other examples of fine needlework. The collection, which includes a Centennial Quilt made in 1876, is displayed on antique furnishings in the home of Ruth Wells, a master knitter in the United States Knitting Guild. Call ahead and Ruth will give you directions and receive you in her beautiful home.

Less than a mile past Centerville, Bocage and Frances plantations (both private) grace the roadside. Paul F. Stahls, Jr., author of *Plantation Homes of the Teche Country,* notes that Bocage is the largest home ever moved by barge on Bayou Teche. It originally stood on the east bank of the bayou, near Franklin, before its history-making relocation in 1969. Frances dates to the early 1800s and was restored in 1963.

In Garden City, next to Centerville, you can visit one of the few "Mom-and-Pop" stores that was among the thousands that once dotted America's countryside. In the 1930s, **Stroud's Cajun Store** was a busy purveyor of groceries and needed household items, as well as a popular meeting place. Today, herbs and health products, reflecting the preferred life-style of the owner, are mixed in with the groceries. Local crafts, glassware, and antiques also line the old-fashioned shelves.

As you follow Louisiana 182 into Franklin you will catch glimpses of more antebellum architecture through openings in the thick shrubbery lining the road. If you call ahead for an appointment, the owners of **Arlington Plantation,** the only tour-receptive home between Centerville and Franklin, will graciously share the history of their home, acquaint you with its architecture and furnishings, and explain the problems and rewards of living in a pre-Civil War structure.

Just past Arlington and the Alice C Plantation (private), branches from centuries-old oak trees entwine above Franklin's distinguished Main Street. White-globed lamps with cast-iron pedestals line the median. Their imprinted caution: Do Not Hitch, reminds us of a gentler time when horse-drawn carriages brought callers to the "white way's" palatial mansions.

From October through December, when the sugarcane harvest is in full swing, trucks heavily laden with cane pass down Main Street on their way to the mill. The cherished lanterns are then swiveled sideways so they will not be damaged.

Unlike her French-founded neighbors to the east and west, Franklin was settled by Anglo-Saxon planters and merchants bearing names such as Lewis, Carlin, and Sanders. The community grew into a thriving steamboat port and, following the advent of the railroad, a prosperous sawmill town. Today, more than 400 noteworthy commercial and residential structures, built during these two eras, are part of Franklin's impressive historic district.

The **City of Franklin Tourist Information Center,** in City Hall—located in historic Cromwell School—has information on these architectural treasures. To reach it, turn left onto Iberia Street at the second traffic light on Main Street.

Start a walking/driving tour of Franklin at Shadowlawn (private). The imposing mansion at 906 Main St. is the only steamboat-era home north of the city's turn-of-the-century business district. It was built in the 1830s by Simeon Smith, owner of the first large schooner based in Franklin.

Franklin's oldest house of worship, Ashbury Methodist Church, is across from Shadowlawn. The 1838 church has been lovingly maintained by a devoted congregation. Members did extensive interior remodeling in 1900, and repaired the

steeple and building after Hurricane Hilda roared through
Franklin in 1964. More repairs were necessary after Hurricane
Andrew in 1992.

As you pass through Franklin's downtown district, you will
notice modern buildings that seem painfully out of place.
Fortunately, the decorative tin storefront on Popkin's Jewelry
Store and the stepped gables, arched windows, and ornamental brick work on other buildings sustain an overall turn-of-the-
century look.

Along the "white way"—named for the creamy glow cast by
the street lamps—antebellum and Victorian homes dominate
two blocks of graceful dwellings. Just off Main Street, along
First and Second streets, cottages constructed during the railroad era are interspersed with larger, Greek Revival homes.
Rising from their midst on First Street is "Carpenter Gothic"
St. Mary's Episcopal Church, an irresistible subject for amateur and professional photographers. Those interested in seeing the simple interior of this carpenter-laced, wooden chapel
may inquire at the parish hall behind the 1871 church.

In such a historic town, it is natural for folks to congregate at
a nineteenth-century grocery. Join locals at **Iberia Cash
Grocery,** on the corner of Third and Iberia streets. Enjoy a
good sandwich, a cup of coffee, and some friendly conversation; then, head north on Main Street where you can browse
through the store's collection of Louisiana-themed books and
gifts at **Splash Page** on the corner of Main and Sterling streets.
Then, turn right onto Sterling Road just past Franklin cemetery
and circle east to **Grevemberg House,** an 1851 Greek Revival
mansion that was sold to the Grevemberg family in 1857.

The St. Mary Parish Chapter of the Louisiana Landmarks
Society restored the exterior of the locally renowned home to
its original buff color. Members furnished it with antiques and
memorabilia donated by local citizens, but one room—full of
Civil War relics—recalls the battle of Irish Bend that took place
in the surrounding countryside near **Oaklawn Manor,** a plantation five miles farther along Sterling Road.

Oaklawn's thick, brick walls stood strong against the ravages
of war, hurricanes, and the misfortunes of nineteenth-century

owners and is presently the family home of Louisiana governor Mike Foster. Now restored to its original splendor, the estate is a delight. You feel as if you are driving through an enchanted forest as you follow the winding road that curves from Oaklawn's gate through a sylvan park that provides a proper setting for this grand dame of the Teche.

At the manor, there is a priceless collection of Audubon folios, exquisite antiques collected by the current owners, and Oaklawn's prized chandeliers. After your tour, explore the plantation's modeled-after-Versailles gardens and the aviary Warner Brothers Studios built for the filming of the movie *Drowning Pool.*

When you leave Oaklawn, turn right and follow Sterling Road (Louisiana 28) until it intersects with Louisiana 182. Turn left and drive back to Franklin. On the way, you will pass the Chamber of Commerce building where tourist information is also available.

You may want to overnight at **Best Western's Forest Motel,** just past the Chamber of Commerce. The accommodations are comfortable and the hostelry's **Forest Restaurant** is renowned for its appetizing cuisine.

On an extended stay, you may also have time to sample the delicious dinners prepared at the **Yellow Bowl Restaurant,** a forty-three-year-old, Louisiana 182 landmark. The Yellow Bowl, the Jeanerette Museum, and other attractions described in "A Liberal Sprinkling of Salt and Pepper" are only about fifteen miles from Franklin. **Emery's Antiques** in Baldwin, on Louisiana 182 between Franklin and Jeanerette, is a good wayside stop.

The Chitimacha Indian Reservation in Charenton is also close by, a few miles north of Baldwin via Louisiana 326. Most visitors go to the reservation to try their luck at **Cypress Bayou Casino's** 450 Las Vegas-style slot machines, but some come to learn about the history and culture of the Chitimachas at the **Chitimacha Tribal Center** or to purchase crafts at two informal shops on the reservation. (Ask for directions to the shops at the Tribal Center.)

Marcus de la Houssaye's **Expeditions Atchafalaya** also attracts a number of visitors to Charenton. This native of the Atchafalaya Basin offers personalized tours of the basin, Lake Fausse Point, and Lake Chitimacha. His boat is smaller than the usual pontoon tour boats, allowing visitors to see some interesting areas. Marcus can show you a small village accessible only by water, Indian shell mounds left by Native Americans who lived in Louisiana's wetlands approximately 300 B.C., and many animals and birds who live in the swamp.

Area Codes:

Morgan City, Berwick, Patterson (504)

Franklin, Baldwin, Charenton, Garden City (318)

Getting There:

Access Morgan City and Franklin From U.S. 90, which dips southward from Interstate 10 between Lafayette and New Orleans.

Where and When:

Arlington Plantation, 56 E. Main St., Franklin, LA 70538. 828-2644. Call for appointment. Admission.

Brownell Memorial Park, Louisiana 70 (P.O. Box 949), Morgan City, LA 70381. 384-2283. Daily, 9 A.M.-4 P.M.

Cajun Jack's Swamp Tours, 112 Main St., Patterson, LA 70392 (P.O. Box 225, Berwick, LA 70342). 395-7420. Tours daily, 9 A.M. and 2:30 P.M. Summer sunset cruise, 5:30 P.M. Admission.

Chitimacha Tribal Center, P.O. Box 661, Charenton, LA 70523. 923-4973 or 923-4974. Museum hours: Mon.-Fri., 8 A.M.-4:30 P.M.

Cypress Bayou Casino, 832 Martin Luther King Rd., Charenton, LA 70523. 923-7284 or 1-800-284-4386. Open daily, 10 A.M.-'til.

Expeditions Atchafalaya, Box 181, Charenton, LA 70523. 923-7149. Call for tour reservation and directions. Brochure available at City of Franklin Tourist Information Center or sent on request. Night tours, fishing trips, sunrise/sunset photo safaris, camping, lodging, meals, and canoe trips also offered.

Emery's Antiques, 401 E. Main St., Baldwin, LA 70514. 923-4795. Mon.-Fri., 8 A.M.-5 P.M.; Sat., 9 A.M.-5 P.M.; Sun., 1-5 P.M. Admission.

Grevemberg House, Sterling Road, Franklin, LA. St. Mary Chapter Louisiana Landmarks Society, P.O. Box 400, Franklin, LA 70538. 828-2092. Thurs.-Sun., 10 A.M.-4 P.M. Admission.

Oaklawn Manor, 3296 E. Oaklawn Dr., Franklin, LA 70538. 828-0434. Daily, 10 A.M.-4 P.M. Admission.

Oakwood on the Teche, 610 St. Mary 131, Franklin, LA 70538. 836-5442. Open daily by appointment. Admission.

The Original Swamp Gardens, 725 Myrtle St., Morgan City, LA 70380. 384-3343. Tours: Mon., 1:30 P.M., 2:30 P.M., and 3:30 P.M.; Tues.-Fri., 10:30 A.M., 1:30 P.M., 2:30 P.M., and 3:30 P.M.; Sat., 10:30 A.M., 1 P.M., 2 P.M., and 3 P.M.; Sun., 1 P.M., 2 P.M., and 3 P.M. Admission. Tickets sold at Morgan City Tourist Information Center.

Scully's, Rural Route 4, Box 222, Morgan City, LA 70380. 385-2388. Restaurant: Mon.-Sat., 9:30 A.M.-9 P.M. Boat tours: Mon.-Sat., 10 A.M., 12:30 P.M., and 3 P.M. Call for reservation. Admission for boat tours.

St. Mary's Episcopal Church, 805 First St., Franklin, LA 70538. 828-0918. Inquire at rectory to see interior.

Splash Page, 212 Sterling Rd., Franklin, LA 70538. 828-0201. Mon.-Sat., 9 A.M.-5 P.M.

Stroud's Cajun Store, Louisiana 182, Garden City, LA 70540. 828-1200. Mon.-Sat., 8 A.M.-5:30 P.M.

Turn-of-the-Century House, 715 Second St., Morgan City, LA 70380. Mon.-Fri., 9 A.M.-5 P.M.; Sat. and Sun., 1-5 P.M. Admission.

Wedell-Williams Memorial Aviation Museum, Louisiana 182 (P.O. Box 655), Patterson, LA 70392. 395-7067. Tues.-Sat., 10 A.M.-4 P.M. Admission.

Information:

City of Franklin Tourist Commission, 300 Iberia St. (P.O. Box 567), Franklin, LA 70538. 828-6323 or 1-800-962-6889. Mon.-Fri., 9 A.M.-5 P.M.

Morgan City Tourist Information Center, 725 Myrtle St., Morgan City, LA 70380. 384-3343. Mon.-Fri., 8 A.M.-4 P.M.; Sat. and Sun., 9 A.M.-4 P.M.

St. Mary Parish Tourist Commission, 112 Main St., Patterson, LA (P.O. Box 2332, Dept. B, Morgan City, LA 70381). 1-800-256-2931 or 395-4905. Mon.-Fri., 8:30 A.M.-4:30 P.M.

West St. Mary Chamber of Commerce Tourist Information Center, 15301 LA 182 West, Franklin, LA 75038. 828-5608. Mon.-Fri., 9 A.M.-4:30 P.M.

Guide Services:

Not available for this getaway.

Accommodations:

Chain and independent motels in Morgan City.

Best Western's Forest Motel, Louisiana 182, Franklin, LA 70538. 828-1810. Reservations only: 1-800-352-1234.

Restaurants:

Bee Bee's, 100 LA 182, Berwick, LA 70342. 385-5717. Daily, 10 A.M.-10 P.M.

Dixie Grill, 1924 U.S. 90 East, Morgan City, LA 70380. 385-1302. Daily, 24 hours.

Forest Restaurant, Best Western's Forest Motel, Louisiana 182, Franklin, LA 70538. 828-1810. Mon.-Sat., 6:30 A.M.-9:30 P.M. Closed Sundays.

Harbor Seafood, 500 Universe St., Bayou Vista, LA 70392. 395-3474. Tues.-Thurs., 11 A.M.-9:30 P.M.; Fri., 11 A.M.-10 P.M.; Sat., 5-10 P.M.; Sun., 11 A.M.-2 P.M. Closed Mondays.

Iberia Cash Grocery, 501 Iberia St., Franklin, LA 70538. 828-0392. Mon.-Fri., 8 A.M.-6 P.M.; Sat., 9 A.M.-3 P.M.

Manny's, 7027 U.S. 90 East, Morgan City, LA 70380. 384-2359. Daily, 5 A.M.-10 P.M.

Richard's Restaurant and Lounge, 2618 LA 182, Bayou Vista, LA 70380. Mon.-Thurs., 4-9 P.M.; Fri. and Sat., 4-10 P.M.; Sun., 4-7 P.M.

Scully's Restaurant, Rural Route 4, Box 222, Morgan City, LA 70380. 385-2388. Mon.-Sat., 9:30 A.M.-9 P.M.

Yellow Bowl Restaurant, Louisiana 182 (Route 2, Box 1), Jeanerette, LA 70544. 276-5512. Thurs. and Fri., 11 A.M.-1:30 P.M., 4:30-10 P.M.; Sat., 4:30-10 P.M.; Sun., 11 A.M.-2:30 P.M.

Major Annual Events:

Big Bass Classic, Morgan City—April.

Festivale Sur La Teche, Franklin—Memorial Day weekend.

Le Festival du Poisson Arme, Baldwin—April.

Louisiana Shrimp and Petroleum Festival, Morgan City—Labor Day weekend.

Magnolia Festival, Franklin—May.

Mardi Gras, all areas—Tuesday before Ash Wednesday.

Patterson Cypress Sawmill Festival, Patterson—Second weekend in March.

Patterson Rotary Christmas Lights on the Bayou, Patterson—December.

34

THE LONGEST STREET IN THE WORLD

Bayou Lafourche, once used as a "highway" by roadless pioneer settlers, branches off from the Mississippi River at Donaldsonville. Its waters meander more than 100 miles through the "toe" of boot-shaped Louisiana, and tumble into the Gulf of Mexico at Pointe Fourchon. It is known as "the longest street in the world."

It is great fun to follow Louisiana 1 and Louisiana 308 along this tranquil waterway. The pleasures include stopping at historic sites, supping on spicy seafood, and viewing tranquil bayou scenery. And, of course, there is that added bonus of the people you will meet along the way.

To begin this odyssey, take Exit 182 off of Interstate 10 and cross the Mississippi River on the Sunshine Bridge. Then follow "Bayou Plantation" signs to Louisiana 70, and Spur 70 to Louisiana 308.

Six miles down Louisiana 308, stop to tour **Madewood,** a majestic plantation deservedly called the "Queen of the Bayou." If you plan your getaway in advance, and call for a reservation, you can spend a night with the "Queen." Her gracious staff will treat you like a member of the royal family. Madewood's coddled guests assemble for an aperitif of wine and cheese in the library, a delectable dinner in the mansion's elegant dining room, and coffee and brandy in the grand parlor.

Madewood Plantation. (Photo courtesy Lafourche Parish Tourist Commission)

Laurel Valley Village. (Photo courtesy Lafourche Parish Tourist Commission)

In the morning, fortified with Madewood's delicious breakfast buffet, continue on Louisiana 308 for a few miles, cross one of the bridges over Bayou Lafourche, and follow scenic, oak-lined Louisiana 1 until it intersects with Canal Boulevard in Thibodaux. Turn right onto Canal and go about six blocks to the **Thibodaux Chamber of Commerce Tourist Information Center.** Here, you can request a tour map pinpointing the town's architectural gems. They include several graceful Queen Anne-style homes; **St. John's Episcopal Church,** the oldest Episcopal church west of the Mississippi River; and **St. Joseph's Co-Cathedral,** which has a glorious stained-glass Rose Window modeled after the one in the Cathedral of Notre Dame in Paris.

Religion's role in the Cajun life-style is illustrated at the **Jean Lafitte National Historical Park and Preserve Wetlands Acadian Cultural Center** on St. Mary Street (Louisiana 1). The center interprets the rituals, cuisine, and traditions of Acadiana through demonstrations, performances, and audiovisual exhibits.

In Thibodaux, you can sample Cajun cooking firsthand at **Politz's Restaurant,** three blocks west of the cultural center, or at **Bubba's II Seafood Restaurant** on Highway 308 (across the bayou in back of the cultural center). Or, you might try **Flanagan's,** a block or so down Audubon Avenue from where it intersects Louisiana 1 alongside Nicholls State University.

History buffs and baseball fans will enjoy exhibits in the Allen J. Ellender room on the first floor of Nicholl's **Ellender Memorial Library.** The long, eventful career of U.S. Sen. Allen J. Ellender is showcased here. And the room also includes exhibits that focus on the university's history and the semipro baseball leagues that once played in Thibodaux and Houma.

Just beyond Nicholls, you will come across Acadia Plantation (private). This residence, nestled in a parklike setting fronting the bayou, is believed to have been formed from three homes built by famed Alamo defender, Jim Bowie.

From Acadia, cross the Audubon Avenue bridge to the other side of the bayou to view works by local artists available at **The Gallery.** Continue left, following the bayou's banks, to Rienzi (private), a spectacular home whose graceful staircases were meant to be ascended by Queen Maria Louisa of Spain. The monarch ordered the home built as a refuge in case her troops were defeated by Napoleon.

More humble abodes are the focus at **Laurel Valley Village,** the largest, most intact turn-of-the-century sugar plantation complex in the United States. Retrace your path down Louisiana 308, past the Audubon Avenue crossing, to see Laurel Valley General Store's collection of antique utensils, tools, farm machinery, and locally made foods and crafts.

Between the general store and the neighboring plantation schoolhouse, two small engines from a "dummy" railroad that once hauled cane out of Laurel Valley's fields recall busy harvests when dozens of hands were needed to cut cane and transport it to the mill. You can turn onto the road next to the school for a drive-by view of tenant houses, a blacksmith shop, the ruins of the sugar mill, and other century-old structures awaiting restoration.

Back on Louisiana 308, follow the bayou south as it curves past Chatchie (private), an 1865 mansion built on the site of a home burned during the Battle of Lafourche Crossing, a two-day Civil War skirmish for control of the railroad bridge over Bayou Lafourche just past Chatchie. About ten miles from Chatchie, you will pass Rosella (private), a beautifully refurbished, French Normandy-style raised cottage on the outskirts of Raceland. The town was named for horse races held at a local track in the early nineteenth century.

From Raceland, turn left onto Louisiana 3199 to start an adventurous, circular route that will take you to Kraemer—one of the few remaining Cajun villages—and back to Thibodaux where you can spend the night. Go 2½ miles on Louisiana 3199, past the Raceland Sugar Mill. Near the mill, you will see mounds of bagasse (a by-product of the sugar milling process used to make wall boards and insulation) piled alongside the road.

Turn left over railroad tracks onto Louisiana 308, a road that curves through acres of sugarcane fields until it is suddenly hemmed in by wetlands. Drive cautiously nine miles into the swamp until you emerge at Kraemer on the banks of beautiful Bayou Boeuf. Many residents of this close-knit settlement still tend traps as their fathers did before them; others, such as the Torres and Tregle families who operate **Torres'** and **Zam's** swamp tours on either side of the Bayou Boeuf bridge, have found different ways to earn a living and still remain on the bayou.

If you only have time for one swamp tour, you will have to flip a coin, but no matter which boatman you choose, take in the lagniappe offered by both friendly competitors. Roland Torres shares his outdoor exhibit of exotic birds from all parts of the world with all who come his way. Zam Tregle and her husband offer a yard tour of swamp wildlife and a trading post filled with Cajun life-style exhibits. Their daughter, Edwina, serves up spicy Acadian dishes at her bayou-side eatery, **Edwina's Restaurant.**

After you have had a look at the abundant flora and fauna on Bayou Boeuf, continue on Louisiana 308 approximately twenty-five miles to Louisiana 20. This route will take you into Thibodaux.

Before you leave Thibodaux, you may want to travel two miles south of town on Louisiana 20 to **Bourgeois's Meat Market.** This landmark store offers Acadian specialties such as homemade hogshead cheese, beef jerky, *andouille* (a coarse ground pork sausage used in gumbo), *boudin* (made from pork shoulder mixed with rice), cracklins (fried pork skins), and several other kinds of freshly made sausage. After you have toured Thibodaux, explore the other neighborhoods on the longest street in the world. As you meander from town to town, be sure to stay well within the *strictly enforced speed limits.*

Get under way by taking Louisiana 1 to Raceland. There, you may want to pause to relish the serenity of St. Mary's Catholic Church. You can also contemplate the graveyard architecture in St. Mary's Cemetery. Freddie John Falgout, the first American casualty in World War II, is buried there.

Just beyond the intersection of Louisiana 1 and U.S. 90, on the far side of Raceland, stop at the **Lafourche Parish Tourist Commission's** Information Center. Here, you can get information on the handful of south Lafourche Parish municipalities that line Louisiana 1 all the way down to Grand Isle.

These towns evolved from early land grants known as "line settlements." They were proportioned to give each land owner a bayou frontage of less than 600 feet, with a lot depth reaching as much as 1½ miles. Heirs often divided these plots into smaller strips of bayou frontage and the land behind it.

You will be in the small hamlet of Mathews as you leave the tourist center and pull up to **Adams Fruit Market,** two miles down on your left. The name of this eclectic establishment gives no hint that alligator *boudin,* crawfish pies, fresh cane syrup, and various fishing and grocery items are sold inside. Nor does it herald the store's wildlife minimuseum or let on that some of the best fishing tips on the bayou can be garnered from *confrères* (friends) who regularly congregate at a corner table.

In Lockport, nearly five miles from Adams Fruit Market, bulky locks span Bayou Lafourche and control water flow into a canal connecting with Lake Salvador. Just below the village, you will pass Bouverans (private), a nineteenth-century, raised Creole cottage built by Pierre Claudet. It is still embellished with the outer stairway the Claudet youngsters used to climb to their beds in attic lofts.

Claudet and his contemporaries were mostly farmers and fishermen, but in the 1930s and 1940s, oil joined agriculture as an important Lafourche Parish industry. As you pass Bollinger's Shipyard, one mile past Bouverans on the opposite shore of the bayou, you may see vessels utilized in the offshore oil industry berthed in the bayou. Two miles farther, in front of **Orgeron's Marsh Equipment,** amphibious marsh buggies used to reach marshland pipelines and wellheads are displayed alongside the road.

Oil provides work for many bayou residents, but it has not totally eclipsed the way of life embraced by many generations. The water itself provides the residents' livelihood. Along the picturesque miles of bayou that flow below Lockport, white-booted shrimpers still mend their nets and oystermen dock their wide-decked, flat-bottomed boats.

At a Louisiana 1 retail store on the edge of his crawfish farm, Henri Boulet, of **Henri Boulet, Jim Boulet Export,** sells boiled crawfish to passersby. If you would enjoy a picnic interlude from your bayou browse, buy some of Henri's crawfish, cross the high-rise bridge over the Intracoastal Waterway (that carries marine traffic from Jacksonville, Florida, to San Diego, California), a half-mile down the road, and turn right to Larose Park. Feast on your mudbugs in this relaxed, outdoor setting, then return to Louisiana 1 and continue south.

After you pass several stands that sell fresh vegetables in season, you will arrive in Cut Off, named for a cutoff canal near the town. Have dessert at **Cajun Pecan House,** headquarters of a popular mail-order business selling pecan-flavored pies, pastries, candies, and coffee. It also offers many other items decorated or enhanced with the versatile nut.

Côte Blanche (white coast) was the name originally given to Cut Off, a coastal town of white-painted houses. The historic title was later adopted by **Côte Blanche Productions' Louisiana Catalog & Store,** just across from the Cajun Pecan House. Here you can thumb through hundreds of books on Louisiana history, cooking, culture, and other topics, and select from gift items and games saluting the Bayou State.

With advance reservations, you can overnight in Cut Off at **Hassel House.** A unique, well-appointed Bed and Breakfast, it has an alligator lolling in a prairie-banked pond in front of the main house. Hassel House also offers a private nature trail that extends into the forest behind the comfortable guest quarters.

It is hard to tell where Cut Off ends and Galliano, the next community along the bayou, begins. But you know you are leaving Galliano and entering Golden Meadow when the number of shrimp boats anchored in the bayou increases.

While you are in Golden Meadow, taste some of the goodies sold at **Dufrene's Bakery,** a favorite stop for weekenders going to Grand Isle, or try the scrumptious seafood at **Randolph's** (both on Louisiana 1). A block from the restaurant, compare the dimensions of *Petit Corporal,* a nearly 150-year-old wooden shrimp boat named for Napoleon, with the butterfly-netted, fiberglass crafts now navigating the open Gulf.

Just as *Petit Corporal,* the oldest vessel on the bayou, memorializes the skill and bravery of seafarers, Holy Mary Shrine, across from Golden Meadow Town Hall, and the Smith Shrine, a tiny chapel alongside the bayou south of town, are testaments to the faith that sees Bayou Lafourche families through trying times. Some of those difficult days occur when gentle Gulf breezes are whipped into hurricane frenzy. Shrimpers who unload their catches at seafood processing plants in Leeville, next to Golden Meadow, sometimes tell stories about the terrible storm that ravaged the town in 1915. Newly built locks and levees, seen from Louisiana 1, may save many bayou communities from the destruction once vented on their neighbor.

As you cross the Leeville high-rise bridge over the bayou, look to your left to see fences anchored in the water and entwined with discarded Christmas trees. Coastal Louisianans are using this method to reclaim wetlands lost to erosion, salt water intrusion, and oil field canals. The trees catch sediment that eventually builds up into marshland.

On the narrow strip of land at the foot of the bridge, in Cheniere Caminada, a tiny cemetery on a rise is all that remains of the original town. The once-busy fishing village lost half of its nearly 1,500 residents in a fierce 1893 storm.

Local patrons of **Cigar's Marina & Cajun Cuisine,** a Caminada Bay restaurant and marina noted for its boiled and fried seafood, hasten up the bayou at first notice of a hurricane, but they nearly always return to the waterside life they love, even if it means rebuilding their homes and camps. One of their favorite places to gather is the old bridge leading to Grand Isle. It was left in place when the new bridge was built and serves as a fishing pier.

On the "Cajun Riviera," as Grand Isle has been dubbed, there are no T-shirt shops, dune buggy rentals, or luxury hotels with lounge chairs lined up on the beach. But, on this sandy island—Louisiana's only Gulf resort—there are accommodations ranging from modest motels to plush condominiums.

Wooden walkways, bordered with picnic gazebos, offer plenty of access to the beach where swimming, crabbing, and fishing are popular pastimes. On the beachfront, in **Grand Isle State Park,** a long fishing pier over the Gulf of Mexico and a shorter one over an inland bay are good vantage points from which to see hundreds of migratory birds that visit Grand Isle every autumn and spring. If frolicking on the beach in the invigorating Gulf breeze stirs up your appetite, **Sarah's Sandwich Shop,** an open-around-the-clock Grand Isle landmark, will be ready to serve you.

Some year-rounders who live on Grand Isle take Louisiana 3090 to their jobs at Port Fourchon, or they work on offshore oil rigs like the ones visible from Pointe Fourchon beach. Besides being workhorses for the oil industry, rigs are artificial reefs that attract tarpon and other game fish. They are one of the reasons the Fourchon-Grand Isle area is reputed to be among the top 10 fishing spots in the world. If you want to test your angling skill, see **Charlie Hardison & Sons, Inc.,** for charter boat and shoreline facilities on Pointe Fourchon.

At Pointe Fourchon, nature seems uninhibited by the conglomeration of equipment that services LOOP (Louisiana Offshore Oil Port), a "superport" for huge tankers too big to dock in existing harbors. In late summer and fall, hundreds of aquatic birds such as herons, ibises, and pelicans wade the island's shallow coastal waters.

When it is time to leave Pointe Fourchon and Grand Isle, hold onto that "vacation" feeling a bit longer with a leisurely drive up the Louisiana 308-side of Bayou Lafourche. From this quiet, residential side of the bayou, you will get a different perspective on all you have seen. However, if you must hurry home, take four-lane Louisiana 3225, which parallels Louisiana 1 from Golden Meadow to just past Galliano.

Area Code: (504)

Getting There:

To begin this getaway at Madewood, take Exit 182 from Interstate 10 and cross the Sunshine Bridge. Follow "Bayou Plantation" signs to Louisiana 70, Spur 70, and Louisiana 308. Stay on Louisiana 308 for six miles to Madewood.

To begin the getaway in Thibodaux, take Interstate 310 from Interstate 10, or U.S. 61 to U.S. 90 South. Exit U.S. 90 at Louisiana 1 and drive west on Louisiana 1 for 15 miles to Thibodaux.

Where and When:

Adams Fruit Market, 5013 LA 1 South, Raceland, LA 70394. 532-3165. Daily, 7 A.M.-6:30 P.M.

Bourgeois's Meat Market, 519 Schriever Hwy., Thibodaux, LA 70301. 447-7128. Mon.-Fri., 7 A.M.-5:30 P.M.; Sat., 7 A.M.-2:30 P.M.

Cajun Pecan House, 3006 W. Main St., Cut Off, LA 70345. 632-2337 or 1-800-432-2586. Oct.-Easter: Daily, 7 A.M.-6 P.M.

Charlie Hardison & Sons, Inc., Route 1, Box 360, Golden Meadow, LA 70357. For information call 396-2442, 8-11 A.M. and 2-6 P.M.

Côte Blanche Productions' Louisiana Catalog & Store, Route 3, Box 614, Cut Off, LA 70345. 632-4100 or 1-800-375-4100. Mon.-Sat., 10 A.M.-5 P.M.

Dufrene's Bakery, Louisiana 1, Golden Meadow, LA 70357. 475-5450. Summer: 4 A.M.-8 P.M.; Winter: 4 A.M.-6 P.M.

Ellender Memorial Library, Nicholls State University, P.O. Box 2004, Thibodaux, LA 70310. 448-4621. Mon.-Fri., 8 A.M.-4:30 P.M.; 1st Sat., noon-4 P.M. Free.

The Gallery, 573 LA 308 (P.O. Box 5493), Thibodaux, LA 70301. 448-2201. Tues.-Sat., 10 A.M.-5 P.M.; Sun., 1-5 P.M.

Grand Isle State Park, Grand Isle, LA 70358. 787-2559. Apr. 1-Sept. 30: Daily, 6 A.M.-10 P.M.; Oct. 1-Mar. 31: Daily, 8 A.M.-7 P.M. Admission.

Henri Boulet, Jim Boulet Export, P.O. Box 267, Larose, LA 70373. 798-7799. Daily, in season (usually end of January-June) 11 A.M.-noon, 3-7 P.M.

Jean Lafitte National Historical Park and Preserve Wetlands Acadian Cultural Center, 314 St. Mary St., Thibodaux, LA 70301. 448-1375. Tues.-Sun., 9 A.M.-6 P.M.; Mon., 9 A.M.-7 P.M.

Laurel Valley Village, Louisiana 308, Thibodaux, LA 70301. For information on guided tours, call 447-2902, 447-5216, or 446-7456. Mon.-Fri, 10 A.M.-4 P.M.; Sat. and Sun., 11 A.M.-5 P.M. Donations appreciated.

Madewood Plantation, Louisiana 308, Napoleonville, LA (#319 Magazine St., New Orleans, LA 70130—mailing address). 369-7151 (568-1988—New Orleans). Tours: Daily, 10 A.M.-5 P.M. Admission.

Orgeron's Marsh Equipment, Louisiana 1, RFD, Lockport, LA 70374. 532-3555. Call for information.

St. John's Episcopal Church, 718 Jackson St., Thibodaux, LA 70301. Tours available by appointment.

St. Joseph's Co-Cathedral, Canal Boulevard, Thibodaux, LA 70301. 446-1387. A brochure, available at St. Joseph's Parish Center, describes the cathedral's artfully decorated interior. Parish Center will direct you to open entrance. Parish Center and Co-Cathedral hours: Mon.-Fri., 8 A.M.-4 P.M. Co-Cathedral open Sat., 8 A.M.-4 P.M.

Torres' Cajun Swamp Tours, Corner of Louisiana 308 and 101 Torres Rd., Kraemer, LA 70301. 633-7739. Two-hour tours. Daily, by reservation. Admission.

Zam's Bayou Swamp Tours, 135 Bayou Rd., Kraemer, LA 70371. 633-7881. No appointment necessary. Two-hour tours at 10:30 A.M., 1:30 P.M., and 3:30 P.M. Admission.

Information:

Lafourche Parish Tourist Commission, P.O. Box 340, Raceland, LA 70394-0340. 537-5800. Mon.-Fri., 9 A.M.-4 P.M.

Thibodaux Chamber of Commerce Tourist Information Center, 1058 Canal Blvd., Thibodaux, LA 70301. 446-1187. Mon.-Fri., 8:30 A.M.-noon, 1-4:30 P.M.

Guide Services:

Contact the Lafourche Parish Tourist Commission.

Accommodations:

Chain and independent motels in Thibodaux; independent motels in Galliano, Golden Meadow, Larose, Leeville, and Raceland.

Bed and Breakfasts:

Hassel House, Route 2, Box 532-Z, Cut Off, LA 70345. 632-8088.

Madewood Plantation, Louisiana 308, Napoleonville, LA (402 Julia St., New Orleans, LA 70130—mailing address). 369-7151 (524-1988—New Orleans).

For information on accommodations, contact the Lafourche Parish Tourist Commission or the Thibodaux Chamber of Commerce Tourist Information Center.

Restaurants:

Bubba's II Seafood Restaurant, 764 Bayou Rd. (LA 308), Thibodaux, LA 70301. 446-5117. Lunch: Daily, 11 A.M.-2 P.M. Dinner: Mon., Wed., Thurs., 5-9:30 P.M.; Fri. and Sat., 5-10 P.M. Closed Tuesday evenings.

Cigar's Marina & Cajun Cuisine, P.O. Box 393, Grand Isle, LA 70358. 787-2188. Daily, 10 A.M.-10 P.M.

Edwina's Restaurant, 135 Bayou Rd., Kraemer, LA 70371. 633-7881. Mon.-Thurs., 9 A.M.-5 P.M.; Fri. and Sat., 9 A.M.-9 P.M.

Flanagan's, 1111 Audubon Dr., Thibodaux, LA 70301. 447-7771. Mon.-Fri., 11 A.M.-10 P.M.; Sat., 11 A.M.-11 P.M.; Sun., 10 A.M.-9 P.M. Live Cajun music on Wednesday nights, champagne jazz brunch on Sundays.

Politz's Restaurant, 100 Landry St., Thibodaux, LA 70301. 448-0944. Lunch: Tues.-Fri., 11 A.M.-1:30 P.M. Dinner: Tues.-Thurs., 5-9 P.M.; Fri. and Sat., 5-9:30 P.M.

Randolph's, 806 S. Bayou Dr., Golden Meadow, LA 70357. 475-5272. Wed.-Sun., 11 A.M.-9 P.M.

Sara's Sandwich Shop, P.O. Box 231, Grand Isle, LA 70358. 787-2955. Open 24 hours, daily.

For a complete list of Lafourche Parish restaurants, contact the Lafourche Parish Tourist Commission.

Major Annual Events:

A Bayou Christmas, Galliano—Second weekend in December.

Bull Club Fair & Blessing of the Fleet, Golden Meadow—First weekend in August.

French Food Festival, Larose—Last weekend in October.

Grand Isle Tarpon Rodeo, Grand Isle—Mid-July.

La Vie Lafourchaise, Mathews—Third weekend in October.

Sauce Piquante Festival, Raceland—First weekend in October.

Spring Food Fest, Lockport—Second weekend in May.

Thibodaux Firemen's Fair & Parade, Thibodaux—First weekend in May.

La Trouvaille. (Photo by Mary Fonseca)

35

GOOD PEOPLE, GOOD EARTH

Early French settlers, the first to describe fertile, water-laced south Louisiana as *terrebonne* (the good earth), were followed into the isolated region by eighteenth-century Acadian exiles attracted by the region's abundant wildlife and seafood. Today, some twentieth-century travelers hurry through Terrebonne Parish to fish the bayous and go after "the big ones" in the Gulf of Mexico. But smart junketeers pause awhile to "pass a good time" with the good people who inherited the good earth.

Houma, a city crisscrossed with so many waterways it is called the "Venice of the South," is the gateway to the good earth. Signs stationed along U.S. 90 direct visitors to the **Houma-Terrebonne Tourist Commission's** Information Center, just off U.S. 90 on St. Charles Street. Here you can watch a get-acquainted video and collect brochures on the area's enticing attractions.

One drawing card you should not miss is **Southdown Plantation/Terrebonne Museum.** The pink and green-trimmed mansion at the intersection of Louisiana 311 and St. Charles Street (a short drive from the tourist center) was originally a one-story Greek Revival home. It was topped with a second floor and Queen Anne regalia in 1893 by Henry C. Minor, son of the original owner. Under the plantation's turreted roof, a resplendent collection of Boehm and Doughty porcelain birds is quartered alongside a replica of U.S. Sen. Allen J. Ellender's Washington office and changing exhibits pertinent to Terrebonne's Acadian heritage.

Four more plantation manors line a twelve-mile section of Louisiana 311 between Houma and Schriever: Crescent Farm, a Creole raised cottage (private); Ellendale, a Victorian bungalow (private); Ardoyne, possibly the most elaborate Victorian home in Louisiana (private); and Magnolia Plantation, an antebellum jewel in a setting of moss-draped oaks (private).

These palaces, built by prosperous sugar planters, differ vastly from homes owned by most pioneer families. Acadian immigrants constructed modest, bayou-bank dwellings and culled furs, alligator hides, and seafood from Terrebonne's bayous and swamps.

You can meet some amiable descendants of these colonists in Gibson, southwest of Houma on U.S. 90. They will introduce you to the untamed beauty of the bayous and share stories about living and working in the wetlands.

At **Bayou Delight Restaurant,** five miles west on U.S. 90 from the Houma-Terrebonne Tourist Information Center, board a shuttle van to the Bayou Black excursion boat captained by "Alligator" Annie Miller, of **Annie Miller's Swamp & Marsh Tours.** This homegrown naturalist, fur trapper, storyteller, former deputy sheriff, and licensed commercial pilot launched the swamp tour business in Louisiana.

Five miles farther, watch for a sign at the intersection of U.S. 90 and Antill Lane that directs visitors to **A Cajun Man's Swamp Cruise.** Captain "Black" Guidry, a Cajun musician and raconteur, regales his swamp-tour customers with jokes, songs, and a comical lecture on Acadian-built accordions. Black's tour offers more than fun and games, however. He names all of the pastel wild flowers lining the waters parted by his barge boat, as well as several species of shorebirds who sometimes end up on the lunch platters of watchful gators gliding noiselessly through the duckweed.

Jimmy and Betty Provost, owners of **Wildlife Gardens,** know a lot about alligators and other swamp dwellers. A few of the critters live in enclosures at the couple's five-acre swamp park

on North Bayou Black Drive near Gibson. Within this unique
setting, several varieties of Louisiana irises border paths to rustic bed-and-breakfast cabins on the edge of a stream.
Overnighters can settle into a chair, rest a fishing pole on the
porch rail, and wait for supper to swim by. They can also enjoy
an exciting, after-dark swamp tour the Provosts offer only to
their bed-and-breakfast guests.

Wildlife Gardens is just one of many delightful Bed and
Breakfasts that may be enjoyed on this getaway. A Houma-
Terrebonne Tourist Commission flyer details the amenities
offered at approximately fifteen inviting inns. One, **Le Jardin
Sur Le Bayou Bed and Breakfast and Gardens,** is situated on a
registered wildlife sanctuary. Dave and Jo Ann Coignet offer
complimentary tours of the lush gardens, including hum-
mingbird and butterfly gardens they have established under
century-old live oaks on their twenty-six-acre property.

Terrebonne Parish's bayous are turned into water gardens
in the spring when purple, yellow, and red Louisiana irises
brighten their banks. If you are enthralled by their delicate
beauty, visit **Bois d'Arc Gardens** on Bull Run Road in
Schriever and purchase some for your own garden. Ask
Tourist Commission representatives for directions to this
Louisiana iris nursery where Ed and Rusty Ostheimer share
growing tips with customers who come to buy plants for their
own flower beds.

While you are on Bull Run Road, you can check out
Munson's Cypress Swamp Tour and browse through the
antiques, crafts, and gifts sold at **Hebert's Artifacts.**

On a springtime getaway, you will probably see more
Louisiana irises along the bayou-rimmed highways traversed
on the **Houma-Terrebonne Tourist Commission's** eighty-mile
bayou circle drive. This eye-opening trek through the water-
and-wetland labyrinth below Houma passes boats of every
description and acquaints you with seafood processing plants,
migratory birds, and aquatic exhibits at the **Louisiana
Universities Marine Consortium.** Before starting this journey,
request an "ABC Driving Tour" pamphlet from the tourist center and make sure your gas tank is full.

If you want to linger in the wetlands to fish, crab, or simply relax by the water, Johnny Glover's **Co-Co Marina, Pointe Cocodrie Inn,** or **Sportsman's Paradise** are good choices for any of these activities. Co-Co Marina offers reasonably priced condominiums, studio apartments, motel-type rooms, a grocery, the tastefully decorated Lighthouse Restaurant and Bar, plus fishing and sight-seeing services. Guests at the recently opened Pointe Cocodrie Inn enjoy charter fishing services and an attractive hotel that offers many amenities. Sportsman's Paradise, just up the road from these two facilities, offers clean, comfortable motel rooms, charter fishing, and a popular seafood restaurant.

Patrons of these marinas congregate with regulars and visitors at **Lapeyrouse's Seafood Bar, Grocery & Campground** on Friday nights. Customers love to sample the complimentary shrimp étouffée, jambalaya, or red beans and rice Terry and Rosalie Lapeyrouse serve to good-timers who sway to jukebox music in their more than fifty-year-old camp store.

Lagniappe at the **Boudreaux Canal General Store,** a mile or so from Lapeyrouse's, is not edible—it is historical. This tongue-in-groove building, successively owned by four generations of the St. Martin family, still has the original teller windows where shrimpers and trappers were paid for their catch with tokens accepted at the company store. Shelves in the 1865 commissary are lined with shrimper's "tennies" (boots), outsized cast-iron pots, foodstuffs, nets, and other gear necessary to sustain its mostly water-based clientele.

Across from the store, workers utilize the Lapeyre automatic shrimp peeler in the Indian Ridge seafood processing plant where it was invented. Every year, at the beginning of the shrimp season, boats festooned with flags and decorations pass in review as the Blessing of the Shrimp Fleet procession glides along the bayou in front of the factory.

You may want to time the end of your "ABC driving tour" so you will arrive at **La Trouvaille** restaurant in time for lunch. During the months of October–May, Wylma Dusenbery and her family cook a traditional Cajun meal and serve it to customers on Wednesdays, Thursdays, and Fridays. On the *first*

Sunday of every month, October–May, they prepare special dishes and entertain guests with a lively performance of Cajun folk songs.

You can tap your feet to more live Cajun music at **A-Bear's Cafe, Dave's Cajun Kitchen, Dula & Edwin's Cajun Restaurant,** and **Gino's** in Houma, and **Bayou Delight Restaurant** in Gibson.

Culinary artists may be found in nearly every Terrebonne Parish neighborhood. To the music hall/eateries already mentioned, add **Savoie's,** a popular eatery operated by the Savoie family for more than thirty years; and **Miss Brandi's Restaurant,** a cozy cafe decorated with a curious blend of cast nets, boat models, and crab traps, to this getaway's list of Acadian restaurants. Houma also offers a choice of Italian, Chinese, and Mexican eateries. Their delectable fares will cause you to loosen your belt a notch by the time you head for home.

Cajun waltzes and two-steps are not the only melodies you may hear in Terrebonne. Gospel music enthusiasts clap to the joyful sounds made by choirs at **St. Lucy's Catholic Church** and **New Rising Sun Baptist Church.** You can listen to the choirs at their open rehearsals or scheduled church services. Music lovers will have many moments to remember when they leave Terrebonne Parish.

Weekenders who want to take home souvenirs find them in the craft and gift shops listed on a handout distributed by the Houma Terrebonne Tourist Commission. The jewelry and ornaments fashioned from garfish scales, nutria teeth, bullfrog skins, and other atypical materials at **Jane's Shell Shop** are among the unique items you will find in the shops. Ingenious handiwork is also sold at **Dupont's Louisiana Crafters,** an arts-and-crafts store on the edge of downtown Houma's Historic District. Original works by local painters and artisans are showcased at the nearby **Guild Gallery.**

If you want to bring home palatable reminders of your Terrebonne Parish getaway, park under the replica of a Longhorn steer at **Billu's Grocery** on Louise Street and pick up a bit of *boudin* or other Cajun meat specialties. The store is just off East Main Street, near Houma's Intracoastal Canal Bridge.

Area Code: (504)

Getting There:

From New Orleans, take Interstate 310 from Interstate 10 or U.S. 61 (Airline Highway) to U.S. 90 West into Houma.

From Baton Rouge, take Exit 182 from Interstate 10 to Louisiana 22, one-quarter mile to Louisiana 70. Cross the Sunshine Bridge to Louisiana 1 South to Thibodaux, take Louisiana 20 South to Schriever, then Louisiana 24 South to Houma.

Where and When:

A Cajun Man's Swamp Cruise, 3109 Southdown Mandelay Rd., Houma, LA 70360. 868-4625. Call for reservation. Admission.

Annie Miller's Swamp & Marsh Tours, 100 Alligator Lane, Houma, LA 70360. 879-3934. Call for reservation. Admission.

Billu's Grocery, 108 Louise St. (P.O. Box 522), Houma, LA 70361. Mon.-Fri., 8 A.M.-6 P.M.; Sat., 8 A.M.-1 P.M.

Bois d'Arc Gardens, 1831 Bull Run Rd., Schriever, LA 70395. 446-2329. Call for appointment, except during the April bloom season when the gardens are open to visitors from 4-6 P.M. (except for the weekend nearest the 15th of April that is not Easter). Spectacular display of wild and hybrid irises. Free.

Boudreaux Canal General Store, Louisiana 56, Chauvin, LA 70344. 594-3421. Mon.-Fri., 7:30 A.M.-4 P.M.; Sat., 7:30 A.M.-noon.

Dupont's Louisiana Crafters, 650 E. Main St., Houma, LA 70360. 851-1005. Mon.-Sat., 9 A.M.-5 P.M.

Guild Gallery, Terrebonne Fine Arts Guild, 1017 Lee Ave., Houma, LA 70360. 851-2198. Tues.- Fri., 10 A.M.-3 P.M.

Hebert's Artifacts, Louisiana 311 and Bull Run Road,

Schriever, LA 70395. 868-7279. Tues.-Sat., 9 A.M.-5 P.M.

Jane's Shell Shop, 209 E. Main St., Houma, LA 70360. 872-1258. Tues.-Sat., 10 A.M.-6 P.M.

Lapeyrouse Seafood Bar, Grocery & Campground, 6890 LA 56, Chauvin, LA 70344. 594-2600. Daily, 5:30 A.M.-11 P.M. or later.

Le Jardin Sur La Bayou Bed and Breakfast and Gardens, 256 Lower Country Drive, Bourg, LA 70343. Tours by appointment only. Call 594-2722.

Louisiana Universities Marine Consortium, Chauvin, LA 70344. 851-2800. Aquarium and observation tower open daily, 8 A.M.-4:30 P.M. Free. Information may also be obtained from LUMC's Council Office, 150 Riverside Mall, Baton Rouge, LA 70801. 342-1488. Mon.-Fri., 8 A.M.-4 P.M.

Munson's Cypress Bayou Swamp Tours, 979 Bull Run Rd., Schriever, LA 70395. 851-3569. Call for reservations.

New Rising Sun Baptist Church Choir, New Rising Sun Baptist Church, 110 St. Charles St., Houma, LA 70360. Choir Director—Howard Nixon, 876-1175. Rehearsal—Tues., 8 P.M. Services—Sun., 11:30 A.M.

St. Lucy's Catholic Church Gospel Choir, St. Lucy's Catholic Church, 1220 Aycock St., Houma, LA 70360. Choir Director—Jess Mckenzie, 876-5287. Rehearsal—Wed., 7 P.M. Mass—Sun., 9 A.M.

Southdown Plantation/Terrebonne Museum, P.O. Box 2095, Houma, LA 70361. 851-0154. Daily, 10 A.M.-4 P.M. Daily tours on the hour through 3 P.M. Admission.

Wildlife Gardens, 5306 N. Bayou Black Dr., Gibson, LA 70356. 575-3676. Tours: Tues.-Sat., 10 A.M., 1 P.M., and 3:30 P.M. Closed on Sundays, Mondays, and major holidays.

Note: Two more swamp tours are available in Terrebonne Parish.

Atchafalaya Basin Backwater Adventure, P.O. Box 128, Gibson, LA 70356. 575-2371. Call for reservations. This tour travels totally on non-navigable waterways and features tours in unspoiled areas, without theatrics.

The Bayou Black Swamp Tour, Bayou Black Marina, Houma, LA. Call 575-2315 for reservations for 1½-hour swamp boat and airboat tours.

Information:

Houma-Terrebonne Tourist Commission, 1701 St. Charles St. (P.O. Box 1792), Houma, LA 70361. 868-2732 or 1-800-688-2732. Mon.-Fri., 9 A.M.-5 P.M.

Guide Services:

Cajun Tours of Terrebonne, 709 May St., Houma, LA 70363. 872-6157 or 872-6146.

Hammond's Air Services—Call 872-1423 for information and rates on "a bird's-eye view" of Cajun Country.

For a listing of charter fishing and fishing guide services, contact the Houma-Terrebonne Tourist Commission.

Accommodations:

Chain and independent motels in Houma.

Co-Co Marina, 106 Pier 56, Chauvin, LA 70344. 594-6626.

Pointe Cocodrie Inn, 8250 LA 56, Chauvin, LA 70344. 594-4568.

Sportsman's Paradise 6830 LA 56, Chauvin, LA 70344. 594-2414.

Bed and Breakfasts:

Allie's Cajun B&B, 120 Lewald Dr., Houma, LA 70360. 868-5543.

Amanda Magenta Plantation House, 1233 LA 55, Montegut, LA 70377. 594-8298 or 594-9686.

Audrey's Lil Cajun Mansion, 815 Funderburk Ave., Houma, LA 70364. 879-3285.

Bayou Cabins, 4326 Grand Caillou Rd., Houma, LA 70363. 879-1328.

Cajun House of Hospitality, 48 Killarney Court, Houma, LA 70363. 868-3725 or 872-2384.

Capri Bed & Breakfast, 101 Capri Court (LA 316 West), Houma, LA 70364. 879-4288 or 1-800-428-8026.

Chateau Ecosse, 3865 Bayou Black Dr. (U.S. 90 West), Houma, LA 70360. 872-2591.

Chez Maudrey, 311 Pecan St., Houma, LA 70364. 868-9519 or 879-3285.

Crochet House, 301 Midland Dr., Houma, LA 70360. 879-3033.

Houma Grand Manor, 217 Lynwood Dr., Houma, LA 70360. 876-5493.

Julia's Cajun Country, 4021 Benton Dr., Bourg, LA 70343. 851-3540.

Le Jardin Sur Le Bayou, 256 Lower Country Dr., Bourg, LA 70343. 594-2722.

Whispering Pines, 306 Agnes St., Houma, LA 70363. 876-4925.

Wildlife Gardens, 5306 N. Bayou Black Dr., Gibson, LA 70356. 575-3676.

Restaurants:

A-Bear's Cafe, 809 Bayou Black Dr., Houma, LA 70360. 872-6306. Mon.-Thurs., 7 A.M.-5 P.M.; Fri., 7 A.M.-10 P.M.; Sat., 10:30 A.M.-2 P.M. Live music Fri. from 6:30-9:30 P.M.—reservations advised.

Bayou Delight Restaurant, 4038 Bayou Black Dr. (U.S. 90 West), Houma, LA 70360. 876-4879. Sun.-Thurs., 10 A.M.-9 P.M.; Fri. and Sat., 10 A.M.-10 P.M. Live music Fri. and Sat., 6-10 P.M.

Dave's Cajun Kitchen, 2433 W. Main St., Houma, LA 70360. 868-3870. Mon., 10:30 A.M.-2 P.M.; Tues.-Thurs., 10:30 A.M.-9 P.M.; Fri., 10:30 A.M.-10 P.M.; Sat., 10:30 A.M.-9 P.M. Live music on Thurs., 7-11 P.M.

Dula & Edwin's Cajun Restaurant, 2821 Bayou Blue Rd. (Louisiana 316 North), Houma, LA 70364. 876-0271. Tues.-Fri., 10 A.M.-10 P.M.; Sat., 11 A.M.-10 P.M.; Sun., 10 A.M.-10 P.M. Live music Tues., 7-10 P.M.

Gino's, 3019 Grand Caillou Rd. (Louisiana 57), Houma, LA 70363. 876-4896. Sun.-Thurs., 11 A.M.-9 P.M.; Fri. and Sat., 11 A.M.-10 P.M.; Mon., 11 A.M.-10 P.M. Live music Wed. and Fri., starting at 7 P.M. Reservations advised.

La Trouvaille, 4696 LA 56, Chauvin, LA 70344. 594-9503 or 873-8005. Open Oct.-May. Lunch: Wed.-Fri., 11:30 A.M.-1:30 P.M. *First* Sunday, Oct.-May, Lunch: 11:30 A.M.-12:30 P.M., followed by performance. Reservations advised.

Miss Brandi's Restaurant, 1023 W. Tunnel Blvd., Houma, LA 70360. 872-9608. Mon., 11 A.M.-2 P.M.; Tues.-Fri., 11 A.M.-9:30 P.M.; Sat., 5-10 P.M.

Savoie's, 1377 Tunnel Blvd. (Louisiana 3040) (P.O. Box 1667), Houma, LA 70361. 872-9819. Lunch: Mon.-Fri., 11 A.M.-2 P.M. Dinner: Mon.-Thurs., 5-10 P.M.; Fri. and Sat., 5-10:30 P.M.

For information on additional restaurants and places to hear live music, contact the Houma-Terrebonne Tourist Commission.

Major Annual Events:

Blessing of the Shrimp Fleet, Chauvin—April.

Blessing of the Shrimp Fleet, Dulac—April.

The Calling of the Tribes Pow-Wow, Houma—Mid-March and mid-September.

Christmas Parade and Arts & Crafts, Houma—First weekend in December.

Downtown on the Bayou, Houma—Second weekend in October.

Freedom Festival, Houma—4th of July

Louisiana Praline Festival, Houma—First weekend in May.

Southdown Marketplace, Houma—Second Saturday before

Easter Sunday and the first Saturday in November.
TARC Christmas Wonderland, Houma—December.

A marsh scene at Little Pecan Island. (Photo by Mary Fonseca)

The sign at Little Pecan Island. (Photo by Mary Fonseca)

36

FOR ADVENTURERS, AND THOSE WHO WOULD LIKE TO BE

Some people harbor a longing for adventure that is never satisfied. They dream about riding the rapids on the Colorado River or backpacking in the Smokies, but such trips are either beyond their skills or their travel budget.

If the spirit of Indiana Jones lies dormant within you, put on your wide-brimmed hat, pull on your leather boots, re-read *The Little Engine That Could,* and boldly depart on one of the Louisiana getaways outlined in this chapter. Each is just daring enough to prepare you for more exciting adventures in the great outdoors.

Cycling into Cajun Culture

Since 1970, Joan and Dick Williams have escorted cyclists from all over the United States and several foreign countries on tours in Louisiana, Mississippi, and Mexico, and their trips have received kudos from bicycle tourists of all levels.

French Louisiana Bike Tours, a company they formed in 1989, currently offers three appealing Louisiana excursions: "Tour of Cajun Country," an extended sojourn to six Acadian communities; "Bike to the Mardi Gras," a long weekend centered on the Cajun *Courir du Mardi Gras;* and a Thursday through Monday "Cajun Music and Food Tour," which is described in this chapter to give you a better understanding of

447

the delightful time you can have on a French Louisiana bike tour.

Cyclists from several states assemble at the Williams' Lafayette home prior to the start of their popular "Cajun Music and Food Tour." The tour leaders pick up their charges at the topnotch Bed and Breakfasts they reserve for participants and bring them home for the Cajun cooking lesson and dinner that kicks off the tour.

Hot gumbo and crawfish *étouffée* are powerful ice breakers, so by the end of the meal, the thirty-somethings who flew in from California are at ease with the retirees from New York, and experienced bike tourists are counseling first-timers who fear they will not be able to keep up the pace.

The next morning, a few hours after the group wheels out of the parking lot at Pack & Paddle, the Williams' outdoor out-fitting store, novices realize they have nothing to worry about. Dick, Joan, or Allen Boudreaux, their assistant, constantly cruise the bike route in a van, picking up tired cyclists or helping those needing adjustments to their bikes. Cyclists ride with the leaders as long as they want, their bicycles securely fastened to a trailer behind the van. Nearly every participant on the four-night adventure rode in the van a part of each day, bearing in mind, as one traveler put it, that they were there "to have a good time, not win an endurance contest."

The Williams plan their French Louisiana bicycle tours with that fun-oriented concept in mind. Except for the first day's route from Lafayette to Washington, which is fifty miles, daily distances on the "Cajun Music and Food Tour" average between 30 and 35 miles, with additional stretches available for gung-ho cyclists who want to spend more time on their bikes. The highways and back roads the routes follow pass through flat prairies; some are scenic, some show Louisiana's need to enforce its litter laws.

On short breaks, the cycling group gathers around the van to refresh themselves with the fruit, juices, and water the Williams supply. In keeping with the theme of the tour, dinners are scheduled at top-quality Cajun restaurants such as the Steamboat Warehouse in Washington and Prejean's in

Lafayette. Lunches are at casual, but appetizing, restaurants along the route. Extra treats arranged by the Williams, such as mint juleps preceding a complimentary tour of Chretien Point Plantation in Sunset and a picnic on the grounds of the Academy of the Sacred Heart in Grand Coteau, are delightful surprises.

Everyone listens or dances to Cajun or zydeco music in enjoyable settings such as Slim's Y-Ki-Ki in Opelousas, Fred's Lounge in Mamou, Guidry's dance hall in Lewisburg, and the Liberty Theater in Eunice. When even the most energetic two-steppers are ready to call it a day, everybody snuggles into comfortable digs at first-class Bed and Breakfasts.

Strangers who met only a few days before hugged like old friends at the end of the tour and vowed to return to bicycle in Louisiana again. Many of them agreed with one girl from California who said, "I'm drawn here because it is the last exotic place in America."

Information:

French Louisiana Bike Tours offers each of its Cajun-culture bicycle tours several times a year. Fees for all tours cover lodging at first-rate Bed and Breakfasts, all breakfasts, snacks enroute, and dinners, plus transportation to restaurants and dance halls and to and from the Lafayette Airport.

Bike rental fees include a helmet, bike pack, backrack, souvenir water bottle, Avocet bike computer, and repairs.

For a complimentary French Louisiana Bike Tours brochure, contact **French Louisiana Bike Tours,** 601 E. Pinhook Rd., Lafayette, LA 70501. (318) 232-5854 or call Pack and Paddle, 1-800-458-4560.

Tips for Novice Adventurers:

• When you can bicycle steadily for 45 minutes, you are ready to try a bicycle tour.

• Wear snug-fitting, padded bicycle shorts that eliminate or reduce friction; bright-colored clothing easily spotted by drivers; a helmet; and cycling gloves.

- Remember that cyclists are subject to the same traffic laws that govern motorists.
- Bring sunscreen and rain gear.

Ropin' and Ridin' at the Double G Ranch

Thousands of kids have attended equestrian summer camps at **Double G Ranch** in Grayson, a rural community in the rolling hills south of Columbia. Armed with the skills Buddy Gill has taught for more than forty years, Double G graduates merit honors in hundreds of equestrian competitions, and more than twenty youngsters have won championships at state, regional, and national equestrian events.

During the remaining seasons of the year, Buddy Gill and his wife, Dianne, welcome couples, and children ages six and older, to their facility for an exciting, ranch-style getaway. Dianne fixes a hearty breakfast for everyone before they wander outside to see what is going on in the barn. There is usually plenty of activity and everyone is welcome to help with the chores. Youngsters love to feed the chickens, but at first they are a little uncertain about collecting eggs. One thing that is certain, however, is their affection for Sugar, the Gills' performing miniature horse.

This tiny star may be the best-loved horse at the Double-G, but Hollywood, Painter, and the rest of the Gills' gentle quarter horses garner their share of attention. Buddy and Diane teach weekenders the basics of riding on these trusty mounts and lead them on trail rides through 320 acres of pine-forested hills. Experienced riders can set off by themselves on a borrowed mount or bring their own along. If you are unable to ride, you can still enjoy a hike in the woods or bring your fishing equipment and angle in a nearby lake.

Buddy delights in showing young people how to rope like cowboys did when the West was young and some kids practice for hours on the wooden calf in the center of the yard. Others enjoy a dip in the pool in warm weather, a game of horseshoes or volleyball, or a ride to Columbia with their families.

On chilly evenings, everyone congregates around the inviting fireplace in the ranch's great room. Later, when the fire dies down, everyone trundles off to bed. Children head outside to enjoy the novelty of sleeping in one of the bunkhouses used by campers, while adults in the party make themselves at home in attractive rooms in the ranch house.

Information:

Double G Ranch, Route 1, Box 14C, Grayson, LA 71435. (318) 649-9363. Breakfast included, other meals upon request.

Tips for Novice Adventurers:

• Bring long pants and boots, or shoes with heels, so you have a firm footing in the stirrups.

• A flashlight and insect repellent are useful during night-time activities.

A Wilderness Adventure

Experience scenic, historic northwest Louisiana by canoe. Let someone else do all the preparation and scouting. Use our equipment and get basic instruction and help along the way. Overnight trips with moonlight dinners. Environmental Tours. Photographic "Safaris." Fishing. Exploring. Primitive Camping. Trips designed to give you a relaxing, fun adventure.

This **Norris Outfitters** flyer offers a lot. But can the company deliver what it promises? My husband, Ron, and I went on an overnight canoe trip with Mark Norris and his wife, Laura, to find out.

With our car parked safely in the Norris' locked yard, we set out on our boating adventure. We left Laura's car at the Corps of Engineers Park where we would end our six-mile float on Bayou Bodcau, then we all rode in Norris Outfitters' van to the put-in point. While I took pictures and Ron carried a few packs to the shore, Mark and Laura loaded the canoes. As we watched them pack our gear, we were impressed—for the first of many times—with the strength and ability of our young guides. In about twenty minutes they had everything lashed into the canoes and we were ready to go.

With Mark and Laura leading the way, we paddled down the bayou while the setting sun glimmered on the water. Ron and I soon settled into a steady rhythm and managed to navigate over and under fallen trees that occasionally litter the bayou. Although there are a few "white water" streams in Louisiana, these "snags," as they are called, may be the most difficult challenge canoeists meet in the state's mostly tranquil waters. In a few places, it was necessary to portage the canoes over the trees, but our veteran guides handled such situations with ease. Mark is a muscular six-footer with strength that has been honed by the outdoor life he has led since childhood. Laura reminisced that her first canoe trip took place while she was bear hunting in Canada with her father when she was thirteen years old.

When it was time to set up camp, Ron and I were amazed at what our two guides had packed into the waterproof sacks they had inside the canoes. In addition to our clothes and sleeping bags, there was an 8'-by-10' tent for us, and a two-man tent for Mark and Laura, plus all the fixings for a gourmet supper and a hearty breakfast. Laura passed around raw veggies and dip while our beef shish kebabs were broiling over a charcoal fire contained in an aluminum roasting pan, an easily transported arrangement that would leave no messy firepit to scar the earth. After enjoying three scrumptious side dishes that were also served, we declined Laura's offer of candies for dessert.

We spent a pleasant evening chatting with our guides about other excursions they offer and about the many international visitors they have taken on outings. "You don't need to know how to canoe to book a trip with us," said Mark. "We've taught dozens of people how to paddle, and we're very helpful to beginners."

A professional biologist joins Norris Outfitters ecological/environmental tours. "He keeps people fascinated by teaching them about influences on plant and animal life, and about the ecology of Bayou Bodcau, Red Chute Bayou, or other wetland areas east of Shreveport," says Mark.

Norris Outfitters recently purchased a 37-foot Montreal

canoe that will accommodate large groups on daytrips and eight to ten people and their equipment on overnight excursions. "We're very excited about using this comfortable canoe on local bayous and area lakes such as Lake Bistineau and Caddo Lake," says Mark.

Even though buzzing insects and "open air" bathrooms are inescapable adjuncts to such outings, the exciting trips Mark plans overshadow these slight inconveniences and present great opportunities for families to enjoy the outdoors together.

After a restful night, and a good, hot breakfast, we set off down the bayou again. The waterway became more beautiful and intriguing as we paddled along. We listened to birds call through the forest and watched cranes and herons feed near the shore. By early afternoon, our wilderness adventure was over. But we've promised ourselves another. We're thinking about the photo safari, or the environmental tour, or maybe we'll just go fishing, or maybe . . . I wonder if we can fit it all into a long weekend?

Information:

Norris Outfitters, Louisiana 80 East (P.O. Box 40), Princeton, LA 71067. (318)-949-9522.

Tips for Novice Adventurers:

• Drinking and boating are a bad mix. Norris Outfitters does not allow alcohol on any excursion.

• Overnight excursions are not recommended for children under six.

• Wear a life jacket at all times while boating.

• Follow your guide's directions.

• Stay with the group.

• Bring sunscreen, insect repellent, rubber boots, rain gear, and a flashlight.

• Powdered sulfur applied to your ankles and around your waist may repel ticks and chiggers.

Houseboating on the Atchafalaya River

From **Basin Landing & Marina's** dock on the Atchafalaya River Levee in Henderson, you can gaze across the vast, exotic basin and see feathery cypress trees pointing to the heavens, fields of lavender water lilies floating on the undulating surface, and herons gracefully gliding across the water. The springtime scene is so lovely and peaceful you wish you could enjoy it for more than an hour or two. And you can, if you rent *The Henderson Princess,* the *Le Bon Temp Bateau,* or one of the other whimsically named houseboats the landing offers for rent. All are supplied with linens and kitchen equipment and, depending on the boat, beds for four to eight people.

Once your party is on board, you can settle in and remain tied to the dock, or have employees tow you a few hundred feet out into the basin, secure your houseboat, and if necessary, teach you how to operate all the equipment on the houseboat and the electric motor skiff that is tied to your home away from home. Then, if you wish, you can spend the whole weekend sipping cool drinks and fishing from your porch. Or, as the folks at Basin Landing & Marina put it, you can opt to enjoy "just a little peace, a little quiet, and a lot of Mother Nature."

Some houseboaters like to bring binoculars and study the many birds and animals that live in the basin. Those who want to explore farther into the waterway often engage the services of "Half Pint," Basin Landing & Marina's seasoned guide who has scouted the entire basin in his boat or on hikes into its mysterious interior. "With my push boat I can go places the larger swamp tour boats can't," says Half Pint. "On my two-hour tours, I show folks eagle nests, beaver dams, and a variety of wildlife and scenery. If they want, they can use my camcorder to video the outing and I will transfer it to a tape."

While some houseboaters spend the whole weekend fishing or photographing the basin's scenic panorama, others prefer to balance their peace and quiet with a few shoreside outings. Joining fellow fishermen to trade tips and stories in Basin Landing & Marina's tiny cafe and camp store is a favorite pastime for anglers, especially on Thursday nights when the marina sponsors a "dogfight" bass tournament. It was so named, the manager good-naturedly says, "because these fellows fight like cats and dogs over the winning entry."

Several inviting restaurants close to the landing also attract houseboaters, some even offer live Cajun music on weekends. And there are a few small-craft and souvenir shops, plus an art gallery featuring paintings by "blue dog artist" George Rodrigue in Landry's Cajun Village, just off the Henderson Exit of Interstate 10.

On Levee Road, which extends from Louisiana 347 in Henderson to the Atchafalaya Basin Levee, there are stores that offer services even a carefree houseboater may need, such as a sporting goods store, a bakery, a grocery, and a lauderette. Then it is back to the basin for more peace, more quiet, and a lot of Mother Nature.

Information:

Basin Landing & Marina, Inc., 1219 Henderson Levee Rd., Breaux Bridge, LA 70517. (318) 228-7880.

Tips for Novice Adventurers:

• Basin Landing & Marina recommends a houseboat with a screened porch for families with young children.

• Wear life jackets in the skiff, even for the short ride to the dock.

Island Hopping with the Nature Conservancy of Louisiana

When I toured the Creole Nature Trail that runs along the coast of Louisiana, south of Lake Charles, I thought I had traveled to the wildest, most remote section of the state. But a daytrip to the Nature Conservancy of Louisiana's Little Pecan Island Preserve showed me I was wrong. Heeding the instructions sent by the Conservancy, I followed Louisiana 14 and Louisiana 27 south from Interstate 10 for about 27 miles, crossed the Intracoastal Waterway, and turned onto Little Chenier Road.

I felt like I was driving to the end of the earth when the paved road gave way to a gravel trail that continued for miles along the shore. But finally, after a fourteen-mile drive, I spotted the wharf and the modified crew boat waiting to take the Lake Charles-based group I was joining to Little Pecan Island Preserve, the Nature Conservancy's 1,810-acre chenier in southeastern Cameron Parish.

As we cruised down the Mermentau River and turned into Little Pecan Bayou, Allen May, our Nature Conservancy guide, revealed why the organization considers Little Pecan Island one of its most important acquisitions. "Little Pecan Island has been identified by our Heritage Program as one of the most significant wetland chenier tracts in the state," noted May, who further explained that "a chenier is a large wooded area that forms on a beach ridge that becomes isolated from the coast by changes in sea level and deposition of sediments transported by the Mississippi River."

Allen finished his explanation just as we pulled up to a dock where two stoneware pelicans guarded a sign that read, "Little Pecan Island, elevation five feet." We walked up a slope behind it to the Nature Conservancy's comfortable lodge and spent a few minutes exploring the game room, a family-style den where visitors gather around a fireplace to chat or watch television, and several bedrooms that sleep up to 14 people during the Nature Conservancy's popular weekend workshops. Six more field-trippers can be accommodated in a small annex near the lodge.

After awhile, we split into two groups and set off to explore the island. About six of us climbed into a boat that looked and sounded like Bogart and Hepburn's *African Queen,* and went chugging along canals that run through the wetlands. In the spring and fall, these marshes swarm with migratory waterfowl, and the chenier is host to colorful, Neotropical birds that draw dozens of birding enthusiasts to Little Pecan Island's lodge for a two-night getaway. Besides the birdlife, you are likely to see alligators, snakes, white-tailed deer, and other animals, plus fields of radiant Louisiana irises and delicate wild flowers. The island's flora and birds are favorite subjects of avid photographers who sign up for two-days of nature photography instruction.

Our one-day trip allowed just enough time for a tour of the island, so after our wetland excursion, we enjoyed a casual lunch on the lodge's screened porch, and followed it with a jaunt on a trailer pulled by a four-wheeler. At first, we viewed Little Pecan Island's woodsy chenier from our perches atop the trailer, then we hiked through the undergrowth to the remnants of a sawmill that once operated on the island.

"No one has been able to determine how Little Pecan Island got its name, but the island has a long history of settlement and has provided natural resources to humans for centuries," our guide told us. "Preliminary archaeological exploration indicates that humans first settled here as early as 2,000 years ago."

The sawmill we viewed was used to harvest cypress in the late 1800s, and more recently, the island was part of a private waterfowl refuge/hunting preserve. Then, it was bought by the Nature Conservancy with funds provided by the Brown Foundation of New Orleans and other donors. A gift from Amoco has also funded a research facility that will allow Little Pecan Island to be used for many scientific projects and ecological studies, as well as a setting for numerous field trips presently enjoyed by the public.

Many of the popular outings appeal to sportsmen, but they are especially enthusiastic about the saltwater fly-fishing workshops offered in October in a nearby saltwater marsh and the freshwater session on Little Pecan Island in June.

To some folks, Little Pecan Island is simply the ideal place to "get away from it all." They bypass the workshops and reserve the lodge for family reunions and company retreats highlighted by appetizing meals, leisurely hikes, adventurous canoe trips, and exciting fishing expeditions.

Information:

Nature Conservancy of Louisiana, P.O. Box 4125, Baton Rouge, LA 70821. (504) 338-1040.

Tips for Novice Adventurers:

• Wear a life jacket at all times while boating.
• Follow your guide's directions.
• Stay with the group.
• Bring sunscreen, insect repellent, rain gear, and a flashlight.
• Powdered sulfur applied to your ankles and around your waist may repel ticks and chiggers.

REFERENCES

Back Road Tours of French Louisiana by Joan Williams

Baldwin's Guide to Inns of the Deep South: Louisiana and Western Mississippi by Jack and Winnie Baldwin

Beautiful Crescent: A History of New Orleans by Joan B. Garvey and Mary Lou Widmer

Cajun Country Tour Guide and Festival Guide—Acadiana Profile

The Deep South: Georgia, Florida, Alabama, Mississippi, Louisiana by William Bryant Logan and Vance Muse

Directory of Louisiana Museums and Historic Sites—Louisiana Association of Museums

A History Lover's Guide to Louisiana by Mary Ann Wells

Huey Long by T. Harry Williams

The Longest Street: A History of Lafourche Parish and Grand Isle by Tanya Ditto

Louisiana: A History by Joe G. Taylor

Louisiana: Off the Beaten Path by Gay Martin

Louisiana: The Pelican State by Edwin A. Davis

The Pelican Guide to Louisiana by Mary Ann Sternberg

Plantation Homes of the Teche Country by Paul Stahls, Jr.

A Short History of New Orleans by Mel Leavitt

A Tourist's Guide to West Feliciana Parish by Anne Butler Hamilton

Yesterday, Today, and Tomorrow by the Jackson Assembly, Jackson, Louisiana

INDEX

461